PENGUIN BOOKS

Home

Former president of the Council for British Archaeology, Dr Francis Pryor has spent over thirty years studying our prehistory. He has excavated sites as diverse as Bronze Age farms, field systems and entire Iron Age villages. He appears frequently on TV's *Time Team* and is the author of *The Making of the British Landscape* and *Seahenge*, as well as *Britain BC* and *Britain AD*, both of which he adapted and presented as Channel 4 series.

FRANCIS PRYOR

Home

*A Time Traveller's Tales from
British Prehistory*

PENGUIN BOOKS

PENGUIN BOOKS

UK | USA | Canada | Ireland | Australia
India | New Zealand | South Africa

Penguin Books is part of the Penguin Random House group of companies
whose addresses can be found at global.penguinrandomhouse.com.

First published by Allen Lane 2014
Published in Penguin Books 2015
008

Copyright © Francis Pryor, 2014

The moral right of the author has been asserted

Set in 9.24/12.38 pt Sabon LT Std
Typeset by Jouve (UK), Milton Keynes
Printed and bound in Great Britain by Clays Ltd, Elcograf S.p.A.

A CIP catalogue record for this book is available from the British Library

ISBN: 978-0-241-95588-8

www.greenpenguin.co.uk

For Mike and Lou Bamforth,
to celebrate their wedding, 13 September 2014

Contents

List of Illustrations

PLATES

Unless otherwise indicated, photographs are courtesy of the author.

Every effort has been made to contact copyright holders. The author and publisher would be glad to amend in future editions any errors or omissions brought to their attention.

Acknowledgements

The idea for this book was originally suggested to me by my then editor at Allen Lane, Georgina Laycock, who also helped me steer it through its initial (and rather turbulent) development stages. Her successor, Thomas Penn, has been a great source of advice and encouragement subsequently. The first two chapters have benefited hugely from discussions with Professor Nicky Milner (York University) and the sections on Stonehenge owe much to Professor Mike Parker Pearson, of University College London. Other prehistorians who have been very free with their advice include Chris Evans, Clive Waddington, Martin Bell and Maisie Taylor. On the production side at Penguin, I have worked with a great team including Richard Duguid and Lisa Simmonds, illustrator Jeff Edwards, copy editor Monica Schmoller and indexer Marian Aird; Casiana Ionita ensured that the production process ran smoothly. As ever I owe a huge debt of gratitude to my agent Bill Hamilton, at A. M. Heath and Co. It has been far too long, but maybe now Maisie and I can have a holiday together.

Introduction

The Greatest Organization
Ever Created

'I'm a family man . . . I regard the family as the greatest organization ever created by human beings.'[1] I couldn't believe my ears. It was Sir Michael Caine. A familiar voice from my youth was expressing the thoughts I had been trying to frame for weeks. I was awake at an ungodly hour and Caine's words issued from a small radio on my wife Maisie's side of the bed. As often happened, she had woken earlier, switched on the World Service, volume turned right down, and had then drifted back to sleep. It was now nearly five o'clock and it was my turn to wake up. I was suffering from a bad case of early morning 'busy brain'. What is it about the wee small hours that makes your mind get everything out of proportion? Everyday problems become complex-verging-on-the-insuperable and everyone seems to be out to get you. Then, a couple of hours later, you can't understand why you were getting so het up.

I rolled out of bed and stumbled downstairs repeating Caine's simple, but profoundly important, words over and over again. At my desk I scribbled them down. That done, I leaned back in my office chair. I looked down at my scribbled note. I knew he'd hit a nail on the head, but for a strange sleep-befuddled moment, I couldn't think which one. At face value the words were bland. Nobody would disagree with him. Nobody. So why did I rush downstairs in such a panic? I suppose my brain was trying to make sense of my unconscious. For a brief moment, I considered returning upstairs to get more sleep, but for some reason I hesitated. Then slowly it all started to come back to me: instinctively, I turned on my laptop. I had begun to research this book.

It goes back to my very first days in archaeology, in 1963, before I even went to university. I was working as a volunteer on an Iron Age hillfort in Bedfordshire which was directed by James Dyer, an inspirational leader if ever there was one. It was there that I learned, probably from James, that archaeology is about the past as experienced by ordinary people. So it was very unlikely that our hillfort had ever been visited by anyone famous – by Julius Caesar or even Queen Boudicca. But that didn't matter. Even if such figures had visited the place, it wouldn't have altered anything. Through history monarchs could, and often did, visit lowly parish churches, but the buildings remained unaltered, as did the lives of the parishioners who attended services there every Sunday. I would be more than surprised if any of those visits left even the slightest archaeological trace.

Back at home at weekends people would ask me about the dig: word spreads fast in a rural village and people were fascinated by what I was doing. In those days, *Time Team* hadn't done its amazing job of public education, and folk in Weston (Hertfordshire) still thought that excavations only happened abroad. I remember explaining – to wide-eyed astonishment – that I was helping excavate the remains of an Iron Age round-house. To most British people in the early sixties, prehistory[2] was indeed another country: aside from a few students and professionals, nobody knew that there had been houses before the Romans arrived.

I was aged 18, and my tales of the Bedfordshire dig soon became famous in the local pub, the Barley Mow, where a pint of bitter cost 1/10d (roughly 8p). On many nights I'd be carried home after too many beers, bought for me by my new-found audience. Today we tend to look back on post-war pub life as male dominated and either stiff or drunken; but in reality, and especially in rural areas at a weekend, the local became a home-from-home for many people. I recall lively domestic arguments between husbands and wives across the dominoes table, and daughters beating their fathers at darts. And yes, boys flirted with girls and teenagers got drunk; but it was all part of pub life – and ordinary life, too. It started to dawn on me that history doesn't just have to be about the acts of kings and queens. Details of ordinary people, their lives and homes – how their hearths were built, the direction in which their front doors faced – were, to me, much more fascinating, simply because here were details that everyone could identify with and recognize.

The simple notion that, even way back in prehistory, the idea of home life somehow mattered to people, has always intrigued me – not least because today it is something the vast majority of us take for granted, maybe because life in our business or professional worlds has become so frenetic and at times unstable. The things we talk about at work say little about our home lives: what we ate at a dinner party, where we went on Sunday. But we rarely discuss what really matters: the reality of our upbringing, schooling and home life. Yes, I have heard people hint that their father was very dominant or their mother was mostly away at work; it's as if an unhappy childhood was less relevant, less character-forming than three years at a particular university. In today's fast-paced urban world, it's all about achievement and potential 'going forward'. We seem to be losing sight of our daily lives in the here and now. You would never sell many copies of a book on *How We Raised Three Healthy Children in Hampstead*. It was the extraordinariness of the ordinary that fascinated me and, I now realize, Michael Caine, too.

Long after I'd graduated and was earning my living as a director of large-scale excavations, I began to appreciate the importance of pre-history to the development of British society and culture. The Romans arrived in north-western Europe at the start of the 1st century BC. Things were never to be the same again. In effect, their writing codified the age that they dominated, whether in narrative accounts – like those of Tacitus or Caesar – or in other, simpler forms, such as inscriptions, tombstones or letters written home by soldiers in barracks on Hadrian's Wall. Inevitably, the more formal written histories make references to the institutions and political structures then in existence. This in turn leads to what historians call a 'top-down' view of the world: we view the past, even the past we have experienced ourselves through the filter of labelled and compartmentalized, organized time. In this way, we wonder what we might have been doing during the assassination of President Kennedy or the terrible events of 9/11. But we think less often about their 'bottom-up' equivalents: how we lived our lives in the early 1960s or 2000s.

The very existence of recorded dates and periods helps to

perpetuate this hierarchical view of the past. Much of the 19th century, for instance, is referred to as 'Victorian' in honour of a Queen who, it must be admitted, never did anything very remarkable herself. In reality, the epoch might be better represented by a term like 'Navvian': during this time, Britain was transformed by the thousands of navvies whose back-breaking toil built the canals, turnpikes and railways that altered its landscape so comprehensively.

Viewed in this way, prehistory presents us with a less hierarchical view of society. Taken at face value, of course, this is also a distortion of reality. For example, prior to the final decades of the Iron Age there is no record of kings and queens, simply because writing barely existed in pre-Roman Britain. (The very earliest written words found in Britain, which appear on coins and which pre-date the arrival of the Romans by several generations, include the names of Iron Age kings, such as Cunobelin or Epaticcus, often with the abbreviated name of the place where the coin was minted, such as CAM for Camulodunum – present-day Colchester, in Essex.[3]) So prehistory treats us to an archaeological record of many millennia, in which the day-to-day activities (and achievements) of ordinary people are all we have to go on.

The surviving prehistoric sites and monuments of Britain are not just about ordinary domestic life. Indeed, the vast majority of the many thousand pre-Roman farms and houses we now know about have only been revealed since the birth of modern archaeology, from about 1860 onwards. However, the best-known, most popular and widely viewed monuments do indeed hint at home or family life, such as the great collective tombs beneath barrow mounds at places like Maes Howe in Orkney, or West Kennet in Wiltshire, both of which I will discuss later. There are also henges and other field monuments, like stone rows and hillforts, where one can make the connection, albeit (as we will see), less directly. And while we can infer that priests and chieftains planned or supervised the erection of structures like Stonehenge, we cannot prove it. On the other hand, we can say with some certainty that a small round-house, of about 7 or 8 metres (23–26 feet) in diameter, with a central hearth and evidence of the cooking and consumption of food, was a family home. Put another way, prehistory is essentially a bottom-up, as opposed to a top-down, history. And that, in short, is what inspired me to write this book.

In prehistoric times British people organized their communities, clan and tribal structures around families. As we will see, families provided education and the inspiration for new ideas. It was the family, too, that maintained communications with relatives in nearby and far-flung settlements. Maybe it is because most of us went through the teenage process of establishing our personal independence that we tend to see the home as a conservative, even a reactionary, influence. But was it? It is my contention, supported I believe by archaeology, that ancient and historical homes were places where human energy and personal ambition were encouraged. My argument is that in their quiet, unassuming manner families have always been the main source of ideas and innovation for local communities, whose emerging institutions, such as the parish in post-Roman times, have reflected this fact.

Today, in the West, when we think about family we tend to think of the nuclear family – a couple and their 2.4 children. But, as the increasingly popular interest in family history is showing, our relatives by blood and marriage can provide a much wider network. Anthropology suggests that in the past these broader family networks were the basis for nearly all social, tribal and community organizations. In Britain today the final vestiges of this very ancient way of doing things survives in the hereditary peers in the House of Lords and, of course, in the Royal Family and Her Majesty the Queen.

As societies developed and became more sophisticated, new influences become evident; these included new classes of more powerful individuals, and emerging military and political institutions. But again, these new social structures were organized along extended or broader family lines, and as such their origins lay much closer to home: tribal warriors and political leaders had always been both protectors of the family and organizers of the community. Despite what some might have us believe, these new top-down organizations never dominated *all* aspects of daily life: ordinary family members, and people in the local community, must have continued to play a prominent role in the growth and development of early British societies.

It is commonly supposed that the focus of domestic life is only about the raising of children. Indeed, when a young couple announce that they are to marry, doting relatives often quickly bring the conversation round to when they plan to 'start a family'. But families are about more than procreation alone: they are also about personal support, relationships with entirely new groups of people and simpler, more enduring things too, such as the love and companionship of a partner and close relatives. Families give structure to human life. In the quite recent past they also gave structure to communities, and were the main source of education, discipline and welfare. So they are not – nor have they ever been – merely about wiping babies' bottoms. We will see in the chapters that follow how in prehistoric times they were an important source of new ideas; indeed, even today, without families, society would soon collapse.

Too often families are under-acknowledged in history books, which usually approach the past from the other, top-down direction – a view that is structured around major political events, such as wars and battles and the reigns of kings and queens. But archaeology is closer allied to the recent sub-discipline of social history, which I'm glad to say is becoming increasingly popular, both in books and on television.[4] I find social history far more appealing and relevant to life than the deeds of the great and the good – and that isn't just because at school I could never remember dates (with the notable exception of 1066).

Before continuing, I want to consider a deceptively simple question: why do we have homes and families? There are, after all, many other ways of raising the next generation – witness any passing ant, fish or hare. Indeed, why have the communal lifestyles beloved of hippies and earlier social experimenters never really caught on? Young mammals – including humans – of course require quite a long period with their mother, during which time she feeds them the all-important milk that both nourishes them and transfers to them her immunity to disease. But there is more to it than that. Much more.

It is easy to overlook family ties in other mammals, even those close to us. Having grown up in the country, I used to think that sheep came in huge, undifferentiated flocks: it was not until I began to farm them myself that I realized the subtleties of their behaviour. I think we were in our third year's lambing when it struck me that three of the ewes in the lambing pens around us were bleating at others a few pens away. Out of curiosity, Maisie checked their ear-tags and found they were a mother and her two daughters. So we moved them to adjoining pens. Somehow it seemed more humane, but we also discovered a practical benefit: that constant bleating immediately stopped. Then, on another hunch, Maisie checked the lambing records for a second time and discovered that the previous season all three ewes had lambed within a few hours of each other. And it happened again that season. We noted similar strong mother–daughter bonds several more times that lambing and now it's something we always look out for. Sometimes, if I happened to be walking through a field of sheep with a dog, I've observed that an older ewe will gather together several lambs and stand defiantly between them and my dog, and I've often wondered whether she was protecting a group of her grand- and great-grand-lambs, or whether they were just random lambs from the flock. On the whole, I now suspect the former. As with long-vanished human communities, we tend to underestimate the intelligence and protective instincts of other animals, who, in my experience, rarely do anything truly at random.

As with sheep, flock or pack behaviour explains why the great apes, our closest biological relatives, have close families too.[5] There is also evidence to suggest that ancestral forms of human beings, such as *Australopithecus*, who lived in Africa two to four million years ago, and more recently their distant descendants, the Neanderthals, also lived in family groups.[6] Ultimately, it's down to Darwin and evolution: herding is an essential survival instinct. It's especially important if, as a species, you have evolved a larger brain as your means of survival, rather than thick skin, ferocious claws or teeth. Thanks to evolution, our bodies are remarkably flexible, and are good at putting the brain's ideas into practice. Nevertheless, we lack the tiger's teeth, the elephant's hide or the bear's muscularity. Our strength lies in numbers and, even more important, the ability to work together for the communal good. And families are the basis – and I choose the words carefully – for that vital co-operation. I would suggest that the in-built human herd instinct, the need to communicate clearly and bond with others, lies behind most of mankind's subsequent achievements.

The herding instinct can also help restrain or focus its main rival, the human competitive instinct, whose roots ultimately lie in the sexual challenge to find a better mate. This is what gives rise to tensions within families. And these tensions, like the bonds they can shatter, are also universal, through time and space. (The best known is of course the friction between sons and daughters and their respective mothers- and fathers-in-law.) It's something that has obsessed anthropologists since Victorian times. In some societies this tension finds expression in a ban on marriage between 'cross-cousins' from either side of a family.

Family life demands a form of intimate communication. Shepherds still refer to a particular sort of soft bleating that a ewe makes to her newly born lambs as 'talking'. It's part of the bonding process and will help the mother keep an eye on her offspring when it returns to the flock. And as we have seen, those bonds can last for very much longer. We cannot be certain when human speech began, but most physical anthropologists would agree that it extends back hundreds of thousands of years.

Our long-extinct cousins, the Neanderthals (or *Homo sapiens neanderthalensis*), had language too and are known to have enjoyed a rich ceremonial and symbolic life – if, that is, their elaborate burial rites are anything to go by. And as for ourselves, *Homo sapiens sapiens*, to give us our full and double-wise name, we are always supposed to be a small step brighter and more adaptable than the Neanderthals, which of course is why we have survived and they, sadly, have died out. I would dearly have liked to have met one. Incidentally, there is now increasing genetic evidence that modern humans and Neanderthals did interbreed in Europe, if not elsewhere, following their migration from Africa, maybe fifty thousand years ago.[7]

But for how long has home life been important and what precisely do we mean by that cosy term 'domesticity'? How has that changed? Have the British always been settled and domestic: a nation of shopkeepers? Incidentally, that vastly over-used phrase has always intrigued me. We British have used it as a self-deprecatory term. We accept that it was first coined by Napoleon in exile on Elba (his precise phrase was: *L'Angleterre est une nation de boutiquiers*) and we rather enjoy turning it back on ourselves; but in actual fact those words were first coined by the great Scottish economist and philosopher Adam Smith in his *Wealth of Nations* (1776):

> To found a great empire for the sole purpose of raising up a people of customers, may at first sight appear a project fit only for a nation of shopkeepers. It is, however, a project altogether unfit for a nation of shopkeepers; but extremely fit for a nation whose government is influenced by shopkeepers.

Characteristically, Smith gets straight to the point. I'm sure there have been periods, and I'm thinking here, for example, of the immediately post-Norman centuries, when governments were supported by sundry aristocratic war-lords, and when ordinary British people only had a minimal say in the way they were being ruled. But even in prehistoric times the evidence does not suggest that the various tribes and emerging kingdoms were ruled by entirely self-centred despots who disregarded public opinion. These were times when tribal social structures, themselves based on family or bottom-up values, were all important. Ambitious people would have had to operate within clearly defined rules of appropriate behaviour. Viewed in the short term, tribal societies appear to be very conservative. This caution is needed both to retain social cohesion and to protect technologically less-advanced communities from assault by the forces of nature and indeed by other groups of humans. So people evolved rules of behaviour that emphasized communal security, yet at the same time they understood and acknowledged the importance of wider communication. And we can see these social systems mirrored in the physical layout of prehistoric farms, villages, fields and roadways right across Britain.

Houses were usually of much the same size, and tended to be carefully arranged in a way that respected the neighbours. There were also very few distinctively large or grand buildings. Indeed, I can think of only one bona fide pre-Roman palace, and that sits within its own compound and is not part of a larger settlement.[8] Interestingly, it dates to the Late Iron Age and the turbulent years immediately prior to the Roman Conquest of AD 43.

The top-down view of British history has tended to overemphasize the role of rulers and war-lords. The Vikings are a good example. With names like Thorfinn the Skullsplitter they have acquired a very hard, warlike reputation. If ever, it could be argued, there was a top-down, male-dominated society, it was during the so-called 'Viking Age'. But this was also the time that saw the foundation, or growth, of cities like Dublin and York – hardly enduring monuments to brutality. Indeed, archaeology has clearly shown that it didn't take long for even the most blood-curdling of Viking warriors to settle down in a nice little house in either town or country.[9] In Lincolnshire, for example, one of the most commonly found Viking artefacts is not a battle-axe, sword, dagger or (hornless) helmet, but brooches, some of them actually imported from Denmark. The majority of these brooches were almost certainly worn by women.[10]

Most of what archaeology has revealed about past houses and family life has been excavated from the ground. The results have been spectacular: I think it probably fair to say that we know as much about the structure and organization of domestic space in an Iron Age house of, say, 100 BC as we do of a rural British cottage of the early 20th century, or indeed of working-class housing throughout much of the industrial era.

In the 1980s we used to welcome many school parties to Flag Fen, east of Peterborough. Even when the National Curriculum arrived in 1988 and we all discovered to our amazement that now English history 'officially' began with the arrival of the Romans, prehistory still mattered. So parties came to view life in the Bronze Age. To help them we reconstructed a number of Bronze and Iron Age round-houses, where we lit fires and did our best to re-create a prehistoric atmosphere. I remember one teacher asking me what life expectancy was in the Bronze Age. This is a subject that is constantly being debated, so I gave him the then best estimate – somewhere into their mid to late 20s, as I recall – and followed this with the usual proviso that some people would have lived for very much longer, maybe into their 70s or 80s. The big problem, and the single factor that would have skewed the figures, was infant and childbirth mortality, which would have been very much higher. For a few moments the children thought about what I had just said. Then a girl raised her hand and asked the crucial question that has kept me thinking ever since: 'If babies and children were always dying, did their mothers feel their loss less badly?'

And what about home comforts in the remote past? Was life really so 'nasty, brutish and short' as Thomas Hobbes would have us believe? I don't think so for one moment. For a start, Hobbes' view of the past assumed (correctly) that people were illiterate, but he confused lack of literacy with lack of culture.

As a farmer I frequently find myself out in the fields in winter, maybe disentangling a sheep's head from a wire fence. Often I seem to spot such problems when driving somewhere else and don't have time to go back to the house and dress for the weather. So I'm out there in my shirtsleeves while snow is blowing across our flat Fenland fields, straight from Siberia – or so it seems at the time. Half an hour spent like that is more than enough, and as soon as I get home I lean up against the Aga (you can't get urbanites to understand why country people love those stoves) and pour myself a cup of strong tea. As the blood returns to my fingers, then hands and arms, I wonder whether Ice Age hunters could have retreated from the cold like this, or were conditions more like what my grandfather had to endure in the trenches of the Somme, during the Great War (without, I might add, his family)? Was life at home in post-Glacial times entirely about endurance and survival, rather than contentment, pleasure and a sense of achievement? Did hunter-gatherer families ever sit down to a meal of roasted venison at midwinter and discuss the events of the day in a civilized fashion; or did they merely grunt, as a film director once suggested to me (in all seriousness)?

Until very recently it was widely believed, even in well-informed archaeological circles, that hunter-gatherers in the millennia follow-ing the retreat of the Ice Ages, some ten thousand years ago, lived in light, skin-covered temporary shelters resembling the 'benders' of hip-pies and eco-warriors. It's hard to conceive what family life would have been like in such a dwelling – I hesitate to use the term 'house' – especially during a cold winter. But now we have good evidence that early post-Glacial families had warm, thatch- or hide-roofed houses, the earliest of which (8500 BC) was discovered very recently, at Star Carr, in North Yorkshire. It's interesting, if not a little ironic, that the name of this, the earliest-known site of Britain's post-Ice Age re-settlement, derives from two Danish words *star kjær* meaning 'sedge fen'.[11] Nordic place names in eastern England were of course introduced by the Vikings, much later 're-settlers' from mainland Europe.

We have known since before the last war that the pre-Roman population of Britain generally lived in round buildings; this shape was the dominant ground plan of houses along the Atlantic fringe of western Europe – a pattern that remained consistent in Britain until the Roman period. By contrast, on the continental mainland, people tended to prefer larger, more barn- or hall-like, rectangular buildings, often with the family space at one end and livestock at the other. It used to be fashionable to attribute many aspects of social structure to something as fixed and tangible as house form, size and layout – and indeed there may have been some truth in such speculations. But on the other hand, the shape and form of houses owes a great deal to local tradition and the availability of building materials, not to mention climate (especially wind speed).

I excavated a number of prehistoric settlements along the Fen margins at Peterborough in the 1970s. Most of these houses – I would estimate there were 50 to 60 of them – had approximately the same floor space as the terrace dwellings provided by the Great Northern Railway for its workforce in the same city in 1850. Today those terrace houses, so convenient for the station, are much sought after by young professionals, many of whom commute to work in London.

Shortly after we reconstructed a Bronze Age (*c.* 1500 BC) round-house at Flag Fen, we were struck by the infamous hurricane of 1987. I have an abiding memory of standing in the doorway looking out while sheets of corrugated steel and laminated plastic blew around us from off a nearby industrial estate, like so many pieces of monstrous confetti. Yet the superficially 'crude' Bronze Age house, which then stood entirely on its own, without the benefit of the trees and hedges which we had only just planted and were yet to become established, was completely unaffected by that terrible storm. This incident proved to me beyond a shadow of doubt that prehistoric houses were warm, secure and sound, just like their Roman, post-Roman, medieval and modern equivalents – they were perfect settings for family life.

Today we take it for granted that an archaeologist could be sheltering from a hurricane in a Bronze Age round-house, whereas just a generation ago such an announcement might have caused quite a stir. One reason for this was a change in academic attitudes towards the past, which happened in the 1960s and '70s. I shall discuss what we then labelled the New Archaeology in Chapter 4, but here I'm more concerned with how it altered the approaches and indeed the lives of those of us who were affected by it. Personally, I was too young and lacked the academic confidence to play an active part in what history must surely judge a major, if not a revolutionary, change. But I found myself completely gripped by what was going on around me. I went to conferences assiduously and read everything I could lay my hands on. They were fascinating times and not, of course, just in archaeology. By my mid-20s, in 1969, I found the confidence to emigrate to Canada, advised to do this by my sister's godfather, an eminent academic who was concerned that I was under a lot of pressure to continue in the family firm, where I had found myself when penniless after graduating from Cambridge (in those days the very few archaeological jobs available went to people with first-class degrees; I had earned a solid 2:2!).

At The Royal Ontario Museum I rapidly re-engaged with archaeology, a decision I have never regretted. After a gap of less than two years I was astonished by the extent to which the subject had changed. One of the aspects of archaeology that had irritated me was what seemed like an obsession with object classification. All the emphasis had been on *things* and the way they might have changed through time; very few researchers seemed at all concerned about the human beings who made and used the things. There was even less concern with what the objects might have meant to people living at the time.

It was assumed that everything then was as it is today; a spoon is just that, a spoon, to be used for soup or cereal – an implement with no wider significance. Put another way, it was just an artefact without any life or meaning of its own as, say, a keepsake, a marriage gift, a

family heirloom, a mark of attainment or a memorial to a dead relative. I have to say I found it a colourless and rather drab view of the
past, which might explain why I decided to join the family firm when
I did. The other explanation, of course, is that the family firm was
Truman's Brewery, in Brick Lane, East London. They were nice people
and they brewed fabulous beer in lively surroundings.

But when I returned to archaeology in Canada, I found I was doing
so on my own terms, as a graduate professional. More importantly, I
had freed myself from the close educational and family networks that
were so constricting back in Britain. In Toronto, I soon began to feel
more self-confident and at the same time I rediscovered how the New
Archaeology was approaching the past in a wholly new way: artefacts
were no longer merely objects for dating and classification; instead
they had begun to acquire much wider significance as symbols of
power, rank, social status and family identity. Some of these ideas
have not stood the test of time, but many have, and I strongly believe
we are all the richer for them.

I returned to England every summer for nine years to run the Museum's excavations on the edges of the Fens, at Fengate, near
Peterborough. In the autumn and winter I would fly back to Canada
to work on material and write reports. As time passed, I found I was
becoming more and more interested in the relevance of archaeology
to the public at large. Soon I realized that its appeal was universal. I
gave several series of public lectures in Toronto, which proved hugely
popular and were trailed extensively on the then-emerging, and
semi-underground, FM radio stations, such as CHUM-FM, where I
began to have something of a regular guest slot.

During the later 1970s I had several informal invitations to return
to Britain, but all these were 'proper' jobs, usually in universities, and
by now I had a strong disinclination to allow myself to be tied down.
I had managed to escape by taking drastic steps and I was not about
to undo all that. With hindsight, I think I found myself increasingly
identifying with the independence of the people and the communities
I was studying. I was surviving on my wits, as did they; but of course
I now realize that we both had networks of friends and relatives to
support us. Then in 1979 a semi-freelance job was announced where
the successful applicant would be in charge of large-scale excavations

in gravel quarries along the edges of the Fens. It could have been designed for me (and I now have reason to believe it probably was). So by the end of the decade I found myself back in Peterborough and digging full time. Soon I began to establish links with local media, just as I had done in Toronto, but sadly the place of the lively, anarchic North American FM radio network had been taken by 'Auntie' BBC; even so, I was able to turn to the local newspaper, the *Peterborough Evening Telegraph*, where I wrote a series of stories and articles, and a popular booklet, with the sci-fi title *People of the Dawn*.

The Fengate dig had had an on-site museum in a converted site hut, but this would not prove possible in the more dangerous surroundings of working gravel quarries. So we organized an extensive series of open days, which attracted media attention. Soon I was presenting documentary series for Anglia Television and even made a 6-part series *Now Then* for BBC Children's Television. In 1982 we discovered Flag Fen which we operated through a charitable limited company we set up for the purpose in 1987. It was to be a public excavation and it opened that summer; I'm pleased to say it is still open, although now run by an independent trust for the city council.

I can only speak for myself, of course, but I'm in little doubt that my team's efforts to reveal modern field archaeology to a wider audience were a consequence of our more theoretical views on the subject that we all shared in common. We were all products of the New Archaeology and we were keen to introduce a degree of scientific rigour to our work – and we were very proud of what we were doing. We were also a small team (rarely more than a dozen people) and we lived together in various houses abandoned by their occupants ahead of development; these were situated on the outskirts of Peterborough, and in a strange way we too lived something of a 'fringe' existence. We worked long hours and visited town very briefly each day. In those days it was rare to see cut-off jeans, let alone mud-spattered, long-haired and very weather-beaten people in what was still a small provincial city. We created quite a stir. But on the other hand I made a point of servicing the dig from local suppliers and we also employed local people wherever we could. And of course we spent most of our personal money in local pubs. Over the years we established excellent relations with the people of Peterborough, so that when Flag Fen opened its doors in the summer of 1987, thousands of people paid to see what we were doing.

For the archaeologists and students on the team there was just one rule, and no exceptions: everyone must be prepared to give site tours. It was our way of putting the concept of bottom-up archaeology into practice. In the first season I drew up a list of topics to be covered, but soon abandoned it when I realized it was stifling individual creativity. At first, some of the students in the excavation would laugh or giggle at an inexperienced tour guide, but when their own turn came to show people around, the silliness ceased, for good. Those tours were extraordinarily helpful to team morale and to us all, as individuals. With every influx of new students there would be a few very insecure, shy or retiring youngsters who tried to get out of doing tours. My wife Maisie was very good at spotting them and she would always send them out for their first tour when there were just two or three visitors. On their return we would congratulate the guide warmly – and then we would send them out again. By the end of their first week, their body-language would be more confident and by the end of the season it was not unusual to have tearful farewells. It is no exaggeration to say that public archaeology and Flag Fen changed some people's lives for ever.

Over the years I have lost count of the number of archaeologists I have met whose interest in the subject was triggered by a visit to Flag Fen. Many slightly older visitors would return regularly to view progress and to see how our ideas were changing. They liked the fact that we abandoned interpretations and explanations when new evidence arose to refute them. I suppose you could think of this as the fallible, the human, face of archaeology. They also liked the fact that different tour guides viewed the site and its significance in various, and sometimes contradictory, ways. They found this a huge contrast to the prepared and pre-packed, often rather corporate tours they were given at other, more commercial, historical visitor attractions. Again, it was all about establishing direct one-to-one relationships. In those days we were all instinctively averse to any top-down preaching or spin. There was no 'party line' that had to be followed, which is not to say, of course, that we lacked beliefs or convictions ourselves. We had them – lots of them – but we all agreed we would never ram them down our visitors' throats. We knew from the dozens, even hundreds, of tours we had all done, that new ideas only take firm hold when the listeners arrived at them by themselves – alone and unaided. I well recall giving a tour to one man on his own. We used to dread such tours as they were far harder work than a group. As we walked around the excavation he didn't appear to respond much to what I was saying, and I assumed I was wasting his, and my, time. Then, right at the very end, after I had shaken his hand and begun to leave, he tapped me on the shoulder. I turned round and he was standing very close behind me, wide eyed. His stare was profound. 'Those people,' he said, 'those Bronze Age people were civilized . . .' He drew the last word out, then almost under his breath, added: 'Just like us . . .'

I can remember visiting a factory on the outskirts of Peterborough around 1980. We had come to do an excavation in advance of a new building, and people working there were fascinated by our presence. Everyone seemed genuinely mystified: wasn't archaeology something that happened in Greece, Egypt or Peru? Hadn't we come to the wrong place? Of course I showed them air photos and explained that the factory was sited on an Iron Age settlement, and they were eventually convinced. But it was an uphill task, nonetheless. Scroll forward to another factory in the same industrial suburb sixteen years later. This time I arrive and explain why I am there, to be greeted with the question: 'And who's doing the geophysics?' That massive leap in the public's awareness and understanding of archaeology was entirely due to one programme: *Time Team*, which began the first of 20 annual series in 1993.

I firmly believe that an idea such as *Time Team* would not have been possible in the intellectual climate that preceded the New Archaeology. Laying aside the fact that the programmes would have been tedious in the extreme, the prevailing climate of opinion was all wrong: archaeology was the province of a few initiates. It was not for the mass of the population. Of course there were exceptions, such as the hugely popular *Animal, Vegetable, Mineral?* (a television game-show of the 1950s), but that was essentially a show which encouraged its (often colourful) participants to display their knowledge of obscure subjects and civilizations. Put another way, it allowed the wider public a brief glimpse into the rich world of academic archaeology, but it certainly did not encourage anyone to get personally involved. More recently, I viewed some archive editions of the show and was forcibly struck by their all-pervading sense of Them and Us. But all of that was to change for ever with *Time Team*.

My personal involvement with *Time Team* began in Series 6, and over the following 15 years (we did a season of documentaries after Series 20) I must have taken part in about 60 films, including live shows and documentaries. In addition, I have also made mini-series based on my own books. I certainly enjoy television and I'm delighted that *Time Team* managed to reach such a huge audience, but having said all that, television by its very nature is a mass-medium in which one-to-one contact is impossible – and it was that individual contact that made Flag Fen such a joy. In theory, of course, books are also a means of mass communication, but when I get the chance to talk unexpectedly to readers – say on the train (as quite often happens) – it seems like I have been talking to them for years; we share many thoughts in common. It's the strangest sensation – rather like meeting a long-lost and dear friend. I know it sounds peculiar, but as a result of these chance encounters with my readers, I have come to regard writing as a direct and often very intimate means of communicating ideas and concepts. In a way it's ironic: television, so often seen as the great leveller, is actually a better medium for preaching top-down messages than the more personal pages you are now reading. And of the two, I know which I prefer.

So the following chapters are going to be about a number of occasions, when British history was changed by the actions of ordinary people – in the language of this book, from the bottom-up. Very often these actions give the impression of being concerted, which is why some prehistorians have suggested that they were controlled by centralized and hierarchical (i.e. class-based) authorities, or hypothetical 'Big Men'. I object to these suggestions because (a) I don't think they are necessary, or are supported by site evidence, and (b) because all the archaeological data we possess on communities of the various periods, such as the layout and arrangement of their fields, their settlements and their relationships with surrounding groups, suggest that wider social networks operated very effectively, and without such 'higher level', or top-down, controls. The more remote a community might be, the greater its need to stay in touch with others.

How does one explain the synchronicity of these diverse events? At a crude level, they have to be cases of stimulus and response: new opportunities arose; maybe something, or some things, needed to be changed and people came together to exploit or to change them. I imagine that many potential 'revolutions' failed to catch on; maybe they were ideas ahead of their time. But what we do know is that those that 'worked' then spread fast – and had a lasting influence. And again, it would be a huge mistake to suppose that communications, even in the earliest post-Glacial times, were inadequate. People needed to stay in touch. Humans are social beings, and by the later Neolithic (say 3000 BC) Britain was criss-crossed by a network of long-established routes and trackways; rivers too would have been important.

Finally, I come to one of the principal themes of this book: what is the relevance of prehistoric home life to us?

As I did the initial research for this book, it slowly dawned on me that I was working on a broad theme that was as relevant in prehistory as it is today. As Michael Caine understood so well, families have always mattered. But there was something else, more fundamental, which has to do with the very organization, not just of families, but of communities and societies too. Indeed, it's the highly complex structure and arrangement of our cultures that sets humans apart from other animals. That, ultimately, is what this book is about.

It would be reasonable to ask how such a bottom-up analysis of ancient British communities can be relevant to modern Britain. And the answer to that may be found in the structure of the contemporary political world which is supposed to give our nation its structure. Just look at the reaction of people around you when you turn on a radio or TV set and witness the braying, the leering 'hear-hears', and the Victorian Public School jeering of MPs during Prime Minister's Questions. Normal people find the scene horrible: an irrelevant insult to the nation's long history. The press, too, are over-obsessed by the latest Westminster Village gossip. But that isn't what concerns people who live outside the Westminster political 'bubble'. Our own problems are far more pressing: how do I find money for a mortgage? How can I stay in work? The growing gap between the top and the rest of the social pyramid is what worries me, bearing in mind that for thousands of years British societies governed themselves very well indeed, but without any centralized help, or co-ordination. Their social structures, based on family values, gave them the stability and cohesion they required. So I firmly believe that the prehistoric communities of Britain have important things to teach us today, if, that is, we have the humility to learn from them.

But enough of introductory thoughts. It is time to begin a journey that will take us back to another period of rapid change, over ten thousand years ago, in the immediate aftermath of the last great Ice Age.

I

After the Ages of Ice
(9600–8000 BC)

Britain at the end of the Ice Ages was a very different place from now. For a start, it was still attached to the continental mainland, but, rather surprisingly, the climate was not *that* different. Certainly it was cooler, but we are not looking here at something resembling the icy plains of Siberia. The post-Glacial warming had been sharp and rapid; and although Britain was not surrounded by sea, it was still very much within a sphere of maritime influence. We should not forget, either, that because of the way the planet revolves on its orbit around the sun, weather systems would still have travelled west to east, taking with them, to what would later become the British Isles, the warmer, moist air they had picked up over the Atlantic.

Since the last war, our knowledge of early post-Glacial times has grown rapidly, largely thanks to a number of new scientific techniques, ranging from analysis of ice cores, sea- and lake-bed muds and pollen, to some extraordinary recent research into the pre-maritime history of the North Sea. It is probably fair to say that these science-based studies were ahead of archaeological knowledge until the final years of the 20th century, since when there have been a number of important discoveries which have transformed our understanding of what we can now appreciate was a very dynamic period indeed.

THE SETTING: BRITAIN
BECOMES AN ISLAND

Let us start with the land beneath our feet; then we will turn to climate. Although the maps we have been familiar with all our lives show the British Isles to be perched on the very edge of Europe, the Continental Shelf, which raises Europe high above the depths of the Atlantic Ocean, is actually very much larger around north-western Europe and Scandinavia. Indeed, the entire North Sea Basin is actually on the Continental Shelf.[1] Satellite images clearly show the Shelf to continue about 125 miles (a couple of hundred km) west of Ireland, then it swings north, leaving Scotland, and its many off-shore islands, well 'inland', surrounded by shallow seas. These shallow waters are important because they are readily warmed by the sun; they are also enriched with nutrients washed in by the many rivers that are fed by the moist maritime climate. The warmth and the nutrients feed plankton and seaweeds, which in turn nourish a huge food-chain of shellfish, fish and, ultimately, ourselves.

As I have just suggested, post-Glacial warming does not seem to have been a gradual process. In fact, it probably happened in less than a century. The way we currently understand it, there was a sharp rise in temperature, of some 10 degrees Celsius, that signalled the end of the Ice Age, around 9600 BC.[2] By 8000 BC, conditions may even have been slightly warmer than they are today.[3] This would have meant that the earliest inhabitants of post-Glacial Britain did not have to contend with sub-Arctic conditions when they arrived. They were also moving into, or recolonizing, a completely uninhabited landscape, so they could pick and choose when and where they settled, as they headed northwards into that part of the north-western European plain that was shortly to become the North Sea and the British Isles. So we must abandon any idea that these people led lifestyles comparable with the Inuit (the modern term for the people we used to call Eskimos), as the climate would have been only a little cooler than it is now – perhaps the equivalent of parts of southern Scandinavia today. At this time much of the British landscape was wooded, but the trees were predominantly birch and pine, rather than the oak, beech and ash of today. What are now the traditional hardwood trees of the British Isles took longer to recolonize the land than did the people.

Archaeologists have long been curious about what might once have been happening below the low-lying plains that later became the North Sea. It all began with the discovery, in 1931, of a bone spearhead which was pulled up from the bed of the sea by the crew of the *Colinda*, a sailing trawler, about 25 miles (40 km) off the Norfolk coast.[4] The object had been embedded in peat, about 20 fathoms (36.6 metres, 120 feet) below the surface.[5] The style of the spearhead is identical to examples that Professor Grahame Clark and his team were later to excavate at Star Carr, in Yorkshire – a site we will return to often – so presumably it was of roughly the same age. In actual fact it was later dated by radiocarbon, which showed it to be approximately a millennium earlier, at about 9500 BC. Sea-levels would have been even lower at that time because so much water was still locked up in the enlarged ice-caps around the North Pole and in Scandinavia.

A number of other finds were made from submerged peat beds, especially around the Dutch coast,[6] but systematic survey work only became possible in the later 20th century, when companies started to prospect for new sources of North Sea oil. And then, of course, money was thrown at the problem. The result has been a detailed surface map of the submerged southern North Sea plain, an area known as 'Doggerland', named after its final remnant, the Dogger Bank, now beneath the waters of the North Sea. This term was coined by Professor Bryony Coles of Exeter University, who in 1998 had the foresight and imagination to attempt a hypothetical reconstruction (based on the best available geological evidence) of what might lie hidden beneath the waters.[7] Her map actually coincides very well with the much later survey that was published by archaeologists using the new three-dimensional seismic data produced by the oil industry. Both surveys clearly show that there were huge landscapes of fertile ground which would have been a rich resource of animal and plant foods.

Most of the population around 9000 BC probably lived out on the low-lying plains that today sit at the bottom of the North Sea.[8] These people would have looked west with some trepidation. Much of the land which is now Britain would have seemed inhospitable to them: dry, craggy and bleak – and very much their hinterland. By contrast, their marshy, low-lying world was extraordinarily abundant, rich in fish and eels, shellfish, wildfowl, and game of all sorts, ranging from hares to red deer. In the uplands that are now Britain, and on drier areas of the North Sea plain, the principal threats to humans were from bears and wolves, both of which are discouraged when confronted by organized groups of people. (See Fig. 1.1.)

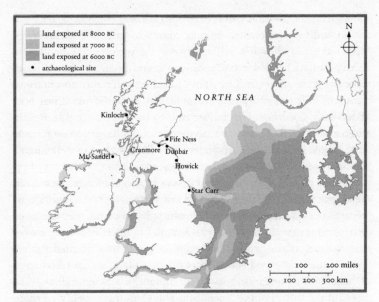

Fig. 1.1 A map showing how Britain gradually separated from the continent at the end of the Ice Age, between about 6000 and 4000 BC.

We cannot discuss the social organization of these communities if we have no idea how they managed to keep themselves alive. The problem here is that sites of the earlier Mesolithic, from about 8500 to 6500 BC, have been very hard to find in Britain, largely, one suspects, because most now lie beneath the sea, but the conventional wisdom has for a long time suggested (and to my mind counter-intuitively) that communities living on the land which was about to become the British Isles subsisted entirely on dryland resources, despite the fact that they were rapidly being surrounded by sea water. We know for a fact that they inhabited coastal camps and made hunting and foraging expeditions inland during the warmer months of the year, but even so, they don't appear to have eaten fish or shellfish on their travels.[9]

By complete contrast, the evidence from Scandinavia, where for various reasons the conditions for preservation are rather better, suggests that people only tended to exploit the resources of the marine zone, especially shellfish and fish. I suspect, and common sense would surely support me, that in Britain coastal communities, especially those living along the lower-lying coasts of eastern England and East Anglia, must have led broadly similar lifestyles. At the same time, those living further inland could have exploited their own, non-marine, resources. But sadly, Britain's storm-lashed east coast does not preserve many good post-Glacial archaeological sites. Rising sea-levels and constant erosion have done tremendous damage. Even very much later prehistoric sites like 'Seahenge', which once rested safely inland behind a sheltering screen of sand banks, are now being destroyed by the waves. But the same erosional processes are also revealing far, far earlier material, once safely hidden below the active tidal zone. Indeed, the earliest evidence for human occupation in Britain, recently redated to some time around a million years ago, has been found on a heavily eroding beach along the north Norfolk coast, at Happisburgh.[10]

Again, it used to be believed that the first post-Ice Age recolonists of Britain had no choice but to live in 'bender'-like portable structures, made from hooped poles and skins, as the hostility of their surroundings forced them to adopt an itinerant, nomad-like lifestyle. Laying aside what we now know about the considerable comfort such lightweight houses can provide, the new evidence suggests that in fact they were anything but flimsy. As is so often the case in archaeology, our first attempts to come to grips with life in a remote period of the past underestimated what the people were actually capable of achieving. And as so often happens too, it turns out that the real story, now being carefully revealed, is far more exciting than anything we had previously imagined.

THE STORY SO FAR . . .

I have been writing general books on British prehistory for about fifteen years, and during that relatively brief time the evidence for man's earliest presence in Britain has been pushed back from 500,000 to 600,000 to over 1,000,000 years ago.[11] The last Ice Age ended just over 10,000 years ago. So the period I will discuss both in this chapter and further on in this book is, in effect, a very thin layer of sugar on the top of a thick, multi-layered cake. To mix metaphors, we are not dealing here with a blank canvas. In effect we will be repainting a pre-existing picture, but one which is still only partially understood – and that doubtless explains the rapid revisions of the basic dates.

When the Ice Age ended, Britain was indeed a very different place, but the people who reoccupied the lands that were later to become the British Isles were both physically and mentally identical to us. Recent genetic studies have shown that initially, when conditions were coldest, they came from southern and western Atlantic Europe, but later from France and then further east.[12] But what about their daily lives? Did they have routines, or were their lives one long, ghastly struggle for survival? Indeed, did they have families at all? Over the years I have noted the persistence of what I think of as the 'Flintstones' view of the Palaeolithic, or Old Stone Age, where people are supposed to have eked out a meagre existence, while living in grim caves and hovels. The reality was very different, but again our understanding of the times has also gone through many changes. But first, a brief word about chronology.

The Stone Age represents 99.99 per cent of mankind's existence on this planet. We now know that there have been human beings for some two million years and they probably used stone tools of one sort or another from the outset. On the other hand, metal, in the form of copper, usually followed by bronze, only appears on the scene around eight to nine thousand years ago – and doesn't reach Britain until just before 2500 BC. Because it is such a huge period of time, the Stone Age is conventionally sub-divided into three shorter periods. In Britain the Old Stone Age, or Palaeolithic, begins, as we have just seen, around a million years ago and it ends with the last of the Ice Ages, around 10,000 BC. The Palaeolithic is followed by the Mesolithic or Middle Stone Age, which runs from the end of the Ice Age through to the arrival of farmers around 4200 BC. Finally, the Neolithic, or New Stone Age, starts at 4200 BC and ends with the arrival of copper and bronze in about 2500 BC.

This way of sub-dividing time is far from perfect. For a start, the Old Stone Age is disproportionately long, when compared with the Mesolithic and Neolithic, and is further sub-divided into Upper, Middle and Lower Palaeolithic; these, in turn are divided up into a series of smaller periods. For our purposes, these various sub-periods are largely irrelevant, but I mention them to make the point that the Stone Age wasn't an amorphous chronological 'blob', when people huddled in their caves fearful of marauding sabre-toothed tigers, but did little else, other than endure the Ice Age cold. In reality, the Ice Ages were interrupted by warm periods – indeed we are probably living in one now – and Palaeolithic people developed a succession of remarkable stone, bone, antler and probably wooden tools, which show that their societies were constantly growing and evolving.[13] In short, people back then were just as inventive as they are today. Innovation, it would seem, is part of the human condition.

It used to be believed that hunter-gatherer communities had little time for anything other than chasing around after food. This view was part of what one might term a progressive attitude to human history or prehistory. It went along with school-room wall-charts showing the Long March of Mankind which began with tiny crouching little monkeys that slowly grew larger, then began to straighten up and ultimately strode confidently from the shadows of Prehistory into the Future, as modern human beings. Those rather hunched and heavily browed fellows were generally speaking early forms of humans, whereas the striding chap at their head was one of us, a farmer. At least that was how the story was taught to me, or perhaps (to be fair to my teachers), that was how I remembered it.

In reality, Eurasian farming began around ten thousand years ago, at about the same time that the Ice Age was ending in Britain. The very first farmers lived in the Middle East, in places like modern Iraq. But the ideas and practices of farming took just under four thousand years to reach the fringes of north-western and Atlantic Europe, arriving in Britain shortly before 4000 BC. By this time, the British Isles had been fully separated from the mainland for at least a couple of millennia. Those are the basic facts, but as we will see, they only tell a part of the story.

Although the inventiveness of Stone Age communities has been known since the pioneering days of modern archaeology, in the early 19th century, that knowledge has generally failed to inform our ideas about how people in these remote periods of the past lived out their daily lives, which are *still* generally perceived as being nasty and brutish, etc. The widespread belief persists that our hunter-gatherer (i.e. pre-farmer) ancestors led impoverished lives. They would spend all day chasing around after scarce and flighty game, only to arrive back in the hovel, or cave, at night-time empty handed, or at best, with a moth-eaten hare or a hibernating hedgehog. Meanwhile, the wife and children had been out in the woods grubbing around for a few edible roots, or buried nuts. They gobbled down this unenviable repast over a flickering fire, then collapsed, still hungry, into a fitful sleep, always keeping one eye open in case the fire died down and a passing cave-bear might be feeling peckish.

As a student I remember learning that the hunter-gatherer lifestyle was distinctly grim in winter, but got slightly better in summer. There were more nuts and berries for the family to collect and the leaves of trees and shrubs provided the men with better cover to stalk their prey, which were fatter and more meaty than in the leaner months of winter. But even so, this foraging family would have had little or no time for what one might term the finer things of life: for religion and for abstract thought. And that was why they never managed to construct formal cemeteries, nor the great henges and other ceremonial sites that suddenly seemed to mushroom across the landscape when the first farmers arrived on the scene.

On the face of it, this caricature of the hunter-gatherer life is not wholly misleading. There was, for example, a big seasonal difference in the availability of resources, and in wintertime pickings could be lean, unless you happened to be living close to fresh water, in which case they were rather more plentiful, thanks to fish, eels and wildfowl. But our understanding of the period has been transformed through two important developments.

The first was the emergence of a number of new science-based techniques. This happened just before, but then with greater vigour after, the last war, and led directly to a far better understanding of the post-Ice Age environment. Second, and just as significant, was a more profound appreciation of what was involved in the hunter-gatherer way of life. Again, certain pioneers, especially the late, great Professor Grahame Clark, of Cambridge, had begun to take the anthropological side of their researches more seriously. This started to happen before the war, but gathered huge momentum in the mid-60s. This was when archaeologists in North America widened their attention, away from the way hunters tracked and killed their prey, and instead examined what else they did with their lives, when, that is, they were not chasing after, or eating, food. And what they discovered came as a revelation to many of us who thought we understood what life was like for those few people who had returned to Britain as the ice sheets melted, some ten thousand years ago. Just to remind you, this is the period known as the Mesolithic, or Middle Stone Age – and it is where our story really begins.

SETTLEMENT, FAITH AND
A NOMADIC LIFESTYLE

The new science-based techniques, such as radiocarbon dating and pollen analysis, showed that many of the known post-Glacial hunter-gatherer sites (dating to between *c.* 9000 and 4500 BC) were only occupied at certain times of the year. There was also evidence that these places had been returned to repeatedly, year after year. At the time it was widely believed by many prehistorians that nomadic communities, such as the Mongols, wandered across the vast land-scapes of, say, the Asian Steppes more or less at random, following the migrations of game and the availability of other natural resources. So they assumed, and who can blame them, that Britain's Mesolithic people moved around in the same, seemingly aimless, fashion.

The trouble was that the Mongols, and indeed all other nomads, did actually lead highly structured lives and there was no pointless wandering at all. Put another way, people followed known routes rather than their noses. And those routes would cover much the same areas of land from one year to the next. They were planned so as not to interfere with the migrations of other, most probably related, groups of nomads, and there would be regular tribal meetings to sort out any developing conflicts over resources. From time to time, of course, things did break down and skirmishes would have happened, but these confrontations were the exception not the rule. Hollywood aside, the Steppes were never the sole domain of marauding bands of warriors.

When anthropological archaeologists turned their attention to smaller hunter-gatherer communities, which were organized on a scale more like those of the British Mesolithic, they again found little that was haphazard or random about their lives. People like the Bushmen of the Kalahari Desert of southern Africa also followed fixed migratory routes that took advantage of various seasonally available resources. But (and this is what surprised everyone at the time), the new research also revealed that the evident order of hunter-gatherer social life extended into rich conceptual realms. So shared creation myths and tales of the ancestors underpinned and supported the structure of their communities and families. It was a way of using the past to give meaning and structure to the present. These legends were taught to their children and grand-children by the older generation in regular sessions – surely an educational system by any other name?

But in the 1950s, and for most of the '60s, British archaeologists accepted that Mesolithic hunter-gatherers had little or no time for thinking, or for using their imagination – or indeed for being human, as we would see it. It was believed that these early communities simply lacked the time, and with it the inclination, for such things. While I was being taught these 'facts' at university, I also recall lecturers telling me, most emphatically, that physically and mentally these were people just like us in every respect. I remember thinking it was very odd: *I* couldn't imagine living such an impoverished way of life. So why did they? I can even recall imagining that somewhere out in those long-vanished Mesolithic campsites there must have been tents where the intellectual equivalents of people like Bach, Newton and Shakespeare would have lived. Today it seems patently absurd that men and women of genius would have stared into a fire, night after night, their minds a complete blank. Yet sadly, that is what we were expected to believe.

The main element that was thought lacking from the Mesolithic hunter-gatherer lifestyle was religion and ceremonial, for which the first, good, tangible evidence appears at the start of the following period, the Neolithic, around 4200 BC. Again, the view at the time was that the new religions, for want of a better word, arrived along with farming and settled life. Put another way, when they started to *produce*, rather than merely *gather*, their food, people suddenly acquired the leisure to think about Higher Things. But that idea depended on the single observation that food-gathering is more time-consuming than food production. Research in the later 1960s was to show that this was a false assumption.[14]

We will see, time and again, that families and religion go hand-in-hand: everything from grace before meals, to family prayers, to sitting in family pews in the parish church. Some houses in the Middle Ages and later had a small shrine in a central place; great country houses had their own chapels, and it is interesting that there were similar structures in both Roman and prehistoric houses – the best examples of the latter being in Neolithic and Bronze Age Orkney (see Chapter 3). So it is hard to imagine family life, as we would understand the term today, in a period where religion (or ritual, as we prehistorians like to call it) was absent. So, clearly something was wrong or missing in our understanding of life in the British Mesolithic. But as we will see in the next chapter, the long-lost evidence for Mesolithic religion is at last starting to emerge from the ground, and the waters.

But before I discuss what is surely Britain's first significant housing boom, we must return to the question of mobility that I started to address earlier. Put another way, to what extent were Mesolithic people nomadic? As I discussed earlier, nomadic people did not move around at random, but they did move – and quite often, too. Weekly stays in one place would not have been uncommon. One clue to such a shifting lifestyle lies in the build and size of their houses. Put crudely, lightweight structures suggest impermanence. But immediately this flags up another warning: the more substantial a house, the greater and more durable will its archaeological remains be.

Again, it's common sense: a lightweight structure (such as a hippy bender) will leave only a very slight trace in the ground when the group of travellers decides to move on. Your best chance of proving that they had ever been there in the first place would be by spotting the rubbish they might have left behind them. By the same token, permanent or semi-permanent settlement sites soon accumulate huge quantities of debris, whereas one-off, short-stay camps are well nigh impossible to detect archaeologically. This means that archaeological surveys are inevitably biased in favour of permanence, and against mobility. And here it's worth noting that the sheer quantity of material from some of the newly discovered Mesolithic settlements suggests either a degree of permanence, or frequent re-visits – or both.

There is, however, evidence, and plenty of it, for shifting, short-term settlement in Mesolithic Britain, but as most of it consists of a few scattered flints in a field, it can be difficult to draw hard-and-fast conclusions. Having said that, we should not simply assume that the lifestyle of more nomadic families was somehow inferior. Lightweight buildings can be very comfortable and the travelling life does indeed have its compensations: sites are cleaner, so diseases are rarer, and often game can be more abundant. On the down-side, of course, it's riskier, mainly because the more productive, i.e. 'safer', landscapes would probably have been occupied by settled communities quite early on. Like settled and travelling groups throughout time, the permanent occupants would not have welcomed intruders, even – no, especially – in times of scarcity. It has been estimated that many of the Mesolithic families in southern Britain could have moved their homes as often as fifty times a year.[15] But it would be a great mistake to suppose that somehow this was the norm, which is certainly what was assumed when I was a student in the '60s. Today, however, our ideas are rather different.

BRITAIN'S FIRST HOUSING BOOM

There have been a number of mini-revolutions in British archaeology during the fifty or so years I have been studying it, and I have had the great good fortune to have been actively involved in two of them: the transformation of wetland archaeology and the discovery of intact Bronze Age field systems in lowland landscapes. There have, of course, been others since the last war, such as the meteoric rise of urban archaeology, the transformation of timescales brought about by radio-carbon and now the insights provided by DNA analysis. But of all these mini-revolutions I think the most exciting is still taking place. Indeed, there was an item on a recent Radio 4 *Today* programme that nearly made me choke on my breakfast; but I'll have more to say about the astonishing find at South Queensferry shortly. The mini-revolution I am thinking about dates to the very start of life in post-Glacial Britain; the more I look at what was happening, the more it appears to be Britain's earliest housing boom. And make no mistake: these were all proper family homes – but built at an almost unbelievably early period.

Now I cannot claim to have played even a small part in the discovery of these early Mesolithic dwellings, but they have been revealed during a period when I have been writing a series of general books on British prehistory and landscape development. So I have had the time and the motivation to follow them up. Perhaps more to the point, as we will see shortly, my wife, Maisie Taylor, is the leading specialist in prehistoric British wood-working and she has been closely involved with at least two of these projects. Sometimes I'm allowed to tag along on her site visits; on these occasions, I pretend I'm her photographer.

So instead of the usual textbook style of description followed by discussion, I thought I would offer a narrative account of how these exciting new finds came to my attention. It was never a straightforward process: the truth took a long time to dawn on me, and when it did, it happened slowly, by degrees. In a busy world, where there is increasing competition for people's attention, new archaeological discoveries are offered to the public cut and dried, with few loose ends – and of course any uncertainty makes for a weak news story. But in my experience, when you are on, or close to, the cutting-edge of advancing knowledge, things are never so plain to see. Clarity comes through repetition, editing, revision and experience. And of course this is also where error and misconception enter the picture. It would be great if we could always get the initial research dead right; it would save so much head-scratching and recrimination later. But sadly, that is not the way we humans do things. Anyhow, for better or for worse, what follows is an account of how Britain's earliest domestic revolution came to my attention.

Now it might be supposed that the very earliest houses in post-Glacial Britain would be sited in the warmer south, preferably in a low-lying, sheltered river valley. Maybe they were, but so far they have not been found there. One reason for that might well be the devastating effects of much later ploughing which we know has removed most of the evidence for Neolithic houses (I will discuss this further in Chapter 3). Another reason, of course, was that the focus for settlement in these very early times lay well to the east, out there in the

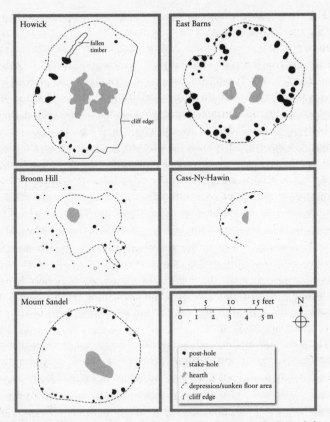

Fig. 1.2 Floor plans of houses built by hunter-gatherers in the Mesolithic period. These are substantial dwellings that were probably occupied permanently (perhaps for more than a decade at a time).

fertile plains of the southern North Sea Basin, in landscapes long since inundated. But whatever the reason, the earliest houses in Britain have survived on higher ground and often in seemingly hostile land-scapes, near cliffs, for example. I suspect that the modern distribution of these very early buildings has been grossly distorted by the passage of time and erosion by both man and the elements. But now to our story.

The world of British archaeology is very tight-knit. It is also very small, and like all human groups of its sort, it is riven with gossip. Rumours abound; and I think I must have heard about the extraordinary discoveries in Northumberland some time around or shortly after 2002, probably while the work was actually taking place. Everyone was talking about these early Mesolithic discoveries and how they were going to transform our understanding of the period, even if nobody, myself included, seemed to know precisely how.

But the stories and rumours continued to surface and although I was meant to be deeply involved with the research and writing of *Britain AD*, a book on post-Roman times, my attention kept being caught by these earlier Mesolithic discoveries, which were still happening. They fascinated me, but I was never at all clear why. Then, very gradually, as I began to come to grips with the layout and construction of these newly revealed structures, it came to me that they were real houses – substantial structures, built to last. Somehow I had to visit one. Then five years ago, I managed to persuade the BBC to make a programme about early settlement around the North Sea, and I put Howick at the top of the list of key sites that we would have to cover. (See Fig. 1.2.)

The beauty of making radio and television programmes is that you get to talk to the person who made the initial discovery. And nothing is better than that. Books, leaflets and information panels are all very well, but they cannot compete with a first-hand account. And Clive Waddington does a very good first-hand account. His task was made easier by the beauty and drama of the landscape around us. Howick is a very dramatic place, high above rocky cliffs on the Northumbrian coast (see Plate 1). It was a breezy day and my initial reaction wasn't good: frankly, I found it impossibly exposed and bleak. Clive then reminded me that the cliffs had eroded back some distance since the house had been built and it may well have been more sheltered than today. The sea would also have been further away, although not that far, as by the time in question – shortly after 8000 BC – the main mass of the North Sea had extended well south of Northumberland, which would have already been coastal for several centuries.

I had been on site for about half an hour when the June sun came out and the place became transformed. There were larks in the air. As we walked, Clive pointed out that the ground was dry and well drained. He went on to describe the excavations: how they had revealed that the floor of the house had been slightly lowered and there was clear evidence in the form of burning and charcoal for a central hearth, or more probably hearths. Buildings of this sort don't have a chimney and smoke escapes through the roof-covering, which would probably have been of dry bracken, heather, reeds, or a mixture of these and other types of thatch, probably tied into place and weighted down with stones or turves. The only thing they would have lacked would have been straw – cereals and farming were not to arrive in Britain for at least another three and a half millennia.

The early date of the Howick house caused surprise in the archaeological world when it was first announced, but what made me sit up and take notice was the fact that the radiocarbon dates showed it to have been occupied for about 200 years.[16] But that was just one of many discoveries: excavations were happening everywhere, as the economic boom of the early 21st century was still forging ahead, and sites like Howick had to face stiff competition for space in the archaeological media. Indeed, Clive Waddington was able to point to at least two other British sites that had revealed substantial houses of the early 8th millennium BC. But that early date and the fact that the Howick house had been built so robustly was most remarkable. I can remember thinking that a round-house like that would not have been out of place over five thousand years later, in the Iron Age, when the British landscape was fully developed and most people were living settled lives in fixed villages. But in the early Mesolithic? Surely, we all thought, that was when people had only just re-settled Britain and were barely able to scratch a hand-to-mouth existence? The idea that they built themselves permanent houses seemed almost absurd. But there was no arguing with the evidence, which lay before me as clear as day.

It was there, and there could be no doubt about it. Clive's team's meticulous excavation showed the house must have been occupied for long periods – years rather than days. There were clear signs of repair and rebuilding, which show that the house must have been continuously occupied. For what it's worth, the other substantial early

8th-millennium BC house then known, at East Barns,[17] East Lothian, and slightly later examples, at Mount Sandel, in Northern Ireland, also showed clear evidence for continuous repair and maintenance. I shall have more to say about Mount Sandel shortly. It's also worth noting here that substantial houses made from natural materials require constant maintenance: birds peck holes in thatch, mud walls crack and collapse and of course posts rot, especially below ground. The Bronze Age houses we built at Flag Fen require small jobs doing to them weekly, if not daily – and most particularly in winter, when frosts and winds can cause minor havoc. When it comes to such buildings, 'a stitch in time' is the watchword: leave damage alone, and it will soon get worse. Minor problems can rapidly become major headaches.

Clive's team had painstakingly rebuilt the Howick house, but it had been burnt to the ground by vandals a few months before my visit.[18] What I saw was a charred tangle of beams and branches. In some respects that was even more moving than the reconstruction. In a strange way, those sad remnants seemed somehow more real. For a moment I felt like a member of the original family who had just returned from a day's fishing to discover his precious home a pile of ashes. Maybe one of the children had been playing too close to the hearth. Maybe a spit-roast joint of fatty wild boar piglet had caught fire – as happens too often on my barbecue – but whatever had caused it, the place burnt down, and we know from numerous excavations that such fires were relatively common throughout prehistory. But for a moment, as I stood and looked at what was left of their house, I couldn't help feeling sympathy for so many families in the remote and distant past.

Howick was in every respect a house, not a 'hut', as these dwellings are generally described by specialists in the Mesolithic. I have to say, I dislike the use of that patronizing term, which denigrates places people once thought of as home; 'shack' is almost as bad. No, it is clear that the Howick house would have been a family home – and a pleasant one at that. There would have been ample space for two parents and their children and maybe even room for grandparents too. It is worth remembering here that most of people's lives would have been lived outside the home, either in the woods hunting or gathering food, or closer by. Young children and elderly people would probably not have ventured so far away.

Reconstruction of an ancient building on the basis of the floor plan and a series of post-holes is never straightforward. The pitch of the roof is always a problem, but there are one or two basic facts which cannot be avoided. Thatch, whether of reed or straw, only sheds water efficiently if the slope of the roof is greater than 45 degrees. Any flatter than that and the water tends to trickle through, rather than along the thatching material. Similarly, if the roof-covering is of turf or bracken, then a pitch as steep as 45 degrees would soon see the roof-covering sliding off. Experience has shown that these roofs need a flatter pitch, of about 35 degrees, or less. You can play around with these pitches by using various combinations of roofing material: at Flag Fen, for example, we found that a combination of reed straw and turf, at an angle of 35 degrees, has worked very effectively. But more on this later.

When I saw pictures of Clive's reconstruction of the Howick house, I noted that he had the roof set very steep indeed: closer to 55 than 45 degrees. I can remember thinking, in the light of my own practical experience roofing a Bronze Age house at Flag Fen, that this might cause problems. In roofs of this sort all the covering material has to be tied into place and this in turn creates leakages, because water runs down the ties; but again, the roof pitch is so steep that heavy rain will tend to flow down the rafters, even on their undersides, so you don't get as much dripping inside these houses as you do with flatter pitches. But whatever the pitch, people would have used the most appropriate roof-covering for their particular region: in the west the rainfall is far heavier, but the wind can be less fierce than in the flatter landscapes of the east, where winters, too, tend to be colder.

And of course there are social preferences to consider. People are rarely entirely rational about their homes, where current fashion can apply, as much as in dress. Some things would have been seen as 'up-market' and as indicators, perhaps, of rank and status. We can only guess at what these symbols might have been: most probably the treatment of doors and doorways, but also roof-covering, which would have been highly visible. Sadly these things are only rarely preserved on archaeological sites.

Part of the Howick house had been eaten away by the cliff, but the extent of the floor was clearly visible and was further marked by a spread of Mesolithic flints. The hearths, too, were clearly discernible. Sometimes houses with low or very flat-pitched roofs have trouble getting rid of smoke, so hearths are often placed just outside the doorway. This makes the house less warm, but again, such houses tend to be smaller, which means they enclose less air; as a consequence, they would have been more readily warmed by radiant heat given off by the glowing embers of the external fire – and of course by the body-heat of the people inside. Chimneys and fireplaces are not found in British houses until Roman times. Instead, smoke was allowed to filter-out through the roof-covering – and again, the steepness of the pitch would have helped, here. In the 1950s some early reconstructed prehistoric houses were given small holes in the roof to allow the smoke to escape. These experiments were short lived, as the blast-furnace-like updraught proved far too strong, and the fire went out of control and lit the thatch.

The steepness of the Howick house's roof was doubtless a response to having a hearth inside it, but sadly it could also have been the reason why it was torched by vandals, who might not have been attracted by a lower, less striking structure. And this raises another topic: security. The newly discovered early Mesolithic houses seem to have made no attempts at concealment. They all appear to sit proudly within their landscapes and this must suggest that their builders and owners felt secure in their tenure of the land around them. I don't want to make too much of this, but it must surely be evidence for a more settled, less mobile way of life – and at such a very early date.

The programme I was making when I first visited Howick was about 'Britain's lost Atlantis'. We were interested in the archaeology beneath the North Sea and at the time the Howick house was the earliest yet found in Britain. But as I have already hinted, even at that very early date (8000 BC), the inhabitants of the house would not have been able to walk out of their front door, straight across what is now the North Sea, to Denmark. Instead, they would first have travelled a long way south, down the coasts of Durham, Cleveland and Yorkshire, then across the Humber to Lincolnshire, before they could safely have turned east. Even as early as 8000 BC, Britain was well on the way to becoming an island.

STAR CARR: RETHINKING THE MESOLITHIC

Britain has produced just one or two archaeological sites that are icons of a particular period, and Star Carr, North Yorkshire, is one of them. It has been known about as an early Mesolithic site since before the last war and has been the subject of more-or-less continuous academic research ever since.[19]

When I was a student, Star Carr was held out as *the* example of how modern archaeology should be carried out. Admittedly, the professor and head of our department at Cambridge was Grahame Clark, the man who had master-minded the Star Carr project, but the fact remains that it was one of the first, and best, examples of archaeological teamwork. Consequently, many other members of the project staff were also giving us lectures on everything from bone and antler, to flintwork, to pollen analysis and palaeogeography. You name it, Star Carr had it. But there was even more to it than that: the approach to Star Carr was new. It is probably fair to say it was closer to being a scientific experiment than a traditional excavation: ideas were constantly being put forward and then tested in the field, which is why research continued for so long. Much of this research, however, was to do with the geological history of the area, and how the environment there had altered as the climate grew progressively warmer.

The best-known excavations took place at Star Carr between 1949 and 1951, but research has continued there, on and off, ever since. This was intensive, research-orientated, meticulous excavation. Meanwhile, in the 1960s, '70s and '80s, British archaeology was quietly transforming itself, but in rather different directions. A new generation of field archaeologists were pioneering techniques of large-scale, 'open area' excavation, where entire settlements, field systems and even landscapes were being surveyed and excavated. As a consequence of this new work, prehistorians were starting to grasp the impact of ancient communities on entire landscapes. Put another way, the focus of research was shifting in both direction and scale.

But while these new landscape-scale approaches were being developed, very few new trenches were being opened at Star Carr, largely, I suspect, because of the site's iconic status. Indeed, that status is continuing to cause researchers there problems. Meanwhile, it was becoming increasingly clear to many practical prehistorians that the ancient environment and the changing natural setting of this important site were now quite thoroughly understood. What we lacked was a broad assessment of the nature of the human occupation there: the debris and other remains left in the ground by Mesolithic people. We didn't even know if the site was a short-lived hunters' camp (which was widely believed), or a more permanent settlement. All we had to go by was a single trench, excavated in the early 1950s by Professor Clark. And there is a limit to what you can say about a single, small trench. To make matters worse, it has been known for at least thirty years that the site was steadily drying out. And that was potentially catastrophic for the preservation of the very fragile remains that still lay in the peats of the sub-soil.

Clark and his collaborators' work on the changing environment of post-Glacial Star Carr was only made possible because the site had remained permanently waterlogged since Ice Age times. This water-logging, and the acidic nature of the peats that had accumulated there, meant that delicate organic material, such as leaves, seeds, twigs and pollen grains, had all been preserved. In the normal run of events, such stuff would have been destroyed by rot, wind and rain in a few weeks or months, at the most. See how leaves and twigs that accumulate on lawns and in parks over autumn have largely disappeared by the following spring. So the news that Star Carr was drying out came as something of a wake-up call to the academic community. The result was a new research group, based at the University of York, and co-led by three archaeologists, all distinguished in their own specialized fields of interest. As such projects go, it is widely regarded as first rate, but then I would say that, as Maisie is their wood consultant. And as we will see shortly, despite its drier and more degraded state, Star Carr is still producing quantities of wood, and much of it clearly worked by the hand of man.

I can still just recall visiting the field where Professor Clark had excavated those early Mesolithic flints and timbers, back in the 1950s. To us students, the site was iconic-verging-on-the-supernatural, and every aspiring young archaeologist had to make a pilgrimage there. Mine was some time around 1967. Sadly, my Mecca Moment was a miserable, wet and foggy one, and I honestly can't remember much at all, other than peaty soil and some windy, dripping Scots pines. Over the years, I have driven along the A64 through the Vale of Pickering many times, but I have never seen fit to turn off the road again, until, that is, my second visit in 2006, which was *much* more memorable.

I can remember looking up as we felt the first few drops of rain. Maisie and I were walking along the edge of a harvested wheat field. The pines I had remembered from my first visit were now behind us. It was the third week in August and it had been a fine morning, but lately the weather had grown unsettled. So before we left the car we had taken the precaution of putting on wellies, which was just as well because soon it was pouring down. We pressed on, and as we walked I was surprised to discover that the wet soil was not sticking to our soles. On rainy days in the Fens, where we live, the clay-rich, silty soil soon builds up, making walking difficult – a phenomenon we've taken to calling 'moonboots', after Neil Armstrong's gravity-defying foot-wear. For us, moonboots are an exhausting feature of everyday life in winter. But the wet peat soil at Star Carr remained light and fluffy. In an odd way, my lightweight feet seemed somehow to lift my spirits. I was feeling very optimistic.

Looking back on that morning, I suppose we should have been feel-ing pretty dreadful. The previous night we had barely slept at all, as our hotel had hosted a lavish wedding reception, and right through to dawn, paralytically drunk guests had slammed doors, vomited noisily, brawled and generally made a racket. Sleep was impossible, so we should have been tired and irritable, but somehow we weren't. Our wet walk across the field was proving exhilarating; we were stepping lightly. For anyone with even a slight interest in British prehistory the place we were approaching has a special meaning – no, that's the wrong word – a special magic of its own. It's where everything seems to have begun: it wasn't just a return to Britain after the ages of ice, but modern archaeology itself was reborn here after the grim austerity of the last war. To prehistorians, Star Carr is probably the most famous site in Britain. And I couldn't believe it: we were now heading across the field towards a group of archaeologists who had actually begun to re-excavate this special spot.

We paused for a moment while I removed my camera from its case. I squatted down and manoeuvred Maisie to act as a barrier against a passing light shower. I couldn't see her face, but I could imagine her indulgent smile. She was used to being used to screen the forces of nature on my photographic expeditions. From close to the ground the wide-angle lens made the subtle relief of the landscape stand out. As I adjusted the focus and depth-of-field I could see we were near the bottom of a shallow depression and the excavations were taking place on a very slight rise over towards the hedge. Those tiny ups and downs in the landscape would quite literally have been the difference between life and death to a prehistoric family: on or above them, you were safe and dry, below them your home might perish. But to modern eyes, or to somebody unfamiliar with such landscapes, the whole place seemed flat.

I stood up, put the camera back in its case, and Maisie led the way. I followed a few paces in the rear; I had no wish to push myself forward. It was Maisie who was a key member of the project and I was there as her guest. But I cannot say this worried me: as I get older, I find I'm often happier just watching life around me. And besides, this wasn't my show: I was an observer.

We reached the trench and I could see that the Star Carr dig was running smoothly. People who know what they're doing have a purposeful air to them, even if they don't seem to be particularly active. And that was the situation when we arrived. There was only one person in the trench and it was Nicky Milner herself, one of the project's three co-directors. She was soaking wet but completely at ease, wearing shorts and wellies, but no socks. Like the rest of the team, she was spattered in mud and had given herself the job of opening the dig for the day's work. And I could see why. You had to have detailed knowledge of everything in the trench if you were not to do damage with your feet.

Bear in mind that this was not ordinary, whack-a-nail-in-it wood; this was 10,000-year-old wood, preserved in waterlogged peat. But over the years the lignin, which gives timber its hardness and flexibility, had been dissolved out, to be replaced by other, softer minerals. Now Nicky is by no means a heavy person, but if she had put a foot wrong she would have atomized pieces of wood that had taken the team weeks to expose. I'm familiar with 3000-year-old Bronze Age wood, and I can easily break a 15-centimetre (6-inch) thick branch across my knee – but here the wood was three times as old and far, far softer. I noticed that nobody said a word to her as she moved the pump pipe from one wet patch to another. Concentration was vital. Plainly Nicky knew where every carefully exposed piece of wood lay. Then the shower passed and people headed off to get their tools for the day's work.

The trench had been carefully positioned and we were standing along its southern side. This would have been the 'downhill' end, ten thousand years ago. Today this part of the field was flat, but just to the north, the land was starting to rise. So the trench had been positioned at the very edge of a glacial lake, subsequently labelled Lake Flixton, which was only finally drained in the 19th century. In Mesolithic times, the trench would have cut through a band of reeds and sedge that thrived around the lake's gently sloping shores. Birch trees grew on the slightly higher ground, back from the water's edge. Today the land looks like any other intensively farmed arable field in eastern England. It's well drained by deep ditches, but as late as the 1950s, when Clark and his team were working here, it was still remarkably boggy, as the sharply focused, black-and-white photos in his report show only too clearly.[20] The wood he revealed looked fresh, solid and in good condition. One glance at the wood in the trench in front of me was enough: it was nowhere near so well preserved – and I'm in no doubt that was entirely down to drainage. To be quite frank, I am now fairly certain that nothing will be worth excavating there in a very few years' time, unless somehow the groundwater levels can be raised.

I have already mentioned the natural richness of Britain's wetland environments, but we tend to forget that such plenty could be on an industrial scale: two or three thousand ducks a week were sent to London in the 18th century from Fenland decoys.[21] Having said that, it is quite another things to imagine what it would have been like to have lived on the edges of a glacial lake. To Mesolithic communities they must have seemed like inland seas, with their own set of communities, who, even at this very early stage, would soon have established their ancestral claims to different tracts of the land around the shoreline. Today their presence can be detected from the scatters of flint tools that once littered the surface about their settlements.

One should think of glaciers as vast geological bulldozers. During the Ice Ages they forced their way along valleys, planing off the sides and bottom, to leave a smooth, open U-shaped profile behind them. With the immense power of expanding ice, they pushed this debris before them, where it accumulated as a vast, slowly churning bank of rocks and debris. But when the climate started to grow warmer, the glaciers began to retreat and the bank of debris was left stranded, a great barrier, marking the ice's point of maximum expansion. These huge banks, known as terminal moraines, are a major feature of once-glaciated landscapes and there is a particularly big one, which blocks off the Vale of Pickering, just a few miles inland from Scarborough and the North Sea. As a result, the natural drainage pattern was reversed, and streams in the area now flow backwards, towards the west. Glacial Lake Flixton was the main result of the great glacial blockage.

Britain has lost most of its lowland lakes and meres. The largest of all, Whittlesey Mere in the Fens, just south of Peterborough, covered some 2 square miles and was one of the most extensive lakes in Britain, prior to its drainage in the 1850s.[22] But some do survive. The great glacial lake at Hornsea Mere in the wetlands of Holderness, to the north-east of Hull, is one such example (see Plate 2). A few thousand years ago the trees surrounding it changed, as birch was replaced by alder, oak and willow, which pushed their way northwards in the warmer climate; but the great, shallow lake itself is still there. I can remember on my first visit being irritated by the presence of fishermen, who somehow seemed to break the stillness of the place. Then I paused. I was being ridiculously over-aesthetic. After all, there had been fishermen around this lake since Mesolithic times. So why break with tradition?

It is worth bearing in mind that shallow waters can be easier to fish than, say, the deep, steep-sided lochs of Scotland, such as Loch Ness. You could almost have waded across some of the Fenland meres and the warm waters would have been home to huge populations of freshwater mussels, crayfish and, of course, eels. One can imagine eagle-eyed herons standing along the lake shores at regular distances, each one stock still, like so many tail-coated sentries.

This, then, was the setting for the re-settlement of Britain after the Ice Ages. Contrary to popular opinion, it was not a tundra-like world of bleak plains and endless winters. If we could travel back ten millennia we would find it slightly cooler – perhaps the equivalent of southern Scotland rather than, say, East Anglia. But no worse. And these generally benign surroundings are reflected in the earliest post-Glacial houses, which were built out in the open and did not seem to have made much use of caves, cliffs or other natural shelters.

As we have seen, the opening years of the 21st century witnessed a sudden rash of new discoveries of Mesolithic houses. Prior to that, they were extremely rare and sometimes quite controversial. Indeed, many eminent scholars believed that people lived in shelters that were so flimsy they have left no archaeological trace. But I have to say I have always been very suspicious when I hear this argument, which is sometimes an excuse for poor observation. Then in 2011 came the news, which actually made it to national bulletins on Radio 4 for two days (no less), that Star Carr had revealed the remains of what is still Britain's earliest house. I was delighted: if any site could do it, it would be Star Carr. I have to say that I had known about the discovery for some time, as Maisie was a part of the team, but we, like everyone else, were sworn to secrecy. Nowadays the best-run research projects manage the PR aspects of new discoveries carefully: a big media splash always comforts funding bodies, whom one then hears being shamelessly plugged by archaeologists desperate to secure future budgets.

I admire the way the Star Carr team announced the discovery of the house to the archaeological world. In fact it is still happening as I'm writing this. A couple of days ago I emailed Nicky Milner to find out when there would be a published plan of the house which I could use in this book. I knew Maisie was heading up to York for a Star

Carr team meeting and the end-of-dig dinner and I privately hoped she could collect it while she was away. Then, to my amazement, Nicky emailed me an offprint of the article she had co-authored with her two directors, and Maisie, for the prestigious journal, *Antiquity*. It arrived shortly before we set out for Peterborough station. On my return home I had various urgent jobs to do on the farm, so I only managed to read it last night. I should have begun earlier: it is sensational.

The report was not just about the house, but it explained the site's setting and revealed it was part of a far larger settlement than anyone had hitherto thought possible in 9000 BC.[23] The latest estimate is that the site still covers an astonishing 20,000 square metres (5 acres, or 2 hectares).[24] And remember, the climate had only warmed up 600 years previously – the equivalent for us of the later Middle Ages! It took a couple of large whiskies for my mind to settle down enough for sleep. I woke bright and early, but still thinking about that paper, which I reread before grabbing a quick breakfast. Meanwhile, Maisie had been texting me with details of train times and what they ate at the dinner, while 100 miles to the south-east, all I could do was think about the archaeology they had all been revealing. I've noticed something similar before, when we've been right on the cutting-edge of research: you can never both be walking around with your heads in the clouds. One of you has to remain rooted in reality.

Two summers ago, I had an interview with Nicky, which was one of the things that set my mind in motion. At the time, the book you are reading was meant to be a straightforward account of prehistoric domestic life. It was a simple enough idea, but if I'm honest, it wasn't working for me. Yes, I knew I could get it written, and with the right marketing it would probably sell quite well. But it lacked something: excitement, perhaps? When I was working on *Britain BC* or *The Making of the British Landscape*, I had arguments and ideas constantly in my head, and these drove the story along. In many respects those books wrote themselves; in fact the most difficult task was editing them down to a manageable size. But this time it was different, and I knew it would be a struggle to reach the word-count I had agreed with the publisher. I don't think I recognized it while I was researching, but in retrospect my interview with Nicky started to pull the rug from beneath my feet. I had decided the book would be about the slow, gradual, almost irresistible growth of family life and the communities that supported it. But what she told me undermined those certainties. Then I began to question all of my assumptions, and most particularly the idea that new ideas come from the top of society, and then somehow filter down to ordinary households. She also challenged the notion that change, even as long ago as 9000 BC, was inevitably slow and piecemeal. I wasn't aware of it at the time, but my preconceptions were about to be turned on their head and the book I then found myself writing was far more radical and less comfortable. Only then did I realize that families were actually about innovation and progress; security and stability that we take for granted today were merely by-products from earlier, less complacent times.

In order to set Nicky's remarks into context, I shall first outline what her team have revealed about the settlement at Star Carr. And I shall use the paper I read with such huge excitement last night and again this morning.[25] Let us start with the title: 'Substantial settlement in the European Early Mesolithic: new research at Star Carr'. The word 'substantial' is crucial here. In settlement terms it contrasts with insubstantial or fleeting. Like all students of archaeology I had been brought up to accept that when Star Carr was first excavated by Grahame Clark it was believed to have been a seasonally occupied hunting camp, that people returned to year after year, for a short time – possibly for a month or two. This explanation fitted with what was found there: hunting spearheads and the sort of flint tools one would use to prepare carcasses for the pot. And then, of course, there were those strange antler head-dresses that I first learned about as a student. Essentially they consisted of the upper surfaces of a red deer stag's skull, with antlers intact. The underside of the skull bone had been smoothed off and two holes had been bored through, presumably for a thong, which would have tied it to the head. Some people believe they were worn as disguises or camouflage for hunters;[26] although most people, myself included, would see them as the sort of strange head-dresses worn by shamans during pre-, or possibly post-, hunting rituals and dances.

The short-stay hunting camp theory made much sense when Clark first proposed it, but as research continued through the 1980s, a number of clues began to emerge, which should have suggested that the reality might actually be more complex. A large number of new sites were found around the shores of Lake Flixton and these revealed a range of flint tools that would not have been out of place on straightforward domestic, or living, sites; they did not appear to be specialized hunting camps. But nobody questioned for one moment that they had been lived in by any more than small, shifting and insubstantial groups of itinerant hunters, who did their best to eke out a living following the thinly dispersed game, which we know from modern observations is characteristic of open birch woodland. Moreover, botanical research in the post-war years had carefully revealed the precise nature of the tree cover at the time. So everything appeared to be fully grounded in solid fact and observation. The trouble was, those facts and observations were obtained in a way that was appropriate to the supposedly small scale of settlement they were meant to be observing. So everything was done in huge detail, and on a very small scale. A broader picture was urgently required.

Meanwhile, as I have already hinted, archaeologists working on sites of later prehistoric periods had been developing techniques of excavation, survey and recording that enabled them to look at very much larger areas: hectares or acres, rather than a few square metres or feet. At first the new Star Carr research team excavated some trenches that were smaller than those dug by Clark half a century earlier. They would have loved to have opened larger areas, but the powers that be who controlled all access to the site wouldn't hear of it. In fact, they did very well to open the tiny trenches they did: every move they made, almost every scrape of the trowel was scrutinized by senior people in the profession who, frankly, should have known better. I have always thought that the task of men and women in their sixties and older should be to encourage the next generation, not make their lives impossible.

A few years before the current research team began its work, Maisie had established (in the laboratory, not in the field) that a substantial proportion of the wood revealed by Clark had in fact been worked by man.[27] Clark had failed to recognize this, not because he was incompetent, but because knowledge of wood-working was then far less

well advanced. Knowing that Maisie had made this unexpected discovery in the late 1990s, Nicky invited her to join the new team and
it was the first time that a wood-working specialist had been present
in the field, so she was able to identify worked wood as soon as it was
revealed. As a result, they soon realized that the spread of brushwood
at the edge of Lake Flixton was not an insubstantial consolidation of
the shore by a passing group of hunters, maybe making use of a collapsed beaver dam, but was actually something much more substantial:
a carefully constructed platform which extended as far as 20 metres
(66 feet) out into the lake. The team could not be certain, given the
tiny size of the trenches they were permitted to open, whether this was
one or several platforms, but there could be little doubt that it was
large, reaching along the edge of a natural sandy headland for some
30 metres. I can remember thinking at the time that this sort of careful
construction, involving split and felled timbers below layers of brushwood, was precisely what we had revealed at Bronze Age Flag Fen, a
site some seven thousand years younger (see Fig. 1.3).

I just mentioned a sandy headland, which now becomes crucial. As
they were prevented from opening useful-sized trenches along the
lakeside, the team turned its attention to the small hillock, or rise,
some 2.5 metres (8 feet) high that was just set back from the lake-
edge. Here they carried out a detailed survey of the topsoil, recording
the position of every piece of flint or bone they could find. They also
peppered the area with small test pits where they sieved the topsoil
and recovered everything. This survey revealed that the lakeside
timber platform was in fact a south-westerly extension of a very substantial settlement, covering an area of almost 2 hectares (5 acres) and
measuring about 190 metres east–west and around 100 metres north–
south, with long extensions running north-west and south-east. The
latter covering a natural bank or 'peninsula' that extended out into
the lake for some 90 metres, where there were hints of further timber
platforms on its southern and eastern sides. All in all, this settlement,
or more likely settlements, would have been of good size in the Bronze
or Iron Ages and it was certainly very much bigger than the occupation area (18 by 18 metres, 60 by 60 feet) that Clark believed he had
discovered in the 1950s.

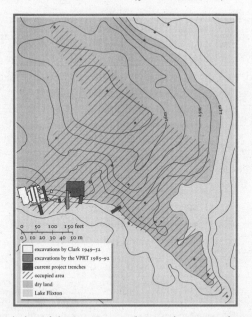

Fig. 1.3 A general plan of the Star Carr settlement showing surface contours and, to the south, the edge of the lake. This plan also shows the location of trenches. (VPRT: Vale of Pickering Research Trust.)

One of the arguments that had supported the general belief that Star Carr was a short-lived hunters' camp was the density of finds revealed in Clark's excavations, where an average of about 230 pieces of flint per square metre were recovered. By comparison, the recent survey found an extraordinary 358 flints per square metre. This density compares very favourably with that found on other Mesolithic sites in Britain and north-western Europe, where everyone is agreed there was settlement, indeed, sometimes long-term settlement. So it would seem that the size of the occupied area and the number of finds both strongly suggest that Star Carr was a permanent settlement.

I will consider the evidence for the house in a moment, but first I want to think about that idea of 'permanence' more closely. Put another way, did people live there all year round? Proving 'permanence' is a perpetual problem for archaeologists. Think about it for a moment: if you decided to take a long break and leave your home for, say, three months, how would an archaeologist in the future discover you had been away? The answer is, he would never find out. But if, on the other hand, you left home every year from, say, December to March, then you would leave all sorts of clues in your wake. For example, the shellfish you consumed on your barbecue would leave tell-tale traces in their shells that they had been caught in summer. The same would go for the meat bones, especially lamb and game; although less immediately recognizable, you could still work it out, more or less. Fish bones and scales, too, can be fixed to seasons, as, of course, can firewood – only here there is a problem caused by storage, because nobody would try to burn freshly felled firewood.

Radiocarbon dates suggested that the settlement on the sandy hillock had been occupied in two episodes, the first of about 80 years, followed by a gap of about a century and then a second, of about 150 years. As the team put it: '. . . the large size of the site and the density of occupation debris suggest more than simply repeated occupation by small family groups.'[28] In reality, my own guess is that the size of the settlement area would easily be large enough for 10 to 50 houses at any one time. Fewer than, say, 10 households would call into question why so large a platform needed to be built on the lakeside. It may well have happened that a proportion of the community moved somewhere else at certain times of the year – maybe younger males went to the coast to catch fish or seals. Who knows, but it seems highly probable that most of the buildings were occupied by at least some people all year round – if only for security. Again, the story has moved on a long way from those small bands of itinerant hunters.

One reason that I'm inclined to think that the settlement area was quite well populated with buildings is the simple fact that a relatively tiny trench of just 225 square metres (740 square feet; i.e. about 1 per cent of the total settlement area) revealed clear evidence for a house. If there were, say, just five or ten houses, the chances of coming down directly on top of one would be very small. Despite its small size, the

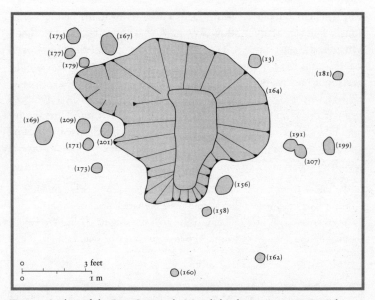

Fig. 1.4 A plan of the Star Carr early Mesolithic house (9000 BC), with 18 post-holes for roof supports, surrounding a sunken floor area.

trench revealed some 8,000 flints and 210 pieces of bone. Incidentally, pottery was not found, as it was only introduced to Britain in the Neolithic period, some 5,000 years later. (See Fig. 1.4.)

The Star Carr house was roughly oval and was defined by an increased density of finds and a scatter of 18 post-holes, which would have supported the walls and roof. This oval building measured slightly over 4 metres (13 feet) across – roughly the same shape as, but slightly smaller than, the early Mesolithic houses at Howick and East Barns. At the centre of the oval setting of post-holes was a sunken floor, about 3 metres (10 feet) in diameter and 20 centimetres (8 inches) deep. This floor was filled with a dark earthy deposit that probably represents a floor covering of long-since-rotted bark, brushwood and reeds – similar floors, but with the reeds better preserved, have been found in continental houses of this period. There was also a darker area in the filling of the floor deposit, which may mark the spot where a hearth had once been positioned. This was near the centre of the house. The top of the hollow was packed with flint tools and flakes which had been unable to fall any further because of the floor covering. Around the hollow floor were the bottoms of the holes for the posts that had supported the roof.

In 2013 the directors of the Star Carr project published a superb popular book on the project: *Star Carr: Life in Britain After the Ice Age*. I'd like to close this chapter on Britain's earliest house by quoting this book's final words (and I can almost hear Nicky Milner's voice as I read):

> We know from the scatters of burnt flint that people were building hearths or fires, where they would have prepared food, or sat around together as they ate, telling stories and exchanging news. We can imagine the sounds as people shouted greetings to one another, the

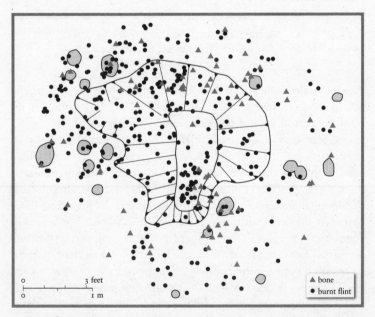

Fig. 1.5 The distribution of burnt flint and bone fragments plotted against the features of the Star Carr house.

excitement as hunters returned with their kill, the laughter as people told jokes, the rustling of branches and reeds in the wind and the water of the lake lapping at the shore. The air would have been thick with the smell of smoke and cooking food, the dampness of the swamp and the woodland undergrowth. This was a place that people experienced with their senses; it was a place that was familiar to them; it was their home.[29]

2

The Re-Settlement Gathers Pace
(8000–4000 BC)

It is probably fair to say that the Mesolithic, hitherto a period that was regarded by many prehistorians as the domain of over-focused specialists who only seemed to care about the evolving shape of tiny flints, known as microliths, has been transformed by a series of remarkable revelations which began in the 1990s and then gathered pace, as we have just seen, with discoveries like the houses at Howick, and more recently at Star Carr. But to everyone's surprise, these revelations have continued, almost unabated. I don't think that anyone actively working on the Mesolithic, at the turn of this century, could have foreseen the huge advances in knowledge that we now take almost for granted. So I shall start this chapter with a discovery that actually happened on the stainless-steel draining-board of our own scullery, or utility room (its name seems to change with the passing seasons). I blame my wife Maisie, of course: it was entirely her fault.

BRITAIN'S EARLIEST WOODEN IMPLEMENT?

The meticulous excavations at Star Carr had plotted the precise find-spot of everything and it is interesting to see how the finds' distribution so closely mirrors the shape of the building. Most notable was a concentration of bone and burnt flints, which are usually taken to be reliable indicators of domestic life (see Fig. 1.5). Buildings also tend to accumulate items that people cherished, or wanted to look after, and it is interesting that two of the three fragments of flint axes were found within the area of the house.

So far the Star Carr house itself has not produced any wood, but this does not surprise me, because even eleven thousand years ago, people preferred to position their dwellings on ground that was dry underfoot all year round. And dry conditions don't favour the preservation of wood. Most of the wood from the recent excavations was in a fairly poor condition, certainly when compared with what Clark found 60 years previously. This deterioration was of course caused by drying out. The pieces of worked wood from the foundations of the platform were axed or split, and one or two may well have been planks. But until very recently, none could be considered domestic, nor indeed an artefact. Then, in the season of 2010, the team came across something most unusual quite low down in the timbers supporting the lakeside platform – and not very far away from the house. A sharp-eyed archaeologist recognized it as special while he was digging, and treated it with special care. It was dug superbly: without so much as a scratch. Next, like all the worked wood, it was lifted, wrapped wet and sealed. Then at the end of the season it was all transported down to our farm, where Maisie could examine it more closely.

The winter before last, Maisie was working on wood found the previous summer, in her workshop in our barn. It was a cold day in the run-up to Christmas, and the afternoon was growing frosty, so she carried the unusual object into the house and laid it out on the draining-board. Over the years, we've both grown used to doing the washing-up in the kitchen sink, when prehistoric wood takes over the scullery. So when I happened to wander in, in search of milk for my tea, I found Maisie leaning over the sink studying very intently what looked like a grotty stick. I asked what was so special about it. There was a pause before she answered. She was concentrating hard.

She stood back to let me take a closer look. As I said, superficially it looked a bit like a pointed stick, but on closer inspection she showed me how it had been carefully worked-down from a dowel (a piece of deliberately split wood), which came from a birch trunk, or large branch. Being worked-down from a split dowel it would have been far stronger than a piece of natural roundwood, which it superficially resembled. It was almost complete, just a tiny bit of the tip being missing. One end was knob-like and fist sized, a good counterbalance and ideally suited for gripping; the other, clearly the 'business end', had been carefully shaved-down and faceted.

Maisie reckoned it was probably a purpose-built digging-stick. That rang bells, but not very loudly. So I went to my anthropology shelves, but could find no photos that were good or close enough to be useful. Despite this, we could neither of us think of a better explanation. To the best of our knowledge, too, nothing like it had yet been found in Britain. But we were still not at all clear on how, or indeed why, it would have been used.

It just so happened that towards the end of that winter, Professor Brian Fagan, an old friend, was staying with us for a conference in London. Brian now lives and works in California, but we both knew he had done his doctoral research in Africa, where he had made pioneering and imaginative use of modern material from hunter-gatherer societies. Maisie showed him her sketch of the object and his eyes immediately lit up. In 1966 he had published a paper in a learned journal, which I happened to have in my library.[1] I found it and put it on the table. Even after a good supper and several glasses of wine, we could all see that the Star Carr object was identical to examples illustrated in Brian's article. The very closest parallels – in fact they were almost identical – had been made and used by the Bushmen of the Kalahari Desert, to dig up roots in soft ground. It was almost too good to be true.

I can remember the thought briefly crossed my mind that the academic world would never believe us. They would say – and especially those who knew nothing about wood-working – that it was a fluke of nature and not man-made. And besides, they would scoff, how can you possibly draw convincing parallels between a dry African desert in modern times and a waterlogged post-Ice Age settlement in Yorkshire? The fact that our object had been carefully made and was perfectly suited to the task would not convince anyone who had never had to do anything practical in their entire lives. No, I knew these people only too well. Nothing is harder to shift than the scepticism born of self-confident ignorance. I was now quite worried.

Maisie could see I was having doubts. So I told her. She just sat back and laughed.

'Haven't you forgotten, there were two of them?'

She was smiling broadly.

She was absolutely right. I had. The second one was far less well preserved and was incomplete, but enough had survived, especially of the carefully faceted sharp end, to be in no doubt that it was another digging-stick: even more important, it was also carefully fashioned from a dowel. That convinced me. Coincidence was impossible. Nobody, not even the bloodiest-minded, most-cloistered of academics, could argue with *two* nearly identical digging-sticks.

So the site was now looking far more complex than we had once believed. Of course we cannot be certain, but in many tribal societies the men do the hunting, while the women look after children and carry out tasks closer to home, like gathering nuts and fruit, or digging for edible roots, such as the tubers of the herb lesser celandine; that way, the community gets to eat a more balanced diet.[2] So the presence of digging-sticks potentially implied that Star Carr was surely more than a small hunting camp, only visited by a few male hunters. Indeed, if the complex antler head-dresses had been worn by shamans, it is likely that the ceremonies themselves would have been quite elaborate affairs – the sort of thing that would have been attended by the whole community. Again, this suggested a far larger and more complex community than a mere handful of hunters.

THE RICHNESS AND COMPLEXITY OF THE HUNTER-GATHERER LIFESTYLE

When Maisie was working on those digging-sticks, it was quite plain to anyone involved with Star Carr that the site was starting to undermine some long- and fondly held beliefs. We all knew, too, that it would be a great mistake to let the new information reach the academic world, a small piece at a time. What was needed was a well-made, multi-faceted case with plenty of good, solid evidence to back it up. Unfortunately some of the bureaucratic and administrative hold-ups meant that progress had been quite slow, but in retrospect I wonder whether that has been altogether bad, because it has enabled the team to prepare the water-tight case that has just appeared in *Antiquity*, and which I discussed towards the end of the previous chapter.[3]

So that was the situation when I met Nicky Milner in the summer of 2011. My own thoughts about Star Carr were starting to alter, and I was keen to discover if she shared any of my doubts – and excitement. I shouldn't have worried. She was well ahead of me.

Back in that rainy field at Star Carr, a couple of years previously we had all been chatting away at tea-break when someone mentioned that Nicky actually came from Yorkshire. She had been brought up on a farm and felt a close sense of personal involvement with the area. As we sipped our mugs of site-hut tea, I could see she was far too busy with practicalities to get involved in a detailed conversation with a visiting specialist's husband. So I listened closely, observed, and decided to contact her later, when plans for this book were clearer in my mind.

I wrote the interview up as soon as I returned from York University, where Nicky has an office in the superb medieval building known as King's Manor. It's architecturally as spectacular as any Oxbridge college and within sight and sound of the towering Minster. You couldn't ask for a more auspicious setting. But make no mistake, this was a big opportunity and I had decided to go about it professionally. I'm not a trained journalist and cannot do shorthand, so I'd bought a small sound recorder which I'd taught myself to work. Even though she wasn't actually excavating, Nicky was still busy sorting and co-ordinating the department's course work for the next academic year, but she could spare a couple of hours over lunch, as her next meeting was not until two in the afternoon. I thought I was being very generous when I bought us both lunch in the refectory, which set me back a whole five pounds.

We sat down and I produced my machine which I placed on the table between us. It could have been a ticking bomb for the inhibiting effect it had on both of us. So I pushed it out of the way, well to one side. After we'd finished, I rewound and found I'd recorded two hours of the refrigerator hum from a nearby soft drinks vending machine. I made this ghastly discovery at the railway station, where I immediately bought a small notebook in which I wrote down my memories of what had been said. My recollections were remarkably vivid; I found I could clearly remember huge chunks of our conversation. Anyhow, all of that took me over an hour, during which time I missed three trains. The one I did eventually manage to catch was full of ebullient football fans on their way south from Newcastle. They had enjoyed that great city's brown ale, but had a very limited repertoire of songs. After three hours I bitterly regretted I hadn't caught an earlier one.

My first question to Nicky was meant to be provocative: did they have families in the Mesolithic? But her slightly pitying look said it all. Was I mad? Of course they did you half-wit. But she put it more kindly than that. Trying to make amends, I then mentioned that the few Mesolithic houses we know about are all roughly the right size to hold the basic family unit of two parents, plus their children. She agreed, but pointed out that houses don't actually define families. She felt, and I think this was based on her own personal experience of growing up in the Yorkshire Dales, that the wider family – grandparents, aunts and uncles – would have played a more important role than today.

That set me thinking. But surely, I suggested, the Star Carr house stood on its own, didn't it? To my surprise she seemed rather doubtful even about this. But I insisted: if she was right, then everything I'd ever been taught about the site had been wrong – or worse, very misleading.

She began her reply by pointing out the constraints they'd been obliged to work under. For a start they had only been allowed to put a single trench in that particular area. And even so, they came straight down on the house. She paused for a moment. It was my turn to go on the defensive. As a field archaeologist myself, I knew only too well that your first trench rarely hits a lone target, unless, that is, there happen to be more of them than you'd originally anticipated. She gave this time to sink in and then asked very mildly whether I didn't think that rather coincidental?

I certainly did.

My next question was obvious: had they tried geophysics? That was a bit naughty of me, as I was aware they had. But I hadn't realized that the survey hadn't been very successful – almost certainly, she told me, because of the porous sandy soil. But it worked well enough to tell them there was something there, though precisely what wasn't clear.

Next I asked her about their field-walking survey. These surveys are routine on modern excavations; they're the archaeological equivalent of a police forensic fingertip search, where everything found on the ground – every thread, every hair, every bloodstained dagger – is kept and recorded in great detail. In archaeology these finds are usually flints, bone fragments or pieces of pottery.

She smiled. She could see I was feeling rather awkward. I fear I will never make a career out of interviewing. But her reply did surprise me: as I guessed, they had found vast numbers of flints there – and they covered a very large area.

Was that area larger than a single house? I asked. Again she smiled. I think she was beginning to enjoy my lack of knowledge. She immediately agreed and went on to suggest that there had to be several other, maybe even many, houses there.

Next I wanted to discuss what was worrying me a great deal at that time, the then-prevalent notion that the earliest people in Mesolithic Britain began by being mobile, and subsequently began to settle down as the population expanded. She smiled. I could see the question was not unexpected.

She paused for a moment, assembling her thoughts.

Her reply was comprehensive. She explained how the environment had changed and how the climate had grown warmer much faster than we once thought. So she didn't believe there was a pressing physical or practical need for people to live a shifting, nomadic lifestyle in many parts of Britain. It would have been pointless: shifting for its own sake. In many places – and Star Carr was one of them – game and plant foods were there all year round. So why move?

We were now approaching the heart of the matter. If that were the case, I wondered, what would their lives have been like?

By now she was warming to the subject. She agreed: they certainly didn't regularly move away from the lake and its surroundings. Maybe small parties would head off at certain times of the year, but most of the community stayed put.

This was extraordinary. Everything I thought I knew about the site and about the earliest settlers in post-Ice Age Britain was going up in smoke: so it wasn't a hunting camp, as we've always been told?

She was enjoying my rapid induction into the world of modern Mesolithic studies. She went on to suggest that life was far more elaborate than that. And Star Carr wasn't alone, even if it was a very early example. There were other, almost as early, sites like it too, such as Howick. She pointed to the similarity in size and shape of the houses at both places. The house at Howick had a series of hearths and that strongly suggested that it had been occupied for some time. Again, it couldn't have been a temporary hunting camp.

This set me thinking. Even later Mesolithic sites, places like Thatcham and Mount Sandel, were more like mini-villages than camps. But the houses were far less substantial than Howick or Star Carr. I shall have more to say about Mount Sandel shortly. Thatcham was a settlement close by the River Kennet in West Berkshire.[4] As at Howick and Mount Sandel, there were a series of hearths and tens of thousands of flint tools and waste flakes. But no substantial, post-built houses. For whatever reason, it would appear that the community here opted for lighter-weight structures. Maybe the availability of bendy boughs of riverside willow played a part in their decision. But we didn't have time to discuss these sites. I had to cut to the chase. I put it to her that these larger, permanent settlements suggest that our estimates of Mesolithic population had to be wrong. When I was writing *Britain BC*, I remember quoting a figure – on reflection a strangely precise one – of around 1,200 people living in Britain in 9000 BC.[5]

I could tell by the look on her face she'd heard that figure many times before. She went on to suggest that there could have been hundreds of people living in the Vale of Pickering alone. Maybe, she suggested, the overall population of Britain could have been ten times what those earlier estimates suggested. Perhaps even more.

'What,' I asked, 'at the *start* of the Mesolithic?'

She was smiling at my incredulity. Her reply was simple:

'Yes. And I don't see why it shouldn't have been much larger at the end, as well.'

I had to agree: the one followed the other. The usual guestimate for the population at the end of the Mesolithic is about five thousand. But fifty thousand would make much better sense. It would also account for the huge number of later Mesolithic flint scatters which occur right across Britain. It would further explain the impact of the first farmers arriving in Britain from the continental mainland just before 4000 BC. If those incoming farmers had encountered a substantial population of hunter-gatherers who had heard about the new way of life and were well predisposed towards it, then it might be a reason why the new way of life spread across Britain in just a few generations – which was what the very latest evidence was suggesting.[6] Frankly, my head was buzzing.

We stopped for a moment, for Nicky to fetch us more tea from the counter. While she was away, I continued to ponder what we had discussed: a far larger Mesolithic population would explain so much. It was all starting to make sense. But I still needed to move the conversation on. I reminded myself that the interview was about home life, and not population demographics. It was time to focus in on what might have been happening inside that Star Carr house.

She returned with the tea and when she had sat down I decided to change the direction of our conversation. Nearly all the questions on my list had been ticked off and the ones that remained – mostly about trade and communication between the different communities – didn't somehow seem so relevant. Yes, they were of archaeological interest, but they didn't help me understand what life would have been like beneath those steeply thatched roofs. At a very basic level, the relationship, both physical and emotional, between men and women was fundamental to everything that happened in the early post-Glacial family home. I began by asking her what she thought about current ideas on gender issues in the Mesolithic.

She paused to gather her thoughts. And I don't blame her: it was a very broad question. Then she neatly side-stepped it. I hadn't expected that; but her reply also surprised me: no, she didn't believe the two sexes were as closely defined as they are today. I have to say, that went against my gut feeling: somehow I had always imagined that life in the pine woods around Lake Pickering all those years ago would have depended on men being men and hunting all the hours they had, while women stayed at home rearing the next generation and providing extra food to fuel the hunters. Put crudely, it was about feed and breed. But I couldn't have been more wrong.

I didn't put it quite so bluntly, but I hinted at something of the sort. I should have known better: she had heard it all before, because she soon cut me short. She pointed out that in many communities today, women take an active part in hunting, often helping to herd animals and divert fish towards nets. And by the same token, men often help to gather plant foods. People in such societies are pragmatic. They do what's needed, when it's needed. They don't worry about whether it's a man or a woman's 'job' to do it.

She paused to take a sip from her now rapidly cooling mug. I imagined I had touched on a subject close to her heart. I was about to ask something else, but decided not to. Sometimes silence can extract reluctant or buried thoughts. She then started to reminisce about her childhood in the Yorkshire Dales. From about the age of ten she often found herself driving the tractor. I could picture the scene. And yes, she was dead right. I can remember bottle feeding lambs, and loving it. Even today, with automatic feeders available, that's usually women's work.

When she had finished, I suggested that she didn't seem to be drawing a simple link between what was found on house floors and the people who dropped those items back in prehistory. She smiled; she could see I was struggling. No, she didn't think that all the flints from old spearheads were dropped on the floor by men. As I thought about it, I had to agree, yes, it was common sense.

It was my turn to break in:

'. . . and the hearths . . . so the cooking wasn't done exclusively by women?'

She smiled and asked by way of reply whether I ever cooked at home, which of course I did – and she knew it, as Maisie had mentioned more than once that I'd have supper ready when she got back home from Star Carr. Then she went on to point out what I was thinking: that for some reason we have a rigid view of life in the past, which is loosely based on our lives today, but not as we actually live them. It tells us something about our views of ourselves, which are almost always too clear cut. She ended by explaining that it was common sense that you would find flint knives and scrapers closer to the hearth, where food was being prepared, but that did not necessarily mean that the area was forbidden to men.

In the past I had spent a great deal of time plotting where flint tools and other debris were found on house floors. So from a purely selfish point of view, I wondered whether we had been wasting our time, and worse, the project's hard-won finances.

She could see my concerns, but didn't share them. Far from it, in fact. She believed strongly that plotting the precise position of everything was important, especially today when GPS is making all planning so much simpler. But we had to limit the inferences we could draw from our distribution plans. So you could show that cooking was happening in a hearth, but it helps if you have additional evidence as well, like traces of animal fat in the earth surrounding the fireplace.

She was referring to some recent discoveries then being rumoured from an important Neolithic settlement in Wiltshire, which I will discuss in detail in the final section of Chapter 3.

'But you think it's too big a step to say that this work was necessarily done by women?'

'It may well have been, but that's an assumption, isn't it?'

I nodded my agreement; I was deep in thought; she was quite right, of course. By now she was smiling broadly. I think she was rather enjoying herself. But I had to press on: 'So how do you think men and women regarded themselves in Mesolithic times?'

I don't think this question came as much of a surprise, and it was clearly something she had thought about a lot as her replies were quick and to the point. She began by returning to something she had mentioned earlier. If anything, she thought that gender distinction in the Mesolithic was probably less, not more, clear-cut than it is today. There was even some evidence, from graves in Scandinavia, for a third gender.

I had heard hints of this and I knew from my anthropology that in some tribal societies holy men and shamans were seen as somehow beyond the here and now – and were believed by some to be neither male nor female. But I was keen to learn more.

I asked her if these burials were of shamans.

Most likely they were. These particular burials were quite different from others and the graves contained both beads *and* microliths.

We have already come across microliths, which were tiny and very sharp fragments of flint blades that were inserted into Mesolithic hunters' spearheads. They are very common on Mesolithic sites right across Europe, including the British Isles. Beads, made of bone or sometimes of amber, have been found in women's graves of the period. I needed to be sure, so I asked the obvious question: that beads signified women and microliths men?

In common with most British Mesolithic specialists, Nicky had a very good grasp of early Scandinavian prehistory, so her reply was particularly interesting and it would appear that my simplistic distinction of beads with women and microliths with men had been demonstrated on numerous occasions in Swedish graves.

So there could be little doubt that in those shamans' graves the male/female 'rule' had been deliberately broken. At the time I wondered whether this would apply in Britain as well, but as we haven't yet excavated a British hunter-gatherer cemetery it was difficult to say anything positive. In fact we didn't even know whether one existed at all, until, that is, very recently. But more about that, shortly.

I had time for one final question. It wasn't altogether fair, but it had intrigued me ever since I realized that home life had been so important in Mesolithic times. In a nutshell, what did she think it was that held these early families together?

I was expecting an anthropological answer, something along the lines of 'ties of consanguinity' (in other words, blood, or family bonds), but what she said astonished me. Just one word: food.

Food? For a crazy moment my mind went literal and I had a rapid vision of families being held together by glutinous toffee pudding. Then sanity returned. I suggested its preparation must have been important, too, just as it is today.

She agreed and went on to suggest that there was some indirect evidence to indicate that from time to time people shared meals, maybe even large ones, with lots of people and plenty to eat.

I replied that I had always thought their diet must have been fairly restricted: venison starters, followed by venison main course . . .

She shook her head. It was clear she disagreed. She explained how she had recently worked on a television programme with Ray Mears which had demonstrated just how many roots and rhizomes were edible. They didn't have to survive on a few nuts and berries. There's a lot of wild food out there. And then there were the herbs ...

I suggested thyme, wild mint and hedge garlic.

She agreed and suggested there were many more. Indeed, she was quite convinced they wouldn't have eaten their meat plain, especially not at family gatherings. Then suddenly I realized it was a Yorkshire farmer's daughter talking to me. As she spoke, I could see that she had family Sunday lunches very much in mind, with roast lamb and thyme with plenty of mint sauce. And it didn't matter if those precise herbs had been present in the Mesolithic. It was the thought, the personal memory, of those meals that was colouring her words.

I could see she was warming to the subject and went on to wonder why it was thought somehow academically 'safer' to assume that Mesolithic people *didn't* know how to use herbs. They weren't stupid. They could smell the plants around them. One day, she supposed, we might know the answer, but in the meantime she preferred to think they were intelligent – like ourselves. And as we don't enjoy bland food, why should they have done? Then she made explicit what I had suspected. She went on to describe big family parties when the meat was always served up with herbs and spices. And of course it was delicious. I could almost hear the fire crackling in the grate.

I was glad to see that Nicky did not belong to the dour, hair-shirt school of university lecturers who had dominated life when I was at college. For them, life in the past was harsh, frugal and not very human or light hearted. Maybe that's why some of us students reacted so strongly against it.

'You reckon life was good in the Mesolithic, then?' I asked.

She pushed her chair back. It was time to go.

'Yes,' she said as we gathered up our things and I pocketed the useless recorder, 'I think it was – certainly at Star Carr. It would be hard to find an area so naturally rich in food and of course clean water. Yes, life would have been good. I'm sure of it.'

It's difficult to miss the huge Italianate railway station at York, but I almost walked straight past it. My mind was so full.

WELCOME TO THE COMPLEX
WORLD OF HAZEL

Traditionally archaeologists have tended to overemphasize the role of hunting in Mesolithic life, and this probably reflected the fact that most of the prehistorians who were studying the period in the later 20th century were male. To add to this inherent bias, the tools needed to dig or process plant foods were made of wood and have rarely survived. In addition, the tiny flints used to make hunting and fishing spears, and arrowheads, slowly changed shape as time passed and acquired great importance – I would suggest far too much importance – as chronological indicators. Scholars became obsessed, indeed many still are, with their 'typology', which is a jargon way of saying that they evolved in a way that can be followed, charted and dated. Anyhow, as a result of these, and other unconnected factors, the less glamorous food-gathering side of the hunter-gatherer lifestyle has been largely ignored.[7]

Quantities of hazelnut shells, usually charred, have been found at many early Mesolithic sites, including Star Carr. They are often found with other food and domestic debris and it has been argued that they must have formed an important part of the Mesolithic diet – and from the earliest times.[8] For what it's worth, they are also very commonly found in similar circumstances on Neolithic, Bronze and even Iron Age sites; but in these later periods, they are also sometimes revealed as deposits deliberately 'placed' in pits. The way these pit fillings can sometimes be structured suggests that some of them may have been religious or ceremonial offerings. Again, this suggests that while hazelnuts formed an important element in the prehistoric diet, as time passed they may have come to acquire even greater significance in people's minds. It's also worth noting here that hazelnuts are a significant source of fat (in the form of oils) and, of course, of protein. It isn't coincidental that vegetarians eat (having once tried one, I cannot say 'enjoy') nut cutlets.

But hazelnuts are archaeologically fascinating for two reasons, other than their food value alone. First, we still don't understand why they are so often found charred. I suspect this is something to do with survival conditions. Unburnt nutshells do eventually rot unless ground conditions are particularly dry (I have found unburnt prehistoric hazelnuts on, for example, chalk soils). Burning, on the other hand, converts the rottable, woody shell into pure carbon, or charcoal, which is quite fragile and easy to crush, but completely resistant to rot. And on very ancient sites, like those of the early Mesolithic, almost everything that could rot, will rot. A frequently heard alternative explanation is that heating over a fire was a way of preserving nuts for better storage over the following year. However, I have carried out a simple experiment that shows this is not the case.[9] Hazelnuts store perfectly well, if kept dry, airy and away from mice and other rodents. In fact, they actually improve in taste and texture when stored for two or three months. One other explanation is of course that people enjoyed some of their nuts roasted. And I agree; I eat many of my own, after roasting in a hot oven for about twenty minutes, but I also cheat and add a little salt and olive oil (which would not have been available to our hunter-gatherer families, although delicious wild boar dripping would).

The second concerns the way they have to be grown. But at this point I must introduce the topic of coppicing. Essentially, coppicing involves the cutting back of a tree or shrub during the dormant season (i.e. between September and March), to ground level. If the plant is cut higher up its stems or trunk (usually to avoid young shoots being nibbled off by browsing livestock, such as cattle, sheep, goats and horses), the process is known as pollarding. The purpose of this cutting back is to promote the growth of sturdy, fast-growing shoots in the spring. The young, straight, whippy shoots are known as withies (usually one or two years old), more sturdy ones (say one to two years old) are rods, while older, thicker rods develop into poles. Poles, depending on their size, are used as structural timbers in house roofs, but I have also seen them in the big V-shaped dams used for fish traps. In fact, they have a variety of uses around the fields and yards of a farm.

Today, coppice rods are used in vegetable gardens to support runner bean frames and in the past they were used as wattles which were woven into hurdles, or fences, and they formed the central support for a house's wattle-and-daub walls. Daub is a mixture of clay, straw and fresh cow or horse dung – and when dry it sets almost as hard as plaster. It's wonderful stuff, and makes excellent insulation, but must be kept damp free. The youngest, finest rods (withies) were woven into basketry and many have been found in old river-beds, dating back to Mesolithic and later prehistoric times, where they were once woven into elaborate fish and eel traps. Recent discoveries of prehistoric fish traps at Must Farm, near Peterborough, were identical to ones made by modern eel-catchers in the area. They were also built into permanent sets of weirs or dams, which suggests that by the Bronze Age Fenland fisheries were becoming very intensive.

The rapid, straight growth of coppice shoots is the plant's stress response, following a serious injury. Now it used to be thought that coppicing began in the Neolithic, and may have been introduced to Britain with farming. But to be honest I have never had much sympathy with that view, simply because it suggests that Mesolithic people were stupid. Any observant person out for a walk in a wood after a serious gale would soon have observed the way wind-damaged and broken tree trunks responded in the spring – and it would not have taken a genius to realize that if a tree was cut back with an axe (and Mesolithic communities possessed highly effective flint axes), then vigorous young shoots would soon sprout, to repair the damage. Hazel bushes respond well to coppicing and produce a wealth of straight, fast-grown withies and rods. Although not quite such a fast grower, hazel resists rot much better than willow (which also coppices well) and, in my experience, hurdles made from it will last two to three times as long. It's also a much stronger wood. But there is a complication: coppiced hazel does not produce many nuts.

For a start, coppiced hazel bushes are best grown in quite deep woodland, often alongside taller forest trees, known as 'standards'. These are usually oak or ash and they provide enough cover to restrict daylight, which causes the shooting coppiced hazel bushes to grow upwards (i.e. tall and straight), towards the light. As such growth is essentially a stress response, the plant puts less energy into flowering and fruiting – and when after several years it does eventually start to carry nuts, these are often held high in the air, well out of the reach of any pickers.

This is why traditional cobnut (the cultivated relative of the wild hazelnut) orchards are planted out in the open. These are still to be found in Suffolk and Kent. Here the bushes are pruned, rather than chopped back as in coppicing. The general aim is to replicate plants growing in a woodland edge (as opposed to woodland heart) environment. The pruning is intended to form well-shaped (i.e. easy to pick) bushes and no importance is attached to the growing of long, straight poles. In fact shorter, branching wood produces more flowers and hence more nuts.

Now it seems quite inconceivable to me that prehistoric, even early Mesolithic, people were ignorant of the different growing and cultivation conditions that the two uses of hazel required. It also strikes me as blindingly self-evident, having stumbled across hundreds of them myself, that Mesolithic woodsmen would not have been aware that the vigorous seedlings that can be seen to sprout from out of a hazelnut shell could be moved to somewhere more convenient. I think this more than likely, given the fact that wood mice like to bury little caches of nuts, which they often forget about over winter; these germinate in the spring and form small clumps of seedlings which are impossible to miss.

The mouse caches are often mixed with leaves, moss and fine twigs, and consequently the seedlings may easily be lifted out and taken away. No, as I said, it seems self-evident to me that Mesolithic people could have transplanted hazel seedlings from wood to woodland edge, or even closer to their houses and settlements, if they so wished. Indeed, this is even more likely, now that we are starting to appreciate that some Mesolithic groups lived in more-or-less fixed settlements. Even better for my argument, the extraordinary site at Star Carr has produced two stout wooden digging-sticks (see above, pp. 37–9), which would have made perfect replanting tools. But there is an academic snag. The movement of seedlings technically constitutes cultivation, and that is a part of farming; whereas Mesolithic people are supposed to be hunter-gatherers and some archaeological theorists insist that the two cannot be combined. You're either one or the other, so they say. By now, readers might have guessed that I don't have much time for such silly hair-splitting.

There is now increasing evidence to suggest that Mesolithic communities manipulated their environment in quite subtle ways to encourage the growth of plants they needed to nurture. In other words, it wasn't just a matter of producing better hunting grounds: places where prey was tempted to congregate and where there was a good field of vision, for waiting men, armed with spears, bows and arrows. Work in the lush wetlands that were forming around the tidal shore and flood-plain of the River Severn in South Wales has produced unambiguous evidence that fire was being used regularly, if not routinely, to cut back and coppice plants that were useful to Mesolithic communities.[10]

It seems to me that Britain's Mesolithic communities possessed an extraordinary wealth and variety of skills. We now know they were highly proficient wood-workers and woodsmen. They understood the tending and cultivation of hazel, not to mention a huge variety of other plant foods, ranging from roots and rhizomes to leaves and berries. There is evidence on the continent that they were fine boat-builders – indeed, they had crossed the choppy seas around the Isle of Man by 8000 BC to colonize Ireland, so they must have known much about seamanship. We know for a fact that they were expert fishermen and were able to operate using hooks and line, as well as woven basketry traps. They were superb craftsmen in bone and flint and were able to make a variety of complex, composite spearheads, not to mention useful household tools such as blades (i.e. knives) and scrapers. And, as we have known for a long time, they were excellent hunters, capable of catching a large variety of prey. The original excavations at Star Carr produced abundant evidence for the working of red deer antler – a very hard material – to produce barbed spearheads and fish spears. And of course we also now know they were capable of building substantial houses, which often included hearths for heating, cooking and even the smoking of food.

Surely it is now time we abandoned ideas that life in post-Glacial Britain was somehow grim, primitive and impoverished? I would not be at all surprised to learn that families would have organized informal schools to teach youngsters about the complex world they were about to join. But these lessons would probably not have been entirely practical – to do with hazel harvesting, fire-making or eel trapping alone. No, if modern hunter-gatherer societies can be used as a guide, everyday home life would have been structured around a framework of small rituals and ceremonies, that in turn would reflect what people believed about creation myths, together with the accepted ideas on the laws of nature and society.

As was probably the case in the Neolithic and Bronze Age, the line between life and death was not seen as clear cut, and the shades of the ancestors might have been invoked to enforce certain rules, such as settlement boundaries or hunting territories. Communities living at these levels of sophistication and complexity would have passed their skills on from one generation to another, by way of commonly accepted religious and ideological practices; in other words, something would have been needed to hold it all together. A framework of accepted beliefs would also have provided society with sanctions to enforce its laws and to punish those who ignored them. Such ideas are fine, and we have already mentioned shamanism, but is there other archaeological evidence for Mesolithic religion?

RELIGION AND BELIEF IN MESOLITHIC TIMES

Laying aside the vexed question of burials, which we will return to shortly, Britain has, in fact, revealed two good examples of what one might term the religious or non-practical side of Mesolithic life. As we have seen, the 1950s' excavations at Star Carr revealed antler head-dresses comprising the top of a red deer's skull, complete with the antlers.[11] The best explanation is that these were worn by shamans, most probably during ceremonies to do with hunting. Again, there are numerous modern parallels for such activities among hunting communities. It's also tempting to cite those antler-carrying Morris dancers from Abbots Bromley in Staffordshire. Nobody seems to know precisely when this strange dance began, but it probably has its roots in the distant past when such things were more widespread.

The other strange, seemingly non-functional discovery was made when land was being excavated ahead of the construction of the 1966 Stonehenge car park, alongside the A344.[12] It is still hard to understand why the discovery of three pits for massive pine posts did not create a bigger sensation at the time, because radiocarbon dates have shown they were dug some time around 8000 BC – when it would still have been possible to walk across the North Sea to the continental mainland. At this period, oaks had yet to recolonize Britain after the last cold period of the Ice Age, which was the reason why pine was used. The three holes were in a row, but there are indications that they could have formed part of a much longer structure – in effect, a large fence, palisade or barrier. There can be no doubt at all that the post-holes were deliberately dug and the posts were wedged into them by back-filling with earth and rubble. The timbers were far too large to have formed part of a house, and as farming was still four millennia in the future, we can rule out anything to do with agriculture, such as barns, gates or field boundaries. So when everything practical has been ruled out, archaeologists have to fall back on one thing: religion, or to use that jargon term, 'ritual'.

Had the Stonehenge posts been placed out in the middle of nowhere, it might be harder to argue that they were part of a ritual structure; but their location alongside what is perhaps the best-known prehistoric ceremonial site in the world must surely indicate a connection of some sort. It is also very interesting that the posts are aligned with Beacon Hill to the east – the highest point in the landscape.[13] The only problem, and it is a big one, is chronology. Stonehenge seems to have begun life around 3000 BC, some five thousand years after the car park posts. Having said that, there are Neolithic monuments nearby that could close the gap by another millennium, or so. But even so, four thousand years is still a very long time.

I will have much more to say about the recent Stonehenge Riverside Project in the next chapter, but for the time being it's enough to note that it has completely transformed our thinking about how and why Neolithic people built Europe's most remarkable prehistoric monument. One of the questions they tackled – and heaven knows it had been the 'elephant in the room' for British prehistorians for nearly half a century – was the existence of those massive pine posts in the car park. One problem – the easy one – was soon addressed: where were the Mesolithic people living? Although not actively researching this early period, the team came across two substantial areas of Mesolithic settlement debris, one of which was only 400 metres (1,300 feet) south of the car park posts.[14] Almost certainly there are others out there, waiting to be found.

The 4000-year 'gap' between the pine posts and the first Neolithic activity on Salisbury Plain might be more apparent than real. There is now a growing body of solid evidence that certain so-called 'natural places' were viewed by Neolithic communities as being special in some way. These places were often spectacular and on the fringes of the settled landscape: high in the Cumbrian Fells, or on remote Scottish islands. But they influenced rituals in the more populous areas of Britain by means of their products. Thus distinctive greenstone, quarried in Cumbria, was much used for polished axes in the East Midlands and around the Fens. The famous Bluestones from high in the Preseli Hills of south-west Wales were transported all the way to Stonehenge. It has been suggested that some of the mystery, the 'magic', of the revered natural places was believed to reside in the transported rocks themselves.

Further research by the Stonehenge Riverside Project has produced evidence to suggest that some of the standing stones, such as the outlying Cuckoo Stone, were most probably large rocks that had been left on the land surface after the Ice Age, which Neolithic people had then trimmed and erected as an outlying part of the religious monument.[15] We know for a fact that sarsens were an obstacle that farmers had to clear off their land from earliest times, through to the 18th and 19th centuries, but a small, largely uncleared area still survives in the National Trust's care, at Lockeridge Dene, Wiltshire. This gives a vivid impression of what parts of the Stonehenge area might have looked like in Mesolithic times.

There are no reasons to believe that the veneration of 'special places' began with the arrival of farming, indeed there are indications that a substantial number of earlier Neolithic sites have roots that extend much further back. If, for argument's sake, we assume that the area around Stonehenge was particularly densely packed with large sarsen rocks, similar to the Cuckoo Stone, then it might well have been selected as a special place. Some of the recumbent stones lying on the surface could then have been either moved to another position, or erected on the spot – by digging a large pit at one end and then tipping the stone into it.

If we take this longer-term view, then the large posts in the car park might well have been erected when the special place, that was later to become Stonehenge, became formalized in people's minds and imaginations. Religions tend to come and go, but places retain a more secure hold on people's consciousness. But that does not mean that worshippers and visitors need leave a mark on the place. Indeed, their reverence for it could have the opposite effect: so visitors strived to leave it pristine – as a sign of their respect. One thinks here of those remarkable Buddhist gardens in places like Japan. A good example of such long-term veneration is the tall standing stone in the churchyard at Rudston in the North Yorkshire Wolds.[16] This Neolithic monument is just the visible element of an ancient 'ritual landscape', still visible as cropmarks from the air, whose many features seem to focus on, and around, the very much later church. But is this coincidence or continuity? We will probably never know, but for far too long we have simply assumed the former. In my view, this reflects our own obsession with change-for-change's sake. It is time we tried to think ourselves back to a different, an older, mind-set, where time was seen in cycles, based around the coming and going of the seasons. Viewed thus, what do a few centuries – the odd millennium – signify?

Archaeologists tend to look for simple explanations to account for very complex phenomena, such as the long-term reverence and respect for a sacred place. 'It's near a spring' or 'it commands the landscape' are the sort of things one hears in the bar at conferences. But if you were to ask an Australian Aboriginal person why his or her community respected Uluru, or Ayers Rock, you would get a very long and metaphysical explanation. Similarly, simply to state that large sarsens could be seen on the ground on Salisbury Plain is not enough to explain the posts in the car park, nor indeed the later Stones. In fact much larger sarsens can be found over 30 miles to the north, in the Marlborough Downs, from whence many of the massive Stonehenge uprights and lintels were transported. So other factors, some of them beyond the reach of even the subtlest of modern archaeologists, must come into play. And Mike Parker Pearson's Stonehenge Riverside Project has come up with a superb example. You can believe it, or not, as you see fit. Personally, I am in little doubt.

I mentioned that people in prehistory, and indeed throughout most of history, conceived of time as essentially cyclical.[17] It was all about the passage of the seasons and the renewal of life every springtime.

Human lives were seen in these terms too. So the emphasis was on return to the earth and one's Maker. This cyclical view of existence still find expression in the Christian Church's calendar, but for much of modern British society it is relegated to Christmas. The modern approach to time arose after the Middle Ages, with the rise of science, industry and commerce. This new view, which is now universal in the developed world, is essentially linear: human, indeed national lives are seen in terms of progress towards an indefinable future, which could be good or bad, depending on one's world-view. But the process of achieving these ends, both personal and national, is one of continuous progress or regression; of success or failure; it's not about return and revisiting. And the steady passage of time is the independent 'control' that marks the success or otherwise of people's lives. It is an unrelenting and essentially unforgiving way of regarding the world, and I sometimes wonder whether we wouldn't be better off if we stood back and regarded life more cyclically.

If your whole existence is structured around a cyclical view of existence based on the concept of annual rebirth and regeneration, then the end of winter darkness is of fundamental importance. It has long been recognized that Stonehenge is all about the two solstices, the longest and shortest days of the year, and the Avenue leading up to the great Stones is precisely aligned on the two points where the sun rises and sets on the midsummer solstice. This alignment on the summer or winter solstice is known from many British Neolithic and Bronze Age ceremonial sites, so it must have been a fundamentally important idea underlying many religious beliefs at the time.

When I was a student we were told that early farmers necessarily took the midwinter solstice seriously: it was a portent of change. When days started to grow longer they could think about spring, about sowing crops, about the new season's calves and lambs. But no mention was made of the hunter-gatherer people of earlier periods: what about them? We have known for some time that recent hunter-gatherers were deeply concerned with the passage of the seasons because it affected the movement of game and ripening of fruits, nuts and other wild foods. It also affected the availability of certain landscapes and other resources, which in wintertime would have been flooded. Indeed, the word 'seasonality' has long featured prominently in the literature on Mesolithic hunters.[18] So it seems entirely natural that they, too, would have shared an interest in the solstices as definable moments of change in the eternal cycle of the seasons.

During the later stages of their research, the Stonehenge Riverside team discovered that the ground beneath the Avenue that led into Stonehenge from the north-east was naturally ridged and by an extraordinary accident of late-Glacial geology, these ridges were aligned on the axis of midwinter sunset and midsummer sunrise at the two annual solstices.[19] A couple of the taller ridges would probably have poked above the thinner topsoil of Neolithic times, but in the early post-Glacial period, when the great pine posts were erected, they would not yet have acquired even this thin covering and would have been *very* much more prominent. Mike Parker Pearson believes that the alignment of these ridges had been spotted by visiting Mesolithic groups and that this was one of the reasons they began to regard the area as special.[20] I have to say I find his suggestion compelling. And it certainly helps explain why people went to enormous effort to erect that row of huge pine posts.

REMEMBERING THE ANCESTORS

If home life is about living together under one roof, it is also about coming together and remembering the loss of a dear one. Of course, in the past those gatherings were rather more frequent than they are today, and would also have concerned people very much younger. So death is an integral part of family life. But it is also educational: it teaches us about our immediate ancestors, and through funerals and commemorative gatherings we meet and mix with more distant relatives of our own generation. In short, it helps us build networks that will be useful in later life. On an entirely personal level, coming to terms with death is how we learn about our own mortality and how to deal with it.

With the exception of a couple of cave sites revealed in the late 18th and early 20th centuries, there has been very little direct evidence for death and burial in Mesolithic Britain, which, it should be remembered, lasted for very much longer than the Neolithic (5000 as opposed to 1500 years), the age of farming, which replaced it.[21] The first farmers brought with them new continental burial rites, including the use of large collective tombs under earth or rock mounds, known as barrows or cairns. It was the sheer archaeological visibility of the Neolithic barrows – hundreds of which survive to this day – which came as such a contrast and led some prehistorians to take a minimalist view: they believed that somehow Mesolithic people were different from us and did not value their ancestors. All of this went hand in hand with the prevailing ideas that post-Glacial hunter-gatherers led an impoverished, shifting pattern of life, where the dead were buried where they died, by the side, as it were, of the migratory road – and were soon forgotten, once the group had moved on.

Then, in the 1960s and '70s, Mesolithic cemeteries began to be revealed in some profusion on the continent, in places like Denmark, where preservation was sometimes superb, and it became apparent that these hunter-gatherers had a rich and imaginative ceremonial and spiritual life. But what was it about Britain? Specialists in the period were in no doubt that burials would be found there, but when? Many sceptics had nagging doubts: maybe the British Isles really were *that* impoverished.

When I had that conversation with Nicky Milner, as recently as the summer of 2011, Britain had yet to reveal a well-dated Mesolithic burial. It was still one of the strange facts of insular archaeological life. Then a few months later my copy of *Past*[22] arrived in the mail. *Past* is the newsletter of the Prehistoric Society and I can well remember sitting on the society's council back in 1986 when the first issue was published. Some of our older members thought it a pointless innovation: what was wrong with the *Proceedings*, our heavyweight learned journal? The answer, of course, was speed. A paper in the journal could take years to appear in print, whereas *Past* could run a story, if needs be, in days. And now that speed was paying off.

I distinctly remember sitting back in my chair after supper, in front of a roaring log fire and opening that new issue of *Past*. Secretly I suspected I would fall asleep by the end of page 1, as I often do these days after a good meal. But not on that night. The front-page story was about a find of Wessex-style Early Bronze Age gold-work from Ireland. On page 2 there was an interesting account of a new field system of roughly the same period, this time from Kent, and on pages 3 and 4 a fascinating piece about a digital scan of the Stonehenge stones. It was an excellent issue. I was about to set it aside – and who knows, may never have picked it up again – and head up to bed, when my eye was caught by the words 'Early Mesolithic Cemetery' in a headline on page 6. With their laboratory numbers and technical details, radiocarbon dates always stand out from the rest of the text, and these were no different. There were three, taken from skulls, and they were consistent: all fell in the centuries between 8500 and 8200 BC.

The 'new' Mesolithic cemetery was actually nothing of the sort. It had been revealed over 80 years ago by the famous archaeologist Harold St George Gray, by then internationally famous for his work on the Lake Villages of Somerset at Glastonbury and Meare, in the wetlands of the Somerset Levels. Gray liked doing something I used to do too: he would visit the sheds and huts used by local quarrymen to store their tools, have tea and so forth. In modern health-and-safety-conscious quarries such places have vanished, but a few survived into the 1970s and '80s and I always hoped to stumble across something important in one of these cheerful, usually rather ramshackle places; but apart from a few mammoths' teeth and the odd massive aurochs's bone,[23] I was out of luck. But not Gray, who visited the sand quarry at Greylake, another site in the Somerset Levels, on 8 June 1928. Inside the gloomy hut, his eye was immediately caught by five skulls on a shelf in the quarrymen's shed.

Gray learned from the men that they'd been dug from the ground a week previously; they also produced some leg bones, so Gray was in little doubt that these had once been complete skeletons. In those days, indeed, until as recently as the 1980s, quarries routinely trashed archaeological sites, so the discovery of bones in a quarrymen's hut didn't cause much of a stir. Eventually, the Greylake bones found their way into the storerooms of two museums where they remained for 8 decades. Their true significance only began to become clear during a recent research project into the 'Lost Islands of Somerset'. This project was examining islands that had mostly been in existence as late as the 19th century, i.e. prior to the widespread drainage of the Somerset Levels. Greylake was one of these 'lost islands'. It was small, just 700 by 300 metres (2,300 by 980 feet), and lay in the flood-plain of the Parrett Valley. In many respects its situation recalls that of Star Carr. But the story doesn't end there.

In the 1930s a local amateur archaeologist made regular visits to the Greylake sand quarry, where his searches found no fewer than four thousand Mesolithic flints. These included tools, such as an axe and scrapers, as well as the tiny microliths used to make spear-heads. So members of the Lost Islands project re-evaluated these finds and revealed that no less than 83 per cent of the material con-sisted of the by-products (mostly waste flakes, chips and spent cores) of flint implement manufacture. Again, this is just like Star Carr, and it strongly suggests that the Greylake site was a permanent settlement, and not just the transient camp of a migratory hunting band. Again, the presence of a cemetery alongside the settlement, which we now know contained the bodies of both men and women, clearly indicates permanence. Those bodies do in fact tell us a great deal. They show that these very early inhabitants of what was much later to be called Somerset must have believed that their com-munity, their tribe, in effect 'owned' the land where their ancestors were given their final resting places. After all, you don't bury your family's dead in ground that is disputed or is controlled by a hostile community. Your family are buried in 'your' land; their safety, indeed their future, is bound up with yours and that of your whole family. Put another way, you protect your ancestors, just as you hope they will protect you – but this is a topic I will return to in the next two chapters.

HOT FROM THE PRESS: EVEN MORE EARLY HOUSES

More conservative readers might have thought that my use of the term 'housing boom' in Chapter 1 was something of an overstate-ment, given the actual number of buildings involved, but I still stand by my choice of words: allowing for the remoteness of the period and the fragility of the evidence, it is surely remarkable that so much new material is still coming to light. It is worth recalling that these houses are indeed substantial, but they are nothing like as massive as the round-houses built in the Bronze and Iron Ages. The roof support posts, for instance, tend to be about half to a quarter the size of the later ones and the holes needed to support them were proportionately much shallower. This slighter archaeological trace means that modern agricultural practices, such as pan-busting, deep ploughing and under-drainage, can be very destructive – hence my use of 'fragile'. That is why so many of these early houses are being found on marginal land, on the edge of the intensively farmed landscape. But it does not mean that this marginal land was where everybody chose to live. I strongly suspect that the vast majority of the population would have dwelt out in the fertile river valleys and flood-plains, just as they had done in the good old days of Doggerland.

Hardly a month goes by, it seems, without the announcement of some new Mesolithic discovery. Take January 2013. Both the popular magazines devoted to British archaeology carried stories of two new sites, one at Sefton, in Merseyside, the other (which I've already briefly mentioned in Chapter 1), at South Queensferry on the shores of the Firth of Forth. The Liverpool find is slightly more recent (5800 BC) than the very earliest houses, but there are three of them – as yet we cannot be certain whether they were all occupied at the same time – but they are of the same size and shape as the ones we have already seen. One very interesting aspect of this new site is its location on the edge of a reed swamp. There is nothing unusual in that, but the excavators did find evidence that the reeds had actually been burnt, which would indicate that the reed-beds were being managed in some way. It has been suggested that areas of woodland around, for example, watering holes, were kept free of undergrowth by fire in order to get a clear view of prey, such as red deer and wild boar, approaching for a drink. Maybe something similar was happening at Sefton. Again, this suggests a degree of permanence: you don't manage your hunting grounds in this way if you live a very nomadic lifestyle.[24] But that isn't to say that the community, or members of it, lived permanently in one place, because the houses produced large quantities of flintwork, all of which had to have been transported to the site. The nearest source of good flint is in Derbyshire, some 30 miles away. This might also suggest the existence of more specialized people, who traded or distributed such commodities, but so far we have no evidence for this idea.

The other recent discovery was at a place called Echline, at South Queensferry, and it was discovered during a pre-construction survey ahead of a new road crossing of the Firth of Forth. The work was carried out by Headland Archaeology, under the direction of Ed Bailey, and it illustrates well the very flexible approach of modern commercial archaeologists.[25] The areas stripped of topsoil and examined were huge and would have been quite unimaginable in the days of the original Star Carr excavations. But the really clever bit was not just the careful mechanical stripping, but the identification of such a fragile feature early on in the process. This has to have been done from the very moment the topsoil was first removed and would have required two very sharp-eyed people: the immensely skilled digger driver and his banksman or woman, an archaeologist whose job was to watch the ground around the machine's bucket, as it worked. I've done that job over many years and it is very easy to let one's concentration lapse, especially towards the end of a long, hard day.

As time passed, it became clear that Ed Bailey and his team had revealed the floor and posts of an oval house, about 7 metres (23 feet) long, with a gently dished, sunken floor about half a metre deep. There was evidence that the doorway faced downhill, to the west. The outer posts were set at an angle and sloped inwards, towards the centre, suggesting a tall, conical roof similar to that found at Howick. So my earlier thought, that Clive Waddington might have got the Howick reconstruction's roof angle wrong, was also wrong. Inside the angled posts was another oval of vertical posts which would have supported a low external wall, probably of stones, topsoil and turf. As at Howick, the excavators at Echline revealed the remains of several hearths inside the house.

It is currently thought that what is now the earliest house in Scotland was occupied seasonally, in wintertime; whereas Clive Waddington thought Howick was used all year round. And he has much

1. Cliff top at Howick, Northumberland, overlooking the North Sea. Shortly after 8000 BC this site was occupied by a Mesolithic family of hunter-gathers who built their house overlooking the sea. The charred remains of an *in situ* reconstruction of the house can be seen in the foreground, right. At this period Britain was still just linked to the continent by tracts of marshy ground to the south, but much of the coastline of Scotland and north-east England was more or less as it is today.

2. Hornsea Mere, in Holderness, south-east Yorkshire. This large, shallow lake was formed towards the end of the Ice Age, over 10,000 years ago. During the Mesolithic period its shores would have been surrounded by dozens of small settlements of people exploiting the lake's abundant resources of fish and wildfowl.

3. Mesolithic footprints in the muds of the Severn Levels at Goldcliff, south Wales.

4. (*above*) Recording waterlogged deposits in the Etton enclosure ditch. Note the long coppiced rods (probably of willow) extending across the width of the ditch.

5. (*left*) View of a waterlogged segment of enclosure ditch at Etton, showing a concentration of smaller woodchips and other woodworking debris (each piece of wood is marked with a red label). This view is taken from a causeway and shows how the ditch has been slightly expanded as it approaches the causeway.

6. (*below*) A length of twisted flax twine from the enclosure ditch at Etton. This is the earliest piece of string to have been found in Britain (*c.* 3500 BC).

7. (*above*) A piece of partially folded birch bark from the enclosure ditch at Etton (3600 BC).

8. (*right*) Etton enclosure ditch. A (*above*) The fossil sea urchin as we revealed it. B (*below*) After rolling it back onto its flat stone 'mat'.

9. (*left*) A small group of Neolithic pottery fragments from a single vessel. The vessel had been broken and the pieces were then gathered up and stacked one inside another. This tight pile of broken pottery was found in a row of offerings, placed at the bottom of the enclosure ditch, at Etton (3600 BC).

10. (*left*) Broken fragment of quern-stone (corn-grinding stone) in a row of offerings placed at the bottom of the Etton enclosure ditch. It had been arranged in the ground so that its smooth grinding surface, which would have been horizontal during its use-life, was now vertical (3600 BC).

11. This large, complete, saddle quern-stone had been placed on edge in a pit close to the centre of the Etton enclosure (*c.* 3600 BC). The scale is in 10 cm bands.

12. House 1 at Skara Brae, Orkney, seen from the entranceway. This Neolithic house was part of a settlement of nine closely linked houses, built and occupied between 3200 and 2500 BC. This view shows the two-tiered dresser, with a pair of quern-stones in front of it and a small stone 'box' which would have been lined with clay to hold water. To the left

and right are box beds, and above the one to the right is a stone 'cupboard' (a recess in the wall). In the middle (*foreground*) is the rectangular hearth, which stood at the centre of the house. The roof would probably have been of turf and thatch, weighted down against the Atlantic gales.

13. At the bottom of the pit, beneath the complete saddle quern shown in Plate 11, we found the top stone that would normally have been kept above the larger, bottom stone. The reversal was deliberate and symbolized the two stones being taken out of use in this world, possibly for use in the realm of the ancestors (c. 3600 BC).

14. The excavator Professor Mike Parker Pearson kneels in front of the hearth of one of the Neolithic houses his team discovered at Durrington Walls, near Stonehenge. The hearth (note the spread of charcoal around its edges) is slightly raised on a chalk plaster floor. The three deeper slots are for the wooden plank sides of box-beds and other furniture. The post-holes of the house walls can be seen running in a gentle arc in the foreground. Preservation is so good that Mike's knees rest in two shallow indentations in the floor, worn down by kneeling cooks some 4,500 years ago.

corroborative evidence to back him up. At this stage it is probably too early to know for certain, but the problem with any seasonal or episodic explanation is simple: what happens to the house if nobody is there? Laying aside any human interference, empty houses can be very smelly places. Just the scent of cooking fat soaked into the ground around the hearths would soon attract foxes and wolves from miles away. If they behaved anything like my Border Collie sheepdog (who is, of course, descended from a very intelligent line of wolves), the rich smells would soon get them digging with their front feet and the well-defined hearths seen in the excavation trenches would rapidly be disturbed beyond recognition. Personally, I think the jury must remain out on the question of seasonality at South Queensferry until there is further evidence either way.

The Echline team did reveal two very telling pieces of new information. The first does not sound exciting when stated as a bald fact: inside the house they found the bones of a wolf's foot. But then pause and think how this could come about. It could, just possibly, be butchery waste, but so far there is very little evidence that wolves were hunted for the pot in Britain at this period. Far more likely, the wolf had been skinned and its warm pelt worn as a cloak or blanket at night. It is easy to leave the feet on a pelt; they can look quite striking, and can also be used to tie or fasten it to the wearer.

The second unusual discovery was just outside the building, where a small circle of stakes was found surrounding post-holes and two fireplaces. Nearby, they also found a large number of bird and fish bones and the suggestion is that these were meat smoking and drying racks, where the wind was broken by a semi-circular C-shaped screen on the outside. It was probably roofed with hides to contain the smoke better. Other evidence for food included quantities of charred hazelnut shells and the bones of red and roe deer and wild boar. And again, it's worth noting that while smoking does act as a preservative, especially when combined with salting (and there was saline water nearby), it is also a process that enhances flavour enormously. Give me a proper smoked and cured kipper any day, over a plain herring. These people were certainly enjoying a remarkably high standard of living.

FOOTPRINTS IN TIME

It is one thing to speculate about home life in remote times, quite another to prove it. So far, we have considered many things, ranging from the very existence of families, to the different roles of men and women within them. And of course all of these are very difficult to demonstrate with direct archaeological evidence. As we have seen, it is also so easy to come to the wrong conclusions, even after much deliberation. If Grahame Clark were to return from the dead and see how we now regarded Star Carr, he would be astonished. But I also think he would be delighted, despite the fact that at face value he had been proved 'wrong'. But was he? Given the constraints he had to work within, I think he got things as 'right' as he could – and probably better than we could, were we working with him in the 1950s. In my view, ideas of 'right' and 'wrong', or 'correct' and 'incorrect', in such circumstances are missing the point. What matters is the size of the step you take when you move the subject forward. Viewed in this way, most prehistorians would agree that Clark took several large strides.

Archaeology can be a very analytical business and I must have spent many years of my professional life measuring flint flakes and peering at pieces of pottery under a hand lens. One does these superficially tedious tasks because the end results can prove enlightening. And I say 'can' advisedly, because sometimes they cannot. I'm also aware that most archaeologists do what they do for other, less rational, reasons. For many it's the social side of excavation that they enjoy: nothing can match the feeling of camaraderie that a small team feels after finishing a hard dig, especially through the cold, wet months of winter. Then there are those wonderful periods of stillness and reflection at the end of the day, as the sun sets behind the remains of a Bronze Age burial or a Victorian blast furnace. At such times one feels strangely in touch with the past, or more importantly, the people of the past. I suppose it's more a matter of communion than communication. Like my colleagues, I value all of these moments, but what really makes me tingle are those smaller, more intimate things that appear out of nowhere, unexpectedly. They don't happen very often, but when they do, it can be magical.

So after almost two chapters spent describing sites and changing interpretations, I want now to lighten the mood and indulge in a luxury: an archaeological discovery that is non-controversial. And yes, such a thing does exist. In this particular case it proves what we have always strongly suspected, that families existed in Mesolithic times and that through them one generation gave rise to another. But even so, it is nice – no, more than that: it is comforting – to find incontrovertible proof.

I've written about the first time I saw Bronze Age fingerprints on a piece of burnt clay when I was digging sites at Fengate, near Flag Fen, in Peterborough, back in the 1970s.[26] It was another of those personal moments I shall never forget. Just for an instant I sensed I was standing close to a prehistoric man or woman; I could almost feel their breath on my neck. Then something similar happened far more recently, but this time the people involved were Mesolithic, and it wasn't their fingers, but their toes that made my imagination race away.

I remember the day well. I had come to South Wales to look at some of the remarkable discoveries that were being made by Dr Martin Bell and his team from Reading University. It was his team who carried out the research on the burning and manipulation of the Mesolithic environment, which I mentioned earlier in the section on hazelnuts. For a long time Martin had been studying the flat tidal landscapes along the northern shores of the Severn Estuary. In many respects this landscape would have been closely similar to parts of the Fens: it's superficially flat and there are huge expanses of tidal silts, just as there are today around the Wash foreshore. You also need to know your way around them, because these seemingly placid expanses of wet mud can turn out to be quicksands. As around the Wash, they're not likely to drag you completely under, but they can bog you down, and then of course the tide comes roaring in – and you're stuck fast, unable to escape. I was very mindful as I followed closely on Martin's heels, that the Severn tides are higher and faster than others almost anywhere else in the world.

On previous visits, I had experienced some of the archaeological riches that the Severn Levels have to offer: there were inundated Bronze Age, Iron Age and Roman houses, complete with wattle-woven walls and intact floors, all beautifully preserved beneath countless layers of tidal silts. There were also lines of large poles that once formed the sub-structure of numerous fishermen's weirs, which could be almost any date from Saxon, medieval or modern times. But we were not after anything erected or built by the hand of man. We were in search of something smaller and more ephemeral.

We had been walking for about half an hour and were now getting quite close to the water's edge. Out on the main stream I could see two large tankers heading for the refineries at Milford Haven. A cool breeze got up and there were grey clouds heading our way from the north-west. I didn't relish the prospect of being caught out here in a rainstorm, but Martin seemed unconcerned. I had to trust him: if you've worked somewhere for long enough, you develop a 'nose' for hostile weather – you have to.

We walked on for another ten minutes. We were going slower now. Martin paused; he was looking around him, intently.

'Does it change much out here?' I asked.

'Yes,' he replied, 'after every tide. Normally the basic landform stays the same, though . . .' he tailed off. He was concentrating hard as he stared at the dappled grey and brown mudflats that surrounded us. Then, more resolutely this time, he headed off upstream, parallel to the shoreline. After a couple of minutes we stopped. Here the muds were paler. Again, he was looking around. Then his arm shot out.

'Ah,' he said. I could see the excitement in his eyes. 'Look, over there, that small patch of sand . . .'

I could see it quite clearly. From a distance it seemed to be spotted with small puddles – hardly surprising as it had been beneath the waves an hour ago. In my excitement as we hurried across to look at it more closely, my left foot hit a soft patch, sank down fast, and wet salty mud flooded into my boot. I wrenched it out, annoyed with myself for being so careless. Martin was a few steps ahead of me. He knelt down and turned round as I joined him:

'There they are. These are a bit weathered, but you can clearly see what they are . . .'

Yes, I could. They were the prints of bare human feet (see Plate 3). I would guess there were two adults, possibly a man and a woman, as one set was smaller than the other. Each footprint was about a couple of centimetres (an inch) or so deep. You could clearly make out individual toes in the best-preserved ones. Some of the prints had partly filled with pale yellow sand, which contrasted sharply with the uniform greys of the muds they had been walking across. I was trying to see if I could detect lines of footprints, maybe paces, but it was proving difficult. Then Martin broke in: 'Hey, Francis, come over here. I think this might be a child . . .'

He was leaning over a smaller patch of mud a couple of metres closer to the sea. I was with him in an instant.

'Oh, yes . . .'

I was lost for words. There could be no doubt about it. The two – actually it was more like one and a half – footprints were almost half the size of the adults', but they were complete. There was no way these were worn-down or eroded adult prints. They were quite clearly made by a child. I'd guess he or she was about ten or twelve. The adults' footprints had been remarkable enough, but these . . . These were almost too much. For a few precious seconds I was back in the Mesolithic with that small family and it would have been just like today. In the background were the constant cries of seagulls and waders. The wind was blowing more briskly now, as the clouds were growing closer. Martin too stood silently. Even having witnessed similar footprints dozens of times, I could see they still affected him.

After a few minutes of silence, Martin glanced up at the sky.

'Time we were off.'

He was right. I dragged myself away. Storm or no storm, I don't think I've ever been so reluctant to leave an archaeological find. As we headed back, I found it hard to accept that those footprints had survived for perhaps seven thousand years and then been exposed for just two or three hours, before the next tide washed them away, for ever.

MOTIVES AND EXPLANATIONS

In this final section I want to consider what motivated people to re-settle Britain after tens of thousands of years of ice and cold. There seems no reason to suppose that anyone gave an order, simply because there was no 'top-down' social hierarchy to issue the command. So how did it happen and why did a series of independent family-scale decisions appear to have been so well co-ordinated?

I must confess that I have always been suspicious of simple, external causes, such as volcanic eruptions, tsunamis and plagues, as explanations for past human events. Yes, disasters like these can hasten or redirect changes that were due to happen anyhow, but with obvious exceptions, such as island populations confronted by rising sea-levels, they rarely instigate change entirely unaided. A good example is the terrible onslaught of the Black Death in 1348 which, together with subsequent waves of plague, triggered a rapid sequence of social and economic changes throughout Britain and Europe.[27] I will touch on this in the Epilogue, but I can say now that it was never a simple case of cause and effect, of disease instigating change; certainly in the case of Britain, by the mid-14th century something had to snap: population had been relentlessly rising, from as far back as the Neolithic, and the rural economy was barely able to feed the growing numbers; indeed, there were several famines in southern Britain in the decades leading up to 1348.[28] The role of the Black Death was to tip the balance; in effect, it was a catalyst, not a cause.

The best contender for an 'external cause' for the movement of people into Britain was of course the post-Glacial climate warming of 9600 BC, which hastened sea-level rise and with it the formation of the North Sea. Within a relatively short time, the vast fertile plains and marshlands of Doggerland were to become uninhabitable. So people upped sticks (quite literally) and moved towards the hinterlands around the fringes of the North Sea Basin, which includes the British Isles. This was a process that would have been under way between about 9000 and 6000 BC, the period when the North Sea was expanding rapidly.

Migration from lower-lying landscapes was one factor; but it is also more than probable that people had been present in Britain from very shortly after 9600 BC, simply because that was where they wanted to live. The immediate surroundings of the settlements at Star Carr, Howick and South Queensferry, for example, would have changed relatively little, certainly in terms of coastline change (if nothing else), from the period around 9600 BC, when the climate changed so rapidly. Who can say whether the folk at these sites necessarily migrated there from the North Sea Basin? What I'm saying is that we must beware of treating human beings like machines that are entirely predictable in their actions: stimulus A triggers response B, and so on. A good example of this is the post-Glacial settlement of Britain's neighbouring large island, Ireland.

On the face of it, there was no pressing external 'need' or 'cause' that instigated a move of population westward. But nevertheless, it happened. Presumably this was because the coast of Ireland was visible from what is now north-west England, the Isle of Man and south-west Scotland, so people there, being curious, decided to explore. Some support for this idea comes from the similarity of flint tool-making traditions in these areas with the oldest Mesolithic flints in Ireland. Having said that, the similarity is not *that* close: the traditions are related, but far from identical.

It now seems probable that these voyages took place around 8000 BC. Interestingly, there are some reasons to think that the natural food resources available in Ireland were not quite so plentiful as on the mainland of Britain.[29] Despite this, Ireland was soon populated with many Mesolithic settlements. At this point it is probably worth bearing in mind that the number of surviving Mesolithic sites is probably just a tiny proportion of those that were once present. It is only a guess, but I would hazard that the sites shown on the map (see Fig. 2.1) represent less than 5 per cent of the original number. We also know that in Neolithic times Ireland seems to have been well populated, and from the very outset, around 4000 BC. This would also tend to confirm that the earlier, hunter-gatherer, population was substantial, too.

So why did families move to new lands when the climate grew warmer? It's as well to be honest here, and admit that we just don't know for certain – and probably never will. But I also suspect that different people had their own, unique and unpredictable motives, just as they do today. For some, it may have been the need to escape from a nagging mother-in-law, for others it was the romance of the journey and for a few perhaps the mountaineer's non-explanation: 'because it's there'. Whatever their motives, families of people moved

Fig. 2.1 Map of Ireland showing the number of Mesolithic (8000–4000 BC) sites known in 2000 AD.

first into Britain and then into Ireland, where they settled. But the important point to note is that nobody told them to move. On the other hand, people in families rarely act without discussing their plans with other family members and I feel sure that the explorers of new territories must have moved with a great deal of practical help and emotional support from the broader family, some of whom may well have travelled part of the way earlier. And of course, when they did settle down in the new territory, they would have been there to welcome any younger family members who might care to join them later. It was all about communication and mutual support: ideas of intrepid explorers setting off fearlessly into *terra incognita* are probably best left to *Boys' Own* history books.

As we have seen, societies and communities at this early stage in the prehistory of northern Europe were organized on the basis of bands and families. It follows that, ultimately, change was brought about through the accumulation of thousands of independent and spontaneous actions. Despite the speed of the re-settlement, and the illusion of synchronicity and planning, we must conclude that these developments happened for one reason only: it was what people, at various times and places across north-western Europe, wanted to do. And if fundamental 'drivers' have to be sought, I would suggest two: the gradual flooding of the North Sea plain and the steady growth of the Mesolithic population, which until very recently has been grossly underestimated. If ever there was a series of locally co-ordinated, spontaneous, family-based decisions, they happened in the centuries that followed the climatic warming of 9600 BC. And their effects were profound, because they led to the establishment of stable communities across the varied set of landscapes that would shortly become the British Isles.

3

Early Farmers (4000–3000 BC)

The next big social and cultural change that was to affect Britain and Europe was the onset of farming, shortly before 4000 BC. This is perhaps the most celebrated event in British – indeed world – prehistory and it marked the start of the Neolithic period. About a millennium into the new period, from around 3000 BC, a series of major innovations took place which included the construction of great 'henge' sites, such as Stonehenge and Avebury, and a series of new communal tombs; both types of monument were often aligned on the solar solstices of midsummer and midwinter. Current thinking would suggest that the spread of farming, together with the invention and construction of the new monuments, arose as the result of 'bottom-up', or communal, innovation. What makes these two eras of change so remarkable is the way they were co-ordinated across the British Isles, and it is now quite apparent that close ties were actively maintained between all the communities of Neolithic Britain and Ireland. As time passed, these links grew even closer.

THE ARRIVAL AND SPREAD
OF FARMING

In the 1950s and '60s revolutions were quite fashionable. I can remember hearing on the radio that my generation were pioneering a sexual revolution, although none of us, male or female, actually felt very revolutionary at the time. We just got on with our lives, just as I'm doing during the current digital revolution. As if this was not enough for a poor student, I began my first and second year prehistory lectures by discovering the Neolithic Revolution. Indeed, the two words were the title of an excellent book published by no less an organization than the British Museum, in 1959.[1] Then, almost as soon as I had begun practising archaeology as a profession, and throughout the following three to four decades, a huge number of radiocarbon dates suggested that the process of introducing farming to Europe had taken a vast length of time to complete. So the term fell from fashion and has largely disappeared. Indeed, very recently I myself have argued against it.[2] So am I about to change my mind?

The answer to that is the usual reply of the academic who has been caught saying something without thinking through all its implications: 'It depends what you mean by . . .' In this case the word I'm questioning is 'Neolithic'. I certainly conceded that the idea of a European Neolithic Revolution is absurd, if only because the spread of farming from origins in the Near East (around 8000 BC) to Britain (by just before 4000 BC) took a little short of four millennia. And it goes without saying that revolutions don't involve millennia, let alone nearly four of them. But if we step aside from this pan-continental view and consider instead the arrival and spread of farming across Britain then those same radiocarbon dates that served to debunk the original Neolithic Revolution can be used to suggest a much smaller – and very much faster – and I think quite justifiable British Neolithic revolution (although this time I shall avoid using the capital 'R'). The reassessment of the British Neolithic chronology was essentially a statistical recalculation of all the available radiocarbon dates, but it was a Herculean task and the two volumes of the final report are massive.[3] In the end, the results certainly justified all the effort.

Radiocarbon dates have taken a long time to settle down and become routine. The man who started it all was Professor Willard F. Libby, a chemist who worked on the Manhattan Project during the Second World War, helping to develop the atomic bomb. Afterwards he moved to the University of Chicago where he invented the technique of radiocarbon dating, publishing his first result in 1949. In 1960 he was awarded the Nobel Prize for Chemistry for his work on radiocarbon dating.[4] The method depends on the natural breaking-down of radioactive isotopes from one form of carbon to another. This happens at a consistent rate and dates can be calculated by measuring the progress of decay, using extremely sensitive technology. All organic material can be dated, providing it has not rotted away – so the most usual samples are from charcoal, bone, antler and waterlogged wood. But there was a snag.

In the 1960s and '70s it was realized that solar radiation, which created the radioactive element in the carbon, had not been constant through time. Solar flares and sunspots affected the rate in which plants took up radioactive carbon. So then it took another couple of decades to prepare precise graphs of solar radiation against which radiocarbon measurements could be compared, to achieve a more accurate, so-called 'calibrated' date. Then came the final twist in the story. Its roots lay in the work of an 18th-century English Presbyterian minister and mathematician, Thomas Bayes, who published an important work on statistics in 1763. His approach, known as Bayesian statistics, could have been tailor-made for radiocarbon dates. I cannot say I fully understand them myself, but they work on the principle that if you come up with new information about something you already know a little about, you can combine the two to acquire even greater precision. And then every new radiocarbon date adds to the precision of those that have gone before. And that is why archaeologists today never get a single, one-off, date – you always try to afford (and they can be expensive) at least three or four tests, and preferably more.

So the new project on Neolithic dates first recalibrated every date from certain categories of sites, whose broad position in the sequence of Neolithic monuments was already well established. It then subjected the recalculated dates to Bayesian modelling, for various sites, events and groups of sites. It sounds complex, and it was. But the results have been, frankly, astonishing.

Prior to the new work, it used to be believed that the establishment of farming in Britain was a gradual process that may have taken up to two millennia to complete.[5] Now the wheel has turned full circle and the new survey suggests we are looking at a period some ten times as short – maybe two *centuries*, rather than two millennia.[6] If we bear in mind that the then widely accepted Industrial Revolution was supposed to have happened over a broadly similar length of time, I don't think it is pushing the evidence too far to suggest that a change of comparable (some would say, greater) importance was therefore also revolutionary.

So farming, and with it the Neolithic period, arrived shortly before 4000 BC and had spread right across Britain, reaching northern Scotland before 3800.[7] Some prehistorians believe that studies of the DNA in Neolithic bones will soon reveal the genetic make-up of the first British farmers. Or to put it another way, what proportion were 'native' Britons and what proportion were 'incomers' from Europe? My own feeling is that this is a science still in its relative infancy and we should be mindful of the lesson of radiocarbon when on several occasions we thought we understood more than we actually did. As with radiocarbon, the new science of DNA characterization may take another decade or two to settle down – and again, it will not be just the science, but the way we interpret the results that we will need to think about. In the meantime, the best-informed opinions would suggest that the ratio of incomer to native was in the range 1:3 to 1:4, but probably no more.[8] There is, of course, every likelihood that some, maybe many, of the new arrivals were recent converts to the new pattern of life from just across the Channel, and it is very debatable whether their DNA could readily be distinguished from that of the native Britons.

It used to be thought that there would have been much resistance to farming by the native hunter-gatherers – rather in the manner of Hollywood Cowboys and Indians. But the sheer rapidity of the transformation suggested by the new evidence surely implies that if there was resistance, it was not particularly fierce, or prolonged. My own instinct is that by the 5th millennium BC the hunter-gatherer lifestyle would probably have been far more settled and well adapted to local environments than we currently think. If my ideas on hazelnuts are proved to be correct, then that might suggest some blurring of the farmer/hunter boundary already. We know for a fact, too, that dogs had been domesticated from wolves by early Mesolithic times (their bones were found at Star Carr). We also know that in certain areas, such as Fenland, Mesolithic and early Neolithic sites nearly always occur next to each other, and it has been suggested that Mesolithic and Neolithic communities consisted of essentially the same people, living slightly different lifestyles, in slightly different times.[9]

The sheer quantity of Neolithic archaeological sites also suggests that the introduction of farming triggered a sustained period of population growth, which would continue, with a few set-backs (like a possible period of plague in the immediately post-Roman period), for some five millennia, until the mid-14th century AD.

NEOLITHIC ARABLE FARMING: AGRICULTURE OR HORTICULTURE?

When I wrote *Britain BC*, back in 2001 and 2002, we still thought that the spread of farming across the British Isles had been a process that had taken over a millennium to complete. My personal view, which I still hold, is that Mesolithic hunters actually 'managed' their game to such an extent that they were almost livestock farmers: they controlled patterns of grazing (through the use of fire), and as we have seen, they cleared woodland around water-holes to make access better, but also to make selective hunting more straightforward. I suspect, too, that some members of the community, if not everyone, would have followed game as it moved from one area to another and may well have encouraged particularly prized animals, or herds, to stay within certain territories. Efforts would have been made, too, to stimulate breeding and to discourage the killing of juveniles. Indeed, I strongly suspect that most Mesolithic groups would have drawn up their own set of unwritten Game Laws. When your future depends on a particular resource, you do your best to manage it.

Britain has a moist, oceanic climate and is particularly well suited to the growing of grass.[10] So when the first domesticated cattle, sheep and pigs arrived with the Neolithic incomers, they would have been readily accepted by the native British population, who would have adapted and extended the grazing areas they had already provided for wild prey. They also had dogs which would have been used to guard the new, and far more vulnerable, beasts, against attack from predators such as wolves and bears. So I see the adoption of livestock farming as more a shift in lifestyle than a thoroughgoing revolutionary change.

But what about the crops they were growing: the other half of the

British Neolithic revolution? Again, I have long believed that the earliest British fields were actually laid out for the use of livestock. I won't go into the detailed arguments here, but the layout of these fields strongly suggests their primary function was the containment and management of farm animals: they are entered by corner entrance-ways; they may be linked by ditched and hedged droveways, which in turn often lead to yards and sub-divided handling areas, close to the farm or settlement. So where were the crops being grown?

While I was digging at Fengate in the 1970s, and then in the '80s at sites a little bit further north, in the Welland Valley, I began to suspect that Neolithic farms were not organized as they are today in the east of England, with large fields of cereals and much smaller fields of grazing. As I learned more about landscape development, it became clear to me that even the medieval open fields gave no hint as to pre-Roman farming. It was apparent that livestock (mostly cattle and sheep) would have featured far more prominently than was believed at the time. But to return to the central question: where were the crops being grown?

In 1978 I returned to Britain from living in Canada and two years later I bought a small farmhouse in the Fens, near the village of Parson Drove, in north Cambridgeshire. As the village name suggests, animals and their droveways formed an important element in the local agricultural economy of the Middle Ages. But whether inspired by this, or not, we began to keep a few sheep in the two small paddocks alongside the house, encouraged, I should add, by Mr Bliss and his son Sam, the owners of the land, who always failed to collect any rent we owed them. The more we learned about the ways of livestock, the less likely it seemed that crops were being grown in fields out there in the livestock pastures on prehistoric farms. As it was, our animals were regularly slipping out through modern wire fences and I couldn't (and still cannot) conceive how early farmers could have fashioned completely stock-proof field boundaries, out there in the open landscape, from hedges alone. But if, on the other hand, their growing-grounds were alongside or much closer to the settlements themselves, then it might have proved possible to erect a truly stock-proof hedge around *them*, maybe heavily reinforced with dead brambles, thorns and bracken. Children and dogs from the settlement could have patrolled such a short boundary, and after a while the stock would have given up trying to break in. But beware: this does not apply to pigs, who are very intelligent and far harder to contain, and would probably have been kept well away, most likely in woodland around the edges of the farm or village.

I looked everywhere for direct evidence of these hypothetical growing-grounds close by Neolithic settlements, but could find none. I now realize that most of it would have been removed by modern ploughing. Then, in the late 1990s, I did find clear and unambiguous evidence, at a site known as Welland Bank Quarry, which I will describe in more detail in Chapter 7. Sadly, however, Welland Bank was very much later than the Neolithic, dating to the latter part of the Bronze and the Early Iron Age. Even so, I can see no good reason why the practice should have sprung up 'out of the blue', as it were, at such a late date, and I strongly suspect it was a development, most likely an intensification, of a system that had been in existence for a long time.

Then a handful of years ago, I began to hear accounts of some research being carried out jointly at Oxford and Sheffield Universities. It first came to light in February 2010 at a conference at Durham University on the creation of homes in the earliest farming period in Eurasia. One of the contributors to the conference, Glynis Jones (whose work I have long admired), noted that the new research showed that 'home is not the house, but where the garden is.'[11] More recently we have been able to see the results of this project in more detail. Essentially, the research has been based around a technique known as stable isotope analysis, which can characterize the molecular composition of ancient organic material. Dr Amy Bogaard and her team have demonstrated that the earliest farmers of Eurasia regularly manured their land.[12] They also kept it free from weeds and they removed surplus stones to improve tilth and fertility. The tilled land would have been bounded by walls or hedges, to protect it. Indeed, we noticed a sharp and very straight edge to the much darker soil of the prehistoric arable patch at Welland Bank, which I attributed at the time to a hedge.[13] It would seem I may have been right. These various measures would have had the effect of increasing the quality and hereditable value of land, which in turn implies there were rules and conventions regarding land-holding, and continuity; family ownership was a strong probability. In short, the research demonstrates, quite conclusively, that early crop farming was more about fixed-place horticulture than shifting nomadic farming. And although Britain might lie on the fringes of Eurasia, the existing site-based evidence would suggest that the earliest farmers there, too, had adopted the same patterns of crop-growing and family-based land tenure.

It could be argued, of course, that later prehistoric sites like Welland Bank grew up as a response to circumstances that would not have applied three millennia earlier, when the Neolithic population was much smaller, more thinly spread, and life was generally less pressured. But again, that is an assumption too – and you might think it was a safer one, except that recent research is now showing that Neolithic communities could be very different from the thin scatter of isolated farmsteads that prehistorians once imagined. We will see at the end of this chapter how Neolithic settlements, such as the one recently revealed at Durrington Walls, in Wiltshire, could be very substantial – large villages by any standards – and individual buildings could be massive, as is currently being demonstrated at the Ness of Brodgar, in Orkney.[14] I would suspect that nearly all permanent Neolithic settlements were accompanied by large horticultural plots, or arable patches.

GETTING TOGETHER

It would be a mistake to see the British early Neolithic as a prehistoric Wild West: wagon trains were not rolling across the Chiltern Hills. What we are looking at here is the spread of people and ideas through landscapes and communities that may have been welcoming and receptive, and were not necessarily hostile. Word of the changes would have preceded the farmers themselves. Again, we must not think in terms of a young lad running into a clearing shouting in panic that 'The Injuns are coming!' More likely, the idea of farming arrived a generation or two before the farmers themselves. So local communities would have been prepared. I don't wish to overdo the Wild West analogy, but when settlers arrived in the American Midwest, they encountered Amerindian riders who were remarkably skilled horsemen – as even Hollywood concedes. What is relevant here is that horses are not native to America and had been introduced by Spanish colonists a few generations earlier. In other words, people will rapidly adopt a new idea if it fits with the way they are living their lives.

If the sheer rapidity of the transition from hunting and gathering to farming was remarkable, there was more to the British Neolithic revolution than just economic change. I believe that we are witnessing here a truly remarkable period of family-based, bottom-up change. Plainly there must have been much co-ordination, if only to avoid conflict, but it must have been at a local level, and again, I see the larger family – the clan – as the means of communicating and supporting the new social developments. So the question that now arises is this: where is the evidence for clans and local cohesion? In other words, where did people meet to discuss, to negotiate and to plan?

I shall discuss tombs and graves in the next section, as these certainly played an important part in keeping families together. But what about larger gatherings, where people met to acquire essential new blood-lines for their livestock, and indeed for their own families? Communities needed to assemble together in prehistoric times, just as they do today; it's part of being a social animal, and a human.

If you open any book about Britain's prehistoric monuments, the earliest examples are always Neolithic, because very little survives, as visible humps and bumps in the landscape, from earlier times. Unless you had been told they were there, and knew how to identify Mesolithic flints, you would never recognize Star Carr, or indeed Howick, for what they are. But when farming arrived around 4000 BC, all of that was to change. Suddenly people started to erect permanent monuments in the landscape, many of which have survived to this day. We know this took a vast amount of work and planning. So why did they do it? And the answer, I firmly believe, resides within the family.

So let's start with the earliest communal monuments, which are known as causewayed enclosures. This has to be one of the most stuffy, unprepossessing names – even by archaeological standards – for what is actually a rather mysterious, and frankly very intriguing, group of religious or ceremonial sites. The clumsy name stems from the sites' appearance from the air, where they show up as a roughly circular arrangement of short lengths of ditches, separated from each other by narrow spaces, or 'causeways'. The best way to describe the layout of the ditches is as concentric rings of sausages, often placed around the crown of a hill, and usually slightly off centre. But they also occur in large numbers on flat landscapes. In fact, the greatest concentration of them anywhere in Britain is in the lower Welland Valley, in north Cambridgeshire, right on the edges of the Fens. And I had the very great good fortune to excavate one of these, near a little village called Etton, but more on this in the next section.[15]

Like most prehistorians, I have long been fascinated by causewayed enclosures. They are the first great field monuments, where people came together for large gatherings. Later, they were to be replaced by places like Stonehenge, but for the earlier Neolithic they were prime sites, and they can be found, moreover, across much of northern and Atlantic Europe. Probably the best-known causewayed enclosure in Britain is at Windmill Hill, just outside the vast henge site at Avebury, in Wiltshire. That huge site has three rings of causewayed ditches, whereas Etton is a much humbler creation, having just one. But Etton has a big advantage over Windmill Hill, and indeed all other cause-wayed enclosures (with one exception at Staines, in Middlesex), because it was partially waterlogged. As we saw at Star Carr earlier, this made it very special, because organic material, such as wood and bark, were superbly preserved there.

But first a few general remarks about causewayed enclosures, which as a class of monument have long puzzled prehistorians. To date, we know of about 70 British examples, but new ones are regularly being discovered, usually from air photos. They mostly occur in southern Britain, south of a line from the Wash to the Lleyn Peninsula in North Wales.[16] I mentioned the famous example at Windmill Hill, because this was one of the first to be excavated, between 1925 and 1939 when the war put an end to things. The man behind the dig, Alexander Keiller, was the heir to the Keiller of Dundee marmalade fortune. After the war, Keiller's finds and notes were written up by the great prehistorian Isobel Smith, and published in 1965.[17] I think it's the most worn, thumbed and loved book on my shelves. I went to see Isobel many times when I was starting out in archaeology and she was an inspiring yet quiet and gentle person. She was also very modest: her name doesn't even appear on the title-page of the book she wrote;

but there is a full-page picture of Alexander Keiller as the frontispiece. Although she didn't dig the site herself, the report she produced has probably advanced our understanding of the Neolithic more than any other single piece of research, with the sole exception of the Stonehenge Riverside Project, which I'll have more to say about shortly.

Very early in the study of causewayed enclosures, people realized they were not defensive, simply because the ditches were broken by so many causeways that were not protected in any way – by post-built stockades, for example. So they soon acquired the name causewayed camps and were seen as places where people stayed temporarily, for whatever reason. Then in the 1970s, excavations at the causewayed enclosure at Hambledon Hill, in Dorset, revealed a series of human skulls that had been carefully positioned at the centre and bottom of the enclosure ditches, often close by a causeway.[18] You don't need a degree in archaeology to know that these were more than just casual camps: strange things, involving ceremonial, religion and 'ritual', were also happening there.

ETTON: A SPECIAL PLACE ON THE EDGE OF THE FENS

Once you get off the limestone uplands of Northamptonshire and Lincolnshire and head east towards the Fens, the landscape flattens out dramatically; in fact newcomers to the area think these plains are the Fens, until you point out that the drainage dykes are far too shallow and the soil in the fields contains gravel and small stones. This land wasn't formed by water so much as Ice Age ice. Then in immediately post-Glacial times, it became part of a system of vast lowland river valleys and flood-plains that drained huge expanses of north-west Europe. The cities of Cambridge and Peterborough are built on this Fen-edge plain.

About 10 miles north of Peterborough the River Welland, which today forms the boundary between Cambridgeshire and Lincolnshire, enters the Fens east of the small town of Market Deeping. I love this part of the world. It's flat, so you live in the sky. The architecture, too, is superb: the older buildings are made of limestone and the churches are simply without parallel. The pubs are also good, as our team discovered when we began work in a large gravel quarry, in the little village of Maxey, back in 1979. The previous year I had returned from Canada, which had been my base for the winter months, while we excavated the Fen-edge sites at Fengate, now part of Peterborough's Eastern Industry area. During those years I had managed to build up a small team of young professionals and, though I say so myself, we were among the best. We worked closely together and our decisions were reached by agreement (usually after long arguments).

The two people who are relevant to this story are Professor Charles French and Maisie Taylor. Charly was (and is) a leading soil scientist based at Cambridge University, but unlike so many scientific specialists, he was also a very good field archaeologist in his own right.[19] This close contact with two different fields of expertise made him an indispensible member of our group. The other key person was Maisie. The fact that she is also a superb cook and we got married a short time after the dig will not bias my opinion, but she is now the leading specialist in prehistoric wood-working and like Charly she is also a practical and very experienced field archaeologist.[20] At the time she had been working on what little wood she could find from ancient sites, but sadly there wasn't very much of it around. Soon, however, that would change.

The Maxey gravel quarry excavation proved to be a daunting task. In those days the infrastructure of the new town of Greater Peterborough was being built: roads, sewers and houses were appearing at an extraordinary rate – and all of this required vast quantities of sand and gravel for the concrete, cement, road foundations and so forth. Consequently the large Maxey quarry was working flat out. The trouble was that the quarry, like so many others in lowland Britain, was in an area of outstanding archaeological importance. So as soon as the project was given the go-ahead, we had to get cracking. And this was why English Heritage, our funders, were keen that we kept the old Fengate team intact. Only experienced people could have met the new challenges so rapidly.

We worked all year round, through wet and dry, and in some respects it was almost like being away fighting a war: we became, in effect, a Band of Brothers (that included Sisters), and we have kept in touch ever since. The sites we dug were remarkable: a vast Neolithic henge and oval barrow, Iron Age burials, Bronze Age burials, an Iron Age and Roman village.[21] Then in 1981, we learned that the quarry would be expanding eastwards towards the village of Etton.

We got out all the air photos and I have to say we were rather disappointed: as the landscape dipped towards the east, the surface became buried under deeper and deeper layers of river-borne flood-clays, known as alluvium. This tacky clay sticks to fingers and retains moisture well. Consequently, crops grown on it don't produce the distinctive crop-marks that can be spotted from the air and which had betrayed the presence of the henge and other sites at Maxey, just a short distance to the west.[22] But close by the modern canalized course of one of the streams of the River Welland system, known as the Maxey Cut, we could see the outlines of a large oval enclosure. And when we looked more closely, we could see the ditch was causewayed. We knew about a possible enclosure, which had been discovered during the dry summer of 1976, but this picture showed it with remarkable clarity. More to the point, the segments of ditch to the west were showing up as very dark marks, which suggested they might well be waterlogged.

We began work in 1982 in what we knew to be the wettest part of the site. We had about a year before the contractors would begin de-watering of the quarry to extract the gravel. So again, we had to move fast. But once we had started, we were astonished at what we revealed: quite simply everything was there in those ditches. And I mean everything: leaves, twigs, flint tools, animal bones, pieces of broken pottery, just as people had left them around 3600 BC (see Fig. 3.1). I well remember those days of discovery. We were so excited, yet we were also awe-struck. Coming face to face with such preservation was strangely humbling. You could almost feel the presence of the people themselves. It affected us all profoundly.

I've written about Etton before, and this time it seems more relevant than ever, but I'm less concerned now with the dating, as that has been sorted out by the radiocarbon project I have just discussed.[23] In brief, the site was first constructed around 3700 BC and was used for about three to four hundred years, although people returned there, but less often, until about 3200 BC – and possibly even later.[24] Just to

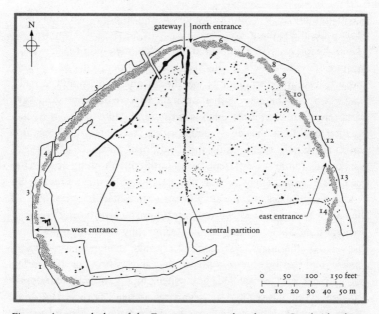

Fig. 3.1 A general plan of the Etton causewayed enclosure, Cambridgeshire. The segmented ditch which encloses the entire site is shown in dark stipple, and the segments are numbered. The enclosure forms a rough oval with the principal entrance to the north, which was marked by a wooden walled gateway. There were other entrances to the east and west and possibly the south, but the southern perimeter is hidden beneath a modern river. The west entrance featured a small guard-house. The site was divided into two equal-sized parts by a central partition fence.

give a flavour of the site: it was quite small, even by British standards, measuring 187 metres (N–S) by 150 metres (E–W) (see Fig. 3.1). I'm also less concerned with the specific roles of causewayed enclosures in Britain, or indeed Europe, as I suspect these would have varied quite widely through time and space. It's their fundamental, underlying purpose that concerns me now, and I think we learned much about that at Etton, partly because the site was waterlogged. Certainly this meant that preservation was better, but more importantly, it also meant that we had to excavate in a rather new and, for the time, quite original manner. I give a lot of the credit for our approach to Etton to Maisie. Let me explain.

If archaeologists are confronted by a ditch, they tend to excavate it in quite narrow trenches. This was the traditional way of working and it has returned to favour today because it is cheap and, usually, cost effective. There are other advantages too: narrow slots save labour and time, but if the ditch is substantial – like the main enclosure ditch at Etton – they also guarantee that you get to sample sections across the whole thing. Using this traditional approach, archaeologists can examine the different layers in the ditch's filling at as many points as possible. The way these different layers go together is known as stratigraphy. And stratigraphy is basic to archaeology because it's the only way you can reveal how a ditch, house, castle or pit developed through time. So, by looking at the stratigraphy revealed in the layers displayed on the side (the 'section') of a trench, an experienced archaeologist ought to be able to discern when it was first cut, how often it was recut and back-filled, and when, finally, it was abandoned altogether. But the trouble with narrow trenches is that they don't make sense if you are trying to investigate large spreads of waterlogged wood, where coppiced rods, for example, can extend for up to 3 or 4 metres (see Plate 4). In those circumstances you need to expose much larger expanses of ditch. At Etton we worked out ways of exposing large areas, yet at the same time recording the stratigraphy using small and temporary sections. This was Charly French's responsibility: it wasn't particularly easy, but it was certainly worth the effort and eventually produced a coherent story that united the different short lengths of ditch.

Etton, like a game of football, was a site of two halves – and we suspect it had always been that way, as it was neatly divided in two by a north–south boundary ditch and fence-line. The western half was the lower-lying and wetter half. Here the encircling enclosure ditch was almost entirely waterlogged with several layers of wet deposits. We currently believe that this half of the enclosure was where livestock were corralled, and probably where people stayed too. The eastern half was more given over to rituals and ceremonial, although I suspect people may have stayed there as well.

We began excavation in the wetter, western side, as we knew the deposits there would be most threatened when the quarry operators turned on their massive de-watering pumps. When we started work we tried to keep open minds, but we were all experienced prehistorians and we were well aware that causewayed enclosures were supposed to be religious or ritual centres. In those days, the discoveries of the skulls at Hambledon Hill were still fresh in people's minds – and it didn't help, either, that Maisie had worked as a digger on that particular site. But even so, we tried not to let that influence us too much; after all, Dorset is, and was, a very long way from Etton. As the early weeks progressed, we were surprised by what we discovered in those waterlogged silts in the ditch. To be quite honest, they seemed much like any other ditch around a settlement – not that many of us had then seen waterlogged settlement ditches, but they contained fairly straightforward rubbish and debris. I could mention a broken wooden axe haft, thousands of axed wood-chips, a few flint flakes, lots of meat bones and fragments of pottery, some of which joined together – just as you'd expect if you chucked half a broken jar in a ditch. I suppose it's fair to say that some of us were slightly underwhelmed.

Maisie, on the other hand, was getting increasingly excited as she was revealing how earlier Neolithic people worked wood. The ditch produced thousands of wood-chips, pieces of coppicing debris and carpenters' off-cuts. And the character of the material changed as we moved around the ditch: some areas revealed many coppice rods, others were rich in wood-chips and smaller fragments (see Plate 5). In other words, different jobs were being done in different places. It was extraordinary: in one particular length of ditch we came across an area where people worked coppice, even finding the axed-off stumps (or 'stools') of coppiced willows, but remarkably, still *in situ*, surrounded by wood-chips and broken coppice rods. Maisie was delighted and soon her enthusiasm spread to the rest of the team.

But as the weeks, then the months, rolled by, things began to change. Every so often something unusual would turn up among all the Neolithic rubbish. Sometimes these things could be explained as unfortunate losses. A good example is a length (56 cm, just under 2 feet) of fine string, or twine, made of the twisted fibres of flax.[25] It was found early on in the excavations, quite high up in the wet ditch filling. The way it was spun (with one end tightly twisted and the other still ragged), and the fist-sized bundle in which it was found, both suggest that it was complete and had never been cut (see Plate 6). That length is precisely what you would expect if you were rolling twine fibres on your knee and pulling the string back towards your shoulders. Later, you could twist, or knot, these shorter lengths together if you needed a greater length of string. The person (probably a woman) making this string might well have sat on the edge of the waterlogged ditch, as she would have needed to keep the flax fibres damp. So it could just have been a casual loss. But again, a complete length of twine represents a lot of work: the fibres first have to be rotted, to extract them from the plant stalk, and then they must be cleaned and combed repeatedly. Preparing flax (the modern flax fabric is of course linen) has always been a labour-intensive process. So after all that effort, would you just shrug your shoulders and mutter 'bother', then walk away and abandon the string in the ditch; or would you make some effort to find it? I'm in no doubt what I'd do. But there was another thing that worried us.

The bundle of twine was found right at the centre of the ditch near a causeway.[26] This must have been an important place, because the ditch had been slightly enlarged, to give it a gentle, club-shaped plan and profile. At the time, I remember thinking that those skulls at Hambledon Hill had been found in a similar position, but admittedly at the very bottom of the ditch. So being well above the bottom, our find of twine could still have been coincidental. But then something else happened, which confirmed my growing suspicions.

Working as meticulously as we had to, it took several weeks to excavate a few inches of ditch deposit, but much later in the autumn the archaeologist who was now working in the same expanded area of ditch came across something dark and quite soft. She called us over to have a look. I'd never seen anything like it. It even puzzled Maisie – briefly. Then she knelt down for a much closer look. I could see she meant business. Out came her hand lens. I thought for one minute she was even going to lick the dark thing, such was her concentration. Then she leaned back and sighed. She announced it was bark, probably birch bark – and the reason we hadn't recognized it was simple: it was upside-down in the ground.[27]

When the excavation gets really delicate, we often put away our trowels and use something a bit softer, like plastic garden labels, or lollipop sticks, which you can buy in large boxes from freezer shops. I can remember watching Maisie and a young Dutch archaeologist crouched over the bark in the feeble autumn sunshine, with three heaps of lolly sticks beside them: one pile wet, one damp, one almost dry. Every half minute or so another stick would be added to the wet pile. But progress was being made. After several hours the little patch had expanded into a complete, partially folded, sheet of birch bark. It was just short of 1.5 metres long (5 feet) by half a metre wide (1 foot 7 inches) and from 3 to 7 millimetres thick. And it didn't have so much as a modern nick on it – and that has to be a huge tribute to the two people who dug it (see Plate 7). This time the sheet of birch bark was lying directly on the bottom of the ditch, about 35 mm east of the string, but slightly below it.[28]

The birch bark had been thinned, scraped and was prepared for use as a mat, or to be folded to form a lightweight waterproof container. Birch-bark boxes are known from British prehistoric sites, and famously birch bark was used in Canada to make canoes. It is naturally rich in tar, which makes it waterproof. As we will see shortly, the complete sheet wasn't the only example of birch bark to come from Etton. But this time its presence could not be explained away as casual loss. It was simply *far* too big. Its position close by a causeway and directly on the bottom of the ditch was also very unusual and like those famous skulls from Hambledon, 'ritual' of some sort seemed the only possible explanation – and for the piece of twine too. So what on earth was going on?

In many tribal societies the preparation of items like birch-bark matting and the spinning of twine or wool was work traditionally carried out by women. The same can be said for pottery-making. A few weeks earlier, at the far end of the neighbouring ditch segment, but once again both next to a causeway and right on the bottom of the ditch, we had found a small (30 cm, 12 inches square) piece of birch-bark mat[29] that had been placed beneath a complete, decorated pottery bowl.[30] The pottery of the earlier Neolithic is restrained and rather elegant, very rounded and rarely has sharp corners. The decoration is often confined, as with this example, to the upper half of the

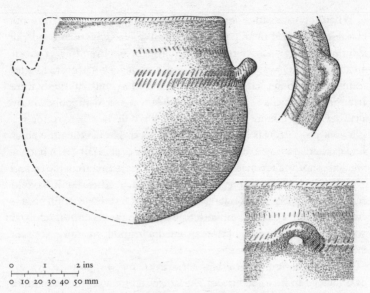

Fig. 3.2 A complete Neolithic pottery jar from Etton, Cambridgeshire. It has been decorated with short oblique impressions on the top of the rim and in bands around the neck and shoulder. The vessel is round-based and has two small handles, or lugs. Date: *c.* 3600 BC.

vessel, so these vessels must have been intended to be viewed from above – like our pot on its mat. But again, it cannot possibly have been a casual loss – not a complete pot on its own individual mat (see Fig. 3.2).

Then, as if to complete the cycle of discoveries, a few seasons later we came across yet another complete pottery jar. Like the first one, this had a smooth, rounded base. It was found on the very bottom of the ditch, close to a causeway. Next to it – and the closest item to the causeway – was a fox's skull, complete with its lower jaw. But what made this find fascinating was the fact that the fox skull had been buried upside-down. And so had the pot alongside it. In fact, when we first came down on the pot (and we did very well not to crush it, as it was very fragile and still had Neolithic air inside it!) we thought it was a child's skull.[31] Now I simply cannot think of a more ritualized, or religious, set of offerings than the inverted pot – which, given the Hambledon skulls, must surely represent a human head – and the inverted fox skull. But that wasn't enough for our Neolithic community, who completed the set of offerings with a finely decorated antler comb and another complete, but smaller, pot. All of these were arranged in a row, one by one, down the centre of the ditch, close by a causeway.[32]

As we excavated our way along the enclosure ditch, we came across many other rows of offerings. In nearly all cases, Charly French identified that they had originally been carefully buried under soil and gravel – doubtless to protect them for posterity. Then the ditch had been filled in almost level with the surface. A few years later, people would return and make more offerings, again arranged in rows – and then bury them in gravel. This happened on three, and in a few cases four, occasions and in each segment of ditch. Again, that earlier question comes to mind: what was going on?

As we worked our way along the ditch deposits we noticed certain repeating themes. Rounded objects, for example, would often be placed close to causeways at the ends of ditch segments. These included round-based jars, a complete human skull (minus its lower jaw) and, in one instance, a fossil sea-urchin, or echinoid, which we found just to one side of a flat stone.[33] The fossil had had a round hole pecked in it, like the opening at the base of a human skull where the spinal cord enters the head. When we had carefully exposed the fossil and the stone alongside it, we gently rolled the sea-urchin towards the stone, and after half a turn, the pecked hole sat precisely at the centre of the stone – which seems to have taken the place of the birch-bark mat we found beneath that first complete pot (see Plate 8). I'm in little doubt that the symbolism here is of the human head, and it is tempting to suggest that it refers to a person, living, dead or mythical. Later I will suggest a possible explanation for the lines of offerings found in the ditch segments, but we did find quite persuasive evidence that the rows of offerings might have been sub-divided into different, roughly equal-sized portions, or 'chapters', if indeed they do represent scenes from family history narratives; as we will see, this might be the case. But the objects chosen to mark these sub-divisions were fascinating in their own right.

If one is asked for a symbol of the family, I suppose one thinks of 'hearth and home'. But in prehistoric times, households would each have possessed a symbol of even greater potency, and I refer here to the family's quern or corn-grinding stone. These were made from special stone suited to the task and were usually quarried from known and established sites. They are heavy (10–25 kilos, 22–55 pounds) and their transport was often over considerable distances (querns at Flag Fen, for example, came from Kent and Wales). So each quern must have represented a major family investment – the equivalent, perhaps, of the modern family car.

Back in the Neolithic and Bronze Age, the standard pattern of quern was the so-called 'saddle' quern – named because the large or bottom stone is dished and slightly resembles the shape of a saddle (i.e. raised at front and rear). The bottom saddle-shaped stone was paired with a smaller top stone, which was grasped in both hands and rubbed against the saddle stone to grind the grain. To do this, the person making the flour kneels astride the saddle stone and puts the weight of the top half of their body behind the action. I've tried it, and it's very effective, but hard work, too. Later, in the Iron Age, rotary querns came into use. These were about a quarter the size of a traditional millstone, but worked in much the same way, with corn poured down a hole at the centre and two flat but circular quern-stones pivoting around a central axle; the top stone was revolved using a stout wooden handle. But as with the saddle querns, these were made to be used at home. Most Romano-British flour milling was also domestic, although animal-powered mills are known in larger towns.[34] The first water mills only appear in early post-Roman, Saxon, times. Incidentally, a very early example (about AD 700) was found during the construction of the Channel Tunnel Rail Link, at Ebbsfleet, in Kent.[35] My point is, that for a very long time indeed, the quern would have been seen as *the* symbol of family life.

Deliberate breakage was an important part of these domestic-based religious ceremonies. It was a theme that would be revived in ceremonies of the later Bronze and Iron Ages, as we will see in Chapters 5 and 6, at Flag Fen and other sites. We cannot be certain what this destruction meant, but it may have symbolized the removal of particular items from the world of the living, as they could then be made whole again, in the realm of the ancestors. That may have been the underlying principle, but its application in ceremonies does not appear to have been consistent, and this surely suggests a degree of subtlety which we cannot detect in the archaeological record. Some pottery vessels, for example, were buried, as we have seen, complete. Others were broken, but the sherds had then been deliberately collected and placed together in the ground, not as a complete pot, but as a tight group of fragments (see Plate 9). So the final offering in the ditch, of broken potsherds, must have symbolized not just the original role of the vessel, but also the act of destruction.

As we all know to our cost, pots are easy to break. But I can assure readers it is very much harder to smash quern-stones. And they rarely break in normal use, not, that is, until they have worn very thin indeed, after many generations of continuous grinding. So it was remarkable that the fragments of quern-stone used to mark out significant portions of the ditch had often been smashed, and most probably deliberately, as they were rarely heavily worn. And as if to emphasize this destruction, at least two broken fragments had then been balanced on edge, so that the grinding surface was vertical – and therefore completely functionally useless (see Plate 10). When excavated, they stood out clearly from the rest of the row of offerings in the ditch, just as they must have done in prehistory.

The symbolic destruction of these iconic symbols of domestic life was taken to an extreme in a pit we discovered at the very centre of the eastern half of the enclosure. You will recall that this was the side of the enclosure specifically given over to religious ceremonial. I first came across the pit when I was driving the mechanical digger, removing topsoil and alluvium. I heard a loud rasping sound and immediately stopped and jumped down. There, directly below the (toothless) bucket was the top of a curved saddle quern. In Neolithic times it must have protruded at least half a metre above the ground and it would have been a prominent focus for this part of the site. When, later, we excavated the stone by hand, we found it was complete and had been set on edge in a pit and the earth rammed in around it (see Plate 11). We excavated and then removed it, and I can recall wondering whether we would find a top stone beneath it. And we did. All the hairs went up on the back of my neck – it was as if I had been communicating directly with the people who buried it. That stone, which was also complete, was very much smaller, and had been placed with its grinding surface resting on the bottom of the pit. You could clearly see parallel striations where it had been used to prepare meals nearly six thousand years ago. But again, the symbolic destruction was two-fold: first, the bottom, or saddle, stone was on edge, and on top; second, the top stone was wedged beneath it: unusable, and deep below the ground.

The prominence given to the pit with the on-edge quern-stone suggests to me that domestic life formed a fundamental part of the religious ceremonies at Etton, because it *could* be argued (mistakenly, in my opinion) that what took place in the outer ditch was symbolically peripheral, or of secondary, importance. But there can be no arguing with that pit and those quern-stones. And for what it's worth, another quern-stone was found nearby.

Prehistorians of the Neolithic have spilled lakes of ink discussing the role and meaning of causewayed enclosures. They write in terms of 'liminality' and separation from the safe, known world of daily life. The sites are seen as being closer to the realm of the ancestors. I'm sure all of this makes lots of sense, and I agree with most of it, but I still don't think it explains much. It's too obvious. It lacks the subtlety of real human experience as revealed in our (and other) excavations. Having lived for many years now with the Etton site and the discoveries we made there, I believe there is something about those deposits that demands more from us than mere analysis.

Now I do not intend to be New Age, or mystical, about any of this. I have been for all my working life a convinced atheist; so for me the spiritual, even the mystical, is meaningless. But having said that, age and experience have taught me a few things. For a start, I've learned to listen to my subconscious. Unlike many in academia, I do not contend that the use of the imagination is somehow undisciplined, or misguided, and that truth can only be revealed through rigorous analysis. And the more I've thought about Etton, the more I've come to realize that the entire site is actually a celebration of humanity. It's about love and death. In a phrase, it's about family life – and I mean here the actual existential process of living – in the family, in both this world and in the next.

Again there have been many attempts to ascribe gender roles to archaeological finds, but inevitably these fall back on the simple distinction between hunting (male) and domestic activities (female).[36] And I cannot say I find that particularly useful, or enlightening, either – and neither did Nicky Milner during our earlier interview, from which I draw some comfort. So if we take that line of offerings on the enclosure ditch bottom alongside the inverted fox skull, then I suppose the skull represents men (hunting) and everything else women: the comb was probably used as part of hand-weaving and the second small pot was teacup sized and could have been a child's toy.[37] The other thing that was remarkable about the dozens of offerings (we called them 'placed deposits' at the time) was the scarcity of wild animal bones – which makes the fox skull the exception that proves the rule. But we know that there were many wild animals out there in the earlier Neolithic countryside, everything from fox and badger, to red deer, wolf, wild boar, wild cattle (a fearsome beast known as the aurochs) and even brown bear. Yet evidence for these beasts rarely appears in causewayed enclosures. Instead, the bones that are found are from domestic animals. So the rites focus on the safe and the domestic – maybe as a celebration of hope over reality – we will never know.

One of the things I like about archaeology is that it never stands still. Ideas and interpretations are constantly changing. When we wrote the final report on Etton, time and money were quite short, so only a sample of the animal bones could be studied in any detail. Much more recently, a younger colleague, Pip Stone, has undertaken an analysis of the entire collection – a massive task, if ever there was one. It has taken her a long time, and is part of her PhD thesis at Exeter University. Every few months I'd receive an email from her that queried my interpretation or phasing of various deposits, so Etton has been much on my mind of late. The original report concluded that 'a significant proportion' of the animal bones found at the site 'derived from non-domestic contexts' and may have had little economic significance. In other words, the sample of bones could tell us little about what people actually ate, or how they farmed their livestock.[38]

Pip's re-examination reverses this conclusion. She considers the material entirely consistent with what one would expect to find on a prehistoric settlement, of almost any period, in lowland Britain. There is abundant evidence for butchery, and animals were managed, culls were taken and younger stock were slaughtered, much as in later periods. But we also know that Etton would have been uninhabitable for the wetter months of winter. That suggests that when it was occupied, maybe for a month or so every year, or few years, then whole households would have moved there, perhaps from different settlements, transferring their ordinary village lives to this special communal place, deep in the river flood-plain.

If Etton had been a 'normal' settlement, I would have expected to have found clear evidence for houses. And believe me, we looked for them – hard. We did find evidence for at least one substantial building, but that was just inside a major causeway/entranceway to the site, and was probably a guard-house or gatehouse lodge of some sort (it lacked any hearth). But instead of houses we found dozens of small pits that had been carefully and deliberately filled with domestic rubbish. As we have seen, the enclosure ditch, too, had been filled with carefully arranged offerings, but there were also many thousands of loose finds – flint flakes, fragments of pottery, and in the wet segments, wood-chips, off-cuts and broken coppiced rods. Taken together, this loose material must represent the refuse of daily life. So I have always firmly believed that people did indeed come to Etton to live and also to work, as we saw in those ditches full of wood-working debris – but probably not for very long. I can only guess how long they stayed there: maybe a week, perhaps a fortnight, even a month, but probably not much longer, or it would prove too disruptive to life back home in the village. They would most likely have lived in lightweight structures – tents, or 'benders', for these short stays. It was probably an autumn or summer 'retreat' too, because any other time of year would have been far too wet, down there on the river flood-plain.

I also believe these annual 'retreats' were to places that were somehow special to the families and clans involved. I say places because Etton is just one of several similar sites in both the Welland and nearby Nene valleys, and it is quite possible that different people sometimes went to different places; maybe a married woman would occasionally revisit the causewayed enclosure of her maternal family (if, that is, their social system was patrilineal, like ours – for which there is absolutely no evidence!). Maybe the oxbow bend in the old river where they sited the Etton enclosure had been special for a long time – probably back to the Mesolithic. Although we didn't find any, Mesolithic flints are not uncommon on causewayed enclosures.[39] I think the purpose of people's visits would have been to honour the ancestors and to ensure that those who had died recently had a safe journey to the Next World. Pip Stone has shown there was abundant evidence for cremations at Etton and there were also many loose human bones – so the commemoration of death must have been an important element in these (probably) annual retreats. But fundamental to everything was the family, which was the message behind those carefully arranged offerings in the ditches, and elsewhere.

We now come to the explanation of the strange segmented layout of the ditch. Those causeways could not possibly have served any practical purpose. Their sole reason for existing was to divide a length of ditch into shorter, self-defined units. When I wrote the report in the mid-1990s, I had become convinced that each segment of ditch would have been the property of a particular clan or family. And when I say 'property', I don't use the word in a narrow modern sense, but more as people still refer to old plots in country churchyards. I can illustrate this with a personal example. If you visit Weston churchyard in north Hertfordshire, you'll find the Pryor family graves just outside the chancel on the south side of the church. My family don't 'own' that land, but they still mow and maintain it, because that's where our graves are: including my parents, grandparents and great-grandparents. You can read something of our family history in the inscriptions on the tombstones – and that's what I think those neatly arranged and covered-over 'placed deposits' in the Etton enclosure ditch are essentially all about. They're permanent records of the doings of long-vanished relatives. I would imagine that every year the members of the family would have stood around their 'own' ditch segment, while a senior, older person recited the deeds – real and mythical – of the ancestors. It was part of the continuing process of educating the young and of binding people together, with their common family histories and shared memories. Had I lived in the earlier Neolithic, my life would doubtless have been commemorated with a carved flint trowel.

Most of the rites that took place at Etton would have involved visiting the family's ditch segment – doubtless decorated in some way – and the freshly marked pits around its periphery, while repeating tales, myths and ballads that celebrated family history; elsewhere, people would have stood in circles, while shamans made contact with the world of the ancestors. Doubtless, too, there would have been feasting and carefully contrived visits to other households who were also spending a few days at the special place. Then – perhaps every other generation – it was agreed that the family story needed to be reinforced. Maybe youngsters were having trouble fixing it in their minds, without more concrete, ritualized reminders. On these special occasions the family's ditch segment was carefully re-opened, so as not to disturb any earlier 'placed' deposits, and new offerings would be placed there, and then buried in gravel. Sometimes it becomes possible to see certain elements repeated, but using similar shaped but different objects as symbols: so in later retellings of the family history, inverted pottery vessels, or that fossil sea-urchin, are used to represent human skulls. Each of the individual 'placed' offerings can be seen to represent a past event or even a whole life (such as my hypothetical flint trowel), which in turn was part of a longer family narrative. And there's one other thing that makes this story fascinating.

The earliest placed deposits are separated by clear, unambiguous blanks, or voids – like the gaps between the fox skull, the inverted pot, the comb and the right-side-up smaller pot. But above them, for the second layer of offerings, the gaps are much harder to define. By the third, highest, layer, they are almost continuous. It is as if people have learned to express their family history with greater confidence and fluency. So Etton has preserved for us the evolution of Neolithic symbolism in a most remarkable form, and it banishes any idea that somehow customs and practice in the remote past necessarily developed slowly. On the contrary, the sequence of 'placed' deposits in the Etton ditch show that the accepted symbolic language, probably like the dialect everyone shared, was constantly developing, as each new generation sought to make its mark, in its own way. And of course the process continues to this day.

There's a strange postscript to this story. In January of 1995, on my 50th birthday, a spark from an angle-grinder set fire to a mouse's nest underneath our temporary offices at Flag Fen. We had just finished work on the Etton Report and had started putting material together for writing-up Flag Fen, so all our notes, records, photographs, plans and archives were in the site offices. Mercifully the main site plans and record cards escaped the blaze, and all the digital data had been backed up and stored off site. But in those days digital photography was still far behind film and my entire slide collection of some ten thousand slides melted, where they hung, in a 'fire-proof' steel cabinet. Those slides were not just my lectures, but my memories of those times, people and places. They meant so much to me, but now they were gone. The Etton slides suffered very badly – which is why I couldn't offer readers colour pictures of those strange lines of offerings in the enclosure ditch, here. Maybe the destruction of the physical pictures meant that I had to build on and re-imagine them in my mind's eye. But what I do know is that I have thought about those ditches, and what they might mean, almost every day since that terrible fire.

Now, obviously, losing slides bears no comparison at all to the loss of a child, but I've been told that such pain is greatly eased by the consolation and love of other members of the family. In my far lesser loss, old colleagues from Etton certainly helped: soon every post seemed to bring with it envelopes containing one or two, sometimes even dozens, of duplicate slides, taken by friends and colleagues when they visited the site. Charly French gave me several hundred. I think this spontaneous rallying round might have been one reason why the idea of family took such a deep hold with me.

It's strange the way the past can somehow move forward and become a part of our present. And, of course, vice versa. It becomes a relationship: not something static, something different or strange – 'another country'. No, that fire failed to dim my memories of Etton; if anything they have been enhanced and stimulated by repeatedly musing and plenty of discussion and debate about what happened in that damp corner of the lower Welland Valley, all those millennia ago. But at least I now know those people were truly like us, and their first communal monuments were about celebrating life at home. Their daily routines might seem foreign to modern eyes, but deep inside, their thoughts and emotions were always with their families – their nearest and dearest.

LIVING IN THE FIRST FARMHOUSES

Etton failed to reveal any evidence for houses and I'm fairly confident we would have spotted any, had they been there. The Neolithic levels of the site had never been ploughed and had lain protected under half a metre of heavy flood-clay. We were well aware of this, and used mechanical excavators as sparingly and as carefully as possible. We stripped the flood-clay off mechanically, then sample-sieved and searched the Neolithic topsoil by hand. Once that had been done, we went down further, again with the machine. I think the fact that we came down on the top of the complete saddle quern suggests that we were not digging too deep, or too fast. So the absence of direct evidence for permanent houses has, I think, to be significant. And again, this suggests that the site's use had been short term and episodic: as I said earlier, Etton was a home away from home. So where were people living for the rest of the year and what were their houses like?

As we have seen, before the 1990s it was generally held that most Mesolithic families lived in small bender-like houses, that were appropriate to their supposedly nomadic lifestyle. At the same time, we knew about the existence of a few Neolithic houses in Britain, while the first of many were already being revealed in Ireland, throughout the 1980s.[40] They generally followed the same pattern: a rectangular floor plan ranging from 42 to 96 square metres in area. Walls were almost invariably built from split oak planks. These substantial structures, which one would have called small halls in medieval times, quite closely resembled contemporary houses on the continental mainland, but they differed markedly from the few that were known from England, which were also rectangular, but generally much smaller.

I had the good fortune to discover a house of this type at Fengate, Peterborough, in 1974.[41] It measured 7 by 8.5 metres (59.5 square metres, 640 square feet), which was small by Irish standards, but broadly similar in size to the handful of earlier Neolithic houses then known from Britain.[42] It produced a radiocarbon date of about 3110 BC.[43] Since then other hall-like buildings dating from between 4000 and 2500 BC have been discovered in England, but again, we are still not at all certain that these large buildings were typical of the sort of houses that ordinary people would have lived in.[44] On the other hand, for houses to change from the small, portable benders of later Mesolithic times, to the more substantial rectangular structures of the Neolithic, fitted in well with prevailing views about the social consequences of the introduction of farming and settled life. In short, it went with the idea of a Neolithic Revolution. It also coincided with what we knew about earlier Neolithic houses on the other side of the English Channel, which tended to be large, often tapering, hall-like structures. It would seem that some time just before 4000 BC semi-nomadic hunters were replaced, very swiftly, by farmers living a more settled life in substantial family dwellings. It was all very nice: the observed facts fitted with the accepted theory. So all should have been well. But it wasn't.

In the early 1990s, younger prehistorians were starting to question this conventional wisdom.[45] One of them, Julian Thomas, simply couldn't accept that so few Neolithic houses had been found in Britain and suggested instead that the population was probably far more mobile and lived in lighter buildings, more like the portable benders of the Mesolithic.[46] The trouble was, nobody had found any yet. So if Julian's theory was correct, it would seem that substantial houses, like the one I had dug at Fengate, were probably the exception, rather than the rule. Then in 1988, I added my two pennyworth by suggesting that the finds from the Fengate house were rather better than what one might expect of ordinary domestic debris and could represent a higher-status activity. Maybe they could even be the result of some 'ritual' – i.e. religion or ceremonial – in which case the house could have more in common with a shrine than a cottage.[47] My evidence for this consisted of a large and finely polished shale bead and fragments of a beautifully made polished stone axe brought to the edge of the Fens from a quarry in Langdale, Cumbria. The axe (but not the bead) had then been deliberately broken up with carefully directed blows; in other words, it hadn't been damaged during use. This seemed like deliberate destruction, similar to what had been happening at Etton. It was all very confusing.

Meanwhile, and in addition to the more spectacular hall-like buildings, smaller Neolithic round-houses continued to be found in

Ireland.[48] Largely because they were less grand and spectacular, they had a minor impact on the archaeological public. But nonetheless, they were there. And they were generally similar in size not only to those of the Mesolithic but also to the houses of the Early Bronze Age, the period that followed directly after the Neolithic. The confusion was growing; but it became even worse in the 1990s, when closely similar small houses began to be found on very much earlier Mesolithic sites, such as Howick.

The situation in Scotland was, if anything, more confused still. Throughout the later '80s, the '90s and into the new century, Neolithic buildings in Scotland seemed to fall into two quite distinct groups.[49] Those larger, hall-like timber houses were being found in ever-increasing numbers.[50] Some were truly remarkable – every bit as impressive as their medieval successors. But were they 'bog standard' Neolithic domestic houses, or were they rather special? So far, the available evidence suggests the latter. They have, however, been radiocarbon dated and were first built after 3800 BC, going out of use in the generation that followed 3700 BC.[51] So, the question still remained: in what sort of buildings were ordinary Scottish people living during the Neolithic? And it would seem we had known the answer since the 1930s, but hadn't fully realized its significance.

Open any book, any textbook, on British or European prehistory and the name of one site will leap off the pages: Skara Brae, in Orkney. This site was excavated by an Australian prehistorian, Vere Gordon Childe, between 1927 and 1931. The preservation of the structure of these remarkable buildings was so good that Childe initially considered them to be Pictish (i.e. post-Roman) in date.[52] Four years later, he realized his mistake and corrected it. The latest reassessment of radiocarbon dates suggests that settlements like that at Skara Brae were built and occupied from around 3200 to 2500 BC.[53] We also know of similar, but slightly larger, houses from Orkney that pre-date Skara Brae by four or five centuries – suggesting that the tradition was already established by 3600 BC.[54] One's instincts, if nothing else, lead one to think that these houses might have origins as early as the Mesolithic – if not older.

Earlier accounts of Skara Brae and other Orcadian settlements tended to treat them simply as Neolithic equivalents of modern houses. In other words, people lived out their daily lives in them, but other activities, such as worship or communal gatherings, took place elsewhere, at places like the great stone circles. It was a view which very much reflected the pattern of 20th-century life, with a clear distinction between the sacred and domestic worlds. More recently, excavations elsewhere in Orkney, at sites like Barnhouse, and more recently at the Links of Noltland, on the island of Westray, have shown that houses could also be shrines, and that religion and ritual played a hugely important part in providing structure to ordinary domestic life.[55] I'm convinced that this fusion – this integration – of the sacred and the domestic was a far more important feature of prehistoric and early historic home life than is generally recognized. Indeed, as we will see in Chapters 5 and 6, after the Middle Bronze Age it became even more important and was extended outside the domestic sphere, where it helped provide structure at the local level for societies of increasing complexity.

It used to be thought that the houses revealed at Skara Brae and elsewhere on Orkney were somehow freakish and exceptional – an Orcadian, an insular, development and not at all typical of the rest of the British Isles. Orkney has long been known to have exceptionally well-preserved prehistoric remains and this has generally been attributed to the materials that were used in the remote past. Timber was rare, not because trees cannot grow there – the climate is actually remarkably benign – but because, once deprived of the protection afforded by other trees in the forest, woodland is very slow to re-establish because of the prevailing strong North Atlantic gales. That's doubtless why Iron Age communities in the Western Isles had to make use of driftwood, some of which ultimately derived from Canada.[56] One of the things this tells us, of course, is that during the six millennia of post-Ice Age prehistory, British woodlands were managed with increasing skill, to provide a constant and renewable source of wood, timber and coppice products for a steadily growing population. And it's worth remembering that this management was done by ordinary people at the community level, without the help of big aristocratic landowners, or the Crown.

Life on Orkney might well not have thrived so vigorously were it not for the remarkable local sandstone which readily cleaves (splits) into superb and very strong flat flagstones that make excellent house and tomb floors and walls. Massive fragments can even be used as standing stones, in monuments like the Stones of Stenness, Orkney.[57] It's a most remarkable material, which outcrops close to the surface and along the seashore – and must indeed have been seen as a godsend in prehistory. However, recent research in the Western Isles and elsewhere has convincingly demonstrated that the remarkable preservation and quality of Orcadian Neolithic structures was no insular 'accident'. Elsewhere, too, preservation could be just as good – and fine buildings could be erected without the superb Orcadian sandstone.[58] We were beginning to realize that the common factor linking together the archaeological preservation of these different far-flung places was quite simple: they had never been subjected to modern, nor indeed to medieval, intensive arable agriculture. It was the plough – first horse-drawn, then (vastly more destructive) tractor-towed – that had destroyed the evidence elsewhere. In other words, these remarkable early houses were lucky survivors. And that, of course, suggests that they might once have been more widespread than we believed in the 1960s and '70s. But now we must return to the changing story of Neolithic houses south of the border.

At the start of the present century, and viewed from an English perspective, the situation in the earlier Neolithic looked, frankly, odd: there were proven substantial round-houses from the earlier Mesolithic, but with the exception of some substantial hall-like buildings, there was precious little that could be called genuinely domestic. What made this so strange was a mass of evidence which strongly indicated that the population had greatly expanded, and of course people were farming. Julian Thomas's suggestion that the English Neolithic population was more mobile had helped to resolve this dilemma, but not for everyone.[59] I, for one, couldn't see how the landscape could have been transformed in such a short time if the first farmers, who were the people making the changes, were so highly mobile. It just didn't add up. And it certainly failed to explain why people in England should be more mobile than in Ireland or Scotland; indeed, common sense might suggest the precise opposite.

As we will see in the next section, we also knew that Neolithic farmers were capable of building huge communal tombs, and, of course, they also constructed causewayed enclosures, some of which, in western Britain, had quite substantial drystone walls.[60] Yet we didn't seem to know where their families lived. I was also very worried by the idea that large communal tombs would have been built by semi-nomadic people. To my mind, such tombs were all about communities laying a claim to a particular area of landscape. The presence of their ancestors, for all to see in their huge tomb carefully sited on the top of a hill, or (somewhat later) arranged in lines along the brow of a ridge, was proclaiming that the land around them was *their* land and was still home to the spirits of their ancestors. But was this the way semi-nomadic people behaved? Frankly, it made many of us feel very uncomfortable; still, there was no arguing with the evidence from the field: genuine Neolithic houses, with clear signs of domestic life, were still inexplicably rare in England.

DURRINGTON WALLS AND THE RISE OF STONEHENGE

What seems like the final twist of this story has been revealed by the team, directed by Professor Mike Parker Pearson, then of Sheffield University, who were researching into the early prehistory of the Stonehenge landscape. We came across their work in the previous chapter when we were discussing the links between Mesolithic and later prehistoric religious practices (p. 54). If we lay aside the discoveries of huge post-holes in the car park, the earliest evidence for monument construction on the actual site of Stonehenge was the digging of the outer, circular ditch and bank, together with the series of post- and stone-holes, including the famous 'Aubrey Holes' (named after the 17th-century antiquarian John Aubrey). This flurry of activity took place between 3000 and 2920 BC.[61] But the team were initially more concerned with what happened a few centuries later, from about 2600 BC, with the erection of the first great stone circles.[62]

In fact, their project made its biggest impact shortly after it began, in its second season of excavation, in 2005. They were investigating a huge henge, known as Durrington Walls. Their project is known as the Stonehenge Riverside Project and its original intention was to investigate the relationship between Stonehenge, the nearby River Avon and other sites and monuments in the vicinity. At its heart was an idea proposed by Ramilisonina, a Madagascan archaeologist and colleague of Mike's. Ramil, as he was generally known, proposed that wooden monuments represented the world of the living and stone, the dead. It was an idea that was based on his own family experience and like all good ideas it was simple – and testable.

Together, Mike and Ramil argued that the realm of the living may have been focused around Woodhenge and Durrington Walls, two sites that had already been quite fully excavated and had produced massive circles of large timber posts. They are situated about 2 miles north-east of Stonehenge, as the crow flies. Mike and Ramil further suggested that the two sites were linked to Stonehenge via a far more circuitous route along the River Avon and up the Stonehenge Avenue, a processional way originally discovered in August 1721, but subsequently extended (from air photos taken in the interwar years), which ran from the river, in a curved, banana-like course from the river to the Stones – a straight-line distance of just over a mile.[63] In the final third of its length, the Avenue approaches Stonehenge from the north-east, along the axis of those natural ridges in the sub-soil, which, as we saw in the previous chapter, just happened to coincide with the alignment of the midwinter sunset and midsummer sunrise. Stonehenge, of course, symbolized the world of the dead, while the river and the Avenue together were the ceremonial route that linked it to that of the living.

But one important element was missing from this persuasive and very clever idea. In fact, its absence could be seen as a fatal flaw. In short, there was no avenue leading the short distance from Durrington Walls and Woodhenge, down to the river at the very start of the hypothetical ceremonial route. Clearly, finding that missing avenue had to be their very first objective when the new project began work, in 2004.[64]

Now I don't want to summarize the Stonehenge Riverside Project, because it has already been done by Professor Mike Parker Pearson himself, and superbly: *Stonehenge: Exploring the Greatest Stone Age Mystery*. What concerns me here are not their discoveries in and around the famous Stones, nor indeed that of an entirely new, and miniature, 'Bluestonehenge', down by the river. No, it was their early work in the realm of the living, which began with the search for that much shorter avenue leading down from Durrington Walls to the river.

As any archaeologist knows, you rarely find what you are looking for straight away. Sometimes it never turns up, other times you recognize it when the project has finished. By then it's often too late. The trick is to keep your mind open and think on your feet, which is what Mike and his team were so good at. I won't detail how they did it, but by the end of the second season they had found their short length of avenue; however, much more importantly, they had also revealed evidence for Neolithic houses – and lots of them. For my money, this was the greatest archaeological discovery in Britain for a hundred years, and far more significant than haphazard finds by metal-detectorists, even great one-off discoveries like the Sutton Hoo treasure. And why? Because the new avenue and those fragile, ephemeral houses told us so much about the way prehistoric people thought, and just as importantly, the way they structured their religious and daily lives. It demonstrated, too, that both were closely interwoven. When all is said and done, archaeology is not about beautiful objects, it's about past societies and the way they functioned. And that, surely, is why this work was *so* extraordinary.

Two members of the Stonehenge team had also worked in northern Scotland. Mike Parker Pearson had excavated in the Outer Hebrides and I had visited his site when we were filming *Britain BC* for Channel 4. I can remember being very impressed by the thoroughness of the work, with sieves everywhere and huge attention being paid to every detail of an Iron Age house interior. Bearing in mind the logistical problems they had to face on South Uist, this was an extraordinary piece of organization. Colin Richards had worked with us in the Welland Valley shortly after graduating from Reading University; he then went on to make his name in Orkney, first discovering, then excavating, an extraordinary semi-ceremonial settlement at Barnhouse, within sight of the famous Stones of Stenness.[65] During this work, which again I was able to visit, his team revealed Neolithic houses broadly similar to those dug at nearby Skara Brae, before the war. But with modern techniques and new approaches he was able to discover far more.

One might reasonably wonder why the experience of excavating on

Scottish island sites might be relevant to Wiltshire. But it was. More than that, it was crucial, because the marks in the soil left by these houses were so very ephemeral they'd been missed by archaeologists working in the area in the past – sometimes even the recent past. And to be quite honest I wonder whether I would have recognized the very slight traces they managed to spot in their second season, back in 2005. It's worth thinking about this briefly. It is one thing just to see something – we do that every moment of the day: town-dwellers see trees, I see ash, oak, hornbeam, and the state of their health. It's because I'm interested in them and have lived with them all my life. So I can identify them, old or young and in all four seasons, with or without leaves, when they look very different. This skill, if that's what it is, is a product of interest and experience; it didn't just happen. Put another way, you can only identify pattern if you have something to go on, such as experiences, memories, faded pictures in old books – or seasons spent excavating prehistoric houses in the Scottish isles. And that is why, when the excavators of Durrington Walls came across a thin layer of white chalk, it immediately rang loud bells, which would have remained silent for most of us.

They had discovered a well-trodden chalk house floor; in South Uist floors had been peat and sand, but the essential structure in the ground was the same. Such floors only work if kept dry – out in the open they would soon revert to mud and slime. The shape of the floor was very diagnostic. Like the Scottish examples, it had clear edges and a space in the middle, complete with plenty of ash and charcoal, for a hearth. The Scottish hearths had been square, the Durrington ones were more rounded, but otherwise they were identical.

The floor didn't cover the whole of the house interior, because the outer parts, close to the external wall, where the roof came down lowest to the ground, were where the family had its permanent furniture. In Scotland much of this was made of stone, which is why the famous 'dresser' at Skara Brae is so readily identifiable (see Plate 12). It could have been made yesterday and one can imagine pots and jars in its neat compartments.[66] In actual fact, it was more likely used as an altar of some sort – to the gods and ancestors of the household. But again, we should beware of assuming that there would have been a clear division between religion and domestic life. As I have already suggested, the two would probably have overlapped. I would not be at all sur-prised if a few salted herrings or joints of ham weren't kept on some of its lower shelves. New excavations at Neolithic houses at Barn-house, not far from Skara Brae, show that the soils in the beds farthest away from the front door had enhanced levels of phosphates. Nor-mally speaking, high phosphates indicate the presence of livestock or latrines, but at Barnhouse the concentrations were very limited in their distribution and the excavator believed, quite plausibly I think, that this nice protected spot away from the front door was where babies and young children would have slept.

Meanwhile, to return to Durrington Walls, it was the sides of the surrounding furniture, facing onto the central hearth, which gave such a characteristically sharp edge to the central chalk floor. The space given over to furniture was just over a metre wide, which was closely comparable to Skara Brae, as indeed was the rest of the house's layout, with wooden box-beds on either side of the main entranceway and clear indications for the presence of a 'dresser' in the most presti-gious part of the house: the back wall, facing onto the only doorway. Immediately beyond that were the stake- and post-holes for the posts that formed the centre of the external walls, which were made from a mixture of pounded chalk and animal dung – a form of 'cob', used for farm buildings in the area as late as Victorian times.[67]

One of the largest and best-preserved houses at Durrington Walls was House 851 (this is an arbitrary number; it doesn't mean there were more than 850 houses; see Fig. 3.3). But there was one extraor-dinary touch which, for me at least, brought this building to life and made it more a family home than an impersonal house. Directly in front of the hearth, and close by the front door, where the light would have been best, were two shallow depressions in the chalk plaster floor. As Mike Parker Pearson demonstrated when we visited him in 2007 (by which time the house was not looking quite as fresh as when first excavated), these must have been made by people kneeling in front of the hearth while cooking (see Plate 14) – an extraordinary thought, if ever there was one.

The similarities between the houses at Skara Brae and Durrington Walls are remarkable. Not only were they of roughly the same size, shape and layout, but their front doors tended to face south and they

Fig. 3.3 A laser scan of the Durrington Walls Neolithic House 851, shown in Plate 14. The clearest feature is the smooth chalk floor, which is bounded by three sets of foundations for wooden planks, arranged in an open-sided rectangle. The open side faces south, towards the entrance. At the centre is a round hearth and immediately next to it, on the south side, are two, roughly triangular, shallow depressions made by the knees of people preparing meals on the hearth. The stake-holes for the outside walls are set back just over a metre from the plank foundations (they can be seen more clearly in Fig. 4.1).

were sometimes accompanied by little outbuildings, which were either close by, or were actually built onto the external walls. Maybe this was where firewood and fuel were kept dry, but safely separated from stray sparks. On current evidence, the first Orcadian houses appear to be a little older than those at Durrington. They were also, in general, slightly larger. To some extent this undoubtedly reflects the fact that Durrington Walls is just a single site, and we have yet to find earlier examples of the same type of building in England. But there are a few hints of earlier origins.

The remarkable houses at Durrington Walls and Skara Brae, and of course elsewhere on Orkney, have survived because they are in landscapes that have long been recognized as special and have consequently been protected by law. At Durrington, the settlement was shortly to be overlain by a massive ditch and bank of Britain's largest henge monument. Similarly in Orkney, Skara Brae and Barnhouse both form part of a so-called 'ritual landscape' characterized by massive collective tombs, such as Maes Howe, and great henges and stone circles, like the wonderfully named Ring of Brodgar and the Stones of Stenness. So to what extent were any of these houses typical of ordinary, day-to-day dwellings, out there in the rural Neolithic landscape?

It's easier to answer that question in Orkney where early houses are known away from the great ritual landscapes, at places like the Knap of Howar, on the tiny island of Papa Westray, which we reached via the world's shortest scheduled flight. Like Skara Brae, the two houses here are close to the sea, but they probably pre-date the earliest houses there by several centuries (c. 3600–3100 BC).[68] The two houses at the Knap of Howar were interconnected and were more oval, and rather larger than those at Skara Brae, but they do share certain common features, such as central square hearths, evidence for box-beds and 'cupboards' set in niches in the walls.

In southern Britain the evidence is harder to find and I, like many prehistorians, am convinced that this astonishing distortion of the evidence is mostly the result of ploughing, both ancient and modern. To support this idea the distinguished prehistorian Richard Bradley has pointed out that several well-known earlier Neolithic sites in England do have some very suspicious voids, surrounded by pits.[69] These voids, or spaces, are roughly the same size and shape as the Durrington Walls houses. Plainly, a void is just a void, but I have to say, I find Richard's suggestion very tempting.

I think we have demonstrated that these houses were indeed family homes, but families have never existed in a vacuum: parents and their children have friends and more distant relatives, who may be living elsewhere in the landscape or closer by, in the same settlement. And this is where the Durrington Walls project has produced some quite extraordinary revelations. But that opens a whole new topic. It is time to start another chapter.

4

The Emergence of Rural Britain
(3000–2000 BC)

In the last chapter I mentioned that the Durrington Walls houses were on the site of the largest henge monument in Britain, which lies just a short distance to the north-east of the very much smaller, but vastly more famous, Stonehenge. The Durrington houses were also contemporary with the main phase of stone erection at Stonehenge and I share Mike Parker Pearson's view that these may well have been the houses of the Stonehenge workforce.[1] But again, we should not think in terms of the modern construction industry. Indeed, in the past many people – archaeologists, civil engineers and others – have tried to work out how Neolithic communities could have shaped, transported and erected the great monoliths of Stonehenge. But almost without exception, they have approached the problem from a modern, functional and rational perspective, and have tried to do the job in the simplest and most efficient fashion.[2]

Simple efficiency, however, was not what motivated the prehistoric workforce, who were performing their extraordinary tasks as acts of faith, maybe in homage both to the ancestors and the natural world: the sun, the moon and living things. Indeed, one of the original purposes of the great works must surely have been to draw people together, across huge tracts of largely 'untamed' countryside, both open and wooded. At this stage of prehistory, communities were still quite widely separated and far flung and it was the coming together to build and frequently rebuild the great monuments like Stonehenge, Avebury, or indeed the huge Ring of Brodgar, in Orkney, that would have helped tie them together. So 'efficiency of construction', as a modern civil engineer would understand the term, would have been far from their thoughts. If anything, they would have sought out ways to perform the tasks that involved the maximum, not the minimum, number of people. And the Durrington Walls settlement illustrates this well, because it was relatively short lived and very, very large.

Until relatively recently, we used to assume that most of the events of prehistory happened slowly; they took centuries, or at best generations, to complete. But the new statistical approaches to dating, discussed in Chapter 3, have given us much greater precision, and this is particularly true of research projects that are currently under way, or have recently taken place, because we now have a far better understanding of what is needed, by way of dates and samples. Armed with this prior knowledge, the Stonehenge Riverside team were able to refine their various date ranges with extraordinary precision.

Had I been excavating the Durrington Walls settlement even twenty years ago I would probably have concluded that it didn't survive long (one can deduce this from purely archaeological evidence: for instance, none of the houses appear to have been built on top of others, nor to cut through them), and would have suggested a lifespan for the entire community of perhaps 150 years. But the reality is actually a far shorter period: roughly ten years; a decade – some time between the years 2500 and 2460 BC.[3] So no wonder that none of the houses are cut through others, as all would have been standing at the same time. But there's something else remarkable, too. My old friend and colleague Charly French was able to examine the chalk plaster floor of House 851. Under the microscope he could clearly see there were in fact a series of successive floors that had been replaced and renewed up to six times over the house's relatively short life.[4] This pattern suggests that Durrington was indeed a special settlement and that people only stayed there for a limited period during the year – most probably at the midwinter or midsummer solstice celebrations.

The large trench at Durrington Walls was positioned quite close to the outside of the great circular henge monument, and the obvious question every archaeologist in the country at the time was asking was whether the seven houses it had revealed were a lucky, isolated discovery – or part of something more substantial. Eventually the team were able to prove that Durrington Walls was the biggest Neolithic settlement yet discovered in north-western Europe.[5]

This isn't the place to reveal precisely how they did it, but they went

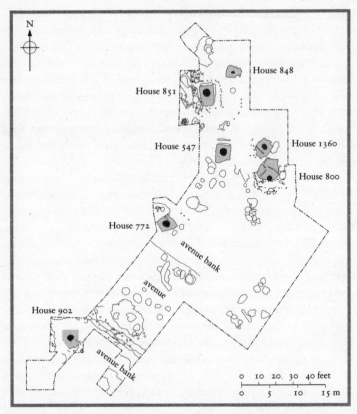

Fig. 4.1 Part of the Neolithic settlement at Durrington Walls, showing the location of seven houses and the position of the banked avenue that led down to the River Avon, some 300 metres (980 feet) to the south-east. Each house has a chalk plaster floor (shaded) and a central hearth (in black).

on to demonstrate that the Durrington Walls settlement must have consisted of over four thousand houses. They were also able to prove their existence at several widely separated places, right across the huge site. Then, as soon as the settlement was no longer needed, the great ditch and outer bank of the henge were erected, some time in the years between 2480 and 2460 BC.[6] Although the digging of the massive ditch would have damaged the archaeological evidence for several houses, it was those later, and highly visible, earthworks which guaranteed the settlement's eventual survival into modern times. And if ever justification were needed for the legal protection of ancient sites, this must surely be the prime example. I have to confess I have never written it before, but just for once: thank God for laws and lawyers.

We are now moving slightly further away from thoughts about homes and houses, pure and simple. Notions like 'settlement' and 'huge earthworks' imply a degree of organization that transcends the family. Perhaps something larger is beginning to emerge?

TOP-DOWN? THE EMERGENCE OF CLASS AND HIERARCHY

In the 1950s, it was widely held that archaeology could never reveal aspects of social organization. It was believed that such notions were well beyond the reach of a subject that was primarily concerned with *things*, with broken pots and flints. It would be like trying to discover what happened within the doors of No. 10 Downing Street by examining the contents of its dustbins. You might conclude that its occupants sometimes had substantial dinners and that every few years the tenants changed, and fish and chips were replaced by *foie gras*. Today, of course, the prime ministerial rubbish would never change, whichever party were in power, and would reflect, instead, the preferences of political professionals living in the fashionable parts of central London.

But as we have seen, archaeology has moved on. We are no longer solely concerned with bits of broken pot and flint. There are a wealth of new techniques available and our understanding of past landscapes and environments has grown by leaps and bounds. While this has been happening, prehistorians have cast their nets more widely and now learn lessons from right across the world; they also draw upon the findings of anthropology and other related disciplines. These changes began in earnest in the early 1960s, when a new generation of prehistorians realized that their subject had been constrained not so much by what it was capable of discovering, as by limited self-belief and self-confidence. Many older scholars held that it was somehow 'wrong' to raise one's gaze beyond the narrow confines of the trench. The result of these debates was the New Archaeology, whose origins I have already discussed in the Introduction. As so often happens in academia and religion, the new movement began to fragment into sub-groups, some of which prospered, while others withered and died.

One of the more productive of these second generation New Archaeology movements was wise enough not to give itself a name, but it was concerned with the important role played by emerging elites, which would lead (sometimes) to the formation of early states. Its principal English protagonist was Professor Colin Renfrew, who is now Lord Renfrew of Kaimsthorn, and sits on the Tory benches in the House of Lords, where he makes the lives of politicians of all parties difficult by actively promoting archaeology and conservation. His own rapid rise to pre-eminence illustrates his archaeological thesis very well. Colin wrote many important papers on the growth of hierarchies and on the importance of top-down control.[7] I have to confess that while I was very glad he had brought a fresh approach to the study of major prehistoric monuments such as Stonehenge and other sites in Wessex, his ideas didn't seem to fit with what I had observed, not just on my own sites, but on digs I had worked on as a student. Although hugely popular at the time (when Mrs Thatcher was in power in Westminster), his were not the only explanations.

There are other ways of viewing the growing complexity of sites and monuments in Neolithic and Early Bronze Age Britain than the suggestion that it was all due to the expansion of new, top-down elites.[8] My brief study of anthropology as an undergraduate in the 1960s had been influential and had shown me that many imposing monuments, such as the vast stone statues on Easter Island, had in fact been carved and erected by tribal groups, without the aid of powerful leaders or Big Men. Yes, the population of Neolithic Britain had been steadily growing for almost two millennia by the time Stonehenge was erected, but I could find no reason to suppose that this was necessarily accompanied by major social upheaval. It seemed to me that Stonehenge, like other emerging henges of the later Neolithic, had roots that ultimately reached back to sites like Etton: the causewayed enclosures, where there was absolutely no evidence for developing elites. Doubtless there were also social influences that archaeology is too crude to reveal, but the basic idea, that people should come together at intervals to link far-flung communities and to cement family ties, does seem to have ancient roots, which might explain why it continued, relatively unaltered, right through the earlier Bronze Age. We can see many links between the ceremonies that took place in earlier Neolithic times, but from the start of the 3rd millennium BC the rites took place in the more formalized, elaborate and structured setting of so-called 'ritual landscapes', where we find a variety of carefully positioned ritual sites, including henges, stone circles, stone rows, chambered tombs and barrows.

To my mind, the top-down, over-hierarchical view of the later Neolithic that was so widely accepted in the 1970s and early '80s was essentially a reflection of later 20th-century priorities, and the spread of 'management culture' beyond the realms of business and commerce. Yes, it certainly made sense – in an analytical way – because it seemed to explain so much. And it fitted with the go-getting yuppie culture of the times. I have to confess, I didn't like these new ideas at all, but I would have been derided by every academic in Britain had I voiced my opinions. Worse than that, my projects would soon have ceased to be funded. So, like other colleagues who were doing full-time fieldwork, I adopted a sort of split personality: I accepted the hierarchical view for big or special sites that I was never likely to excavate myself: monuments like Stonehenge, or Avebury. But at the same time, I knew it didn't apply to places like Etton, nor to the many small henges that my team were then working on in the lower Welland Valley.[9]

Like many younger archaeologists today, I didn't want a major row with the Great and the Good in our profession. So I kept my head down in the trench, where it, and I, belonged. But the question still remained: was this much-vaunted, hierarchical view of Britain's emerging prehistoric identity the truth? By the mid- and late 1980s, it was beginning to worry me a great deal; but I only finally made up my mind when I came to consider the origins of a site we had only just discovered, in November 1982, in a drainage dyke, just east of Peterborough. The site that set me thinking was at Flag Fen, and I shall have a lot more to say about it in the next two chapters.

The new hierarchical view of later Neolithic and Bronze Age societies began to be proposed in the early and mid-1970s. At the time, I
was excavating large tracts of landscape, of precisely those dates,
along the western margins of the Fens in the lower valleys of the rivers
Nene and Welland. It was a fascinating period and place: it was the
time when the inland Fens were actually starting to form; this, in turn,
was a result of the rise in post-Glacial sea-levels (which has ultimately
led to the construction of the Greenwich barrage across the Thames).
And of course Neolithic communities also had to adapt to these
changes. As vast tracts of countryside east of Peterborough became
wetter, the available dry ground inevitably came under pressure. So
the local population divided it up among themselves, along agreed
boundaries.

The more I looked into what was happening, the more convinced I
became that the basic partition or sub-divisions of the landscape were
very ancient and had nothing whatsoever to do with hierarchies. They
first became archaeologically visible when Neolithic and Early Bronze
Age people erected a series of burial mounds at regular intervals along
the edge of the developing wetlands. Sometimes these barrows were
placed in positions that would have been significant in Mesolithic
times, two or even three millennia previously.[10] Usually, they were
spaced along the choicest land of the fen margins at regular intervals,
as permanent physical markers; but as they also contained the bones
or ashes of past ancestors, they were far more than mere landmarks. I
once likened them to 'spiritual electric fences' which were intended to
prevent competing families from trespassing onto their neighbour's
land. Maybe these rules were backed up by ideas about ancestral
vengeance – in the form of disease, flood or fire.

Shortly after about 2500 BC (the same time the Durrington Walls
settlement was being built, far to the south-west), the first field systems began to be laid out, at right angles to the Fens. I'll discuss these
in the next chapter, but here I want to note that the spacing of the new
fields precisely mirrored that of the earlier barrows, which continued
to be used, from time to time, well into the Bronze Age. In other
words, they were the same boundaries, but now marked out in a different way. It is worth mentioning here that the persistence of property
boundaries over very long periods of time is an important indication

of local or communal control: some current house and garden plots in central York, for example, have their origins back in Viking times.[11]

To my mind, what we are witnessing along the Fen-edge in the Neolithic period is growth and continuity, not the disruption that would have attended the rise to power of a major new leader. And I think this all the more remarkable in that the environment was getting wetter and people were having to adapt and respond – precisely the circumstances which, the theorists tell us, might have given rise to a new and more top-down form of governance. But it didn't: instead, the existing social system adapted, and as the centuries rolled by, the western Fenland margins became one of the most prosperous regions in prehistoric Britain. But throughout, communal organization and motivation remained essentially bottom-up: held together and inspired by local tribal or family ties and obligations. That is not to say, of course, that there was no co-ordination. People were not stupid and it must have been in everybody's interest to avoid unnecessary conflict with neighbours. So I'm convinced there must have been regular tribal councils, where differences between different clans and families would have been worked out. But having said that, I can see no evidence whatsoever for any supra-local authority, any Big Man. I shall discuss this in greater detail at the end of Chapter 6, but here it is worth briefly considering what this might mean for Stonehenge.

The idea of a strong controlling authority was attractive and it stuck, as has the notion that sites like Stonehenge positively demand the presence of a specialized priestly class.[12] The latter concept arose from the earlier notion that Stonehenge was a sophisticated computer that could be used to predict astronomical events with remarkable precision.[13] Prehistorians no longer accept these theories as they were originally propounded by the likes of Gerald S. Hawkins: yes, Stonehenge is a remarkable monument, but it can only be understood in its Neolithic contexts; it should never have been used to reflect modern preoccupations with astronomy or computation. As Mike Parker Pearson once told me in a pub: 'If anything, Stonehenge was more about astrology than astronomy.' What he meant is that it was never a predictive or scientific instrument in the modern sense, but rather a place where people came for supernatural assurance about the things that mattered in their lives: that the sun would continue to rise, that winter would eventually end and that grass and crops would grow again, come the springtime.

The great henges would have been respected and visited by people from communities in the region and from farther afield. It's reasonable to wonder how large that region was. Again, we can only guess, but it is interesting that the huge complex of henges, avenues and stone circles at Avebury has to have been of comparable importance to Stonehenge – and this has recently been emphasized by the possible discovery of a Durrington-style settlement there, too.[14] Avebury lies a mere 16 miles due north of Stonehenge, across the great expanses of Salisbury Plain. One might suggest that the people who visited Stonehenge came from the south and west, whereas Avebury covered lands to the north-east. Doubtless, future research will throw further light on the problem. It is also quite possible, of course, that the two ceremonial complexes were visited by the same people, but for different purposes.

The henges and the ritual landscapes of barrows, and other shrines surrounding them, would have been widely respected, and were probably viewed as socially neutral. They would have been the sort of places where leaders of feuding communities could have met to discuss political differences. I find explanations of this sort, rooted in the lives of ordinary people, make more sense than the pseudoscientific notions that became so fashionable in the 1960s and '70s.

I don't want to remove the sense of mystery and magic that any visitor to places like Stonehenge and Avebury must surely feel. I have visited both dozens of times and I never fail to be awed and excited by them. The same can be said for great cathedrals, even though I myself am an atheist. The fact is there is something about such monumental sites that is indeed transcending, or numinous, to use a word that is sadly slipping from general use.[15] You can be rational, and yet experience feelings of awe. Even after the Stonehenge Riverside Project's huge advances, we still only understand a small part of what might have been passing through people's minds as they processed along the Avenue towards the distant Stones. But having said that, I believe it is also time we came up with some fresh pictures for our imaginations, as the ones we have been given, like the 'scientific' theories just discussed, don't do our prehistoric forebears justice.

Fig. 4.2 In the 1920s, Dr MacGregor Reid, Chief Druid of the Church of the Universal Bond, led protests against the banning of Druids from the central stones of Stonehenge on the solstices. The ban was lifted in 1926. Here he is seen, possibly in 1922, conducting a small Druid service wearing robes that look remarkably similar to those of a Church of England vicar.[16]

The pious, almost pompous, berobed 'Druids' who visit Stonehenge every summer solstice are reflections of the very recent past of our own society: as a modern movement they are newcomers, and their rituals and costumes essentially reflect early Victorian and Georgian visions of prehistory.[17] In the 18th and 19th centuries, established religion in England was indeed very top-down, and the Church played an important, and controlling, social role. I have to say I find the resemblance between the Chief Druid's ceremonial get-up and the robes of a Church of England vicar disturbingly close (see Fig 4.2).[18] In reality, I suspect it would have been heads of families or community leaders who would have led at such occasions. Shamans most probably would have played an active part too, and their performance would have been far less restrained than that of a C of E vicar, who may indeed wear clothes that are not gender-specific, but is rarely seen naked, drunk or high on drugs. So which vision do you prefer: the pompous vicar, or the raving shaman? More to the point, think about the nature of the ceremony: the journey from the world of the living to that of the dead. In many societies the grief of the close family is countered by communal celebration and joy, because people believe that a good person has found his or her way to Paradise. We saw this vividly in South Africa during the extended ceremonies after President Mandela's death. My personal feeling is that the ceremonies that took place at Stonehenge would have had more in common with modern Africa than the Church of England.

Stonehenge is an extraordinary monument and it is surrounded by such a remarkable network of henges, barrows and sundry processional ways that we must make some attempt to assess its role in Neolithic and Early Bronze Age Britain. Was it a major regional centre – the prehistoric equivalent of, say, nearby Salisbury Cathedral? If asked that question ten years ago, I would probably have answered yes. But now I'm becoming persuaded that it was even more important than that. Our discussion of the details of the use, layout and construction of houses at Durrington Walls and in the Orkneys shows that there must have been communication between the two areas. Indeed, the closely similar layout of tombs and causewayed enclosures right across Neolithic Britain indicates that people had been in close and regular contact for at least a millennium previously. So it came as no real surprise to many prehistorians when it was announced that scientific analyses of the chemical composition of the animal bones, mostly pig and cattle, found at the Durrington Walls settlement, revealed these to have originated from far away, with a significant proportion coming from northern Scotland.[19] It is thought that pilgrims would have travelled from the distant north, bringing their animals with them. If it were just the bone analyses I would hesitate before suggesting that Stonehenge was the equivalent of Canterbury Cathedral: the principal shrine of the island of Britain. Indeed, the other parallels and similarities now lead me to suspect that might well have been the case.

But now we are moving beyond the world of domestic life into another realm, perhaps more distant, but no less real to those left behind on this earth. We saw hints of the ties that bound the living to the dead, the ancestors to their descendants, in the previous chapter. Now, in the Neolithic, those hints are replaced by something far more solid: by tombs, by bodies and by elaborate rites of passage that marked the journey from this world to the next and which cemented family ties across the generations.

BUILDING HOUSES FOR THE DEAD

When it comes to death and burial, prehistorians rub their hands in glee: there is so much to discover and even more to speculate about, with resonant theories about ancient attitudes to the Next World and the afterlife; and of course it all makes superb grist for the television mills. When I'm confronted by hundreds of metres of featureless Bronze Age field boundary ditches, stretching across a flat Fenland landscape, I have to say I'm positively envious of them, with their bodies, tombs and barrows. In fact, my very first inkling that there might have been a world earlier than the Romans or the Norman Conquest came when, as a boy, I was being driven along the A505, in Hertfordshire, from Baldock to Royston. As English trunk roads go, it isn't the most exciting, but it does run more or less parallel with, and below, the great chalk escarpment, which is the largest single geological feature in Britain. Further south and west, in the Chiltern Hills, it is far more spectacular than here, with the ramparts of huge Iron Age hillforts crowning its heights and dominating the great expanse of flat land to the north.[20] But despite being less imposing, the stretch of escarpment leading into Royston has a charm of its own. In wintertime it's superb for sledging and in the summer you have to keep an eye out for kestrels and golf balls, which fly freely hither and thither.

From the A505, far beneath the steep slope, you can spot a series of quite prominent mounds which I can remember asking my father about. I cannot recall his precise reply, but I'm fairly sure it included the words 'barrow' and 'prehistoric'. I had no idea what either meant, but they sounded deeply mysterious. In retrospect, I wonder whether I ever wanted to discover the actual truth; in childhood, magic is always better if untainted by reality.

I should make it clear from the start that I don't want to get too closely involved with the intricacies of prehistoric tombs or burial rituals. This book is, after all, about home and families; consequently, I'm interested in the dead only inasmuch as they shed light on the living. And at this point I would also like to remind readers that we have already discussed (in the Introduction) the role of ancestors and history in cementing families together. So now I'm concerned with more specific instances that illustrate how family life might have been adapting, as the world around was changing. In prehistoric times, social change might have been somewhat slower than it is today, but as we saw in those ditch deposits at Etton, it was happening, even so. The onset of the Neolithic marked a step change in the pace of social evolution, which continued right through to the middle of the subsequent Bronze Age, when there was a rapid change of direction. Indeed, had it not been for the developments that took place in the two and a half millennia after the introduction of farming, the revolutionary changes that happened around 1500 BC would have been impossible. These, however, must wait until the next chapter. Here I want to consider what it was that made them possible, or even, I now sometimes think, inevitable.

I didn't know it when I looked up from the back seat of the car, but those barrows high on Royston Heath dated to the Early Bronze Age, probably some time between 2500 and 2000 BC, in very general terms. So they actually come towards the end of our story, which begins very much earlier, around 3800 BC, within a couple of centuries of the arrival of the first farmers. The Royston barrows were round and dome shaped. If you examined them more closely you could just detect the slight dip left by a ditch that encircled the mound. This was the quarry ditch that provided most of the chalk rubble which formed that central mound. But the earlier barrows were altogether different from their round Bronze Age descendants. For a start, they were not round. In fact their shape was altogether rather odd.

For some time prehistorians have likened certain forms of Neolithic tombs to 'houses of the dead'. In Orkney, for instance, the plans of a type of chambered tomb, known as a stalled cairn, quite closely resemble those two early houses I mentioned at the Knap of Howar, on the tiny island of Westray.[21] But perhaps the commonest (there are over two thousand of them) and most widespread of the earliest Neolithic burial mounds are known as long barrows. They are generally much larger than the later round barrows, and at first glance look to be rectangular in shape, but on closer inspection they can be seen to taper from a wider, higher end, to a much smaller and narrower 'tail'. Lengths vary a great deal, but 50 metres (160 feet) is not unusual. The wider, higher end is, as you have probably already guessed, the 'business' end. This trapezoidal or kite-like shape is in itself interesting, because the first Neolithic houses on the mainland of Europe are very closely similar in outline, and size. To be frank, I have never understood why the first farmers in much of Europe decided to build their houses in this strange shape, but they did. It puts one in mind of Viking houses, which often have bowed ship-like walls. In that instance, the motivation is obvious: longships and sailing were fundamental to the Viking way of life. So I would imagine that the trapezoid-shaped outline must once have meant something special, but sadly it has been lost in the mists of antiquity. It may hark back to an early pattern of continental house, or it may not. As we will see shortly, the earliest Neolithic tombs are not of this distinctive shape, as one might expect. It would also be far more convincing if we could discover the remains of a genuine trapezoidal house in Britain, and if we do, my money will be on it being in Kent or East Sussex. But it will not be easy, thanks to the terrible destruction wrought by the plough.

The higher, 'business', end of most long barrows was usually built up and reinforced with large stones, drystone walling or timber. Very often, too, the corners of the barrow would be extended to form protruding 'horns', which partially enclosed a protected forecourt in front of the tomb. Often this forecourt was surfaced or paved in some way. This was where the funeral ceremonies took place. And this was usually where the tomb was entered. One of the best-preserved long barrows, with a fine forecourt, is at Wayland's Smithy, just off the great prehistoric road, the Ridgeway, in Oxfordshire (see Plate 15). The long trapezoidal mound and the great forecourt and stone-lined internal chambers that so impress the modern visitor were in fact a second phase of development. It's worth noting here that the first phase (c. 3600–3500 BC) at Wayland's Smithy was much smaller and oval, not trapezoidal. It was only revealed by excavation, as the entire thing had been incorporated into the later barrow, known as Wayland's Smithy 2. Interestingly, some of the bodies interred within

Wayland's Smithy 1 had probably been violently killed. There is other evidence for violence in the early Neolithic, at long barrows and causewayed enclosures, but it is difficult to be certain whether this represents a spate of intercommunal fighting or the usual levels of background feuding that would have gone on at the time. For various reasons, the bodies interred in the earliest barrows have given us a better than usual sample of the population – and how they eventually perished.

After the very earliest phase, bodies were often buried within separate chambers beneath long barrows. These room-like spaces were frequently made with large stone slabs and drystone walling, and one of the best preserved, which visitors can enter, is at West Kennet, a short walk outside the village of Avebury, in Wiltshire.[22] In the Fens, at Haddenham, where there are no available local sources of stone, they built the chamber out of massive planks split from a vast ancient oak tree.[23] These are all very large monuments, but if you want to make a short visit to a more run-of-the-mill long barrow, I can recommend one at Nympsfield in Gloucestershire. In common with many other long barrows, it is located in a prominent position, on Coaley Peak, with magnificent views across the Severn Valley towards the Forest of Dean and the Brecon Beacons, far away on the skyline. Like Wayland's Smithy, this tomb has a small forecourt, from which a passage runs into the mound, to three chambers, one at each side, and one at the end (see Plate 16). So why did people go to the trouble of creating rooms or chambers within the mounds and what do they represent?

To answer that question we need to visit yet another long barrow in the Cotswolds, this time at Hazleton North, in Gloucestershire, a site that was superbly excavated over many years by Alan Saville (see Fig. 4.3).[24] Thanks to Alan's meticulous work, we now understand a great deal more about the rites that took place at these sites, and just as we saw at Etton, it's the details that are so revealing. The two barrows at Hazleton (North and South) are, technically speaking, cairns, the mounds being made up from Cotswold limestone, as opposed to earth, gravel or chalk rubble. Hazleton North is quite early in the long barrow tradition (about 3700 BC) and it was erected on a site that had already seen occupation for at least three centuries

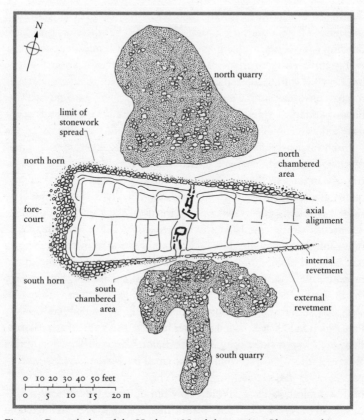

Fig. 4.3 Ground plan of the Hazleton North long cairn, Gloucestershire (c. 3700 BC), showing the trapezoid-shaped mound and the two sets of burial chambers. Stone for the mound (or cairn) was quarried from two large pits, to north and south. The mound was constructed in a series of cellular units which suggest the use of gangs, most probably working at the same time, in several units, which were separated by informal drystone internal walls, or revetments.

(4000–3700 BC), from the very start of the Neolithic.[25] It is also slightly unusual in that it has two separate sets of chambers, which have two opposite entrances in the mound's long sides, to north and south. Just beyond them are two large quarry-pits where stone for the cairn was mined. Interestingly, the barrow has a horned forecourt in the usual place at the wide end of the mound, but there is no passage leading from it to the chambers, as one would normally expect.

I mentioned details, and it was the clear demonstration that the body of the cairn had been carefully constructed in a series of cellular units – on either side of a central axis – that was so fascinating. This layout strongly suggested that the work had been carried out by separate gangs, probably of different sizes, who built up segments of the mound in clearly defined areas that were separated from each other by drystone revetment walls – in effect, cells. Although the use of gangs can be detected, the work was otherwise well co-ordinated and controlled, to give the mound a smooth, gradually sloping profile. The use of two large quarry-pits on either side of the barrow would have ensured a steady supply of rock for teams working on each side of the central axis. Again, this dual layout is reflected in the placing of the two sets of chambers, but again, there is co-ordination: the chambers are all close to each other and funeral ceremonies would have happened in the usual place, in the horned forecourt next to the tallest, widest part of the long mound, to the west. Similar cellular construction has been noted in other long barrows, like that at Skendleby, on the east side of the country, in north Lincolnshire, but in this case the internal revetment was provided by woven wooden wattlework, rather than stone.[26]

The subject of 'gang labour' has been quite fashionable in prehistoric circles for a long time. Hypothetical 'gangs' are often cited to account for the strange appearance of the very few seemingly (because we can never be certain) 'unfinished' Iron Age hillforts in Britain. The best preserved of these is Ladle Hill, high above the chalk escarpment, in Hampshire, which I will discuss again in Chapter 7. Here the ditch is clearly unfinished, because it makes no sense as a defensive work, being dug in uneven segments of about 50 metres (164 feet) in length, accompanied by 'ramparts' that more resemble the untidy spoil heaps of an archaeological excavation. In this instance 'gangs' do seem to be the only sensible explanation. But what do we mean when we use that word?

I suspect when the term was first applied to prehistoric times, the image in people's minds would have been that of the early railway navvy gangs, who were, for the most part, disciplined groups of sub-contractors. In some circles today it's still fashionable to see them as hard-drinking, semi-riotous and (mostly) Irishmen, but in reality, if they were that dysfunctional it's hard to see how Britain's once-huge railway network managed to get built at all, let alone in a single decade (the 1840s). And having directed the only excavation of a Victorian railway-age navvy camp, I can report that the finds included very few booze bottles; instead there were hundreds of sherds of floral plates and teacups.[27] I shall say no more. But essentially the purpose of gang labour, in the modern sense, is to break down the workforce into manageable units that can be used when and where they are required. Put another way, it's a pragmatic, functional arrangement which is very much in tune with the practical age we live in. But did it apply in prehistory, too?

Let's start to answer that question by returning to a site we have already examined in some detail. Etton is fairly typical of other causewayed enclosures, and besides, I feel at home there. Previously, I was concerned with sometimes minute details, now I would like to consider the general picture. As causewayed enclosures go, Etton was not a very grand or spectacular site: it never crowned a great hill and there is only one ring of segmented ditches, but as it was sealed below almost a metre of river flood-clay, we can be fairly certain that many of the features revealed there are indeed ancient, even if they never produced datable finds. I mentioned earlier that I have mentally lived with this site for many years, and every time I return to it I'm reminded that seemingly haphazard features always seem to occur in an ordered, if not an overtly structured, pattern. It's as if the haphazard element is somehow being contained, but there is also nothing to suggest that it was being discouraged, either. Indeed, I sometimes get the impression that the haphazard, the seemingly random, was being encouraged – but within certain limits, which I suggest were agreed by the entire community. I apologize if this sounds rather Delphic and obscure, but the underlying principle is, I think, important – and should become clearer when we examine two case-studies. So let's return to the segmented enclosure ditch at Etton.

The first thing to note is that this ditch was actually quite regular, generally having a flat bottom, of fairly constant depth, of just under a metre. The width, too, was consistent at about 2.5 to 3 metres. Most causeways ranged between 1 and 2 metres wide, except for the main northern entrance, at 25 metres and 10 metres, in its first and second phases; similarly the east and west entrances were also wider (6 and 3.5 metres). Mindful of the fact that I must be careful not to fall into circular arguments (the main entranceways were partly defined on the basis of their greater width), there does seem to be a degree of consistency here (see Fig. 4.1). And yet the lengths of the ditch segments themselves vary hugely, in fact *tenfold*: from 81 metres (Segment 5) to just 8.8 metres (Segment 9).[28]

A similar contrast between one seemingly permissible variable and an otherwise standardized layout can be seen in the internal cells at Hazleton North, which are consistent in the way they respect the central axis and the two sets of chambered tombs, but otherwise vary quite considerably in area (see Fig. 4.3). I would suggest this 'permissible variability' is quite simply a reflection of the different size and status of families within the community, as defined by the Hazelton barrow or the Etton causewayed enclosure. Everyone involved with the construction, frequent modification and 'use' of the two sites was bound together by respect for the rules that governed the communities where they lived. So some families may have been larger and perhaps more powerful, and they would have provided the labour used in the construction of the longest ditch segments or the largest 'cells' within the Hazleton mound. Size of ditch segment or mound cell may have been just one of the factors that signalled a family's status: maybe proximity to the main northern entrance at Etton, or to the forecourt or burial chambers at Hazleton, was seen as important, too.

A recent parallel to such a structured arrangement might be seen in the layout of graves and pews in a Victorian country church. In my own family's case, my uncle, grandfather and great-grandfather were all squires of the village and owned the medieval manor. They were also the principal landowners and possessed the 'gift' of the parish – i.e. they could appoint and nominate vicars. Put another way, they were very big fish in a tiny pond. This status was reflected by the location of the family graves, close to the church, on the south, sunny side. Similarly, the family pews were in the chancel, close to the altar. In hindsight it was a very prehistoric seating plan.

So yes, gang labour was employed, but it wasn't about the gangs themselves: it was the families they represented that mattered. But remember, these things were happening a very long time ago indeed – some 5,700 years, to be more precise. At that stage of prehistory, the British landscape was still being developed. Trees were being felled, roads and trackways were being laid out and possession of good farmland was being divided up among competing communities, sometimes, as I have hinted at, with feuding. Under such circumstances, communal loyalty becomes hugely important and this is what is being expressed symbolically at places like Etton and Hazleton. But the different communities were all family based; it was the families who provided community leaders with support, with manpower and with stability. In return for their loyalty, they were able to express their own identities, which they did, no doubt, competitively.

So do I completely disregard the idea that there were any major, controlling elites in the Neolithic? No I do not. It seems to me self-evident that the complex, interrelated developments we can see in ritual landscapes – at places such as Stonehenge, Avebury, the Boyne Valley in Ireland, or in Mainland, Orkney, and probably, too, at less well-known sites, like Maxey, near Etton, and dozens of others right across Britain – were indeed co-ordinated.[29] But at the same time I cannot see such communities agreeing to be ruled by a single Big Man (or Woman, come to that), 'out of the blue', as it were. Everything we know about Neolithic social organization suggests compromise and discussion. Indeed, this is what we find in tribal societies to this day.

If your community is living close to the land, you cannot afford wholesale conflict. Your labour and the livelihood of your family must come first. Accordingly, when disputes do happen, negotiation is paramount, and, as we will see shortly, the means of mediation are an integral part of the system. Something as horrendous as the Great War would have been impossible in prehistory. Instead, hostilities would have been limited, probably only happening when younger men were freed from farming duties, most probably in the months of autumn, and even then they would have been constrained; inter-tribe or clan feuding would largely have revolved around raiding parties, as illustrated in the evocative, and ultimately prehistoric, poem *The Cattle Raid of Cooley* that has survived in Ireland.[30]

It is also worth noting that the tiered social structure necessary for all negotiation and mediation was already there, represented by the heads of families and their representatives, plus other community leaders. It does not take a major leap of imagination to suppose that people in certain areas, like that around Stonehenge, found it necessary to add another level to the hierarchy: a gathering of the leaders of individual communities – which today we might see as the emergence of tribal councils. I would consider this a perfectly natural social process with its own built-in checks and balances. It isn't a radical change, nor is it irrevocable, although, as we will see in the next chapter, continuous population growth did in fact mean that British societies continued to develop and evolve, but in their own regional ways and on their own terms.

As time passed and the population grew, social organization inevitably became more complex. Religious sites proliferated in a variety of forms, and towards the latter part of the Neolithic, in the early and mid-3rd millennium BC, we see the rise of henges, a distinctively British and Irish form of ceremonial site, which were closely linked – as the Stonehenge Riverside Project has so elegantly demonstrated – to the process of transition from life to death. But relatively late in this process of evolving monumental complexity, there was a development that happened right across Britain, and indeed over large parts of western Europe, too. I believe that, ultimately, it was a new way of expressing family identity, but this time through the individual. To understand what was happening in these later developments (towards the end of the Neolithic and the start of the Bronze Age), we must first pause to consider how people's attitudes to death itself were changing.

WALKING WITH GRANDFATHER'S BONES

Having lived with the Neolithic and Bronze Age for the best part of a lifetime, I have gained the distinct impression that they are very different. I would of course agree that the change from the one to the other was gradual, and that unlike the introduction of farming, Britain did not witness the arrival of a significant proportion of people from overseas. The technological change that archaeologists use to signal the new Age, the introduction of bronze (an alloy of about 90 per cent copper with 10 per cent tin), just happens to coincide with broader social changes. But having said all that, I'm still left with the impression – maybe 'feeling' would be a better word – that the Neolithic was somehow more conservative, more constrained and more risk-averse than the Bronze Age. Of course the bare facts might suggest otherwise: after all, it was the Neolithic that saw the introduction of farming and food production, and suddenly the British Isles became capable of supporting a vastly greater population than in the days of hunting and gathering. That was indeed a hugely radical step and certainly very much greater than the introduction of an alloy. But prehistory is not just about food production, or metalworking, however important they may have been at the time. It's actually about people, their surroundings and how they inhabited the landscape.

It is also worth recalling that ideas only take root when society at large is ready to receive or accept them. One thinks here of Leonardo da Vinci's helicopter, which was four centuries ahead of its time. I believe that although the idea of farming spread very fast, it then took over two millennia for farming families, which in those days meant everybody, to adapt to their landscapes, to clear or manage woodlands and to establish viable permanent communities that were linked together by a network of roads, streams, rivers and trackways. And this, to my mind, was the great achievement of the Neolithic. By about 2500 BC, when the first bronze and copper implements and technologies arrived in Britain the population was ready to receive them and then, with their help, they were able to accelerate and complete the process of landscape development they had begun around 4000 BC. As we will see in the next chapter, that process was substantially completed by 1500 BC.

By the end of the Neolithic, and with new technologies to assist them, Bronze Age communities became more adventurous and less conservative. We see the rise of increasingly powerful individuals, and new social networks also begin to appear. In some tribal communities, anthropological evidence suggests that some smiths and metalworkers would have been outside mainstream society; we don't know whether that applied in Britain, but there is plenty of evidence to suggest that metalworkers were considered to be important and distinctive – all of which implies growing social complexity and diversity.

These essentially evolutionary changes were taking place and were being handled and managed – 'mediated' is the jargon term – by existing family- and community-based social structures. But having said that, there was also something new, and rather harder to define about the social climate in the earlier Bronze Age: as I see it, it became more open and accepting, with a 'can-do' attitude, where communities became less risk averse. Maybe these new approaches were a result of the long-term landscape improvements of the Neolithic, which might well have led to greater feelings of security and well-being at the community level. It was a time of greater intercommunal communication and networking, as I think we can see quite clearly, for example, in the later developments at Stonehenge.

By way of contrast, life in the earlier Neolithic was very strongly focused on the community. It's worth bearing in mind that these were pioneering times. Different settlements were quite far flung, and were separated if not by impenetrable forest, then by large tracts of undeveloped, natural countryside. And of course there were wild animals, such as wolves, bears, wild boar and aurochs (the fearsome wild cattle). Sites like Etton and other causewayed enclosures were certainly needed to keep communities within a given region in touch with each other, but communal tombs, such as the long barrows, were more about individuals, villages and their families.

It is probably true to think of these earlier Neolithic communal tombs as *houses* of the dead. Laying aside their trapezoidal shape, the forecourts and entrance portals resemble those of houses, as do the internal chambers and passages. So were they used like medieval family vaults in parish churches and cathedrals? And the answer to that is no. For a start, corpses in medieval and later times were placed in vaults and left there. They were never removed, unless under the most exceptional circumstances. But in Neolithic times the houses of the dead were treated rather like those of the living. Their entrance portals were not sealed permanently until the very last interment – then a great stone or rock would be rolled into permanent position as a blocker. But before that I suspect people would have visited what they would have seen as their ancestors' homes, whenever it was appropriate. More to the point, the bones within the various chambers were often muddled up: an arm or a leg from one chamber being put back in the wrong one. This mixing-up of bones within long barrows is quite a consistent feature in those tombs where preservation has been good enough to allow analysis.

The mixing-up of bones in chambers of long barrows and other Neolithic communal graves also suggests that the bodies or bones of the ancestors were removed from the tombs, maybe at regular intervals.[31] In modern tribal societies, such practices take place on certain ceremonial occasions, such as the funerals of senior members of the clan or family, when the remains would be taken on procession through the community, maybe to the home of the person who has just died. Then they might accompany the corpse to its new home in the appropriate chamber of the tomb. In some instances, we know that skeletons were carefully positioned in life-like positions – in one case sitting upright, in another with legs flexed against a wall.[32] It would seem that the boundaries between life and death were deliberately being blurred. And this is important in societies living in more challenging or remote environments, where the role of the ancestors was perceived as vital in helping to keep clans and families together. It would have been seen as a case of 'united we stand, divided we fall'.

As time passed, the shape and layout of chambered Neolithic tombs changed. It does not matter for our purposes that long barrows and cairns were replaced by a new form of tomb, known as a passage grave, shortly before 3000 BC; I see these as different expressions of the same underlying beliefs. What concerns me more were the changes that took place at the close of the Neolithic, when there was a sharp shift away from communal tombs to unchambered barrows, where, so far as we can tell, bodies were buried permanently, with or without coffins, directly beneath the mound, but without a protective chamber. As a general rule, these barrows are smaller than their earlier Neolithic counterparts and the single bodies buried within them were often accompanied by an entirely new style of pottery, known as Beakers.

THE RISE OF THE INDIVIDUAL

I would normally try to steer clear of different pottery styles, just as I would try to avoid the intricacies of different styles of barrow, cairn and tomb, but in this instance they cannot, I'm afraid, be avoided. Beakers were first identified in graves, where they are generally found complete. The pots themselves are perhaps the best known of prehistoric European ceramics and are very attractive, being extensively decorated and very well made and fired. They are generally considered to have been drinking vessels, and it is quite possible that the drink might have been alcoholic. The pattern on the pot was arranged in a quite complex design of different zones, and it is very unusual to find identical Beakers. For my money, these vessels are symbolic expressions of personal or family identity. As the archaeologist Julian Thomas put it: they were artefacts 'with personalities'.[33] The earliest Beaker graves in Britain date to around 2350 to 2150 BC.[34]

The Beaker 'phenomenon', as it is sometimes termed, was about more than just attractive pots. Early Beakers are found with early metalwork – copper or bronze – and some have suggested that the pots are representative of a 'people' – the Beaker folk – a community that moved throughout northern and western Europe, taking with them the mysteries of metalworking. Others have suggested that Beakers – and drinking alcohol – were part of a religion, a so-called 'cult package' that newly emerging elite classes somehow bought into. It has even been suggested that the rapid spread of Beakers across Europe represented the need to find wives in neighbouring communities. I have to say I find the latter a bit far-fetched – why start doing such things so suddenly – and everywhere? So it would seem that Beakers still retain some of their mystery. On the whole, I tend to favour the idea that Beakers and the people who used them were indeed linked with metalworking and with the trade and exchange that it generated, but precisely how this happened must remain unclear for now.[35]

One of the earliest (2470–2280 BC) and richest of Beaker burials was found in May 2002. The body was that of a man aged about 35 to 50 years old and his skeleton was accompanied by almost a

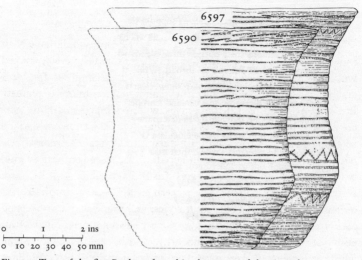

Fig. 4.4 Two of the five Beakers found in the grave of the 'Amesbury Archer'. The close similarity of their form, the arrangement of the decoration and their profiles show that these two vessels were made by the same accomplished potter.

hundred finds, many of them of outstanding quality and associated with archery – for example 15 superb flint arrowheads and two polished stone wrist-guards (to protect the inner face of the arm and wrist from the snap of the bowstring when an arrow was released). As his grave was found about 3 miles south of Stonehenge, the man who was buried has acquired the name the 'Amesbury Archer'; the *Daily Mail* dubbed him 'King of Stonehenge'.[36] Given that sort of reception by the media, I suppose it could be argued that here, surely, there was evidence for Britain's first 'Big Man'. But, as we have seen, the origins of the monument at Stonehenge lie as early as 3000 BC, over half a millennium earlier than the Amesbury Archer. So if he was involved with Stonehenge, which seems very likely, given the grave's proximity to the site, then he belonged to a continuing tradition of builders and modifiers. He wasn't a Richard Branson: he didn't explode onto the scene out of nowhere, have a series of brilliantly commercial ideas and then set about building the greatest prehistoric monument in northern Europe.

No, prehistoric society was very different. People would have been constrained by strong familial ties and obligations. There was, and is, no such thing as true free trade in tribal societies. Goods and services would have been exchanged, not for money, but to honour previously agreed family arrangements, which were often linked closely to marriage settlements. In other instances, goods or services would be exchanged between parties by agreement; for example, so many days' ploughing, in exchange for an agreed measure of seed corn. It's highly unlikely that an entrepreneur, even one as remarkable as Sir Richard, could have arisen under such circumstances. Society simply wasn't organized along free-market lines. Communities had more pressing concerns to contend with, such as social cohesion, protection and economic survival. Although the modern world still relies heavily on the family, it has, nonetheless, moved on, and to many people today, work and security of employment are of comparable, if not equal, importance to their families, which in turn have become more flexible and harder to define.

As I have suggested, we still don't fully understand what caused the Beaker phenomenon. The simplest explanation would be the arrival of a new group of people from the continent, as the pots and the early metalwork accompanying them were so distinctive. But new people bring with them languages, culture and beliefs, too; they don't just bring pots and metalworking. When, for example, the British colonized North America, their churches and churchyards closely resembled those being built at the time in Britain. So one would expect any incomers to arrive with, say, new house plans and new burial rites that could clearly be identified with a specific place or region. But so far as we can tell, this did not happen.

Pottery is usually a reliable indicator of where styles and decoration, if not actually the vessels themselves, might have originated, or been inspired. Fortunately for us, the five pots buried with the Amesbury Archer were studied by Ros Cleal.[37] For me Ros is the best expert on English prehistoric pottery; not only does she know her pots inside-out, she is also a keen practical potter herself, so can bring important insights to her work that so many purely academic studies lack. Ros showed that stylistically these very early British Beakers were heavily influenced by the work of potters in the Netherlands, north-west France and the lower Rhine area. Having said that, a geological examination of the clays used showed they had all been made locally.[38]

But Ros's greatest insights came when she looked at the pots with her potter's eye. It was clear to her that four of the five vessels had been made as pairs, by the same potter. Two had been made together, but had then had different 'histories', as their wear patterns (the scuffs and abrasions on the surface) were very different (see Fig. 4.4). Maybe they had been used in separate households, but they both clearly *had* had a past: in other words they had not been made for the grave. The second pair, on the other hand, were remarkably fresh and had almost certainly been made to be buried. The 'singleton' pot was less distinct-ive, but had been made from a clay that the potter had mixed with crushed potsherds, known in the trade as 'grog'. This might suggest a different origin entirely for this particular vessel.

Finely made, thin-walled Beakers like those buried with the Ames-bury Archer would not make good cooking vessels: they are too fine to take repeated and rapid heating and cooling. In modern terms, they are best seen as tableware. Samples from inside all the pots showed evidence of fatty residues and those from the two 'made for the grave' vessels were identified as degraded animal fats, most probably derived from milk.[39] It's hard to avoid the conclusion that these vessels some-how represent aspects of the dead man's life and status: the worn pots from close family households and the pair 'made for the grave' con-tributed by mourners as a sign of their respect and his high status in the community.

There is little that is consistent about early Beaker burials. Some are buried under mounds, but many are not. The Amesbury Archer grave, for example, was within a timber 'mortuary structure', but there was no barrow, apart from a small pile of turf.[40] I can, however, remember being very excited when I learned that the Amesbury Archer's burial had been accompanied by that of a younger man, aged about 25 to 30. He was not buried with such massive wealth: just a boar's tusk and two gold earrings. Was this a master and his servant? That would certainly fit well with the Big Man theory. But there was a snag.

For a start, although the younger man was not buried with the many wealthy trappings of the Archer himself, there were two gold earrings, close by his head. From their position it does not seem like he had been wearing them. So they had been put there. What makes them remarkable is their close similarity to the two basket-shaped earrings that were found in the Archer's grave, but again, *they* were found by his knees. So it would seem that both sets of earrings had been placed in the graves as offerings. Both sets were very similar in size, shape and decoration. Are these the sorts of items a Bronze Age chieftain might give to a servant? I think not.

But the discovery that clinched the nature of their relationship was only revealed when the two skeletons were studied by Jackie McKinley.[41] She noted that the feet of both skeletons were affected by a rare condition, known as 'bilateral non-osseous calcaneonavicular coalition' (found in 1.2 to 2.9 per cent of the population today). This condition, which would have caused their walking to have appeared rather awkward, 'shows high hereditability within immediate families and over several generations within a family'.[42] This would suggest that the relationship was that of father and son, or of two brothers.

Modern science is also able to add one illuminating detail about the lives of these two men. Human teeth do all of their growing during childhood and the composition of their enamel will be closely similar to that of the water the child drinks. Analysis of their tooth enamel suggested that the older man had been brought up in south-east or west Germany, whereas his son, or much younger brother, grew up in southern England, as his teeth showed he had drunk water from chalklands.[43] Recent research is now suggesting that people travelled far more in prehistory than is generally supposed. By the middle and later Bronze Age, it is becoming quite common to find French and central European objects on English sites (we found many at Flag Fen, around 1300–900 BC). Maybe we are witnessing here an ancient equivalent of the 18th-century Grand Tour, where rich individuals would spend time abroad, renewing relationships with distant cousins. Those relationships would then be remembered, when gifts from far away arrived on ceremonial occasions.

As time passed, the chambered tombs of the earlier Neolithic were replaced by a new style of burial where the body was either cremated or was placed in the grave with the clear intention of remaining there, with or without offerings, or grave goods. Beakers soon became closely identified with these rites, which now began to become more consistent: barrows were universally round and very much smaller. In the majority of cases, there would be a central or 'primary' burial, very often with smaller, less lavish 'secondary' burials – or more usually cremations – inserted into the mound. Sometimes these later burials could be added over four or five centuries – occasionally even longer.

The first Neolithic chambered tombs generally occurred on their own, but from about 3400 BC the style changed: newer forms, including passage graves, were now often placed under round barrows; sometimes these barrows occur in groups, or cemeteries. By the Bronze Age, the new rite of single-grave burial, without a chamber, continued the later Neolithic tradition of round barrows and also of barrow cemeteries. Such cemeteries can be seen in many areas of Wessex and elsewhere, including those barrows that so fascinated me as a child, high on the heath outside Royston. A particularly fine group can be seen near Lambourn, in Berkshire (see Plate 17). So although the new Beaker rite of single burial beneath a small round barrow seems at first to be a rather sudden introduction, it is in fact building on much earlier traditions. And as I said before, this is not what one would expect of an incoming group of settlers. I'm in little doubt, however, that there *were* new arrivals, but these people settled within, and were accepted by, local communities who would, of course, have benefited from the new technologies of metalworking they brought with them. And there were spin-off benefits too: smelting (the extraction of metal from ore) and smithing require better control of fire, furnaces and heat, which in turn led to improvements in other technologies, such as pottery, where many vessels were fired more consistently and became harder.

It might be thought that the new style of burial within unchambered, smaller barrows severed all the earlier symbolic links between the houses of the dead and those of the living. But if one examines Early Bronze Age funerary rites between about 2500 and 1500 BC more closely, it soon becomes clear that the distinction between life and death was not as hard edged as one might suppose. Although there were no chambers in these new-style barrows, it seems likely that they continued to be seen as homes for the ancestors' spirits, even if their bones and bodies had been consumed by cremation pyres. Analysis of fat residues on Beakers found in graves shows that many had contained milky drinks; more to the point, a slightly later and very widespread form of urn for cremated bones, known as the Collared Urn, was used for milky foods and drinks, but also once held pork and probably beef stews or soups. More to the point, the researchers were of the opinion that many of the urns from burials were in fact domestic cooking utensils that were only pressed into service as cremation containers, after a life of use in the kitchen.[44] Maybe the pots had always belonged to the man or woman whose bones they now held. Whatever the actual stories, there could be no clearer indication that family life was thought to continue after death, and certainly within the barrow, if not farther afield in the afterlife, too.

I would see continuing processes of social development as the main driving force behind the complex developments of grave and barrow layout in the Early Bronze Age. As I hinted previously, chambered tombs were about families within communities: at its simplest, the chambers stood for families, whereas the community was represented by the mound and its elaborate forecourt and revetment walls along each side. There are further symbols of family life in the internal construction of the mound, and doubtless, too, in other aspects of the tomb, which we have yet to identify. By contrast when we come to the Early Bronze Age and to Beaker burials in particular, all of that has changed. So does the barrow still represent the village or community? I think not. These later barrows are, in effect, the equivalents of those earlier chambers. So each barrow now represents a family,[45] and communities are represented by barrow cemeteries and perhaps in other ways too: my own work on the edge of the Fens has linked barrows to individual land-holdings. In upland areas barrows often occur along high ridges, in spaced-out lines, rather than cemeteries. Here, I would suggest, the barrows on the ridge 'belonged' to (or were identified with) individual families of communities spread out across open landscapes down in the valleys below.

So it would seem that in the Early Bronze Age families are just as important as they were in Neolithic times, but something has undoubtedly changed. Most obviously, heads of wealthy families now express their power, influence and lavish lifestyles in sumptuous burials, like that of the Amesbury Archer and, indeed, many others in early 3rd-millennium-BC Wessex. It would seem that people are becoming far more outward-looking. There is much evidence for 'trade', or exchange. I put 'trade' in quotes, because as I have already mentioned, tribal societies rarely operate a true market economy: goods change hands for reasons, to do with family, marriage and other social obligations. The converse of co-operation is conflict, and much of the wealth displayed in the rich new graves of Wessex expressed in weaponry: bows and arrows and large copper and bronze daggers. But as before, we are probably talking about raids and posturing à la David and Goliath (a Bronze Age scene, if ever there was one). I believe that the social changes visible within the new-style round-barrow cemeteries reflect population growth and increasing social diversity, which can also be seen in the almost fully developed landscape and the rapid growth of new settlements right across the country. Prehistoric Britain was coming of age.

By 2500 BC, when Stonehenge begins its major phase of rapid development, Britain was a very different place to what it had been when farming began, some two and a half millennia previously. By now, most of the woodland was well on its way to being opened up to livestock and agriculture. The landscape was peppered with small cairns, barrows, standing stones and other long-vanished markers, such as ancient trees which signalled the edges of communal and family holdings. In certain parts of the country, such as the edges of the Fens, the first fields were being laid out, using those earlier markers as guides. Villages were starting to emerge. Landscapes of this sort can only function if they are linked by a network of roads and droveways (for livestock), connected, in turn, to rivers and streams. The whole process was reciprocal, a feed-back loop – call it what you will – between people and their surroundings: social development stimulated landscape change, which in turn affected the way people in different communities were able to interact. But again, all of this was being co-ordinated and pushed forward by families and communities working together, ultimately for the greater good of all. Part of this process was the appearance of more influential and wealthy leaders. But these people were not somehow above everyone else, as was suggested in the 1970s. After all, they had been given their legitimacy and power by the families they headed. Their conspicuous wealth was an expression of the family's success. So they were not above or outside the social system, but were an integral part of it. Had the Amesbury Archer been buried in ancient Egypt, where a true top-down system operated, the young man alongside him might well have been a slave, rather than a close relative, accompanied by family heirlooms.

Throughout the later Neolithic and into the Bronze Age, the processes of social and economic evolution were gathering pace. The centres of economic power and development were also shifting away from Salisbury Plain and Wessex, down into the fertile river valleys of the Thames, East Anglia and the East Midlands. Big changes were afoot and soon something radical would have to happen. It is time to start another chapter.

5

The Age of Stonehenge
(2500–1500 BC)

I want to turn now to the centuries leading up to what I increasingly believe was the most significant cultural change in British, or indeed north European, prehistory. As we will see, the change itself happened quite rapidly, but it was the result – I'm tempted to say the inevitable result – of a series of developments that had been taking place since the arrival of farming and which we started to examine in the previous chapter. The major changes that took place around 1500 BC were undoubtedly momentous and they all happened quite rapidly in the two or so centuries of the mid-second millennium BC. And once societies had altered, there could be no going back. Indeed, I'm firmly convinced that we are living with the consequences to this day.

But before we discuss what I have called the Domestic Revolution of 1500 BC, I want to examine the scale of later Neolithic and Early Bronze Age ceremonies, because they were not all large Stonehenge-style mega-events. As we will see shortly, some were quite small – even family sized. But they were quite distinct from what was to happen after 1500 BC. As a useful shorthand, I shall refer to the earlier practices as the Old Order and those that developed after 1500 BC as the New Order.

SEAHENGE AND THE CELEBRATION OF FAMILY LIFE

It has taken me a lifetime of research to appreciate the simple truth that you cannot paint with a broad brush until you understand the details, because they are what provide the insights into human behaviour. So I make no apologies for yet another intricate case-study. Etton gave us unique glimpses into the rites and practices that would have helped to keep together families living in what was essentially a rather hostile, pioneering, landscape. Earlier on I discussed Stonehenge and the extraordinary short-lived workers' settlement at Durrington Walls, and I'm aware I might have given the impression that as time passed religion became bigger and grander everywhere. In actual fact, I suspect that even the Stonehenge ceremonies were fundamentally community based and bore no resemblance whatsoever to the Druidical New Age rites that adorn our newspapers most summers during the appropriately named 'silly season'.

It is not generally known, but there are literally hundreds of henge sites found throughout the British Isles, and many of them are very small, even tiny.[1] In 1990 our team excavated a 'mini-henge' at Fengate, on the outskirts of eastern Peterborough, that measured just 3 metres across. It was 'nested' within a much larger henge, so I think its identification is most probably correct.[2] But is it sensible to compare a tiny henge scraped into loose gravel, perhaps on just one prehistoric afternoon, with monuments as mighty as Stonehenge, or Avebury, which took centuries to erect and modify? And I think common sense would scream: No. But sadly, archaeology and common sense often part company – indeed, it's one of the things I like about the subject. Let me explain.

Archaeologists have defined henges by their encircling ditch and outer bank, and the fact that the ditch is broken by one, often two, and occasionally even four, gaps or entrances. It's the ditch that is crucial for their definition: timber setting and stones are an added extra. It's rather like Christian churches, which have to be aligned east–west. They usually have a tower at one end and are entered from the south, but the altar can be at the east end, or the centre, and they don't have to have a spire, nor indeed a churchyard (as in many urban chapels). So do the underlying fundamental organizational principles (the ditch with at least one gap, in the case of henges; and the east–west alignment, in churches) suggest that these places were home to broadly similar rituals?

Can a small gathering of people, maybe for a jumble sale or coffee morning, in a local non-conformist chapel in, say, Glasgow, be compared with the Coronation service in Westminster Abbey? Do they have any similarities, apart from the basic beliefs of the two Churches? To my mind, there are precious few – and in some respects the underlying dogma or belief system is irrelevant. The Glasgow gathering is about families living nearby, whereas the Coronation is ultimately about the government of Britain: the chapel get-together has nothing to do with government, nor that at the Abbey with ordinary families. Put another way, their perceived similarities are irrelevant and conceal some very real differences. And I suspect the same can be said for henges.

Although I haven't discussed the rituals that took place at Stonehenge in any detail, I think their scale and complexity should now be apparent. It's the other end of the ceremonial spectrum, the Glasgow chapel end, that concerns me now. One place stands out. The site in question was dubbed by the press 'Seahenge' and the name has stuck, despite the fact that there was no encircling ditch with a gap. So, strictly speaking, it is not a henge at all. But I don't think that matters: it's circular, of the right period and includes many features found in henges. However, as I'm trying to escape the ties of unnecessary definition, I won't take that argument any further.

The Holme-next-the-Sea timber circle, as Seahenge is more correctly known, was excavated under very difficult circumstances: a highly hostile environment, together with a few persistent and rather strange protesters.[3] But it was promptly published,[4] and to a superb standard, and is now on display for all to see in King's Lynn Museum, where it has been magnificently (and very accurately) re-created, using the original, conserved timbers. If ever a site was rescued from destruction by the forces of nature and human ignorance, this was the one. And we have learned so much from it. To this day, I sometimes think I can hear Bronze Age people saying 'thank you' to the team who saved their site for posterity.

This book is about home, families and communities, so I do not want to get too heavily involved with ritual and ceremony, which I have already discussed in some detail for Etton. But I do think it's important to point out that small-scale, sometimes intimate, family-based ceremonies continued to take place in the later Neolithic and Bronze Age, long after the much earlier causewayed enclosures had gone out of use. In other words, the nearly two millennia from around 3400 to 1500 BC were not just the era of the mega-sites: the Stonehenges and Aveburys of this world. Even in those very early times, smaller, more intimate gatherings were taking place. Britain was slowly growing in complexity and diversity; indeed, things were less simple and straightforward than they are sometimes portrayed.

It is time to return to Seahenge, but first I should say that my role in the project was one of general dogsbody: I was wheeled out for press-releases, to deal with the media, and I provided moral support to Maisie and to Mark Brennand who were running the project. I would also take turns helping on the dig and I would often ferry timbers back to the base for study. Later, I was to become the main wood photographer. It was fascinating: I had become an observer, not just of the archaeology, but of the archaeologists and how they reacted to some sometimes horrible provocation. I suppose today you could say I was 'embedded' in the team, who were kind enough to make me very welcome.

Seahenge was located on the north Norfolk coast, near the small village of Holme-next-the-Sea. Its timbers have been dated to 2049 BC. This would place it somewhat later than Stonehenge, but as it was never a henge at all, I don't think that matters. If you crave a classification, I would call it a timber mortuary structure, of which several are known in eastern England. Indeed, we excavated a similar, if earlier, example a few hundred metres west of Etton, at Maxey, back in 1979.[5] Seahenge consisted of a roughly oval-to-round setting of 65 timbers arranged around an upside-down oak tree trunk, that protruded about a metre above the ground, with roots that resembled arms stretching out – as if pleading for help (see Plate 18). It was genuinely eerie, especially when I saw it out on the lonely beach for the very first time, back in the late spring of 1998.

We know the precise date of this extraordinary site, thanks to tree-ring dating (or dendrochronology, as it is known in archaeology). What is less known, but is even more important, is that close examination of the tree-rings revealed that the timbers had all been felled in the late spring or early summer (say, April to June) of the year 2049 BC. Now no carpenter or woodsman, in their right mind, fells trees at that time of year, when sap is running fast and the tree is in full growth.

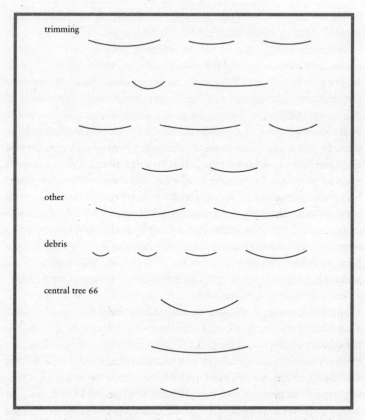

Fig. 5.1 A selection of outlines of tool cutting edges used to work timbers at Seahenge, Norfolk. Axe-marks found on the central tree (66) are shown at the bottom. This tree was surrounded by 65 oak posts. A few tool-marks from posts of the circle are also shown: some produced during the trimming of the timbers (top), and other major work (upper centre). Most of the tools used are axes. Smaller woodworking debris, mostly chips, was also found on site (lower centre); marks included those from two probable chisels (left) and one axe (right).

Being so wet, the timber would take far longer to season and would not be in a fit state to burn for well over a year. This suggests that the central upside-down tree and the posts surrounding it must have been felled for altogether different reasons. Who knows, maybe they wanted them to 'bleed' their sap?

The best explanation is that Seahenge was a small (roughly 6.5 metres across, 21 feet) burial site for a special person, whose corpse may well have been placed on the platform formed by the horizontal roots of the central oak. But we could only begin to understand this enigmatic site, rapidly being destroyed by the sea, if we took it apart and then looked at it *very* closely. It was positioned just above the low-tide mark and we knew it would be a difficult and often a very dangerous task. But eventually all the timbers were excavated and lifted, without so much as a nick or modern scratch. We transported the timbers to our barn at Flag Fen for 'first aid', and here every Bronze Age axe-mark was carefully recorded by Maisie, who came to the conclusion that a grand total of fifty to sixty axes had been used to fell and shape the timbers.[6] At the time nobody, not even prehistorians, seemed to realize how important that finding was, although now, almost ten years later, the penny is beginning to drop.

The variety of tool types used is remarkable at such an early period in the Bronze Age (see Fig. 5.1). They range from narrow chisels or gouge-like hand tools, through medium-sized 'workshop' axes, or choppers, to full-sized, heavy-duty felling axes. As one would expect, smaller tools tended to be used for trimming and finer work. But it's interesting to see that three distinctly different axes were used to work the central tree, once it had been felled. Sadly, we could find no complete tool-marks on its felled surface; these three axes might suggest that the tree had been modified in three distinct stages, by three separate carpenters at one time, or by one man with three axes. On the whole, I tend to favour the first option, as I cannot see why you would need to use different tools for the various jobs. The tree is also quite small and there is barely room for two men to work together safely. But these are just guesses.

Maisie's research into the tool-marks clearly showed that a very small – tiny even – Bronze Age religious site had been important enough to local communities to have attracted a minimum of fifty people, as it is almost inconceivable that, at such an early date in the Metal Age, anyone would own more than one, or at very most two, bronze axes. So let's say, for the sake of argument, that there were 50 people doing carpentry – and we know that it was taking place on site, because the excavations revealed hundreds of axed wood-chips. The men doing the wood-working must have been accompanied by other members of the community, not to mention the family of the man or woman whose dead body was being laid to rest within the circle.

It seems likely from what we have discovered on other sites of this period, that bodies were sometimes laid to rest through a process known as excarnation.[7] It's a process that was quite widespread until recently among certain tribal societies. It involves the exposure of a dead body away from public gaze, either high in mountains, or screened off in some way. At Seahenge the screening was provided by a tall circle of oak posts, set edge to edge. The corpse's flesh is removed by birds such as seagulls and buzzards (both of which would have been common on the north Norfolk coast). The scavenging birds were believed to have been removing the dead person's soul or spirit, along with their flesh. Such a rite would also explain why a body would have been 'buried' by being exposed to the air within the roots of the upside-down central oak tree.

We have already seen that prehistoric people's attitudes to death were very different to ours. Today, when somebody dies, or worse, is killed, they are buried rapidly, usually within a week of death. Sometimes burial may be delayed by a post-mortem or inquest, but in those cases the process is merely deferred – which makes it very much worse for the surviving close relatives, who cannot start the process of grieving. Indeed, we constantly hear bereaved people complain that their loved ones were 'taken away from them' when their bodies were suddenly destroyed by, say, an air crash, bomb or callous murderer who will not reveal where his victims were disposed of. I suspect that many of these problems are caused by the fact that the Church (and this applies to some other faiths, too) in the Middle Ages took possession of the rites of passage, following the introduction of the pernicious doctrine of 'original sin'. I do not want to go into early medieval history, but it was laid down in received dogma that everyone was born into the world a sinner and that those sins had somehow to be expiated. It was a clever idea, from the Church's point of view, because it gave them control of people's lives and subsequent destiny. So you had to be buried in consecrated ground, or else the Church (through Christ) could not intercede on your behalf, as a sinner, on the Day of Judgement. Similar, but less unforgiving, ideas surrounded the ceremonies of the other rites of passage: birth (the Churching of women, baptism), puberty (confirmation) and marriage.

In prehistoric times, families and their communities still retained control over all aspects of their lives, including the big personal events. Accordingly, the social processes that followed death were quite extended. I'm not saying here that this was a deliberate attempt to give people time to grieve, but experience would soon have shown that it worked. People felt better if they could gradually accommodate their minds and emotions to the idea that someone they loved very dearly had moved on. This might help explain why the processes of transition from this world to the next were so drawn out. We see this at Stonehenge, where bodies were transferred from the realm of the living, at Durrington Walls, then along the Durrington Avenue down to the River Avon; thence onto a boat, or raft, and a choppy length of the River Avon, to Bluestonehenge where all would disembark for the final procession along the Avenue to the Stones themselves.

Local communities could not afford either the resources or the land to erect complex processional ways, or shrines, like those around Stonehenge. So they did things differently, but the end results were probably much the same. Most Neolithic ritual sites involve movement or transportation; both in their use and creation. And this does not apply just to Britain: in Brittany, for instance, there are many examples of huge stones being moved from distant quarries. The best-known examples are the so-called 'Bluestones' at Stonehenge, which were transported to the site from a known source in the Preseli Hills of south-west Wales.[8] It has been suggested, quite reasonably, that the source of these rocks was somehow sacred, but I believe there is more to the idea than that alone: surely the physical journey made by the rocks was somehow linked in people's minds to the symbolic journeys made by the spirits of their loved ones.

The quarries rocks come from can be identified by clever geologists equipped with high-powered microscopes. It's much harder to do precisely the same thing with trees, but we are not completely lost. Examination of the quite wide growth-rings of the trees used to build

Seahenge suggests that they had not been growing anywhere near the sandy dune landscape of the North Sea foreshore. The reason for this is simply that sand dunes are very low in nutrition and the salt spray off the sea does not encourage sturdy trees; the ground water in the area, too, is salty and again trees like oak, ash and beech don't like this. The tree-ring specialists reckoned that the Seahenge timber had grown well back from the foreshore, on the higher, drier and more sheltered land 2 or 3 miles from the low-lying coastal plain. We cannot be certain whether they chose trees that were growing as close to the site as possible, or whether distance was no object, but we do have something else to guide us.

The central tree had had two stout 'loops' carved into its trunk. Through one of these we found a length of twisted rope still attached. The rope was made from honeysuckle and it had clearly been used to tow the heavy (2.5 tons) tree from the felling site to the foreshore, because the bark on the underside of the trunk had been entirely worn away and the sapwood beneath had been scraped and scratched. Eventually it took a 20-ton machine to lift it from the ground, to transport it to the conservation site (see Plate 19). When we dragged a similar, but admittedly lighter (1.5 tons), tree from out of the wood where it was felled, all we managed to do in the process was slightly scrape and muddy the bark. Personally, I'm in little doubt that the Seahenge oak had been dragged at least 5 miles and across some rough terrain. Sand dunes are far less abrasive than rock.

From our own experiments with honeysuckle ropes, rollers and movable wooden rails it's quite possible to move a heavy tree with a relatively small number of people: two dozen fit men would probably have been sufficient to move the Seahenge central tree.[9] But it was not as simple as that, because it is highly unlikely that the task would be approached as a normal, everyday job around, say, the farm. It seems reasonable to me that the main central tree, and the 60-odd timbers used to construct the solid ring of oak around it, were probably moved through the countryside together, maybe in some sort of ceremonial procession. This would certainly fit better with what we are beginning to deduce from other sites, such as Stonehenge. If that were the case, then our two dozen tree-movers could easily be doubled.

Our experiences would suggest that the moving of so many trees over, say, 5 miles could not have been done in much under five days. And even a small workforce of around 50 people would need food and water and somewhere dry to sleep at night. Presumably all of this would have been provided by members of their families. Again, it's worth reiterating that we should not view the moving of these trees as a 'normal' task in any way. It was an act of reverence that celebrated a person's life and that of their family. Its purpose was to bring people together and if the man-handling of the trees would have involved a minimum of a hundred people (50 workers and 50 supporters), it's not unreasonable to suppose that another hundred could have attended as invited guests, or as an assembled congregation of supporters. This figure accords remarkably well with what we have already learned from Maisie's examination of the tool-marks. One or two hundred people could 'inhabit' the ground around the small timber circle, as we discovered when we made the Seahenge documentary film for Channel 4, where there was a team of archaeologists, a platoon of army cadets, local volunteers, not to mention the TV cameramen, sound recordists, production assistants and the catering crew. There must have been 150 people on site. I do, however, think it would be stretching the evidence to suggest that the carpenters and the tree-movers, together with their supporting families, were all separate groups of people. In those days, if not today, men were capable of multi-tasking. So I think that a gathering of five hundred would have been too large. Everything suggests that the truth probably lay closer to half that number.

Now a footnote: shortly after we filmed at Seahenge, Maisie and I went to the funeral of a good friend. The lady in question was highly regarded and much loved in our village and she was given a full Fenland funeral. The village street was blocked off (unofficially, by tractors) as the coffin was carried (by eight men) to the small parish church. There wasn't room inside, so we stood in the churchyard, along with, I counted, two hundred other people. I remember thinking that this gathering was of the same scale as Seahenge. The deceased came from a large family, most of whom were there. So it was essentially a family gathering, but other members of the community came along to pay their respects. Afterwards, there was a large party in the village hall. Admittedly, it was tea and cakes (possibly alcohol in the Bronze Age), but I could see several youngsters giggling and flirting, and their farmer fathers were anxiously discussing the price of wheat, as the harvest was approaching. This reminded me that family gatherings rarely have a single purpose; other things will always be happening on the fringes.

In what one might term the Age of Stonehenge, it was not just the massive monument complexes that existed to keep communities together. As time passed, the number of smaller centres and shrines grew, and this surely has to have been a response to the growing population and the increasing development and 'filling-out' of the landscape, which included proliferation of new settlements and the gradual appearance of the first field systems, which began to be laid out in eastern England at more or less the same time that places like Stonehenge and Avebury were starting to decline. As we saw earlier, this was all part of a general shift in economic activity down into the lower-lying fertile plains of the river valleys. It was at ceremonies at these centres – large and small – of what I have called the Old Order that people did the other things that are essential to human life: they prospected for partners from outside the immediate family, they brought in new blood-lines for their livestock and they would have exchanged grain and seed to ensure the genetic health and diversity of their crops and animals. You cannot live or farm in complete isolation. As someone who runs a so-called 'closed' flock, to protect my sheep against easily preventable problems, such as foot-rot, I know only too well that from time to time I have to introduce fresh blood-lines. In our case, we do this by buying in top-quality replacement rams. But there is nothing new here: it's part of a process that has been going on for thousands of years.

OF PEOPLE, SYMBOLS AND THINGS

Man-made objects are never just functional. Take something as ordinary as a hammer or a screwdriver: these items have to be sold, so they must appeal to the buyer; often today they carry prominent branding. Even home-made tools have to look good. I remember inspecting the barrel-making tools of a master cooper when I worked in a traditional brewery in the late 1960s, and being astonished at their workmanship. I now appreciate that those tools, which the cooper had made for himself, were also symbols of his skills as a craftsman. In other words, they were about far more than wood-working alone.

Sometimes the symbolic power of objects can be raised hugely in our minds and our emotions. Even though I do not believe in the existence of God or the Divine, I don't think I could ever bring myself to smash a chalice or an altar cross with a sledge-hammer. I'm certainly not a fervent royalist, but even so, I would never express my views with a felt-tip pen across a portrait of the Queen. These, of course, are conditioned responses, but that does not make them any the less real. What I'm saying is that symbols have a practical effect on our lives; they are not just expressions of abstract concepts. And of course the symbols that mean the most to us are those that refer to close family members: a baby's first shoes, a child's paintings, a mother's wedding-ring, a grandfather's medals. It's when symbolic objects can be linked to an individual that they become most powerful.

The medieval Church understood this very well. Sacred relics could draw huge crowds to view them. There must, for example, have been enough fragments of the 'True Cross' in circulation in the Middle Ages to build a small ship; and as for the Turin Shroud, we know it was not alone: there were others like it. And then there were what one might term the secondary symbolic objects, such as gifts and tokens acquired on long pilgrimages to view these venerated relics. Symbolic meanings can change, too. So a treasured token bought at great cost on pilgrimage can become symbolic of a particular person's piety; then, possibly after that person's death, it becomes, especially in the family's eyes, a symbol of the whole person, rather than of their beliefs alone.

Objects can be symbols of their owner's power or prestige. The best-known examples are, of course, the Crown Jewels, which express a vast array of symbolic values. With military men, their smartest 'dress' swords were of great importance and can still be found proudly displayed on the walls of state rooms in grand houses right across Britain. These spaces were laid out to impress visitors and they became, in effect, shrines devoted to a particular family's glorious past. The items displayed in them were, of course, symbols of individuals' rank and achievement, though as time passed, individuality became less important than the family. But such things can be more personal too. My grandfather served with distinction in the trenches of the Somme and his shooting-stick (which, younger readers may not know, was a walking-stick-cum-seat) is still fondly preserved in his memory, because he used to carry it with him every time he 'went over the top' into the hell of enemy machine-gun fire.

From earliest times, the Church has banned the burial of objects in Christian graves, in the belief that every human is equal in the eyes of God. So if all documents had been wiped out in the ultimate nuclear holocaust, an archaeologist in the distant future, excavating graves in a churchyard, might come to the conclusion that the 20th and 21st centuries were times of remarkable social equality. But of course we know they were not. Far from it: if anything, social disparity is growing. So we must beware of taking symbols at their face value: they can often express a wished-for ideal, rather than reality itself.

And this brings me back to the Amesbury Archer, who was buried with so many fabulous objects. We have already considered the Beakers, but what about those two beautiful stone wrist-guards, the delicately worked arrowheads and the three copper daggers? And bear in mind this grave dates to the very beginnings of metalworking – a time when it is unusual to find one, let alone three, daggers in a grave. What are those objects telling us?

The answer to that question is not simple, but it's important because the 'message' concealed within objects buried in prehistoric graves was not always the same. Like the monuments they built and frequently modified, the beliefs that people held were in a state of gradual evolution. Attitudes to religion, death and the afterlife were changing with ever-increasing speed, as the population grew and the landscape developed. As modern excavation has become more detailed and sophisticated, we can now map the partition of the landscape at a local level. This work has revealed substantial earthwork boundaries between neighbouring communities, and increasingly, too, sub-division within those communities.[10] Most often, the latter is expressed in the layout of fields and the various tracks and droveways which were used to parcel them up.[11]

We see the sophistication and complexity of ideology starting to gather pace at Stonehenge. Whereas in earlier Neolithic times the dead were buried in communal tombs near the settlements where they had lived their lives, by 3000 BC burial rites had changed. Between about 3000 and 2400 BC most communities opted for cremation, and the ashes of many of the most influential (we assume) were actually buried within the area later taken up by the great stones at Stonehenge. It's not a well-known fact, but the site became Britain's largest prehistoric cremation cemetery, with a current total of 63 known cremations.[12] So these people were laid to rest away from their communities. Then, after 2400 BC, cremation slipped from favour and we see a return to burial, often under barrows and often, too, accompanied by objects. The Amesbury Archer is a case in point.

The symbolic complexity increases too, because the period of transition between cremation and the resumption of barrow burial was the time when the Avenue, the Durrington Walls settlement and henge were all in use. The later Beaker barrows were all arranged around the edges of the so-called 'Stonehenge Basin', looking down on the Stones. Indeed, barrows continued to be erected there well into the Early Bronze Age, after Beakers had gone out of use. So the funeral rites of people buried in the outlying barrows must have involved processions along the Avenue and river, much as before, but then their bodies were transported an even greater distance, out to the barrows that still grace the skyline – itself, surely a highly symbolic action. But none of this was happening near the settlements, where the people had lived out their lives, and where their families had now to spend time grieving.

This paradox is, however, more apparent than real. For a start, the vast majority of the population were not buried in smart barrows overlooking Stonehenge. Instead, they were laid to rest in cremation cemeteries or their ashes were inserted into earlier barrows close by their settlements. But the point I'm trying to make is that it is now possible to separate different aspects of the symbolic rites of passage: transport from the village, procession to the Stones, procession to the barrow, burial. Presumably the objects buried in the grave would also have been the objects of smaller rituals in the days leading up to the burial. Certainly the Beakers buried with the Amesbury Archer appear to have led very dissimilar 'lives'. Everything would have been steeped in symbolism. We cannot be certain, for example, that all of the cremations found at Stonehenge were of complete bodies. Maybe a few bones, or pyre ashes, were kept at home and buried nearby. Maybe certain objects that could be closely identified with the dead person also remained at home. Who knows, but perhaps the Amesbury Archer owned another set of fine wrist-guards which were left hanging in pride of place, back in the village? Something similar might well account for his son or brother's otherwise unusual lack of grave-goods.

So to return to my earlier question, what are those objects telling us? Essentially they are about identities of individuals and their families, yet those identities also changed as time passed, like those crossed swords one sees hanging in the halls of country houses. But symbolism does not change through the passage of time alone. Place is important too. We saw this very vividly with the funeral of Princess Diana. When her coffin was in Westminster Abbey, she was the much-loved 'property' of the vast majority of the nation. Then she took that ceremonial journey along the M1 into Northamptonshire. Next the hearse entered the gates of her family home, which closed firmly behind it, excluding the television cameras. And the scale and nature of the symbolism changed profoundly too. We, the Great British Public, were pointedly excluded from the grand stately home, because the funeral had now become a family affair.

At Stonehenge I suspect something similar happened when the body was taken away from the Stones and was moved off to the barrows on the horizon, or indeed, in Amesbury. In the case of less grand barrow burials nearer the community, I suspect the private farewells may have taken place earlier, maybe as the body was removed from the family home. This would have been the time when the carefully collected offerings were placed on the bier or coffin. What we don't know (and possibly never will) was the atmosphere that prevailed at these ceremonies. Clearly, the most directly affected must have been deeply grieving, but what about the rest? Were those Beakers placed on the bier in sadness, or was it like the return from the graveyard at a New Orleans jazz funeral, with the congregation rejoicing that the deceased was now in a better place and celebrating their life with music and dance? I think it's important to stress that we must not assume that ancient attitudes were necessarily the same as ours today: this was, after all, a very, very long time ago.

Again, viewed from four millennia later, the situation between about 3000 and 2000 BC was evolving, but not necessarily steadily nor consistently. We must bear in mind that nobody was dictating 'the direction of travel'. Had one been living at the time, the rites would have seemed permanent: rooted in the very mists of family history. Their purpose was, after all, to provide a core of stability in a changing world. It is also worth restating that these increasingly sophisticated practices and beliefs were created and adopted by ordinary people, living day-to-day lives. Yes, I'm sure that innovations – metalworking is the obvious example – were introduced from outside, but they were modified by the families and people of local communities to fit their own circumstances. Nothing, and I must keep stressing this, was being imposed on them 'from above'.

THE ARCHAEOLOGY OF CHANGE

The Stonehenge Riverside Project has demonstrated very clearly that the millennium and a half leading up to 1500 BC was a time of population growth and social evolution. It was also a crucially important period for the development of the British landscape.[13] Then everything changed, and so far as we can tell, that change was rapid and permanent, which is why I have referred to it as a revolution, indeed, *the* Domestic Revolution. But it's one thing to make sweeping statements; quite another to back them up. So I want to say a few words now on how prehistorians approach the problem of change: how we see it and how we estimate its speed, or pace.

Now I need hardly add that it would be very much more straightforward if we had historical records to guide us, such as the Bayeux Tapestry or Domesday Book. When we take the archaeological evidence on its own, we can discern general trends, but it's far harder to pin down actual events with absolute certainty – even something as crucial as the site of the Battle of Hastings.[14] We also know that Norman-like castles were being built before 1066: how do you prove on the ground that a Saxon landowner had been replaced by a

Norman? All we can say is that some time around the latter part of the mid-11th century there was a dramatic increase in both church and castle building, and that many substantial Saxon cathedrals were replaced by even larger Norman buildings – as at Canterbury itself.[15] From an archaeological perspective, there can be little doubt that someone or something is out to make a mark on the landscape and impress the population. Maybe the fact that the basic settlement pattern and farming practices remained substantially unaltered throughout the conquest period, and later, might indicate rapid top-down change, but it would be difficult to go much further, without some additional, independent evidence.

There are also problems with timing and chronology. There are two types of archaeological dating. The best known is illustrated by radiocarbon, but there are other techniques that can provide independent or 'absolute' dates, which are usually expressed as a range of years, such as 2470–2280 BC for the Amesbury Archer. Tree-ring dates can be even more precise, as we saw in the case of Seahenge, where it was possible to narrow the date down to months. The so-called 'absolute' dates provided by scientific techniques, such as radiocarbon and dendrochronology (and many more), have truly revolutionized archaeology, but you have to be very careful that the material you are dating does indeed relate to the event you are interested in. A radiocarbon date from an old gatepost from the field where the Battle of Hastings took place, for example, would probably turn out to be Victorian, not Norman.

Conventional, or 'relative', archaeological dates are very good at showing how styles of pottery or metalwork changed over time, but they have their limitations, too. The technique has its roots in Victorian times, and ultimately, like so many other aspects of the modern world, owes a great debt to Darwin's ideas on evolution. Essentially, relative dating is about evolving styles and technology. So early phonographs were housed in large mahogany Edwardian-style cabinets. Later, as the technology changed we see the appearance of lighter, more portable sets; meanwhile, larger systems continued in use, but were less ornate. You can see similar things happening with pottery shapes and decoration, both today and in prehistory. Beakers, for example, marked a step change, but then they continued to develop into new styles, which were clearly Beaker in inspiration, for several centuries thereafter.

The next step has been to combine relative and absolute dating, so that we can pin down with far greater precision the different stages in, say, the evolution of a particular style of pottery. At this point I can imagine many readers are laying their books aside and are muttering: 'Very interesting, but so what?' My response is that this quiet transformation of archaeological dating, which has been happening over the past thirty to forty years, has enabled us to start writing meaningful prehistoric narratives. When I started studying archaeology in the 1960s, British prehistory was not so much a coherent story, as a succession of different pottery styles, which could be linked (in the Bronze Age) to barrows and (in the Iron Age) to hillforts. It was a case of: 'These things have been found in these places', but little could be said about the people of the time, nor of their economies. In an attempt to rebalance this 'material-world' view of the distant past, new styles of pottery, for example, were seen as being introduced by waves of invaders, some of them with names, like the Celts. As I recall, there were believed to have been four, possibly even five, waves of incomers to Britain in the Iron Age alone. It's easy to scoff now, but these were genuine attempts to inject a little humanity, a little relevance to modern life, into a subject that was obsessed with objects, seemingly for their own sake.

The other modern development, which again has been happening for thirty to forty years, has been the rise of landscape archaeology. This approach deliberately sets out to study a group of sites and the way they relate to each other and the surrounding landscape, through time. Its aim is to paint a dynamic, rather than a static, picture, which has only become possible as techniques of dating, both relative and absolute, have improved. It has been a dynamic process, in more ways than one. Now it goes without saying that landscape archaeology is expensive and it would be impossible to treat the entire surface of Britain in this way. But it is becoming increasingly apparent through large landscape projects – such as that at Stonehenge, our own work in the Fens, and other big or long-term projects in the Thames and upper Nene valleys, on Salisbury Plain and on major infrastructure schemes, like the Channel Tunnel Rail Link – that there was a profound change at the close of the Early Bronze Age, around 1500 BC. It was a change, moreover, that seems to have taken place right across Britain, as the saying goes, from Land's End to John o' Groats.

Prehistorians have recognized that the changes were widespread and significant for a long time, which is why they are taken to signal the end of the Early Bronze Age and the start of the Middle Bronze Age. But it's worth noting here that these terms don't all convey equal weight. I would defy most archaeologists, for example, to define precisely where on their sites the Middle and the Late Bronze Age transition took place. The same can be said for the change from Bronze to Iron Age. These things are difficult to pin down in the field. But the end of the Early Bronze Age is different, because substantial sites, such as round barrows and henges, are abandoned. And the rites that replace them are very dissimilar. These New Order practices are often based around water, but they are also far smaller in scale and show clear links to aspects of ordinary domestic life. Gone for ever are the massive ritual sites and landscapes. By the end of the Bronze Age (say 1000 BC), Salisbury Plain around Stonehenge had already been partitioned into farmers' fields for many, many generations.[16] (See Fig. 5.2.)

The very earliest field systems had started to be built at about 2500 BC, and as we noted earlier, this was when Stonehenge entered its last, grandest and most elaborate stage of development. In a way I think it was emblematic of deeper social and economic transformations that were already under way: a final fling or flourishing of an earlier way of life. If the unexpressed social purpose of great ritual landscapes like Stonehenge was to keep dispersed communities together and in regular communication, that need became less pressing as time passed. This was when the landscape was developing, with new settlements and new roads to link people together. At the same time, smaller shrines, like Seahenge, grew up and provided local communities with religious centres. Often these new places were in surroundings that had been considered special for many generations; frequently, too, they were slightly removed from the day-to-day agricultural landscape: on poorer soils, or atop windy ridges or, in the case of Seahenge, in a marshy back-swamp behind coastal dunes. Archaeologists refer to these locations as liminal, from the Latin

Fig. 5.2 The Stonehenge landscape in the Late Bronze Age (1300–800 BC).
In the foreground is a farm and its fields; behind, in the open pastures, we
can see the mounds of round barrows which ceased to be used after 1500 BC
(reconstruction by Jane Brayne). Source: J. Richards, *The Stonehenge
Environs Project*, back cover (English Heritage, London, 1990).

limen, meaning a boundary. But they were not just on the edges of
good land, their liminality extended to people's imaginations: they
were seen as being 'removed', on the edge between our world and
that of the ancestors. It was for reasons of liminality, for example, that
dozens of early medieval monastic sites – large abbeys, small priories
and even hermitages – were located on isolated natural islands or by
rivers deep in the heart of the Fens. Even today places like the abbeys
at Crowland, Thorney or Ramsey have a remote, detached and cut-off
feel to them – especially on cold, foggy days in winter.

By 2000 BC, the large sites like Stonehenge had almost served their
original purpose. New, smaller sites were now proliferating. Again,
Seahenge was created at almost exactly this time, together with a
recently discovered burial mound immediately alongside it, which is
of precisely the same date. And similar things were happening right

across the British Isles at literally thousands of different places. These sites, however, were all based in the earlier tradition: to return to that earlier metaphor, they were the Early Bronze Age equivalents of the small Glasgow non-conformist chapels and were linked to the great places by certain common themes: most were circular, some had entrances or portals aligned with the sunrise or sunset at the solstice, and many of the barrows contained burials accompanied by Beakers, or other styles of complete pottery vessels, and occasionally, too, items of metalwork, such as daggers, axes or earrings. Cremations in urns were often placed around the edges of these barrows as so-called 'secondary' burials.

The proliferation of barrows and henges continued after 2000 BC and into the latter part of the Early Bronze Age. But then, quite suddenly around 1500 BC, everything changed. Viewed from some three and a half millennia later, it's as if somebody threw a big switch. As I see it, this was the pivot-point that marked the transition from an initial, or pioneering, phase of British prehistory, to an entirely new era. It would be tempting to call this new time the modern era, but I think that would be to underplay the very real changes that took place from AD 1550, in post-medieval times: developments that saw the emergence of truly modern agriculture and industry. So I prefer a less loaded term. What I'm calling the Domestic Revolution of 1500 BC signalled the transition from the Pioneering to the Developed phase of British prehistory and later, of course, of British history.

I see the Pioneering phase of British prehistory as starting at the end of the Ice Age, with the arrival of new communities who lived often remarkably settled lives, at places like Star Carr and Howick. From just before 4000 BC the pace of pioneering picks up with the arrival of farming. With gathering pace we are witnessing here the development of the British landscape and its essential infrastructure of roads, tracks, settlements and latterly of fields, too. Instead of being placed on their own, out in wild, open countryside, the great ritual and ceremonial sites slowly start to be incorporated within much larger, developed landscapes. Had the people who attended and used these sites realized it, those slowly encroaching drystone walls and new hedgerows were shortly to signal the end of these ancient places of ceremony and ritual; but just as strong pre-Christian themes can still

be detected in the calendar of the modern Church (the two main festivals, Christmas and Easter, have good pagan antecedents), the new
Bronze Age rites also owed much to the past; but at the same time
they clearly expressed some new, and, for us, very informative ideas;
they give us clues as to where those ideas originated. It will come as
no surprise to discover that the sources of the radical rethinking that
went with the New Order were the family, the domestic world and the
community. In short, a new and more confident localism is starting to
emerge. Indeed, the scale of society, like that of the landscape itself,
had changed. These were the results, the outcomes, of fundamental
processes that had been under way since the introduction of farming,
and I need hardly add they were to prove irreversible.

THE DOMESTIC REVOLUTION
OF 1500 BC

Perhaps I had better begin this section with a concise summary of the
archaeological changes that I believe went with a period of quite rapid
social change, around 1500 BC. First, many forms of monument were
either abandoned, or were modified or ceased to be built. The most
important of these were various forms of henge and barrow. It is true
that many barrows continued to be used as places of burial, especially
for small secondary cremations, throughout the Bronze Age and even
into the Iron Age, but the fact remains that new barrows in the old
tradition ceased to be built and that other forms of burial began to
dominate. These included cremation cemeteries and both burials and
cremations in and around settlements. At roughly the same time, we
witness the appearance of the first water-based rites, where offerings
were deliberately deposited in rivers, lakes, marshes and other wet
places. This is also the period when we see the first widespread appearance of large metalwork hoards. Again, these are generally seen as
offerings, although some may also have been metalworkers' stocks of
scrap or traded metal. Personally, I doubt if the people concerned
would have drawn a hard-and-fast distinction between the two: the
clear – even rigid – distinction between practical and ritual is something which has arisen in modern times.

I'm still not absolutely clear about the duration of the Domestic Revolution. There are indications in tidal/coastal areas of South Wales for wetland offerings as early as 1700 BC.[17] And by 1300 BC, when Flag Fen appears on the scene, the process is fully under way. All in all, it would seem that the 'tipping point' would have been somewhere around 1500 BC, which also happens to be the conventional date for the end of the Early, and the beginning of the Middle Bronze Age.

In my view, the new social politics brought about by the Domestic Revolution was essentially to do with localism. With an established national network of roads and tracks, and with the landscape cleared of natural forest, woodland, heath, moor and scrub, people in different regions would have been in regular contact with each other. So it made sense to structure life around that simple fact. As it was now unnecessary to travel so far, people organized their communities around what lay closer to home: their families, their houses and their farms. They also probably paid greater attention to relations between neighbouring settlements and communities, many of which, of course, would have held their relatives. One of the aspects of the Domestic Revolution that surprised me when I began to research the topic was the frequency of seemingly long-distance contacts, which, as we have seen, extended back to earlier Neolithic times. By the latter part of the Bronze Age people were in regular touch across Britain and I suspect there were several cross-Channel voyages every day, weather permitting. Prehistoric Europe was becoming 'joined-up'.

We can see these emerging social networks being expressed symbolically in the new rites, which were far smaller in scale. The evidence suggests the gatherings were often family sized, probably involving dozens, rather than hundreds, of people. Indeed, I suspect, but it would be difficult to prove, that even a smaller congregation of the previous epoch, like that at Seahenge in 2049 BC, would have been larger than most of the ceremonies of the new era. But I also suspect that what they may have lacked in size, they made up for in regularity. Again, it is difficult to prove in absolute terms, but the sheer quantity of offerings found at sites of the New Order suggest regular, perhaps monthly or weekly, gatherings. Having said that, the ceremonies themselves were most probably shamanistic, and as such were very different from any later religious gathering; but at the same time, it is hard not to draw general parallels with regular services at parish churches. Essentially, both were about the solemnizing of family events (birth, marriage and death) and communal celebration of important times in the cyclical annual calendar (harvest festivals, and others at midwinter, spring and midsummer).

The new religious centres have been known about for some time, but they have only recently been subject to careful, modern excavation, and while I cannot pretend that we have 'cracked' all of their meaning, I do think we now understand some of their basic workings and the motives behind their creation. Indeed, I had the very good fortune to be closely involved with the discovery and excavation of one of the largest and best preserved of these new centres, at Flag Fen, Peterborough. Today the site sits on the fringes of an industrial suburb which was mostly constructed in the 1970s and '80s, as part of the new town. Peterborough was one of the second wave of post-war new towns, so its expansion was carefully controlled by a New Town Development Corporation who ensured that we were able to complete our excavations. Before a single brick was laid, the areas scheduled for development were comprehensively surveyed by the Royal Commission on Historical Monuments (now part of English Heritage).[18] Looking back on over forty years of near-continuous research, I'm now convinced that the RCHM survey was crucial to what happened later. Armed with its carefully considered conclusions, we were able to pick our targets and use our small workforce, and even smaller budget, to the maximum effect. Today, there is vastly more by way of facts and figures and statistics to help the planning of a new project, but it's the careful sifting of the essential from the inessential that is so often lacking. We were very lucky to have that report and my very battered copy still sits on my shelves in pride of place.

When we were discussing archaeological change (above p. 164), I mentioned that modern prehistoric narratives have been made possible by improved techniques of dating and what I called the landscape approach to archaeology. Flag Fen illustrates that approach very well, because it is not just a site on its own. It's an integral part of a changing ancient landscape, and to understand its many subtleties I shall describe it chronologically, as we excavated it, starting back in 1970.

We will work in the time-honoured archaeological fashion, from the known to the unknown. In this case that also saw us move from the dry, to the damp, to the very wet indeed. But like all landscape archaeology, it took time: almost thirty years from the first excavations to the last major published report.[19] And like other landscape projects, I'm glad to say that work continues and is still revealing extraordinary surprises, some of them, as we will see shortly, of truly international importance.

EXPLAINING THE FLAG FEN
LANDSCAPE: FROM THE KNOWN . . .

Our story begins in the summer of 1970. At the time I had been working for two years at The Royal Ontario Museum (ROM), Toronto. That museum had, and still has, an international reputation for archaeological research, but all over the world, and not in Canada alone. My boss was a remarkable and much-loved man called Doug Tushingham. Doug's links with Britain went back a long way and he knew most of the English Archaeological establishment, including another great name from the recent past, Sir Mortimer Wheeler. Sir Mortimer, even in his eighties, was a striking figure: tall, erect, with a wide-brimmed hat set at a jaunty angle, and his internationally famous military moustache. During the 1950s, together with its chairman, Dr Glyn Daniel, Sir Mortimer had been a key member of the massive hit BBC TV quiz series, *Animal, Vegetable, Mineral?* Both Sir Mortimer and Glyn were voted TV Personality of the Year – and on more than one occasion. Even in the years of *Time Team*'s greatest fame, archaeology has never had a bigger public profile.

Doug arranged for me to meet Sir Mortimer in his London office, where he quizzed me closely about my plans. I told him I had seen reports that large areas of rural landscape just east of Peterborough were going to be destroyed by the emerging new town and we planned to excavate ahead of them, with a team funded and run by the ROM. The project would have the full approval of the Commission of the New Towns and the then equivalent of English Heritage. A few years later, I would learn how to play these various bodies off against each other. I called it competitive funding and it certainly helped our finances when we needed the money most.

I suppose I must have sounded too earnest and serious, because when I had finished describing my plans the great man gave me quite a sharp pep-talk about the importance of involving the public: PR and Outreach we would call it today. He explained that a high public profile was going to become increasingly important and he urged me to think about an on-site display hut, or mini-museum, which we did manage to put together a couple of years later. He was quite right: that museum attracted newspaper and television reporters on days when other news was scarce. By the mid-1970s our dig at Fengate was becoming a household word. And why? I think it's rather like soap-operas: people like continuing stories. Big announcements are all well and good, but a sudden splash is soon over, whereas a slow-building narrative attracts loyal followers and with them comes money and, just as important, moral support, for those times when the going eventually gets tough.

With hindsight, I'm glad to say the project began quite slowly.[20] In our first season, 1971, the media spotlights were nowhere to be found. And to be honest, I did not need them. I was too busy trying to sort out the meaning of what we had found. At first I could not understand a series of parallel Bronze Age ditches that ran down to the edge of the then still-growing Fens. After another season, it became absolutely clear that these ditches were the boundaries of livestock droveways and the fields of pasture alongside them. At the time we were also developing methods of excavation that involved large earth-moving machines and the stripping of huge open-area trenches. They were exciting times and I managed to produce our first report in 1974 – in those days I did not sleep much.[21]

With the help of the new information from the excavations, I re-examined all the aerial photographs of the area and it became apparent that the newly revealed fields formed part of a larger system. Today, thanks to further research by a team from Cambridge University, it is now clear that there were many systems of Bronze Age fields along the dryland edges of the Peterborough Fens.[22] The same team has also found closely similar field systems in the valley of the River Ouse, closer to Cambridge, and others are known to the north, in south Lincolnshire.[23] And as I have suggested earlier, we now realize that there are broadly similar Bronze Age field systems right across most of lowland southern England.[24]

So how did these field systems 'work'? Like today, they would have varied from place to place, depending on the soil, drainage and aspect of the land. But from their layout, with distinctive corner entrances and double-ditched droveways, we can be reasonably certain that they were primarily intended for livestock – mostly sheep and cattle, to judge from the bones found in and around them. In our area we suspect that the ditches were accompanied by thorn hedges to make stock-proof barriers. The use of the fields may have been partly seasonal, with larger flocks and herds kept in them during the wetter months of winter, when livestock could not be grazed in the lush Fenland meadows, for the simple reason that they would have been flooded. I think it's no coincidence that the Fen-edge fields are located around the fringes of land that would flood in times of high rainfall. This would have been the most valuable land, and the fields were laid out to use it in the most efficient way possible. Farmhouses and small hamlets were distributed evenly throughout this landscape.

A similar pattern of dispersed settlement can be found in other fields of this and slightly later periods, which were generally smaller, and were not always entered at the corners. These fields were for crops, or more probably a mix of crops and livestock, and can be found, for example, on Salisbury Plain (see Fig. 5.2) and in large areas of upland Britain, including the moors of the south-west. At this time in the later 2nd millennium BC, settlements were generally quite small – say up to half a dozen houses; it was not until the Iron Age of the 1st millennium BC that we start to find the first villages. Sometimes, but by no means always, these would be protected by an outer wall or stockade. But again, we must be careful not to jump to the conclusion that an outer wall was necessarily built to keep people away. Very often, like so many town walls in the Middle Ages, they were built to look impressive and their fine, often tower-like gateways were intended to impress and attract, rather than deter.

It took a few years to come into focus, but by 1973 or '74 it was apparent that we were dealing with a fully developed Bronze Age landscape of enormous sophistication. At this stage, most of our research had been concentrated on the dryland edges of a large wet area, which later I was to call the Flag Fen Basin. Our first excavations were along the western edges of the basin in the suburb of Peterborough known as Fengate. We saw previously how this landscape had been laid out using earlier barrows and even a small henge (complete with its own 'mini-henge', see p. 148), as markers. If we assume that the barrows had served to parcel out the landscape, then the holdings, or properties they represented, must have kept the same boundaries for at least a millennium, if not longer. Again, this is not unusual and similar longevity has been demonstrated at towns like York and London, although at a much later period. As I noted in Chapter 4, however, it suggests social stability: you cannot maintain land boundaries over the generations unless your society is stable and people respect the rights of others not just to hold land, but to inherit it, too.

I would further suggest that towards the end of the Early Bronze Age (i.e. in the centuries leading up to 1500 BC), communities had acquired their stability through the pre-existing system, whose roots ultimately lay in Mesolithic times. Indeed, again as we have seen (p. 77), there are hints (and I wouldn't put it any more strongly than that) that the earliest Neolithic landscapes at Fengate were aligned on routes or trackways that survived from the Mesolithic.

I am sometimes asked whether the Neolithic inhabitants of Fengate made regular visits or pilgrimages to the great henge sites. I somehow doubt whether more than a handful would ever have gone to far-off Stonehenge, but we do know of extraordinarily elaborate complexes of henges nearer at hand, close by the Etton causewayed enclosure, at Maxey, in the Welland Valley, just half a day's walk north of Fengate.[25] Another huge site is coming to light on the outskirts of the Roman town of Durobrivae, a few miles to the west, on the modern A1. It is clear, however, that the landscape around Maxey was never intensively settled in Neolithic or earlier Bronze Age times and, rather like Stonehenge, seems to have been reserved for open grazing and ceremonial use. But after 1500 BC, all of that was to change – and again this recalls Stonehenge. Maxey takes its name from the Saxon word *Macuseige* (around AD 963) meaning 'island, or dry ground in marsh, of a man called Maccus'.[26] Taken together the evidence suggests that the sites on Maxey 'island' were a focus for pilgrimages from dispersed communities over, say, a 10–20-mile radius.

The older system in which a spread-out population were held together by the simple expedient of making regular visits to prestigious central locations seems to have worked. It also had the great merit of flexibility. So as time passed, people increasingly focused their attentions on barrows and other smaller shrines closer to where they lived. And I would suggest their visits to the great places of earlier centuries gradually became less frequent. But the all-important social stability persisted. Meanwhile, the landscape around them was growing in complexity: fields were being laid out, there was a growing trade in livestock over large distances and the social structure needed to support these developments was increasingly being provided by the network of communities themselves. Put another way, by 1500 BC there was no need to trek across huge distances: everything required for a full social and economic life could be found much closer to home. Writing about Stonehenge – a very different site in a very different landscape – Mike Parker Pearson puts it thus:

> By 1500 BC that [earlier] world had gone. Southern Britain was parcelled up by land boundaries dividing the communal grazing grounds into plots. Intensive arable farming and sedentary farmsteads were now a feature of economic life ... Economically, Wessex was out-matched for soil fertility . . . by the farmlands of eastern England in the lower Thames Valley, East Anglia and east Midlands. The centre of wealth and power shifted, and Stonehenge was left high and dry.[27]

But humans, like nature, abhor a vacuum, so what replaced the henges and barrows of what we might call the Old Order? And we found our own answer to that question, one foggy morning in early November 1982.

. . . TO THE UNKNOWN

Archaeologists had been aware for a very long time that there was a big difference between the religious rites of the Iron Age (800 BC– AD 43) and those of the earlier Bronze Age, the Age of Stonehenge or what I have called the Old Order. The later rites did not seem to have required elaborate stone-built shrines and very often took place near lakes, rivers or marshes. The best known of these wet sites is in Switzerland, just off Lake Neuchâtel, at a place called La Tène, where literally thousands of objects were placed in the waters between two timber bridges.[28] Many of these objects, especially a series of magnificent swords and their scabbards, gave the name of the site to the most important style of what has come to be known as pre-Roman Celtic Art.

But what was happening in those seven centuries between the Iron Age and the demise of the Old Order, around 1500 BC? Was Britain invaded by hordes of Celts from the continent? Was it they who brought these New Order rites to Britain? This was the accepted view when I was a student in the 1960s, although it must be said there were dissenting voices who urged caution. One of these was Professor Roy Hodson of the Institute of Archaeology (now University College) in London. Ironically, Roy is the leading British authority on continental Iron Age, but in the early 1960s he published two remarkably prescient papers which challenged the very idea of mass Celtic migrations.[29] And I'm delighted to say he has been proved right. It would now appear that the people we labelled as Celtic incomers were nothing of the sort.

By the end of the Bronze Age, which, to remind readers, was some seven hundred years after the events of the Domestic Revolution, the British landscape had continued to grow and develop. Field systems were now extensive, covering large areas of upland and lowland. Settlements had proliferated, and people were showing pride in their communities by constructing elaborately embanked hillforts on the highest ground above their farms and settlements in the valleys below. So even if there had been incursions from abroad, these are unlikely to have been mass attacks involving wholesale population change. Much later, in the more technologically advanced Viking era, the 'native' British population remained substantial, even in counties like Yorkshire and Lincolnshire, where large numbers of raids and landings took place.

The move away from barrows and large central shrines to smaller, more locally based religious centres, many of them involving water, was not confined to Britain alone. Similar changes can be seen across Scandinavia and much of northern Europe. The development of Bronze Age field systems does, however, seem to have begun earlier and been more extensive in Britain than on the continental mainland.[30] Some, but not all, of these New Order watery shrines and sacred places were used in the Iron Age alone, but a substantial number, too, have clear origins well within the Bronze Age – thereby effectively demolishing the argument that these new rites were brought to Britain by invading Celts. The place that demonstrates this continuity most clearly is Flag Fen, and it is a site which has kept me in gainful employment for some thirty years. It is time to return to that foggy morning in early November 1982.

The previous year, I had taken our team to Holland to learn how Dutch archaeologists managed to discover so many prehistoric sites below metres of accumulated peats and silts, which effectively hid them from conventional air-photographic surveys. They had come up with a technique they called 'dyke survey', where two individuals walked along the edges of drainage dykes looking at the wet mud that had been pulled out of them during their regular, usually autumnal, cleaning out. In the Fens we call the process 'slubbing out' and the mud is known as 'slub'. In Holland the authorities ensure that the dykes are kept full of water, as this prevents the peats from drying out and shrinking. In Britain we are less scrupulous (or more greedy) and keep our dykes dry. As a result, we can grow cereals, sugar beet and vegetables, which are all more profitable than dairy cows. But I wonder whether we will be quite so complacent in fifty years' time when the sea will inevitably break through the Wash banks and flood huge areas of Lincolnshire, Cambridgeshire, Suffolk and Norfolk, where the land surface is often well below high-tide level, even today. And of course the land surface is shrinking lower every year while the dykes are maintained so dry.

The policy of dry dykes makes dyke survey very much simpler, because buried land surfaces can be seen in cross-section in the ditch sides. The trouble is, being thus exposed, any waterlogged archaeological remains are likely to dry out and disintegrate. Unless something can be done about this desiccation, thousands of intact Bronze Age timbers at Flag Fen will have vanished, probably in the next half century. Indeed, many have vanished since we found the site, almost exactly thirty years ago.

Having seen the success of dyke survey in the Netherlands, we returned home and I immediately proposed to English Heritage that we should do something similar ourselves. They could see the urgency of the request, and to their great credit produced the necessary funds, then and there. The field phase of the project lasted from 1982 to 1986 and the full report appeared in 1993, but by then we were also heavily involved with our first, and possibly most important, discovery which we made within a few weeks of starting the new survey, in 1982.[31]

One of the reasons I was so keen to look along the sides of freshly machine-cleaned dykes out in Flag Fen was quite simply that the dry lands skirting the edges of the wet basin were, to put it crudely, crawling with Bronze Age archaeology. I had no idea what we might find out in the wet peats, but if any place in Britain stood a good chance of producing waterlogged Bronze Age remains, it had to be there. Then one day, just as we were starting the dyke survey, I happened to spot the jib of a rather aged dragline (a modified crane fitted with a toothed bucket) in the middle of the wettest part of Flag Fen.

I drove my Land-Rover along the high northern bank of the River Nene, which flows well above the surrounding fen at this point, then eased into four-wheel drive and took a smaller track down to the Padholme pumping station. I got out and looked along the Mustdyke, a medieval drain which the builders of the early 17th century had used as their main drain to the sluices and the pumps on the Nene Bank.[32] I walked along the drain to where the dragline was working, and although the teeth on the bucket had not produced a neat finish, I could clearly see on the dyke-sides the point where the later peats overlay the prehistoric land surface. The dragline had also just finished clearing reeds and slub from off a Roman road, the Fen Causeway, which we knew crossed Flag Fen at this point.

The dragline driver was a wonderfully laconic Fenman. I laboriously explained, using nice simple language, who I was and why I was interested in that particular stretch of dyke. When I had finished, he leaned back in his seat and pushed his cap to the back of his head:

'Thought I'd see you here before long . . .'

He then gave me a succinct account of my team's recent work at Fengate, which he had been following avidly in the press. Not for the first or last time in my life, I felt a bit of a fool. Smiling broadly now, he went on to explain who he was working for and their phone number in Crab Marsh, Wisbech. Two days later, Charly French was busily recording dyke-side profiles down by the pumping station, while far to the north I could just see the drag-line's jib as it came to the end of the drain. Meanwhile, I was helping a small group of us clean up the exposed Roman road, ready for an accurate drawing and photograph.

I think we had been working in the dyke for about a week when I stumbled across a piece of oak wood lying in the smelly, stagnant 'slub' at the lip of the dyke. I won't repeat the account of that discovery, but it was to have a profound effect. After a couple of seasons' additional work, it became clear that the piece of oak was from a timber structure that was superficially similar to the post-built timber bridges at La Tène, but this time the 'bridge' had never been raised above the ground, and was more like a causeway. The date of our site was Bronze Age (starting at 1300 BC), which made it significantly earlier than La Tène. Later we were to discover that it continued to be used throughout the Iron Age and just into the Roman period. (See Fig. 5.3.)

By the time we stopped for Christmas (1982), we had revealed a mass of prehistoric timbers that extended for some 80 metres (260 feet) along the dykeside. Then in subsequent years, we were to discover that the site consisted of two components: a massive causeway, about 8 to 10 metres wide, composed of five parallel rows of large posts that had been driven through the soft peats into the harder underlying Ice Age clays and gravels (see Plate 20). Between these posts the ground surface had been raised by laying successive layers of brushwood, tree trunks and split oak planks, to form a series of walkways, whose surfaces were made less slippery by frequently spreading sand and gravel, quarried from the higher, drier land at either end of its remarkable 1200 metre (4000 feet) length. From the outset we decided not to use terms like 'track' or 'causeway' when we realized the site was far more complex than that, and had been used for purposes other than

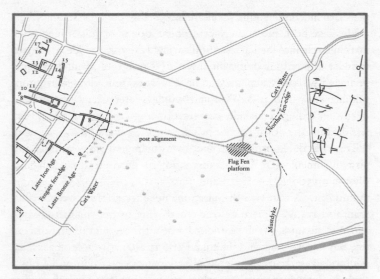

Fig. 5.3 A general plan of Bronze Age features at Flag Fen, showing the course of the post alignment from the fields on the dry land of Fengate (left) to Northey (right).

travel alone. So we opted for the rather unlovely but deliberately non-specific term, 'post alignment'. The post alignment had clearly been positioned to cross a narrow length of wet ground between two areas of dry land on the eastern (i.e. fenward) approaches to the Flag Fen Basin. So it may also have served as a marker, or possibly even as a defended boundary, against incursion from the east.

The second component of the site at Flag Fen, has proved harder to define than the post alignment. Again, we chose a non-specific term: the 'platform'. Essentially it consisted of layers of brushwood, planks and tree trunks that raised a dry platform on either side of the post alignment, which passed directly through it, but slightly off centre. It was a large platform, roughly oval in shape, measuring about 200 by 220 metres (4.4 hectares or just under 11 acres). Our original dyke-side exposure just before Christmas in 1982 is still the only complete cross-section through the platform, one that showed the spread of timber, wood and brushwood to have been continuous; but elsewhere there are indications that small areas, possibly pools or small ponds, might have been deliberately kept open. Along part of its north side there was clear evidence for a substantial revetment made up of tree trunks and planks laid at right angles to the edge, to form, in effect, a perimeter walkway, but we don't believe that this was necessarily continuous: it seemed to be absent from the southern end of the main dyke-side exposure, where the surrounding fen would have been less deep.

Tree-ring dates proved beyond any doubt that the platform and post alignment were built, and rebuilt, at precisely the same time (between 1300 and 900 BC) and must have formed part of the same monument. As that was the case, one might have expected the platform to have been placed at the centre of the post alignment, but it was not. Instead, it was positioned a couple of hundred metres from the alignment's eastern landfall, but in the deepest fen of all. This would suggest that whatever its purpose, the platform must have had something to do with water, which in this area was around a metre deep and would have been quite clear, as pollen was found from both the yellow and the white water-lilies, which don't grow in muddy or stagnant water.

If you look at a plan of Flag Fen it does seem rather less structured and more informally laid out than places of the Old Order, such as Stonehenge, or indeed the much smaller Seahenge. But first impressions can be misleading. Again, tree-ring studies have shown that maintenance was highly co-ordinated. Planks and larger timbers split from the same oak trees have been found at widely separated points along the alignment's length. This would suggest there was some kind of central depot or workplace where trees, brought in from outside (and again, we can be certain of this, because the growth-rings demonstrate that none of the Flag Fen oak timber was grown locally), were split and were then sent to where they were needed most. This would suggest that maintenance of the site was co-ordinated by a central, probably tribal or community-run, committee, or authority. At the later but broadly similar site at Fiskerton, near Lincoln, the controlling authority there was concerned with celestial observations, and concentrated repairs in years when there was a visible lunar eclipse; again, this harks back to the solsticial alignments of many Old

Order shrines and tombs.[33] The calculations were, however, very sophisticated and would have required knowledge that would have been rare, even today; this would in turn suggest that by the mid-Iron Age we are witnessing the appearance, at certain events and cere- monies, of religious or ritual specialists.

There can be little doubt, however, that the scale of operations had altered profoundly. For a start, their tree-rings have shown that all of the many thousands of timbers at Flag Fen had been grown in the east of England – I would guess within 10 or 20 miles of the site. The con- trolling group would almost certainly have been locally based, and it is interesting that the line of the posts actually follows an earlier, pos- sibly later, Neolithic, land division, because a shallow ditch of that date was found far beneath the posts at its Fengate, or western, land- fall. This suggests that much earlier property boundaries were being respected. It also argues strongly against any suggestion that a new group of people had moved into the area and were now running things.

Flag Fen may be the largest site of its sort yet found, but it is by no means unique, although its early start date (1300 BC) is quite unusual. Most similar post alignment and water-based shrines tend to be Iron Age, rather than Bronze Age. We know of no other large post align- ments in the Peterborough area, but others are known in the southern Fens, including four near Ely and one near Haslingfield (Cambridge- shire).[34] In the northern Fens, several are known in the valley of the River Witham, just outside Lincoln, including the excavated example, just mentioned, at Fiskerton.[35] Moving further afield, others are now known at Beccles, in the Waveney Valley flood-plain, Suffolk, and as far away as Eastbourne, in Sussex, at Caldicot in the Severn Levels and at Etton in the Trent Valley, Nottinghamshire (not to be confused with Etton, Cambridgeshire).[36]

There can be little doubt that these New Order sites were focused around the idea of journeying and of travel. But they were not set aside from daily life in the manner of sites like Stonehenge, or indeed Maxey, where the landscapes of ordinary life, field systems for example, were deliberately kept at bay. Many of them, including Flag Fen, also played an integral, even essential, part of daily life. Put another way, in the New Order there was far less of a clear distinction between what one might call the sacred and the secular. Distinctions were becoming blurred. But was this an indication that religion and the supernatural were somehow becoming less important, that British society was becoming more secular, just like today?

I'm in no doubt about the answer to that question, which is a simple no. If anything, what we might loosely term 'religion' was increasing in importance. But instead of being removed from daily life to somewhere less accessible, more and more remote, more liminal, it was brought closer to home, because that was where it was needed. I think it would be a huge mistake to suppose that people's interest in, and concern for, their ancestors and the afterlife was growing weaker. If anything, the opposite was happening: I would suggest that spiritual, or ideological, forces were being invoked with increasing frequency, and indeed regularity, to add authority to the ordinary laws, customs and practices of daily life, which were becoming increasingly complex and widespread, as communities right across Britain grew in size and numbers. So the return of religion back to the people who owned it might be seen as a sign that the daily management of farms, families and settlements in an increasingly populated landscape was becoming more complex and needed greater guidance and control. But again, that control was being self-generated by the people concerned. At the risk of sounding repetitive: it was not being imposed, either from outside, or from the top-down, and in that respect I think it possible to see very broad parallels with the Protestant Reformation of much more recent times – although I would not like to push that analogy too hard.

So to sum up: landscapes and communication were becoming increasingly developed; at the same time, communities and the population were growing, and all of this needed to be co-ordinated, if intercommunal strife were to be avoided. That, I believe, was the principal, if unexpressed, social purpose of the locally based religions of the New Order. People needed to live together in some sort of harmony, and again, there are no grounds to believe these new measures were imposed on them. Taken as a whole, the archaeological evidence strongly suggests that the changes were successful and that British life – in the late 2nd and throughout the 1st millennium BC – was generally harmonious. In the next chapter I will examine what lay behind these new rites and how they might have operated. Then Chapter 7 will return to the people themselves and see how they led their lives in a world that was growing increasingly dynamic and, latterly, towards the end of the 1st millennium BC, unstable.

6

The New Order

(1500–1000 BC)

One of the reasons I enjoy prehistory is that it allows one to look at long-term processes. Very often these seem to be inspired or orchestrated in ways that appear to transcend the people and societies in question. It is, of course, very difficult to identify such long-term processes in one's own time and culture, but I believe the rise of secularism in western Europe is a case in point. Can it ultimately be pinned on Darwin and *On the Origin of Species* (1859), as Christian fundamentalists and Neocons in America would have one believe, or does it have roots that go much further back, to Galileo and the Renaissance in general? Not being an expert on the topic, I'm in no position to decide, but my archaeologist's instincts tell me that such profound, ground-swell movements are rarely the result of a single book or scientific discovery. Such things may well have hastened the process, but they have to appear on the scene at a time when the public mood is ready to accept them. Had Darwin published *The Origin* in 1359, I doubt if it would have made much of an impact – and not just because people had bigger problems (like the Black Death) to contend with.

One of the long-term processes that fascinates me is our ability to create abstract symbols from everyday things. I regard it as a very important part of the human condition, because it allows new customs that transcend individual lives to come into existence and then to persist. The persistence is made possible by the continued existence of the object. An inspired example of this is the use of wine and bread to celebrate Holy Communion; this symbolically rich act of faith is centred around a glass of wine and a plate of wafers, and I often wonder whether the Church could have maintained such a firm grip on society in the Middle Ages without these things. It's worth bearing in mind here, that 90 per cent of medieval church congregations would have been illiterate, but each week they would have seen the objects and the actions of the celebrant at Holy Communion. The fact that the priest was speaking in Latin, a language they probably did not understand, did not matter, because they had learned, often at school, what the objects on the altar symbolized. I'm quite certain that similar object-based symbolic rituals were an important and enduring aspect of the rituals of the New Order.

THE EMERGENCE OF OBJECTS AS PORTABLE SYMBOLS

So objects have always played an important part in symbolic acts, and I believe we can see similar processes in operation, as regards certain archaeological objects and the way they were repeatedly deposited in water. Of course, we will never understand the *precise* meaning these things once possessed, but we can make some informed guesses. To return to the example of the Communion objects, the paten (plate) and the chalice (wine glass): we could reasonably infer they were used in a very important sacred meal, but of course we could never have guessed that the heart of the meal's symbolic menu was the body and blood of the Son of God.

We saw how symbolic rites could evolve in successive deposits within the enclosure ditch segments at Etton. The lowest formed a series of quite distinct 'statements', such as an inverted pot, a skull, a broken quern-stone, each one separated from the next by a clear space. Those initial offerings were then carefully filled in and I think were marked in some way, too, so that when a generation later people came to re-open the ditch and place a new set of offerings in it, they did not disturb the earlier ones – maybe the marker was something quite simple, like a thick layer of leaves. The second set of offerings was less clear cut. There were spaces between them, but they were not always easy to spot. Again, they were carefully filled in, so that the final (surviving) deposit is quite high in the ditch in-filling. By this time the gaps had completely gone, but one can detect from their arrangement that they do indeed relate to what had gone before – yet

I doubt if we would have recognized them for what they were had we not discovered the earlier offerings.

Certain themes could be seen to persist in the ditch deposits, such as the use of broken quern-stones, food debris, potsherds and round objects (including that fossil sea-urchin) close to the causeways. The general form of the offerings, too, remained the same: a fairly tight linear or band-like arrangement along the centre of the ditch. I'm fairly convinced that these offerings are about family histories or legends, and they quite possibly celebrate famous ancestors, but I would hesitate to go much further. By the same token, one could say that the paten and chalice were used in a sacred place, rather than a restaurant, and were to do with worship that involved a meal. I could go a little further and suggest that meals are about drawing people together and have always been central to family life. But again, I couldn't take the story much further forward without undue speculation.

If we now move forward a millennium or so to the Amesbury Archer, we still see certain fundamental themes persisting, especially the link between death, and with it the afterlife, and ordinary, domestic life, as illustrated by those Beakers filled with food or drink. You could see them, I suppose, as merely providing sustenance for the final journey to the next world, but by the mid-3rd millennium BC the theme is already too persistent for so minimalist an explanation which also fails to explain why such graves often include domestic items, like flint tools and copper knives. But what about the archery kit: the quiversful of flint-tipped arrows and the two fine stone wrist-guards; what do they symbolize?

Again, you could take the minimalist view that they were merely there to provide the dead man with food for the afterlife, or to ward off attack by enemies or demons. I'm not saying that these ideas are necessarily wrong, but I do believe they fall short of the richness of the truth. Symbols, especially those surrounding death, have more profound, deeper meaning than the immediately obvious. At such times, and like most people in their late sixties, I speak from personal experience, having witnessed the demise of several close friends. Everyone, even hardened atheists, needs to feel they are loved and supported, and at a profound level. The compassion of family and friends may be enough for some, but many people feel they need extra help and support – and this is where concepts like divine love can play a role. The personal possessions of the departed take on special significance that can persist for a mourner's lifetime. Deep, complex motives and emotions are involved, which is why I prefer to steer clear of simple explanations. So I rather doubt that those arrows were merely about the Archer's need to eat in the afterlife. And yes, they probably indicate that he was once a famous bowman. But again, I think the many objects in that grave are telling us rather more than these rather obvious stories.

For a start, we have moved on from the earlier Neolithic when the focus was very much on the dead person and his or her corpse, which could even be taken out of the tomb and paraded or displayed in the community. By the Early Bronze Age, the items that accompanied the dead body into the grave are the focus of attention. We don't know whether other objects associated in some way with the dead person were also treated in a special way, but at about this time we sometimes find small pits that have been carefully filled with arranged sherds of pottery; this is often decorated in a style known as Grooved Ware. Grooved Ware is closely associated with stone circles and henges across Britain, from Orkney to Durrington Walls. Along with the pottery are buried pork bones, often burnt or cremated, and charred hazelnut shells. It's tempting to see these small offerings as the remains of feasts, but again, we must beware of being simplistic. In this case it is not the feast that is important, so much as why it was held: maybe some of these carefully filled-in pits are a community's way of commemorating a person, whose body was then removed to somewhere special, like Stonehenge, or nearby Amesbury.

But the important point to note is that things – objects – are now starting to play a very diverse set of symbolic roles. So to return to objects buried with the Amesbury Archer: what else can they tell us? The most obvious observation is that this is an exceptional collection of finds, many of which are of superb quality, especially the gold earrings and the two polished stone wrist-guards. The presence of two copper knives is also unusual and suggests that the Archer was a person of high rank. But that again is a simple enough observation to make. Surely it's more important to think about the nature of that rank; in other words, what did it signify? And here, I think, the wide mix of objects can tell us a great deal.

For a start, he probably was indeed a great bowman, but his superbly made arrows and wrist-guards suggest that these were more than utilitarian objects. They were symbols of the man's power and authority which it was hoped he would retain in the afterlife. But what was the nature of that authority? Was he a jumped-up ruthless dictator, like, say, Colonel Gadhafi or Saddam Hussein? Probably not, but there are certain, rather informative similarities.

Both the dictators who fell in the recent uprisings of the so-called 'Arab Spring' had strong tribal support in their families' core areas, which is one of the reasons they were able to hang onto power so tenaciously. So yes, they were tyrants, but they did not appear completely out of the blue – like, say, Hitler. They arose from a family or tribal structure and clawed their way to the top through sheer ruthlessness and a cunning political ability to use and manipulate a hierarchical tribal structure. In some respects they were no different to many European kings of the Middle Ages. Hitler, on the other hand, was a very modern sort of dictator, who genuinely came from nowhere. I cannot see a Hitler-style dictator coming to the fore in prehistoric times. Indeed, it would be quite absurd to suggest that the Amesbury Archer was a Saddam or a Gadhafi, but I do firmly believe his authority was embedded within a closely knit and probably increasingly hierarchical tribal social structure. We can see that in symbolic terms in the other, less spectacular objects in his grave. Take those extraordinary eight Beakers: what, for instance, do they symbolize?

And again, I don't think it's sufficient merely to point out that they held food and drink for the afterlife. Surely we should be asking who provided that sustenance? And again, I think that Ros Cleal's fascinating reconstructed 'life histories' of the various vessels suggests that they may have originated in several distinctly different households and/or communities. Presumably this shows that the dead man enjoyed the active support (and I deliberately avoid using the emotive term 'love') of a family or tribal group of some size. I would further suppose that that family network was also his power-base. So was he an authoritarian-style leader? I don't suppose we will ever know, but the placing of his grave near Stonehenge and the fact that he spent his childhood outside Britain (which we know from analysis of his tooth enamel, see p. 142) tells me that he was a leading member of an important tribe or family. There are other graves in the Stonehenge area of comparable richness, although not quite so early, so I think he was more a pillar of the establishment than a radical dictator; but again, it would be hard to prove or disprove it, either way.

The later graves in the Stonehenge area are fairly typical of Britain as a whole, although somewhat richer. They suggest that from at least around 2500 BC tribal societies were becoming more hierarchical (a process that may have begun as early as 3000 BC), but then around 1500 BC things changed. Was there indeed a physical revolution? Did the down-trodden masses rise up against the likes of the Amesbury Archer in open revolt? I think not. The change, when it came, was peaceful and relatively gradual, taking several generations to achieve. But what lay behind it?

Essentially, it was no longer necessary to co-ordinate tribal networks across large regions of Britain. Instead, the settled landscape had 'filled out', with new communities and new communication networks emerging. So it made more sense to deal directly with your neighbours and establish good local relationships, because that was now where the stress-points lay. This meant that the earlier concern with social connections across long distances became less of a priority. As a result, the emerging hierarchies of the Early Bronze Age ceased to be relevant after the onset of the Middle Bronze Age, around 1500 BC.

If we examine the rituals that were associated with the rich graves of the Early Bronze Age and compare them with what followed, what I have called here the New Order, we can detect many common themes, which suggest to me that the Domestic Revolution was more a very rapid Domestic Evolution. There is no evidence for widespread social upheaval: barrows are not desecrated; Stonehenge is not torn down. There is no Bastille moment, no 14 July. Instead, the changes are more subtle.

From the time after 1500 BC, finds of Bronze Age metalwork rapidly become more frequent and more widespread. There is also abundant evidence that field systems were being laid out across new areas, with increasing rapidity. The general evidence for settlement, too, increases quite rapidly. Finds of domestic pottery, often quite plain and not closely datable, other than attributable to 'the later Bronze Age', become more common; at the same time, new and distinctly non-Neolithic techniques of flint tool manufacture emerge. All of this is accompanied by the move (accentuated by a growing population) from places like Salisbury Plain, down to the flatter, more fertile landscapes of the east.

At this stage, however, I want to stay with the rituals associated with the Old and New Orders, as I plan to discuss settlement and landscape changes in more detail shortly. If one takes a broad view, it seems to me that one of the most significant developments of the Old Order was the emergence of objects as portable symbols in their own right. I believe this was to prove of fundamental importance because it helped people establish and renew social ties and obligations at the local level. Significant objects were no longer reserved for rare occasions, such as funerals. They could now play a greater part in daily life and in cementing together a growing, complex network of family and local allegiances. The offerings made at places like Flag Fen are extraordinarily diverse and cover a range of people and events: men, women and children, with ceremonies that seem somehow to echo what one might find in a parish church: births, marriages and deaths, plus one or two other rites of passage, such as apprenticeships, coming-of-age and perhaps certain civil arrangements, such as land and property deals, which were probably based around marriage settlements. The majority of the symbolic objects come from nearby, probably from the immediate vicinity, but others come from much farther afield: from France, even the Alps.

As we will see, these objects can only be interpreted if the circumstances of their deposition are carefully revealed, which is one of the reasons why I, like most prehistorians, am so strongly opposed to metal-detecting. Understanding the subtleties of the past is all about context. Nothing else matters – and it can only be appreciated through careful, painstaking excavation, by hand. Given the importance of the questions that could be answered by this, anything else is little better than vandalism.

FLAG FEN AND THE RITES
OF THE NEW ORDER

I will use Flag Fen as the site to illustrate the rites of the New Order for the simple reason that our team found and excavated it. As we have seen, other sites are known, but few have been excavated as extensively as Flag Fen, which still provides us with the most comprehensive picture.

I said in the last section that the significance of symbolic objects and offerings can only be understood if they are studied in their contexts. The same can be said for the sites where they occur, which must be seen in their wider landscapes, where they form a part of a slowly evolving story of change. In effect, we are attempting to write a historical narrative, but without the help of named people or documents. Research of this sort is essentially long term and collaborative, and I am delighted to report that the work that we undertook from the 1970s is now being taken forward by teams from the Cambridge University Archaeological Unit (CAU), under the overall direction of Chris Evans. From the later 1990s until 2007, both teams worked in the area, but we kept in close touch and shared many of the same specialists, of whom the two most important were Charly French (soils) and Maisie Taylor (wood-working). The more recent research has been published in two substantial reports.[1] Since 2007, the CAU have been working alone and have made some major discoveries on the south side of the Flag Fen Basin at Bradley Fen and Must Farm. Among many other things, they have revealed that rich archaeological deposits still survive well below modern sea-level, and that the post-Glacial geology of the region is very much more complex than we had previously supposed. Both discoveries have greatly enhanced the potential of the area, which must now be seen as one of the richest and most important archaeological resources still surviving in north-western Europe.

That sketches in what one might call the academic or intellectual context of the region, and we have already discussed in passing how fields developed and the landscape changed. Even so, the remaining story is quite complex and needs to be summarized if we are to understand the wider context of the finds themselves, and how they were placed there in prehistory. I will start with the Fens.

I began this book with a discussion of the formation of the North Sea in early post-Glacial times and the formation of the Fens is just a later chapter in the same story. The million or so acres of north-western East Anglia and southern Lincolnshire, which today form the Fens, were a low-lying plain that had been levelled flat by glacial action in the Ice Age. Large rivers drained down towards the deeper parts of 'Doggerland' from inland. These included the Great Ouse, the Nene, the Welland and the Witham. As North Sea levels continued their relentless rise, the coast crept ever closer, and by 3000 BC the Wash had formed and the Fens, the low-lying land around it, were regularly inundated by tidal flooding.[2] As time passed, this simple picture became more complex, with freshwater flooding and peat formation further inland and the laying down of tidal silts closer to the Wash. It's this complex interplay between fresh and salt water, wet, damp and dry land, that makes Fenland archaeology such a diverse and fascinating topic.[3]

Flag Fen is located towards the centre of the western edges of the Fens, at the point where the River Nene (known as the Nen, upstream of Peterborough) enters the Fenland Basin. By 3000 BC, the rising level of the North Sea was having an effect on the rivers that drained into it. A succession of sand-bars and tidal silts around the fringes of the Wash, over 30 miles to the east, blocked or clogged up the outfalls of rivers like the Great Ouse, Nene and Welland and caused their waters to back up and flood the land. At first only the lowest-lying land (all of it below modern sea-level) was affected, but by 2000 BC freshwater flooding from the backed-up river systems was reaching a metre, sometimes even higher than that, above modern sea-level. The effect was to swamp the landscape directly east of Peterborough. But it would be a huge mistake to see this process negatively, through modern eyes. For a start, the inundation was very variable, some places being much wetter than others. Wetland environments of this sort are actually very rich in resources. During the drier months of summer, for example, they provide some of the richest pastures you can find. Today, Romney Marsh, in Kent, continues to be famous for its sheep, and there is a breed which still bears its name. And the watery areas themselves are full of fish, eels and wildfowl, not to mention reeds for thatching and firewood, and, rather surprisingly, salt was regularly being extracted from the waters of Flag Fen, from around 1300 BC.[4] This would have been a very valuable commodity.

Prehistoric Fenlanders knew their landscape well. And they had to, because although it was very rich in some respects, in others it was less forgiving. If your house flooded, for example, you would be in serious trouble. So they must have carefully followed the changing patterns of the gradually encroaching waters. From about 2000 BC, these patterns settled down and quite a clear-cut distinction could be drawn between the regularly flooded and the flood-free land – and this was where they laid out the fields and built their farmsteads and settlements. It made plenty of sense to live close to the fen, which was such a rich natural resource and larder, especially in those months of winter, when meat and protein were otherwise scarce. As late as the 17th and 18th centuries, during winter, Fenland decoys were exporting tens of thousands of ducks and geese to the growing population of London.[5]

It is still widely believed that the Fens were drained by the Dutch. In actual fact, this is not strictly correct, although we ought to acknowledge here the huge part played by engineers from the Low Countries who developed water-control measures such as efficient sluice- and lock-gates, which in turn made Britain's canal network of the 18th century possible. It was a Dutch engineer, Cornelius Vermuyden, who carried out the first widely co-ordinated drainage of southern Fenland, in the 17th century. Elsewhere, the picture could be very different[6] and in some areas, including the tidal grounds around the Wash, active drainage, often on a parish-by-parish basis, had been under way since Saxon and medieval times.[7] I sometimes think that the drainage of the Fens is a microcosm of the wider theme I'm addressing in this book: at first drainage was carried out from the bottom up, but even then people organized themselves into groups and committees that co-ordinated the local work, which needed to be carried out on quite a large scale to work effectively. Top-down intervention, with central government authority, only became possible after the Dissolution of the Monasteries in 1539, a measure which released some of the vast wealth of the great Fenland foundations, such as Ely, Peterborough, Crowland and Thorney.

Despite its name, for most jobbing field archaeologists, the Bronze Age is not about bronze. Our team started excavating Bronze Age farms and fields at Fengate in 1971, and our first major report, published in 1980, was only able to illustrate a single bronze object: most of the blade of a spearhead.[8] Nearby we also found a tiny solidified spill of molten bronze, which on analysis proved to be of identical composition, strongly suggesting that the spearhead had been cast on site. It's worth bearing in mind that this one find, together with perhaps three or four shoe boxes full of flint and pottery, was all that we recovered from excavating literally hundreds of metres of Bronze Age field boundary ditches. After a season at Fengate in the 1970s, none of our students were under any illusions about the 'glamour' of archaeology.

The main reason, of course, why Bronze Age objects are found so rarely on contemporary settlements is that bronze was a valuable commodity. Accordingly, axes, knives, chisels and other day-to-day tools were carefully looked after and were generally melted down and recast in new, and often more effective, forms at the end of their useful lives. That is why the analysis of metal becomes increasingly ineffective as a means of determining the sources of the ores used. By the end of the Bronze Age, all bronze implements contained huge amounts of recirculated and reused metal. It is also worth noting here that the actual tools used to shape the tens of thousands of timbers recovered from Flag Fen have never been found, although we know more or less what they would have looked like from the curvature of the hundreds of different axe blade marks left on the surface of the wood itself. When an axe shaft shattered, as happens even today from time to time, the broken shaft was abandoned (and we have found several), but the metal axehead was carefully recovered. This must have happened quite often, because many axes of the developed Bronze Age are actually cast with side-loops for bindings, which prevented the axehead from flying off after an accident.

I have just mentioned that most jobbing archaeologists rarely find Bronze Age metal objects, and yet paradoxically the collections of our national and local museums are stuffed with them. Very often, too, the displays feature so-called 'hoards', or groups of metal objects.[9] Indeed, these hoards are very much a feature of the post-1500 BC New Order. One museum in Suffolk actually had to have its first floor reinforced when the largest-known Bronze Age hoard was taken into its care. This hoard, from Isleham, a village on the edges of the Fens in Suffolk, and which was contemporary with the finds from Flag Fen, weighed a massive 95 kilos (210 pounds) and included some 6,500 objects.[10] So if bronze was valuable and treated with such care, we can reasonably assume that when we come across intact objects in the ground, and most particularly, when we come across them in hoards, they were put there deliberately. Very often, too, these hoards or single objects were placed in water or wet ground. I will discuss why people chose to put their valuable metalwork in the ground or in water shortly, but first I want to examine the context of these depositions at Flag Fen. When we understand how and when they were deposited there, we will be in a better position to answer the obvious 'why' question.

I did not realize it at the time, because all our minds were focused on excavating a complex series of Bronze Age farms, fields and stockyards, but that first metal find, a spearhead, should have set bells ringing. I remember thinking that it was a little bit odd: there was absolutely no sign of any local hostilities in the layout of the fields and farms; none were defended with banks or stockades; and their fields communicated with each other via droveways and gates. To my eye it looked just like any other working field system. So why a spear; surely an axe to help maintain the extensive hedge network would have been more appropriate? We discovered the spearhead in 1974 and it took another fifteen years' work to reveal that it was found in the ditches of the main droveway that led down to the post alignment that crossed Flag Fen. In other words, it did not come from an 'ordinary' settlement feature at all. To judge by that spill of bronze alongside it, it was found on dry land, a little set back from the wet (water would have been needed for the small furnace), in a place where metal objects were being made. But why there? Why not closer to a settlement, where people actually lived? Again, time would provide the answers.

Like all prehistorians, I was only too well aware that Bronze Age metalwork was usually found in wet places, which is why I decided – rather controversially at the time – to employ volunteers from a local metal-detector club to 'sweep' the site of a proposed new power station then due to be erected on the edge of the fen at Fengate. The power station was constructed in the last year before archaeological investigation became a planning requirement, so I was delighted when several of the company directors turned out to be archaeological enthusiasts who supported my calls for a large-scale dig. I don't think any of us could possibly have anticipated what we – and more particularly the metal-detectorists – would reveal, but only after some six months of frantic work.

I had met members of the local detectorists' club when I had given a talk to them the previous winter, and although I didn't like some of the shady-looking antiquities dealers who hung around on the fringes in the bar afterwards, most of the members struck me as honest enthusiasts – and I still have no reason to doubt that. By this time, one or two archaeologists were using students to 'sweep' their sites, and when I mentioned to the club members what they were doing, they smiled. Those smiles said it all: the detectorists knew that detecting is not a skill one acquires rapidly. So I abandoned my plan to buy or hire the equipment, and chose instead to invite the club to come down to the site as soon as we had stripped off the topsoil from a reasonably large area, and the machines had stopped working. It was a Saturday, at the very beginning of June – and I will never forget it.

Earlier that year I had found it much more difficult to persuade local authority archaeologists that the site had potential, and for a short time things had looked rather black; but we had started work despite this, knowing that English Heritage and the power station builders themselves were prepared to back us. Slightly anxious at this rather unexpected lack of official support, I had redoubled our efforts to pin down the precise point where the post alignment might have crossed the site. But when it became clear to us that the posts were heading for the centre of the boundary that ran along the very edge of Flag Fen, I decided to throw caution to the wind and go for it.

Normally today, one would start with a geophysical survey, which would be followed by a few selected trial trenches, and when all of that so-called 'assessment' work had been completed (a process that could easily take a year), a larger, open area would be exposed. But we didn't have time to mess around. We tried conventional geophysics, but we knew it would show nothing, as most of the site was deeply covered by layers of washed-in peaty flood-clays. By good fortune I had just heard about ground-penetrating radar, which had been used very successfully at York, but I also discovered that it wasn't cheap. So I got the radar specialists down on a special day-rate, on the off-chance that they would be able to detect something. And they did. After a few hours, it became clear that our posts were running diagonally across the site, stopping a short distance from the spot where the modern power station buildings now stand. That was all I needed to know. I could then have paid a lot of money to have the initial results processed properly, but frankly it was not worth it, and would have taken too long. I don't think they were very happy at this.

Armed with the raw radar data, I calculated the cubic metres of overburden that we could afford to shift with our earth-moving budget and added a bit for luck. The open-area excavation I came up with extended across 2 hectares (5 acres) of the site and extended widely on either side of the posts. Again, certain colleagues thought this unnecessary, but mercifully they were not members of our team, who were all solidly behind me.

I'm guessing the precise length of the post alignment we had stripped by the beginning of June, but it must have been at least half of the spread revealed by the radar: say 75 metres (245 feet), plus a small area on either side. About a dozen detectorists arrived on site on that first Saturday, which was actually slightly more than I had anticipated, but after hunting around for spare clip-boards our students were ready to record what each one found, individually. The previous evening we had surveyed and gridded-out the area to be searched, as I was insistent that each find had to be plotted to the nearest square metre. Today, of course, we would do this instantly and more accurately using GPS technology, but in those days it was a case of tapes and balls of string – but no nails, or steel toe-cap boots, please.

I suppose it's the anthropologist in me, but every time I join a new group of people I instinctively look for certain key people: the leader, the joker, the thinker, the shy one and the trouble-maker. As we hung around drinking flasks of tea and coffee while the group assembled, I spotted most of the 'types' I'd expected, with the exception of the trouble-maker, who I suspect had been filtered out, shall we say, by the group themselves. Their leader, who was also the joker, was a large man with a huge smile, called Terry. Terry had come to Peterborough New Town from London about ten years previously. Sadly he is no longer with us, but it was his energy and enthusiasm which made that first morning such a success. He insisted that all the club members listened closely to my little introductory pep talk, and made sure that everyone knew how important it was that every single find, no matter how small or seemingly trivial, should be recorded by one of our team. As we would shortly discover, he was also a superb detectorist, and perhaps more importantly: he had the luck of the Devil.

When I had finished explaining our task and how we were going to set about it, the group fell quiet. For some time I had been worried that all this preparation could have been in vain: maybe it was just a line of posts, a boundary, a trackway; maybe there was nothing out there? I could see there was doubt in their minds, too. They knew that if we were about to search across a Roman or medieval site, there would be thousands of pins and coins and all sorts, but in the Bronze Age? Three thousand years ago? I couldn't say so at the time, but we were all entering foreign territory here. Then, thank heavens, Terry broke the atmosphere:

'What d'you want first, Francis?' he asked as he pulled his head-phones over his ears.

I thought for a moment: 'A sword, Terry, would do nicely . . .'

I thought he hadn't heard my reply, as he was already heading across to the area we had assigned him, but it managed to raise a small laugh from other members of the club, who were now following him a few paces behind. I stood on the side of the trench and watched as people set to work. Our students were out there with their clip-boards making sure that everyone was more or less in the right place. For some time the silence, to use an old cliché, was deafening. I had sort of expected to hear their machines constantly beeping, as of course topsoil everywhere is full of old nails and other metal debris, put there in the days when farmers routinely spread manure. But we'd already machined all of that away. Maybe, I worried to myself, we had also removed all the prehistoric finds? It was an anxious time – in fact so anxious that I have no accurate idea of its length: a minute, or an hour? I still don't know.

Then my thoughts were interrupted by a shout from Terry: 'That sword, Francis, I think I've found it!'

The students tried to stop them, but every club member immediately dashed across to where Terry was working. I just managed to stop myself from running, but walked as briskly as my legs would allow. Some vestige of directorial restraint is important at such times. When I arrived, Terry was sweeping his detector across quite a substantial area of silt and getting continuous responses along a strip of ground about 40 centimetres (18 inches) in length – a bit short for a sword, but substantial nonetheless. He was about to produce his long-handled gardener's trowel and dig whatever it was up; then he recalled what I had said at the start of the day: no 'rabbit holes'. He replaced it with a wonderfully exaggerated sheepish grin: 'Whoops, sorry Francis, old habits . . .'

I passed him my spare archaeologist's trowel and together we carefully started removing soil; if anything, by now he was even more cautious than me. I remember his hands were shaking with excitement.

I think it was Terry who first exposed metal. I set my trowel aside and worked with my bare fingers. Terry followed me. The soft silts came away easily and in a few seconds we had exposed the tip of a leaf-shaped sword blade. It had to be Late Bronze Age, no other date would fit that shape. A few minutes later and we had revealed about half of a leaf-shaped sword, which had broken about a third of the way down from the hilt.

I leaned back. I could see Terry was awe-struck. By now I had expected some wisecrack along the lines of 'you asked for a sword, Francis, didn't you?' But the reality proved too much. I won't say he was on the verge of tears, but he was clearly very moved. On an impulse I asked: 'Did you get any other signals?'

He paused for a moment. Then picked up his machine and took a pace to one side and began sweeping. In a few moments there was another response – and that proved to be the hilt and upper part of the blade of the same sword. I had some reference books in the Land-Rover, but in this case there was no need to consult them as it belonged to a very well-known Late Bronze Age type, known as a

Wilburton sword, after the site of a massive hoard from the southern Fens, about half an hour's drive from Flag Fen, towards Ely.

At the end of the day I swore the club members to secrecy and they all agreed. I don't think any of us wanted illegal 'night-hawks' to spoil our fun – and make no mistake, it really was very enjoyable and I won't pretend otherwise. It's not often that a dirt archaeologist gets to do anything so genuinely transforming. I was acutely aware that every find was throwing new light on a poorly understood period, and what I didn't realize back then was that the process we had begun would prove irreversible: those early finds are still providing fresh insights, as new discoveries are being made in the area.

The club agreed to return the next day, and by the end of our first week we had revealed some sixty objects, including two complete and two fragmentary swords. When the excavation finished, later that October, we had recovered over three hundred items, mostly Late and Middle Bronze Age, but with a fair scattering dating throughout the Iron Age and just into Roman times.

Subsequently, we have found substantial numbers of bronze and other finds along the post alignment and the rather mysterious timber platform towards its eastern, or Northey, landfall. And although we haven't had an opportunity to examine the Northey fen-edge as closely as we were able to do at the Fengate power station site, we have found good evidence for further finds there, too. At a conservative estimate, I would guess that in prehistoric times somewhere between five to seven thousand metal objects were placed in the ground, or dropped in the waters, along the Flag Fen post alignment.

Earlier on, I mentioned the importance of context if we are going to understand why people placed such valuable things as swords into the muds of Flag Fen. Bear in mind too that these would have been major items, the equivalent in their monetary value of, say, family heirlooms or cars. So whatever was happening was clearly important. Put another way, those activities must have served a purpose; they were not trivial gestures, like tossing small change into a fountain.

We took great pains to ensure that the metal-detector survey extended right across the entire area we had stripped of overburden, but as we worked we became increasingly aware that most of the

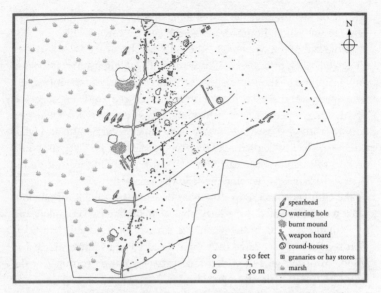

Fig. 6.1 A plan of the site at Bradley Fen, near Whittlesey, Peterborough, showing what happened in the Bronze Age along the edge of the wetland (to the left). Here, individual metal objects and hoards were placed in the ground at the point where the field boundary ditches (running diagonally from upper right) ended. Note also the three 'burnt mounds' alongside wells or watering holes.

finds were coming from over and among the posts and from one side of the trench. Very few were coming from the north side of the posts. Later, we were able to draw a series of distribution maps for the various items found, and it came as no surprise to discover that the handful of objects from north of the posts were all very small: usually tiny rings. I suspect they may have been displaced by water. The slightly wider spread of finds to the extreme west reflects the fact that by this point the posts had reached dry land, where a different distribution pattern, this time following the fen margins, rather than the post alignment, is probably beginning (see Fig. 6.1). This would reflect what recent excavations have revealed on the other (eastern) side of the Flag Fen Basin, at sites like Bradley Fen, where the Cambridge

University team have found a series of metalwork finds, both as single items and in small hoard-like groups at the very point where the dry-land fields end and the open wetland grazing begins.[11] This narrow zone must have been very important, because people were at great pains to mark it out and sub-divide it, not just with finds, but with ditches and with strange heaps of burnt stones and charcoal, which often cover a pit lined with wood. These features are known as 'burnt mounds' and have been interpreted as pits for beer brewing, or as saunas. Most prehistorians would now favour the former – in which case one must question why they were placed so far away from the drier ground where people would have built their houses.

Already the question of context is becoming complex. For a start, we have isolated two quite distinct distribution patterns: one along and to one side of the post alignment, the other parallel to the edge of the fen. It's interesting that the post alignment finds are confined to the area of the posts and to a band about 30 metres (100 feet) wide, along their southern side (see Fig. 6.2). When I first saw that pattern

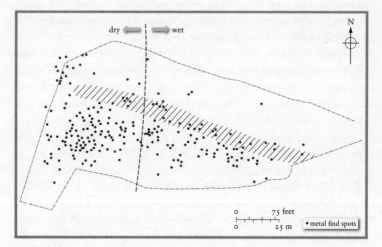

Fig. 6.2 A plan of prehistoric finds from the power station site at Fengate. The course of the post alignment is shaded with diagonal lines. Note, too, the edge of the wetland, where the distribution of finds broadens out.

beginning to emerge, I was immediately struck by the fact that the southern side of the posts was the area of wetland that we know was surrounded by fields, farms and settlements.

In effect, the post alignment was a boundary that cut the Flag Fen Basin off from the open fens to the north. This role might help explain why there were so many posts (in five rows, no less: far more than a causeway alone would require), and why some of them stood taller than a man. So was it a defended boundary? That is a harder question to answer. I would only consider it a real possibility if the line of the posts was continued as a substantial earthwork – a major ditch and bank – when dry land was reached at either end; but there is no sign of anything like that at all. The simplest explanation is that it was intended to be prominent in the landscape and that the objects deposited along its length were probably put there by people from surrounding communities as an act of honouring their shared boundary. This would help explain why all the objects occurred along the southern side – the side where most people would have lived. We now know that the edges of the fen beyond the immediate Flag Fen Basin were quite densely inhabited, so the post alignment and the finds along it can be seen as a statement, with frequent reaffirmations, that the fishing, the grazing and other resources of the basin 'belonged to' (i.e. were controlled by) certain communities.

So far, so good: the motives that lay behind the objects placed in the fen seem reasonably clear, but a moment's reflection should make one suspicious: human rituals are never simple, nor straightforward. And this applied in the Bronze Age, as much as it does today.

THE LONGEVITY OF CEREMONIES

I would be very surprised if the people who came to the post alignment and placed metalwork and other objects there did so in the clear understanding that they were reinforcing an important boundary, and with it, the social cohesion of their community. Religions don't work like that. Other, more personally relevant fears or desires would have motivated them; and of these, birth and death are undoubtedly the most powerful. But ceremonies are never simple in their effects or outcomes, either; nor are they necessarily predictable. In the remote past, just as today, rituals were complex affairs, and it sometimes worries me that archaeologists seem somehow to view them as straightforward: people made offerings and then got on with their daily lives. In reality, of course, the offerings were an integral part of that daily life and would have been taken very seriously indeed – even if very few of the participants fully understood the reasoning behind them.

I remember watching (largely because it was unavoidable in the media) highlights from the near-state funeral of the late Lady Thatcher and I was struck by that elaborate ceremony's underlying motives, largely, I suspect, because they did not quite work out as intended. The family was much in evidence – a process made more media friendly by a glamorous granddaughter – and politicians to the right of centre talked about how Mrs Thatcher had saved the country. Those on the left discussed how she had divided it. As I watched, it became clear to me that the ceremony itself, and the fact that it was based around somebody's death, had allowed public discussion of some important contemporary social issues and problems. It had achieved this, moreover, without any unrest or violence. Had the funeral been centred on, say, the death of the head of state, then its principal underlying purpose – to unite the country (in that case around the monarch's successor) – would have been achieved. But convention had been broken, and in fifty years' time historians *might* decide that the debate that arose after Lady Thatcher's funeral marked an important shift in public sympathy away from the powerful elites that now control the country. Alternatively, they might decide that public reaction to the funeral was a delayed response to the collapse of the bankers' bubble, some five years previously. Others might wonder why the career of the nation's first female prime minister was discussed in essentially male terms. Only time will tell. But it does illustrate how something as seemingly straightforward as a ceremony or ritual can have complex and unpredictable outcomes.

Important ceremonies have long histories, and this reflects the fact that their underlying purposes have always been significant. If ever a time comes when countries are replaced by some other form of social grouping, then coronations and inaugurations will cease to exist, or else they will be modified to reflect the new realities. The same can be said for the institutions that underlie and support them. It matters not that much of the British population is either atheist or agnostic: the Church will continue to survive to support the monarchy and the status quo. But, I believe, a far more reliable guarantee of its continued existence is its position as the principal institutional supporter of family life. If and when people eventually decide that they can do without Christian rites of passage at birth, marriage and death, the Church that administers them will become irrelevant, and only then will it cease to exist – and I cannot see such a thing happening for many centuries.

A number of the ceremonies we now take for granted are extraordinarily ancient. The Coronation can be traced back, in England, to 8th-century Saxon Mercia, and in Scotland, where the traditions of governance were rather different, to the 13th century.[12] Humbler ceremonies, such as Holy Communion, date to the introduction of Christianity in Roman times. Others, such as midwinter and spring festivals, celebrated by Christians as Christmas and Easter, have roots that go deep into prehistory and have to do with fundamental aspects of early farming life: the survival of winter and the rebirth and renewal of the new season. The longevity of these rituals reflects the enduring relevance of their underlying motives, and as I have just said, they will only change or cease to exist when the need for them alters, too.

This basic rule also applied in prehistory. In earlier chapters I discussed the survival and evolution of family-based rituals that went with the re-settlement of Britain and the arrival and establishment of farming. As we saw at Stonehenge, many of these existed for millennia and, indeed, continued, in one form or another, after 1500 BC. But what about the ceremonies introduced with the New Order? Did these possess the longevity of personal and social relevance, or were they merely to prove a flash in the pan?

One of the most striking aspects of the finds from Flag Fen is their date range. Those around the post alignment at the power station site were first deposited in the ground some time around or just before 1300 BC. Thereafter, there was continuous deposition through the rest of the Bronze Age and also throughout the entire Iron Age and just into Roman times. So without stretching the chronology unnecessarily, it would appear that the rites continued for just short of a millennium and a half. To put that in modern terms we are talking about the length of time between the demise of the Roman Empire and the Victorians.

It is also worth noting here that the placing of objects in the ground did not cease suddenly with the arrival of the Romans. The practices continued, although now given a new Romanized appearance. Indeed, ritual deposition and hoards continue into Saxon and even Viking times and sacred areas, such as the Witham Valley near Lincoln, whose well-established roots lay firmly in prehistoric times, positively flourished under monasticism in the Middle Ages.[13]

SCALE, SYMBOLISM AND THE RITES OF THE NEW ORDER

That is enough of generalities: it is time to be more specific. So let us return to that day in early June 1989 and to our metal-detectorist Terry's amazing discovery of a sword in two pieces. A few weeks after this, we learned that the sword blade had broken along a casting flaw, which, if anything, only added to the mystery. So what do the contexts of this find tell us about its deposition? First and foremost: had it been deliberate? And here I think the answer is quite simple: one piece of blade could have been lost accidentally, but not two. And if doubts still persist, we found other items that could only have been put there deliberately: a pair of bronze shears, complete with a specially made wooden box (see Plate 21), and the blade of a bronze dagger which had been buried directly below its beautifully carved antler hilt, or handle (the two pieces were touching). Other swords were buried with broken blades close by. I'm in no doubt whatsoever that the placing of these objects in the silts and waters of Flag Fen was deliberate. I also believe that the same can be said for the hundreds of Bronze and Iron Age metal finds dredged from the rivers of lowland England, most notably the Trent, the Witham (near Lincoln) and, of course, the Thames, especially along its course through London.[14]

The next question is why were they deposited? I have already discussed some of the general, underlying reasons, but if we look closely at their context and at the state of the finds themselves, we can be more specific. Take the sword fragments that Terry revealed. When we came to look at them closely, we discovered that the cutting edges of their blades had been deliberately damaged, by being dashed repeatedly against something like a hard-edged rock. Our consultant specialists were able to demonstrate that this certainly was not the result of battle, where swords generally cut into other blades; such damage, too, tends to be confined to a restricted area of the blade, some distance from the hilt. Two, possibly three, of the Flag Fen swords had been deliberately damaged in the same way, against a sharp rock-edge. Blade tips were also missing and there is evidence that the hilts had been deliberately removed, or torn off, possibly using fire.[15] The sort of hammered-over rivets that were used to secure hilts to sword handles were found lying loose in the ground. This surely suggests that the swords had been deliberately damaged before they were placed in the ground, or water.

If we are to explain such goings-on, we must take a broader view of swords. I have already touched on the symbolic role of weapons when we discussed the daggers buried with the Amesbury Archer, and I think the same general observations – for example, that weapons were symbols of rank and family status – can be applied to the Flag Fen swords, except that by the Late Bronze Age the symbolism had evolved even further.

At the time of the Amesbury Archer, weapons were buried alongside the people whose rank they symbolized. But after 1500 BC there was a profound shift in the way this symbolism was expressed. In rituals of the New Order, objects could now, of themselves, symbolize status. In other words, the object had in a way replaced the need for a person – just as the bread and wine of Holy Communion is believed to represent (or even to become) the body and blood of Christ, the person. So an object could now 'stand for' or symbolize its owner, whose actual corpse may have been buried somewhere else entirely. I sometimes see this as a step in the direction of those sad lists of names inscribed onto war memorials in churches, school chapels and cenotaphs throughout Britain: the bodies lie elsewhere, but the people and their deeds are still remembered, in the appropriate place. But even this seemingly impersonal listing of names can have other personal dimensions. I can think of members of my own family whose names are recorded on such memorials, and I have witnessed the effect they can have on relatives standing close by me. And of course if symbolism is involved, the swords don't necessarily have to be the ones that were actually used and owned by the dead man. Some could have been made especially for the event, as we saw with the Fengate spearhead (and the spill of molten bronze). It's also interesting that Terry's sword had broken along a casting flaw. I cannot see that as being a sword that could have been used much in daily life – let alone in actual combat.

Other weapons had been deliberately damaged before deposition. These included spears whose shafts had been broken and bronze blades bent. We found fragments of cut and smashed sword scabbards (see Plate 22), and then there was the dagger with the antler hilt. That find still fascinates me, because it tells us so much about the scale and general nature of the ceremonies themselves.

Before we discovered Flag Fen, whenever I used to think about prehistoric ceremonies, images of Stonehenge with vast crowds, and men in sheets looking rather like vicars, would of course come to mind – even if I knew in my heart of hearts that modern Druids were entirely irrelevant. Sadly, scenes in the imagination are far harder to expunge than mere facts. So I don't hold out many hopes that what I'm about to say will have any immediate effect, but it might just sow the seeds of doubt. And for what it's worth, I well remember the day it happened.

As the summer of 1989 progressed, the detectorist club would still visit the site of the new power station, but by then we had worked out new methods of operating. They spent more time checking over the ever-growing spoil heaps thrown up by the machines, which we had carefully positioned to ensure that deposits of different ages were kept apart. To give them more time to check the heaps, the detectorists would flag up any signals or possible hotspots out in the main excavation, then we would come in and excavate them.

I have always enjoyed digging; in fact it was the main reason I became an archaeologist. I know it sounds rather sad stated baldly like that, but there was, and is, something about the whole process: the machining, the spading and shovelling and, of course, the fine work with a trowel that I enjoy – and I still grow irritated when I see university graduates who cannot use a shovel properly so never fill their wheelbarrow cleanly, spreading loose earth all around it. I'm aware it's a simple skill, but it requires balance and timing, and if you do take the trouble to get it right, it also saves a huge amount of effort. Trowelling is even more of a skill and it requires a certain gift or knack to do well. Some people have it; sadly others (including a few professors) will never acquire it.

Bad trowellers leave an uneven, bumpy and dusty surface behind them. As with incompetent shovelling, this irritates me intensely. On that particular day, tea-break had been called and I was heading across to the tea shed when I spotted an area that had been very poorly trowelled. There was earth everywhere, so I took out my own trowel and started to clean up the loose soil. Almost immediately I spotted the distinctive green stain of corroded bronze in among the loose earth. Forgetting any thoughts of tea and biscuits, I carefully removed all the earth on the surface and then gently scraped down to reveal a shallow depression, where there was an area of very slight green staining, about 15 centimetres (6 inches) wide. It did not take long to reveal the stain as a blade of a Late Bronze Age tanged dagger. The tang is a tongue-like projection, which fits into a slot in the hilt or handle.

I worked very carefully around the tang end of the blade, hoping to find some indication of the hilt. Some very elaborate daggers found with Beakers in graves of the Early Bronze Age have their hilts decorated with tiny gold pins, which were driven into the wood. So I was working very carefully, but sadly no gold, nor even bronze, pins came to light.

I took a photo, lifted the blade and put it in the finds' tray. Then I noticed that the impression left by the dagger was not particularly smooth or blade-like. Immediately I was suspicious and very gently felt the ground with my fingers. It was hard, and ridged. Sometimes fenny soils can develop layers of hard 'pans' of iron or manganese, especially in areas where the water-table fluctuates, and we had encountered quite a few of these; they are invariably a dark reddish-brown and have a rough, rather gritty feel to them. This was hard, yes, but smooth, if ridged. Frankly I was perplexed. In situations like this there is an old archaeological adage: always work from the known to the unknown. In other words, never dig blind, or 'on spec'.

So I took out my penknife and very gently followed the ridged surface which extended sideways for an inch or so, then started to dive down. At that point I stopped and followed another area of ridging, and again it started to dip. After repeating this process for about half an hour, it became clear to me that the ridging was in fact the surface of antler. I leaned back and surveyed what I had done and immediately the shape in the ground made sense. It was a complete hilt, made from the cut-down main shaft of a red deer antler. And it was perfectly preserved.

Maybe the detailed excavation had put my mind into a slightly different mode, but this time I found myself thinking about the original ceremony, back in the Bronze Age. I looked down at the shallow scoop – at most 30 centimetres (12 inches) long and 10 to 12 centimetres (4 to 5 inches) deep – and thought about the items it had held. The hilt had been pulled off the blade and placed in a shallow scoop in the wet ground, first. Then the blade had been laid, almost balanced, on top of it. These were not violent destructive acts. Later, in the labs at the British Museum, it was revealed that the socket in the hilt still contained the two very fine split-oak wedges that had gripped the tang and held it in place. If this had been a violent ceremony, then those wedges would surely have been torn out or dislodged. But they were still in place.

As I thought about what I had just revealed in the ground, it became clear to me that that particular prehistoric ritual had been a very small-scale, low-key affair. Such a small scoop: the offering within it would not have been visible to a large gathering. Yet I still had this Arthurian-style image of Sir Bedevere hurling the sword Excalibur over the water, to be caught by the pale, beautiful hand of the Lady of the Lake which arose from the depths, to the tumultuous cheers of the vast crowd of ancients who lined the shores on all sides . . . As I pondered the two quite ordinary objects in their humble scoop in the ground before me, that Hollywood-style image began to fade. The scale was all wrong. Again, I looked down at the antler handle and the blade, now in its tray alongside it. Slowly it dawned on me that the group who witnessed their placing in the ground would have been very much smaller, too. Who can tell, but I would have thought a couple of dozen people, but surely no more? This was nothing even remotely comparable with a ceremony like that at Seahenge – which in turn was small scale by the standards of the Old Order.

So who were these people and why were they there? I can only suppose that the dagger once belonged to a relative who had died, and they were placing it at Flag Fen because that was the appropriate place both to remember him and to ensure that the dagger reached him in the afterlife. Maybe too, it was believed that this wet landscape was liminal – an idea, of course, from earlier times – and somehow closer to the world of the ancestors where his soul now resided. And yes, if the concept of the soul was invented in pre-Christian times, then I would suggest that it formed an important part of the New Order, which was more about individuals and families than larger tribal gatherings – and in those respects I believe I have some justification for previously drawing parallels between the changes that took place around 1500 BC and the much later Reformation. Both were essentially about individuals and their relationships with human authority and the supernatural.

This book is about my views on family life, so I don't wish to be diverted into a detailed discussion about Bronze Age religion. But there is also a danger of oversimplification, because make no mistake, the variety of objects, and the many ways they were offered to the waters at Flag Fen, suggests that while the underlying motive for the ceremonies of the New Order may have been more personal than in the past, the ideology – the theology behind the new rites – was indeed complex and had many aspects in common with what had gone before. We know for example that solar and lunar alignment were important in the Old Order, but it was to persist after 1500 BC, as we saw briefly at Fiskerton (pp. 181–2), when the posts were replaced in the years which had a visible lunar eclipse. By the same token – though prior to 1500 BC there was less emphasis on rites that involved water – objects were frequently placed in small pits (as we saw at Etton), most probably as offerings, and the inverted central oak tree at Seahenge strongly suggests that people believed there were ancestral or spirit realms below the ground, too.[16] And again, it is worth noting that both the celestial and landscape alignments and the below-ground offerings take a wide variety of forms, which would suggest that we are dealing with a very complex and multi-layered ideological world. I used to think that if I could be transported back to the Bronze Age, it would be the houses, the infrastructure, the farming and the technology that I would find fascinating; today, I'm in no doubt that it would be their beliefs that I would try to understand.

I hope this very brief overview of Bronze Age religion provides context for the ideological changes that were taking place during the Domestic Revolution. It was not an all-enveloping change, like, for example, the introduction of Christianity and European ways to Africa or South America. That said, it did mark a major turning point and one that, sadly, is still largely unknown outside archaeological circles. But now I want to turn our attention to one of the major new symbolic elements of the New Order, namely, water.

Water is, of course, the ultimate symbol of cleansing, and is used as such at baptism – but there is more to it than just that. Today we live in a work-obsessed world, and we tend to think that the arrival of metal was only important technologically: it allowed the making of stronger, more durable tools and weapons with sharp cutting edges. But when polished, metal becomes reflective, and during the Iron Age we see the manufacture of hand mirrors, usually in bronze, and often with elaborate and wonderfully decorated backs and handles (see Fig. 6.3). These mirrors can be found in the graves of high-status women. The origins of the practice lie in the 4th century BC, then it became very much more popular in the last century BC, and towards Roman times.[17] But it is interesting, and indeed relevant, that the possession of an item which allowed an individual everyday access to their own appearance should have been so prized, and became such a status symbol.

Today we take the minute changes in our personal appearance for granted. I don't think I'm particularly vain, but I certainly examine my face in the bedroom mirror on most mornings and there's a larger one in the bathroom where I keep a weather eye on the size of my waistline, at bath time. As I get older, the mirror ruthlessly shows me signs of mortality, and whether I like it or not, it is indeed a reflection of myself – but one which I interpret freely. To be quite honest, like most men of my age, I generally see what it suits me to see, and it

Fig. 6.3 The decorated back of a Late Iron Age (early 1st century AD) bronze mirror from Holcombe, in Devon. This is a superb example of prehistoric art, done with a light touch: if you invert the image, the clasp which joins the handle to the mirror becomes a grinning face, whose eyes are formed by two studs of red glass.

often takes somebody else, usually my wife, to tell me when, for example, I need to lose weight. But this is interesting, because in common with most people in the western world, my reflected image has become a part of who I am and, more to the point, who I think I am. And this basic human requirement for a self-image is one of the reasons why prehistoric people would have valued, and sought out, tranquil waters. Indeed, I would be surprised if people in Neolithic or Bronze Age times saw their own reflections very often at all. Clear, still water is quite unusual: lakes have reedy margins and floating weed in summertime, and in winter ice and wind frequently disturb puddles and ponds. So I strongly suspect there would have been sheltered pools set aside, where the water was known to be particularly calm, and where people would come to view themselves. And it isn't hard to imagine why these places would soon have acquired religious significance.

But there was a reverse side to the coin too. The surface of water reflects light and, with it, life. But once you pass below that surface, you enter another realm entirely: not one of life, but of darkness and of death. The contrast could not be more stark and the symbolism was certainly apparent to prehistoric people, who were accomplished farmers and would have been very practically aware of water's life-giving qualities, as well as its potential to cause death by drowning. It is no coincidence that water, in one form or another, is a major component of most religions.

Because the symbolism that lay behind the veneration of wet places was so all encompassing and complex, the rites and events that were commemorated there represented most aspects of people's lives. In fact it's very tempting to draw parallels with the range of services conducted at a modern parish church. We have already seen how that antler-hafted dagger and the many swords might have been deposited during funerals, but they could also have been offered as part of the process of taking up, or relinquishing, a new post – the Bronze Age equivalent of, say, high sheriff or village constable. In one particular area we recovered a group of metalworkers' tools: numerous bronze awls (for scribing and marking-out) and small lead anvils, for detailed work. The concentration of this material within a relatively restricted area (roughly 50 by 20 metres, 165 by 100 feet) suggests that this part of the post alignment and the ground around it was reserved for rites to do with the craft of the bronze-smith; maybe this was where successful apprentices were inducted into their trade.

So far I have only discussed ceremonies that most probably involved men, but one of the most remarkable aspects of the New Order is the importance given in its rites and rituals to women and to family life. I have already mentioned the magnificent mirrors of the Iron Age, which most often are found in women's graves. It is difficult to think of objects that might be associated with a child's birth or baptism, but Flag Fen produced a huge number of small rings and tiny lead trinkets which could easily have been offered to the waters at such times.

There are also many pins and bracelets (of bronze and shale) which have almost always been broken, twisted or bent before deposition. We even found a small gold ring, made in a very intricate and distinctive way, using thin, thread-like wires. This beautiful little thing was once part of a more elaborate composite earring. It's a very unusual item and our metalwork expert, the late Dr Dave Coombs, was able to track down where it was made, which to everyone's surprise turned out to be the Alpine region. Several other objects, including some rather strange-looking, thumbnail-sized spoked wheels in pure lead (presumably personal ornaments of some sort), were also made in central Europe. Somewhat later, in the Iron Age, we see bronze brooches being placed in the ground. Some of these were very elaborate indeed, and may well have been offered at the funerals of prominent women, or indeed children.

I mentioned that prehistoric people would have been very aware of their images and appearance and we see this expressed at Flag Fen by the deposition of bronze razors and a remarkable find of bronze shears and their shoe-shaped wooden box. These shears would most probably have been used for cutting hair and beards, rather than sheep's fleeces (which would probably have been plucked, rather than shorn, at this early date). It is tempting to see such items as marking the transition from boyhood to youth, a rite of passage that is still given much prominence in many faiths and societies. Maybe some of the rings and pins we found were offered at rites celebrating girls' puberty, but one good contender here is a small bronze make-up pestle and mortar, which actually dates from very early Roman times. Marriage can be symbolized in different ways and the site has certainly produced many finger-sized rings, but my own preference is for four complete querns, or corn-grinding stones, very similar to the ones we described in Chapter 3, at Etton (see Plate 23). The quern has to be the ultimate symbol of domesticity and home life, and its symbolic value endured throughout later prehistory. Pottery, sometimes even complete pots (see Plate 24), was quite frequently placed into the waters and in at least one case, these pots contained food. We can only guess the original context of such offerings, but they would be entirely appropriate at most ceremonies to do with birth, marriage or death.

Almost all the objects deposited at Flag Fen had been broken or damaged in some way, and as we saw with the dagger and its hilt and the sword's cutting edge, this was quite deliberate and had nothing to do with ordinary wear and tear. So what did it signify? Again, we can only guess, but such rites are usually a way of signifying that the object in question is being taken out of this world and will be restored, whole, in the next. A cynic might add, that it is also a way of thwarting robbers, but this ignores the metal worth of these objects, which would have been great. Indeed, the fact that they have lain undisturbed for over three millennia is a tribute to the enduring power and authority of the rites that took place when they were deposited. Unlike in ancient Egypt, where the upper echelons of society did not share their religion with ordinary people – and hence the almost ubiquitous tomb-robbing which dates from antiquity itself – it would seem that everyone in Bronze and Iron Age Britain subscribed to the same set of beliefs and values.

'TRADE', COMMUNICATION AND AUTHORITY AT THE END OF THE BRONZE AGE

As we have seen, many of the objects placed in the water at Flag Fen came from far away. So was Flag Fen some sort of inland trading station? Given the very rural landscape this might seem unlikely, even given the undoubted prosperity of the region. Instead, I believe the presence of items imported from outside the region is an indication of what one might term the 'background' level of trade that was usual in later Bronze Age Britain. Much of this trade would have been relatively local: we have found items in jet, much of which originates around Whitby, on the Yorkshire coast, and shale, which comes from the other end of the country, around Kimmeridge, in Dorset. One of the complete quern-stones came from a quarry in Kent, with very distinctive stone. The three others probably came from quarries in Wales. These are heavy items and must surely have been transported by boat, first down rivers, and then along the coast. And we know for a fact that good, sea-going boats had been in existence for well over a millennium by that time.

My own feeling is that the 'trade' was part of the normal 'background' pattern of exchange between families and communities – a pattern that persisted throughout the Iron Age, and resumed in late- and post-Roman times, to flourish in the Saxon and Viking eras. It is worth remembering that farmers require frequent trade to continue their work: surpluses must be sold and new sources of seed and fresh blood-lines of livestock must be brought in. Rural economies cannot survive without regular markets; these are also the places where people met socially and where political differences were sorted out by discussion. The trading deals were based around exchange and family obligations, often arrived at as part of marriage settlements. But as we have already noted, true free-market economies require money for their transactions and they only began to appear in later medieval times.[18]

I don't want readers to think for one moment that our work at Flag Fen was unique in its scope, because it certainly was not. Yes, the landscape we were researching was complex and the archaeological remains within it were remarkably well preserved. It was also a piece of very long-term research, but that does not make it unique. Other archaeologists working in well-defined landscapes elsewhere, for example the Somerset Levels, the Vale of Pickering in East Yorkshire or on Dartmoor, in Devon, were discovering similarly complex stories, and in all of these areas research is still continuing.[19] All of these projects, and others too, were demonstrating that whenever a prehistoric landscape was examined at all closely, the ancient settlement patterns proved to be highly intricate and were constantly evolving. It was clear that people adapted themselves to their surroundings and vice versa. Indeed, it is important to stress here that this was a two-way process: prehistoric people did not merely adapt to their surroundings. They changed them too – and usually to their advantage.

If you examine objects from an Anglo-Saxon settlement, you will always find a proportion of material that originated from outside the region. Sometimes, too, this can be quite exotic. Back in the early 1970s, I worked on several Anglo-Saxon sites in East Anglia and for a brief period even considered changing my professional allegiance from prehistory to Saxon England. The more I read on the subject, the more similar Anglo-Saxon sites seemed to their Bronze

Age equivalents. For example, a brief glance at the inventory of things found at the superb excavations at West Stow, near Lackford, in Suffolk, reveals all the usual stuff: pottery, quern-stones etc., but also spearheads, which were spread among the different family units – suggesting, not that the village was at war with itself, but that the spearheads were given when a man reached warrior age.[20] In the cemetery we find fine foreign objects in glass and amber – even silver. These were family treasures and would doubtless have been given pride of place in the Saxon equivalent of the family front room. So I don't think we should rush to the conclusion that foreign objects somehow demand the presence of powerful middlemen or prestigious leaders, as some academics would insist.

In Chapter 5, I mentioned so-called Big Men who were thought by some to have been instrumental in the construction and planning of Stonehenge. Again, as we saw previously, this view has origins in the 1960s and '70s, and Mike Parker Pearson, the leader of the current Stonehenge project, does not accept it. Indeed, his team's detailed research has clearly shown that the history of Stonehenge's development was the result of innovation from within the communities that took part in the ceremonies there. Certainly, there was co-ordination and leadership – it would be ridiculous to deny that – but such leadership was firmly embedded within the social structure of the groups involved. It was not imposed from outside, or by upstart Big Men from within their own ranks. And why not? Presumably because the societies in question were well governed and strong enough, both to resist unwanted outside influence, and to control excessive ambition from within.

Along with the exaggeratedly hierarchical view of prehistoric British societies went the idea that these communities were motivated by so-called 'prestige goods economies'. Essentially, the principle behind this concept is what we witnessed in 1980s' Britain, with the dawn of the yuppies conspicuously quaffing tankards of champagne in smart City wine bars, while their Ferraris, Maseratis and Bentleys were accumulating parking tickets on the double yellow lines outside. In their case, the more conspicuously they spent their money, the greater was their perceived wealth and success – at least in the eyes of other (equally deluded) City people. The anthropological parallel usually cited was the custom known as the Potlatch, in which tribal leaders along the west coast of Canada held feasts where vast quantities of salmon were consumed; after the feast, hugely valuable objects were destroyed in a display of conspicuous consumption that made the London yuppies look Puritan. But it was considered to be worth it, because it gave the donors enormous social prestige, and with that, of course, came respect, power and influence.

These concepts were gaining in popularity in Britain during the early 1970s. I was working in The Royal Ontario Museum, Toronto, at the time and we had an exceptionally fine collection of West Coast ethnographic material, from people such as the Nootka of British Columbia.[21] I loved their superb carvings and vital culture, which of course included the Potlatch, but everything about these people was foreign to me: they were fishers, rather than farmers. They lived along a lush, but narrow, coastal plain with the mass of the Rocky Mountains behind them. So their unique lifestyle had arisen partly as a response to their naturally opulent surroundings. The idea that the people who laboured in the fields around Flag Fen then spent their time in lavish competitive feasting seemed and still seems, frankly, outlandish. Yes, we know that feasting did take place in and around the Fens, and there are prehistoric cauldrons, and the rather gruesomely named 'flesh-hooks' (probably used to remove pieces of cooked meat from the cauldron) to prove it, but there is a wealth of difference between a seasonal or ceremonial family dinner – at, say, a funeral or prehistoric Christmas – and a once-in-a-lifetime let's-all-go-mad Potlatch. I'm sure there was a certain amount of competition, too, between different families and communities; such things are only human nature, when all is said and done. But on the truly massive scale of a Potlatch? The proponents of these ideas argued that highly hierarchical societies based around competitive consumption produce spectacular monuments, such as the massive carved totem poles of the Nootka, or the thousands of stone statues on Easter Island.[22] But one could point to other areas too, such as Madagascar, where the monuments are spectacular, but the societies who built and used them are not particularly hierarchical.[23] Put simply, big monuments do not equal Big Men. And now, at long last, I can report that other eminent prehistorians, and not Mike Parker Pearson alone, are challenging concepts that I have always thought were misapplied to Britain.[24]

It is also worth recalling here that if any part of Britain can boast the natural resources of the West Coast of North America, it must be the Fens, as the recent extraordinary discoveries at Must Farm, near Flag Fen, are demonstrating. The area is similarly rich in fish, eels, wildfowl and grazing. It's a far more opulent landscape than, say, Salisbury Plain or indeed many other upland regions of Britain. Yet I can find no archaeological evidence whatsoever for a prestige goods economy based around conspicuous consumption. So why did these ideas gain such credence, if the supporting evidence out there in the field was largely absent? To answer this question we must briefly examine, not archaeology so much, as archaeologists.

That last remark was a lightly veiled hint that this dispute from within archaeology has general lessons for today. I have always felt that when it comes to Britain, these top-down ideas were themselves proposed top-down by theoretical archaeologists who had a deep knowledge of the anthropological and philosophical literature, but knew less about the monuments, and even less about the landscape and agrarian lifestyle of the societies in question. To my mind, this says something about the social structure of archaeology in Britain, where a clear split has arisen between 'do-ers' and 'thinkers'. Indeed, I suspect this split is not unique by any means to archaeology alone. It's something of a British phenomenon and might perhaps be a distant consequence of, or reaction to, the once-rigid English class system. But whatever its cause, it is nonetheless there. We saw it in the recent banking crisis, where there was a huge divide between the traditional retail, or high street, bankers and the new yuppie City gamblers. Such divisions seem to be something of a growing phenomenon in modern Britain and can be seen in a number of different sectors, where highly paid managers and consultants have far more power and influence than mere practitioners; aside from the financial services and politics, this can be seen most clearly in the National Health Service and the BBC.

So to sum up, the New Order came into existence around 1500 BC, at the onset of the Middle Bronze Age. But over five centuries later, by the end of the Late Bronze Age and into the Iron Age, it had given rise to a series of changes and developments that were to give Britain a most distinctive set of regional identities, which were unified by certain key features to do with their dwellings and domestic arrangements. Although most of the people resident in Britain were probably unaware that they were living on an island, their societies were in close touch with each other, and were in regular contact with the European mainland. As we will see in the last chapter, the last millennium BC was an exciting time of population growth, landscape consolidation and of social and economic development. But we should never forget that it was all made possible by the Domestic Revolution and the consequent New Order.

We must continue our story, which is now approaching historical times. All revolutions, all movements, have consequences, to which we tend to attach less significance, usually because they happen more gradually. But in this instance that would be a big mistake, because what happened in the subsequent Iron Age was to have a major effect on the culture and identity of the people of Britain. It affected not just the way people responded to the Roman Conquest, but also to the rise and growth of Romano-British culture, into subsequent post-Roman and Saxon times, as well. Such labels can themselves be misleading, and over the years people have paid more attention to the 'Roman' and supposedly 'Saxon', at the expense of the British. But recent research now demands that we do not ignore the indigenous cultural contributions to the development of early historic Britain. In the last chapter we will see how these emerging regional identities grew to maturity under the guise of the Celts, during the Iron Age.

7

After the New Order: Celtic Britain
(1000 BC–AD 43)

I have headed this chapter with what some Iron Age specialists refer to privately as 'that C word ...': Celtic. It's a very difficult term to define or to describe, because it is not, and never was (even in antiquity), an ethnographic term like, say, Inuit or Iroquois. But it is nonetheless useful because most modern people recognize that it has something to do with the way people lived in pre-Roman Britain. And that is the sense in which I intend to use it here.[1]

If we take that working definition one step further, I would feel more comfortable calling the culture of Iron Age Britain Celtic than describing the people as Celts. The latter implies a fair amount of what one might term racial integrity, or unity, whereas the archaeological evidence suggests that the population of the British Isles was actually quite diverse and at the same time very ancient. Many of the major historical influxes of people from mainland Europe, especially the Romans, the Saxons and the Vikings, have actually left quite a small trace in the modern population.[2] When I was a student, we were taught that the Celts came to Britain from Central Europe; we now know that this never happened and that a more likely origin for some of the people and certain cultural markers (such as the round-houses I will discuss at length shortly) was the Atlantic rim of western Europe, especially around Iberia and the Basque country. This reflects the fact that western Britain and Ireland have always been part of the Atlantic fringe of Europe. This was land that 'faced the ocean', in Barry Cunliffe's memorable phrase, and the communities who lived along its shores were unified by it.[3] Today we think of sea voyages as long distance, but in prehistory you took short, looping trips along the coast, rarely moving out of sight of land and always ready to disembark should the weather turn foul. This 'looping' pattern of navigation had the effect of drawing coastal communities together; indeed, we saw direct evidence for it in items like those quern-stones at Flag Fen.

So I do not plan to spend much time discussing genetic origins, because although they might have initial relevance, I'm far more interested in how the cultures of Iron Age Britain evolved to assume the identities that we now group together as Celtic. Again, as a student, we were taught that the Iron Age brought about some remarkable changes (like the introduction around 750 BC of ironworking), which indeed it did. But anyone who has ever conducted an excavation of a site dating to the centuries of the Bronze/Iron Age transition (say 900–700 BC) will know only too well that it is impossible to be certain when the change of 'Age' happened. I can think of no site in Britain where there is any evidence that settlements were suddenly abandoned or, come to that, begun at this transitional period. The overwhelming impression is of continuity. In landscape terms, the settlement pattern of the later Bronze Age is identical to that of the Early Iron Age; if there are, or were, any significant differences, they are probably caused by continuing population growth.

The latter part of the Iron Age lies at the overlap period between history and prehistory, when authors in the classical world were writing accounts of places, such as Britain, that were still effectively prehistoric. It is a time that has been labelled 'proto-history', and in some respects its treatment by scholars in the recent past has combined the worst of both history and prehistory, where there has been an obsession with minutiae, and a lack of perspective, even of common sense. I used to wait for my Iron Age lectures at university with some trepidation. If the subject had to do with farming or daily life, they were given by a wonderful teacher, Mary Cra'ster, who unlike some of our lecturers had actually directed excavations and understood field archaeology thoroughly. If Mary was not there, we were often treated to rather lofty accounts of Britain's place in a Romanizing world, which seemed to be about countless waves of invaders whose only effect on British culture was to alter the shape and style of the pottery then in general use.

Even at the time, I could not understand how hypothetical invaders could somehow penetrate to the heart of Britain's Iron Age homes and

15. The forecourt of the magnificent Neolithic long barrow known as Wayland's Smithy, in Oxfordshire. This is the area where funeral ceremonies would have taken place. Note the great stone portal to the right of the second large stone from the left: this was the entranceway into a short passage leading to three burial chambers.

16. Nympsfield long barrow, Gloucestershire. Most of the upper portion of the mound has gone, leaving the chambers exposed, with their roofing capstones and upper walls removed. This view is taken from near the centre of the mound, looking out towards the forecourt area (now a visitor's car park) to the three burial chambers, which were entered by way of a deliberately restricted entranceway between two large threshold slabs. Beyond the threshold is the entranceway passage leading out to a narrow forecourt. The start of the passage into the tomb is marked, in this instance, by just one surviving stone; compare this with the four massive stones at Wayland's Smithy (Plate 15).

17. In the Early Bronze Age, round barrows sometimes occurred in groups, known as cemeteries, such as the Seven Barrows, near Lambourn, Berkshire.

18. 'Seahenge', Holme-next-the-Sea, Norfolk, as first revealed in 1998. A de-barked, upside-down oak tree, whose cut-off roots can clearly be seen, had been deeply set into the ground. It was surrounded by a roughly circular setting of sixty-five closely set oak posts.

19. (*opposite, above*) Lifting the central inverted oak tree during the excavation of Seahenge, in July 1999. The roots are uppermost. Note the tree's flat base, which had been trimmed square after felling.

20. (*opposite, below*) The timbers of the Flag Fen post alignment under excavation in 1988. The archaeologist is clearing peat from a narrow row of posts. Immediately in front of her is a clear path or walkway, about a metre wide, before another, much larger, row of posts (*to the right and centre*). There were three further rows to the right of this picture.

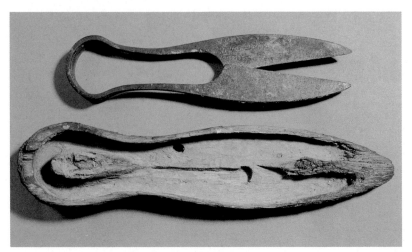

21. Bronze shears and their oak 'shoe' box, from the Power Station at Flag Fen (Iron Age, *c.* 600 BC). Note the slot in the base of the box to hold a small whetstone, and the slight enlargement to help lift it out. The shears were held in place by an iron bar that passed through leather loops fixed to low piers at either end of the box.

22. Three typical damaged Bronze Age items from Flag Fen. (*from the top*) Reinforced tip, or chape, of a sword scabbard; the top (wider) end has been cut and torn, to expose the wooden lining, and a decorative ball has been broken off the bottom (narrow) end. Leaf-shaped spearhead; both blade and socket have been bent and the wooden shaft has been snapped out, leaving a small piece still inside. Knob-headed stick pin; the shaft has been bent and the tip broken off.

23. Set within the lowest level (*c.* 1300 BC) of the timbers of the Flag Fen post alignment were four quern-stones that had been very lightly used, if at all. This one came from quarries in Wales or western England.

24. A small near-complete Late Bronze Age jar, which had been carefully placed among the horizontal timbers of the post alignment. This vessel is made in a thinner, finer ware than the more usual, heavier-duty, coarser pottery also found at Flag Fen. When it was placed in the ground (around 1000 BC), it probably contained a milky porridge.

25. (*above*) The ramparts of the unfinished Iron Age hillfort at Ladle Hill, near Newbury, Hampshire. In a finished hillfort, the banks and ditch would be smooth and continuous; here, however, the banks resemble separate mounds and the ditch a series of deep scoops. This pattern has led to the suggestion that the fort was constructed using 'gang labour'.

26. (*left*) A small 'burial' cairn, or heap of stones, placed within a Middle Bronze Age house (*c.* 1500 BC) on Roughtor, Bodmin Moor, Cornwall.

27. Reconstruction of a Bronze Age house (*c.* 1500 BC) at Flag Fen, Peterborough. Note the notched-log ladder leaning against the doorway and the turf-covered roof, which is 'crowned' by a cone of dry sedge, cut from local dykes.

28. Excavations at Welland Bank Quarry, near Market Deeping, south Lincolnshire. The topsoil and overlying river flood-clay have just been removed by machine (one is still working, extreme left), to reveal a large expanse of 'dark earth' to the left of a large Bronze Age ditch and bank, which runs diagonally to the hedge in the background. Note how the pale soil to the right of the ditch contrasts with the 'dark earth' on the other side.

29. (*overleaf, above*) A close-up of the 'dark earth' at Welland Bank Quarry. At this point the 'dark earth' is being finger-searched for finds, which have been placed in plastic bags. There were so many it proved impossible to search the entire deposit in detail.

30. (*overleaf, below*) The 'dark earth' at Welland Bank Quarry has been removed to the left of the standing figure, and the darker outlines of Bronze Age pits, houses and other settlement features beneath it can clearly be seen.

villages without leaving any other archaeological evidence for their presence. At the very least, the settlements they attacked should have been littered with bodies? Again, it was like the conspicuous consumption of recent theorists: an idea that was not backed up by any real evidence.

We now realize that the changes in pottery styles were almost certainly the result of the regular contacts that were developing during the Iron Age, through trade and social visits to the mainland of Europe. Just like today, people wanted to keep up with the latest trends. The point to emphasize here is that societies, both in Britain and across the Channel, were essentially stable. Sometimes history books and the traces of prehistoric folklore that survive, for example, in certain Irish sources, imply that Iron Age culture was based around warriors – what today we would call warlords. That may have been the case, but we must not then jump to the conclusion that Iron Age Britain was some kind of 'failed state'. The warrior side of life would have been kept under control; it was largely focused on semi-ritualistic cattle raids, where young men of different communities displayed their prowess, for whatever reasons (and I can think of one or two). But if we can use modern tribal societies as an example, these raids would rarely have involved serious casualties and would only have taken place during quiet times of the farming year – usually late autumn, after the hay and cereal harvests had been safely gathered in.[4]

So if the roots of the Celtic way of life don't lie at the start of the Iron Age (around 800 BC), we must then go back to the next possible date: 1500 BC, which means that the Domestic Revolution that gave rise to the New Order was actually the start of Celtic Britain. So the biggest and the last social development of prehistoric Britain did not coincide with any of the major technological transitions (from Stone to Bronze to Iron) of the Three-Age system. And in fairness to the curators who originally proposed the system in the early 19th century, it was only ever intended to be used as a means of ordering their museum collections. It was prehistorians in the late 19th and earlier 20th centuries who were to attach their essentially evolutionary theories to a system of object classification that was never intended to be used in such a manner. Today, I'm glad to say, we are moving in rather different directions. New and more accurate dates are allowing us to draw regional prehistories where terms such as Late Bronze Age are slowly becoming meaningless, being replaced instead by dates. With luck, these clearer, less terminology-ridden narratives will allow many more people to take an informed interest in the ancient history of their own backyards.

But enough of chronology and setting; it is time to return to field archaeology. And this time I want to start with something very British, and, for me, very special. As readers will recall, I came across Iron Age round-houses on my very first excavation and they made a lasting impression on me. As we have seen, they have roots that extend way back to the Neolithic and Mesolithic, but when I first encountered them they were *the* characteristic feature of Iron Age Britain. On the continental mainland, however, Iron Age communities built hall-like, rectangular longhouses. But Britain remained obstinately different. So what was going on?

THE ROUND-HOUSES OF PREHISTORIC BRITAIN

The origins of round-houses are complex, but as we have seen they can be traced back to the very first re-settlers of post-Ice Age Britain. A stricter concept of roundness may have been boosted later in the Neolithic (around 3000 BC) with the appearance of very round barrows which covered tombs reached by a long passage, known as 'passage graves'. Maybe these tombs were a reflection of round-houses, but maybe, too, this process was two way and the shape of houses was influenced by the tombs. I don't suppose we will ever know for certain: it's a classic chicken-and-egg situation. Then of course the smaller, but equally round, barrows of the Beaker-using people of the Neolithic/Bronze Age transition appear on the scene, and again, too, there seems to have been a strong link between tombs and contemporary houses. More chickens and more eggs. But what this close relationship – this symbiosis – surely demonstrates is that the concept of roundness was firmly embedded in British culture.

As I noted earlier, I'm not particularly concerned here with origins, so much as with the way culture developed across Britain; but if you are looking for the ancestors of round-houses, they are to be found along the Atlantic fringes of north-western Europe, especially parts of Spain and Portugal, and around the Bay of Biscay and then along the western approaches of the British Isles, as far north as Orkney and Shetland.[5] And recent research is revealing them on Iron Age sites along the Channel coasts of north-western France.[6] I'm always quite wary of simple functional explanations for something as culturally important as the shape of people's dwellings; but the smaller, more stable and aerodynamically sound, round building with a conical roof must always have appealed to people living along the windy and storm-prone Atlantic shores. Indeed, I stood safely inside a recon-structed Bronze Age round-house in the new Flag Fen Archaeology Park during the terrible hurricane of October 1989, while modern factory buildings all around were being stripped of their steel clad-ding (see Plate 27).[7]

So it would seem that the rapid social changes that comprised the Domestic Revolution of 1500 BC made special use of, indeed empha-sized, aspects of domestic life that were already present. We have seen how the new ceremonies provided a ritual, maybe even quasi-legal, underpinning or legitimation (a word I dislike, but no other will do) for the various rites of passage in people's daily lives. But that order-ing and careful structuring of life extended into the arrangement and layout of people's homes, too. And what is most remarkable is that the layout and floor plan of round-houses seems to have been remark-ably similar, right across Britain, in the 1st millennium BC. Again, one cannot be certain, but the similarities in the arrangement of different buildings is usually the result of a shared set of beliefs and values, as we saw when we discussed Seahenge, henges and indeed churches (pp. 147–9). But this does not just apply to 'special' or ritual struc-tures: beliefs and convictions had a profound effect on the way that people built and used their homes, even their outbuildings, and their villages, too. And that is why it is so important that the arrangement of both Bronze and Iron Age round-houses became very much more uniform, right across Britain, after about 1500 BC.

I cannot provide an overview of the round-houses of Iron Age Brit-ain, because that would take up far too much space, and anyhow it has been done very comprehensively recently.[8] But the point to stress

is that the many thousands of buildings of this period that we know
about were constructed in a huge variety of sizes and materials: wood,
stone, chalk, rocks, boulders and clay. The best preserved of all, the
brochs of north-western Scotland and the Northern and Western Isles,
were tower-houses, built from fine freestone masonry, and some survive which are over two storeys high (see Fig. 7.1).[9] For my money,
they are among the most remarkable buildings in the ancient world.
Similar, but less tall and with a larger ground plan, 'wheel-houses' are
also found in Highland Scotland; these featured stone-walled, cell-like
rooms arranged around a central space. Wheel-houses and brochs
probably housed extended family groups, but the vast majority of
British Iron Age people lived in smaller, single-storey round-houses,
large enough to hold a nuclear family of parents and children, plus,

Fig. 7.1 The Broch of Mousa, Shetland. This Iron Age building, the tallest
prehistoric structure in northern Europe, still stands 13.3 metres (44 feet)
high. It was probably built around 100 BC. Copyright © Crown Copyright
Historical Scotland, reproduced courtesy of Historic Scotland.

perhaps, one or two surviving grandparents. As I noted in the Introduction, these were indeed proper houses, not 'huts', and they illustrate
well the diversity of shape, style and size that a circular ground plan
can adopt. I will shortly discuss some of the features these buildings
had in common, right across the British Isles, but I would like to
pause briefly here and consider how those most remarkable of structures, the Scottish brochs, could have been used.

It used to be thought that these tower buildings provided evidence
for a hierarchical social structure, but the fact remains that large areas
of Highland and Island Scotland are peppered with them; some
570 are known to have survived, and doubtless many more remain to
be discovered below the ground – their stones having been reused for
other purposes. We now realize that they are far too numerous to
have been built by people living in a centralized, or very hierarchical,
society. They certainly can be considered defensive, like the medieval
tower houses further south on the Scottish Borders,[10] but like them,
their defensiveness was more about deterrence in a thinly settled,
open landscape, than repelling attack. A passing band of warriors, for
example, might well think twice before attacking a broch.

The consensus of modern opinion would be that brochs, like so
many other isolated Iron Age round-houses, were built and occupied
by 'independent land-owning families'.[11] I find it fascinating that their
sophisticated construction, with hollow walls that concealed a stair-
case, evolved among quite isolated communities who must surely
have maintained regular contact with each other throughout the
process, and subsequently. It suggests to me that non-hierarchical
communities are just as capable of being innovative as those with a
more top-down structure. The brochs were built over a long period,
too, during the three or four centuries each side of BC/AD. Again, this
illustrates how community and family-based systems can be stable
and enduring.

I can well recall learning as a student that the doorways of Iron Age
round-houses usually faced south-east. It was one of those facts one
slotted away, in the certain knowledge that it would be worth at least
one mark in the final exams. But to be honest, I did not grasp its
deeper significance until very much later, when I was faced with the
task of writing up a village of some 60 round-houses that our team

had excavated at Fengate in the 1970s. I have to say, it was a daunting task, even though I was then living and working full-time in England and my research time was not being interrupted by toing and froing across the Atlantic.

At the time, Maisie and I were living in 'the dig house', a large unoccupied bungalow that had been bought up by the Peterborough New Town Development Corporation ahead of its major programme of factory building at Fengate. The bungalow had been built shortly after the war and it was not the warmest house I have ever lived in. None of the radiators worked, and we heated ourselves as best we could with portable gas stoves and a small, very smoky fire; but even so, I had to scrape frost from the inside of the office windows during the bitterly cold winter of 1980. My office faced due east across our Newark Road excavations, where the early construction work on a new factory had been delayed by the terrible January weather. I can remember spreading plans of the Iron Age village on a table and being vividly struck by the fact that the doorways of the round-houses all faced east or south-east – straight into the teeth of the icy gales that were then blowing from the flat expanses of the open fen. I recall thinking that if I had been building our family home in the Iron Age village, I would have had our front door face west or south-west.

As I continued to research into the Fengate village for the specialist report, I had to examine similar sites right across Britain. And again, I found that nearly all Iron Age round-houses, whether on their own, or within hamlets or villages, faced east, or more usually, south-east.[12] Whenever I went to conferences and met other archaeologists digging or researching Iron Age settlements, I heard the same story: their round-house doors were aligned on the south-east. Britain is an island seemingly perched on the northern Atlantic shores of Europe; it is buffeted by gales in summer and autumn, and in winter the coldest, most destructive winds of all blow from off the North Sea. One might reasonably suppose that Iron Age people would have positioned their buildings' doorways to take advantage of any available shelter, and occasionally we do find this happening, especially in the most exposed locations, such as Orkney, or the Western Isles, but even in these places, doorways more often than not are aligned somewhere between east and south, and very often face due south-east.[13]

We saw in our discussions of the Neolithic and Bronze Ages in Chapters 4 and 5 how religious or ritual sites, such as barrows and henges, were often aligned on one of the solstices. And this, too, must surely explain the alignment of house doorways in the Iron Age; it also demonstrates once again that the hard-and-fast distinction between 'ritual' and 'domestic' simply did not apply in prehistory, where altars and shrines could often be incorporated into houses whose layout, in turn, would reflect current ideas of the spiritual cosmos. The archaeologist Alastair Oswald showed this very elegantly when he plotted the orientation and number of Iron Age round-house doorways and correlated the results against solar orientations (see Fig. 7.2).[14] Indeed, I would see the alignment of Iron Age doorways as an expression of the resident family's 'world-view'. Put another way, the orientation of their houses could be thought of as an element within a larger set of beliefs that were held in common by the community. There was more to it than simple convenience or functional

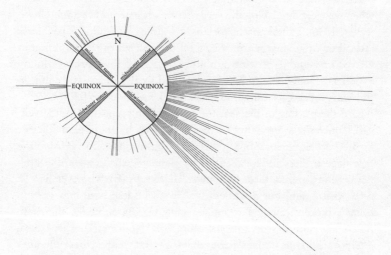

Fig. 7.2 Diagram showing the compass orientation of Iron Age round-house doorways and the direction of midsummer and midwinter solar solstices. The length of each line indicates the number of houses (the shortest lines are for a single house).

necessity. Those doorways were saying important things about the way people lived their lives and structured their days.

Of course there are always difficulties when one starts to discuss the shared beliefs of prehistoric societies, and the main problem is very often one of scale. So was the placing of the doorway an important tenet of religious belief, in the same way that churches today are still aligned east–west? Or was it something more general – as I have already hinted, for example, an illustration of a shared world-view: something that was desirable, but not absolutely essential? I would suggest that the exceptions prove the rule. There are Iron Age round-houses whose doorways face west or even north, but they are extremely uncommon. I'm only guessing, but I would suppose they amount to less than 5 per cent of the whole. But these exceptions are indeed significant, so I'm inclined to believe that doorway alignment was a reflection of a shared world-view, rather than a specific religious belief. For what it's worth, I also consider that this world-view had very ancient roots.

Readers may remember that I discussed the cyclical view of time when we were describing the very first re-settlement of Britain (Chapter 1). I don't think prehistorians are doing anything particularly radical or original when they suggest that early British communities viewed time and its passing as a non-linear, repeatable process. In my experience, many traditional farmers and small-holders still think in this way; indeed, as a small-scale livestock keeper myself, I, too, often regard the passing of the seasons as something repeatable and cyclical. I once drew up a linear, progress-based business plan for our farm's development, but that was only done to satisfy the mortgage-lenders and local authority planners, when we were seeking permission to erect farm buildings. Thankfully, I have never had to refer to it again, but doubtless we would be less devil-may-care in today's more straitened economic climate. Undoubtedly, there are now economic pressures to make one think in a more target-based, analytical and linear fashion; but that isn't to say, either, that time-lines and targets are necessarily an improvement on more traditional and less readily quantifiable methods. In my experience, season-on-season comparisons – the way most traditional farms judge their progress – can be perfectly adequate.

A cyclical view of time and the passing of the seasons is closely tied in with the movement of the sun and its position in the sky. So I see it as entirely natural that places like Stonehenge were so focused on the solstices. We have already seen that when the great henges ceased to be relevant, and the Old Order was replaced by the New, certain fundamental aspects of the earlier world-view continued to find expression, albeit in a slightly different and less formal manner. The practice of religion moved away from henges and great burial mounds to new, more localized, sanctuaries at places like Flag Fen, but the views that supported the religious beliefs were now enshrined in the very layout and orientation of people's homes, which were becoming rapidly more standardized as time passed. This process of standardization was also a reflection of improved building materials, as forest management techniques improved, combined with better carpentry and other practical developments.

Although the technical aspects of house-building in the Iron Age were important, they would have had minimal impact on the way houses were positioned or arranged in the landscape: that was all down to the preferences of individual families and the communities where they lived. So I now firmly believe that the shared south-easterly orientation of the vast majority of Iron Age houses was highly significant, because it suggests that people were increasingly subscribing to a commonly held set of values, that was in turn based around family life and a cyclical view of time. Indeed, the two were probably closely related and would have reflected each other with the daily movement of the sun, the passage of the seasons and family members at various stages of their lives. These were symbolically rich and multi-layered ideas, which then found material expression in the complexity of the various offerings at Flag Fen, but also, as we will see shortly, in the layout of round-house interiors.

By now I'm sure that many readers will be well ahead of me and will have realized that the south-eastern orientation of house doorways was to catch the light of the rising sun. But I don't believe that this was necessarily a practical measure – to make getting up in the morning easier or more pleasurable (although it may have helped). I see it, instead, as a symbol of the sun's important role in structuring the pattern of people's lives. I sometimes get slightly annoyed when I read that the people who built Stonehenge were merely worshippers of a sun god. They may well have been, but that term trivializes something far more profound. It treats the sun as a one-off phenomenon, something up there in the sky, that exists in and of itself; it misses the point that the sun is what lies behind the passage of the seasons and is the source of life and warmth. I think it entirely appropriate that ancient communities appreciated this deeper significance. They were aware that the sun gave structure to their lives and made it a focus of their religious beliefs. Sadly, too, the fact that we find it so hard to give their views the intellectual depth and dignity they deserve says something about ourselves and our attitudes not just to prehistory, but to other cultures in general. And that is why I still find the sight of people dressing-up in sheets and parading around Stonehenge at the midsummer solstice so irritating. Why, I ask myself, is it still acceptable to patronize the past?

In recent years archaeologists investigating Iron Age round-houses have found a number of other repeated patterns in their layout. Everything seems to have been based around the building's main axis, from the front door, via the central hearth to a north-western space, facing onto the front door. This space opposite the doorway became the principal focus of the building, and I suspect that this is where the head of the family would have sat or stood on formal occasions.

I have discussed some of the principles that may have been behind the layout of Iron Age houses in *Britain BC*, from which I have taken Figure 7.3 (see p. 238). Like the shape of the houses, some of these principles have roots in the remote past. The basic organizing idea, that the doorway faces the first light of morning, was unambiguously expressed at the great Neolithic passage grave (*c.* 3200 BC), at Newgrange, County Meath, in Ireland. Here, the first sunlight of the winter solstice actually shines through a small stone-lined window or 'roof-box', set into the ceiling of the outer passage.[15] Outside the week of the solstice the rising sunlight shines down or is reflected by the sides of the passage, illuminating the burial chamber deep within the tomb. Passage graves are often richly decorated and use other features, such as their acoustics, to create the special atmosphere that their interiors, surrounded by the bones of the departed, have.[16] Later in the Neolithic, we find henges and stone circles aligned on sunrise and sunset, as we discussed earlier, at places like Stonehenge, Sea-henge and many more.[17] I'm in absolutely no doubt that these solar alignments were deliberate and were an expression of the daily and seasonal passage of the sun, which had become such an important organizing principle in people's lives.

It is interesting therefore that the so-called 'dressers' of Neolithic houses on Orkney, so vividly illustrated by that well-known example at Skara Brae (see Plate 12), were positioned directly opposite the doorway. Similar examples of stone-built furniture have been found in houses elsewhere in Orkney and most particularly at the Barnhouse settlement close to the Stones of Stenness. Here, some of the buildings, especially one particularly large house, also served a special, probably religious, purpose, connected with the Stones nearby. But perhaps even more remarkably, they all shared organizing principles, with dressers, beds and hearths placed in the same positions, relative to one another.[18] This is not to say, of course, that people's daily lives were somehow 'ritualized', or controlled by a series of pre-rehearsed events or ceremonies (although, like Christmas dinners today, such things would have happened on special occasions). More probably, the simi-larity of house and shrine layouts was a reflection of commonly held beliefs and ideas that structured people's lives. In modern Britain, bed-rooms and bathrooms tend to be upstairs, whereas reception rooms (lounges, sitting-rooms etc.) are on the ground floor. In the recent past even the humblest terrace houses had 'front rooms', which were kept in pristine condition, were often very cold and were very occasionally used to welcome important visitors. These rooms were a reflection of the more formalized social structure of Victorian and Edwardian Brit-ain. They are wonderfully parodied in the brothers Grossmith's superb account of lower-middle-class life in suburban London, *The Diary of a Nobody* (1892).

So by at least 3000 BC buildings were being used and organized in much the same way, and not just in Orkney, but elsewhere in the off-shore islands of Scotland, and indeed, as we saw earlier, in the Stonehenge settlement at Durrington Walls. Again, I'm not saying that the people in such widely separated and far-flung communities led identical daily lives. But I'm suggesting that what I have rather lamely termed their 'world-view', the organizing principles behind the structure of their lives, would have been broadly similar: a cyclical attitude to time that followed the height of the sun and the passage of the seasons. Views and beliefs about such fundamentals as birth and death, sleep and meals, even the conduct of family life and the raising of children, would have been tied in to this framework and would help to explain the similarity of house layouts. It would seem likely that regional identities and differences would have become more apparent below this level of commonly held beliefs. We can observe this illustrated on the ground in the layout, size and arrangement of burial mounds, which, as we have seen, are found across the British Isles prior to 1500 BC. The important point to note here is that they differ significantly from region to region, and this does not merely reflect local geology and the availability of materials. A rocky cairn in North Wales, for example, will differ significantly from a superficially similar monument in, say, the Pennines.

I shall try not to repeat myself, but it's impossible to describe, let alone to understand, the layout and arrangement of Iron Age house interiors without looking at much earlier practices. Those similarities surely demonstrate the essential cultural continuity of British prehistory since the arrival of farming, around 4000 BC. Houses of the Neolithic and earlier Bronze Age shared many aspects in common, but they also displayed regional variations, where they differed quite widely in size, shape and orientation. The evidence becomes a little less clear in the later Neolithic, but regional variability seems to have continued well into the Bronze Age. The situation, however, began to change quite rapidly in the centuries around 1500 BC, when we start to see the emergence of the round-house as the prevailing building type. Again, we must not oversimplify, because we do know about many square and rectangular buildings in the later Bronze and Iron Ages, but these are very much in the minority. Indeed, one could almost say that they are the exceptions that prove the rule.[19] Moreover, many of these, especially the larger examples, were probably shared or communal buildings – perhaps broadly analogous to some of their Neolithic hall-like antecedents.

As the layout and orientation of round-houses became more standardized, the differences that might indicate regional cultural diversity become subtler and harder to detect. I have not done a detailed statistical analysis, although doubtless somebody will soon, but I get the strong impression that house doorways in the Fens, the region I know best, tended to be orientated closer to due east, occasionally even towards the ENE, rather than towards the south-east, which would be more typical of, say, the Thames Valley and elsewhere.[20] This tendency in the Fens is perhaps the more remarkable given the region's notoriously bitterly cold 'north-easters', those infamous 'lazy old winds' that cannot be bothered to blow round you – so go straight through. Again, as I suggested earlier in this section, this strongly suggests that the setting of a house's orientation was deliberate and was based on local culture and practice. Despite all one's instincts to the contrary, it does not seem to have been a practical response to the conditions that prevailed in any given area.

There have been attempts, many based on earlier work by Mike Parker Pearson, to link the underlying solar orientation to the passage of the seasons, and the way life would have been organized in and around Iron Age round-houses (see Fig. 7.3).[21] Again, one must stress that these are not firm conclusions and are best seen as 'best efforts' to understand patterns of life in societies that kept no written records. But it is interesting that since the principles were first proposed, in 1996, they have remained valid; more to the point, no consistent evidence has yet been revealed to debunk them, while newly excavated data is generally supportive. That is about as cautious a way I can find to suggest that they are probably quite accurate.

This is not the place for a detailed discussion of the way that round-houses might have been used, but some features are consistent, right across the British Isles. The location of the hearth at the centre of the house is almost certainly a practical choice. Round-houses have conical roofs and the fireplace has to be positioned near the centre of the floor if the smoke is to filter out through the thatch (a hole at the apex lets out the heat and makes the fire vigorous and impossible to control). Meat, cheese and other food hung in the smoke of the roof space would soon be cured and would store well.

Essentially the space within round-houses was organized as if to follow the daily passage of the sun. The living and eating spaces were to the south and west (Fig. 7.3 (a)). Evidence for food preparation is often found on the north-western side of the building, where light

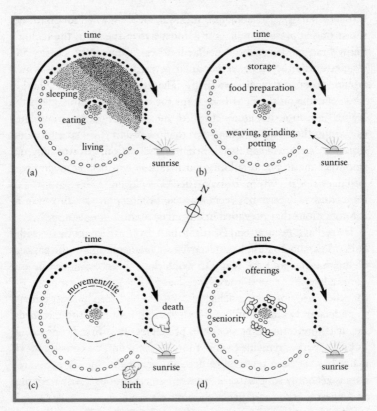

Fig. 7.3 Four ways of linking the cyclical passage of time to the use and layout of Iron Age round-houses and the orientation of sunrise: (a) daily time, (b) seasonal time, (c) lifetime and (d) ancestral time (combined with seniority).

from the doorway would have been best – so decisions were not necessarily based on ideological considerations alone. Most people seemed to have slept around the periphery of the house, and mostly on the northern side. The lifetime cycle (Fig. 7.3 (c)) is admittedly more speculative, but it is not unusual to find burials, even mummi-fied remains, within houses, or beneath their eaves, and these are usually found in the northern sector. I have also come across burials close to buildings, and again, these are often found to the north, although in crowded villages it is often hard to determine whether a grave can be linked to a particular building.[22]

I have long been struck by the fact that as time passed, houses became more standardized in shape, layout and indeed in size. Frankly, it was not what I would have expected. The conventional wisdom would have it that highly stratified, hierarchical societies construct large, almost palatial buildings for their chiefs and leaders. But that is not what we find in Iron Age Britain, where I can think of only one good candidate for a 'palace' and that was constructed away from ordinary settlements in its own ostentatiously enclosed space. It also dates to the very eve of the Roman period and has been linked quite plausibly to the ruling elite of the Iceni of Norfolk; and it appeared so very late: right at the end of the Iron Age. If ever there was such a thing, this huge building at Fison Way, Thetford, and its sumptuous tightly hedged gardens, must surely be the exception that proves the general rule.[23]

IRON AGE HILLFORTS:
SYMBOLS OF IDENTITY

We have seen how the power of emerging Iron Age tribal leaders would have been curtailed by family constraints, and this, I would suggest, was the main reason why we so rarely come across large buildings as symbols of personal power. Instead, as the second becomes the first millennium BC, we see the appearance in the later Bronze Age of the first hillforts. I visualize these, if you like, as communal palaces – as a community's expression of identity and pride. That is not to say, of course, that the tribal hierarchy would not have played a part in their layout and organization, but the labour involved would have been huge and I simply cannot see so many being constructed right across Britain, and indeed on the continental mainland too, by coercion alone. And again, if that were the case, then each hillfort would surely boast a large and very special house for the person who forced through the construction. But such exceptional buildings are entirely lacking; instead, most houses are of roughly the same size, and if there is differentiation, it is often subtly expressed by, for example, doorway orientation, as we will see at Yeavering Bell, shortly.

By about 500 BC, hillforts proliferate across the British landscape. As their name suggests, they were fortified sites, often, but not always, built on the tops of substantial hills – usually in spectacular locations visible from miles around. But if hills were absent they were built on flatter ground, and I can think of two good examples in the Fens.[24] I have given my personal view of why they were built, but there are many other, usually more military, explanations that I do not intend to review here; one thing, however, is abundantly clear: they were intended to impress.[25] Indeed, after about 450 BC we see a process of rationalization beginning to happen: some hillforts are abandoned and others are massively enlarged. Generally speaking, the enlarged hillforts are spaced across the landscape, leading many prehistorians (myself included) to conclude that they represent the territories of emerging tribal confederations.[26]

Given their name, it is reasonable to ask whether they were indeed forts (as they were not always placed on hills). To which I trot out the academic's favourite reply: it depends what you mean by the word 'fort'. They acquired the name because of their construction, which consisted of one or more massive banks and ditches, known as ramparts, which surrounded an area of land often of a few acres and usually on a hill top. On the interior, and usually around the inner edge of the ramparts, we frequently find the remains of ordinary domestic round-houses; but some hillforts appear to be empty, or at best sparsely inhabited, while others, such as Danebury and Maiden Castle in southern England, have even been compared with small towns.[27] Large earthen ramparts also surrounded many earlier medieval castles, which is why it was assumed that the earthworks of hillforts were defensive, too.

I don't consider it appropriate to think of these very varied sites as 'forts' in the modern or post-medieval sense of that word. They were never purely military in either use or intention. Indeed, it would be a great mistake to think of prehistoric warfare as anything resembling its medieval or modern equivalents, in scale, duration, hatred or brutality.[28] Almost never were whole populations involved. So, yes, it is fair to say that hillforts could indeed have been defended, but they were also massively over-constructed and there is still little solid evidence for their regular use in warfare: hundreds have been excavated and direct evidence for conflict is still remarkably elusive (and just as often found out in the landscape, some distance away from the ramparts).

Strange as it might seem, the very best archaeological evidence for organized intercommunal warfare in prehistoric times comes from the earlier Neolithic, from causewayed enclosures in the south-west, in Dorset and Cornwall, where much of the conflict seems to have been with bow and arrow.[29] There is evidence for organized warfare, too, in Bronze Age Europe, where it has been described as 'a defining characteristic', whatever that might mean.[30] By the Iron Age, the idea of combat had became more embedded within the social order, inasmuch as weapons become important symbols of social rank, as we saw at Flag Fen.[31] But despite the presence of some 3,300 hillforts in Britain, the evidence for pitched battles within or near them is remarkably sparse. Indeed, the best-known 'war cemetery' of all, at Maiden Castle, has been conclusively shown to have been a long-lasting, largely civilian, cemetery.[32]

Perhaps the simplest way forward is to take every hillfort as a separate case, and treat each one as a particular expression of a given tribal group's identity. As we will see at the very end of this chapter, I think it probable that their appearance marks a return to earlier practices: we know they must have taken a huge amount of labour to construct, and in some respects – like the henges much earlier – their building, frequent enhancement and modification was also their use. In other words, the raising of massive ramparts was rather like the erection of vast stones, a labour-intensive task intended to draw large numbers of people together for broader social reasons, to do with communal loyalty and coherence. The erection of a hillfort was a clear illustration, not just to visitors, but to other members of the same tribe, that their people were capable of organizing the necessary materials (which would often have included huge quantities of timber) and labour to carry out what even today seem like prodigious feats of engineering. One or two unfinished hillforts are known, and these show clear evidence for 'gang labour'

in their construction.[33] The best-known unfinished hillfort is at
Ladle Hill, near Newbury (see Plate 25). I have already discussed
(Chapter 4) the nature of prehistoric gang labour, when describing
the building of barrows, and I think those observations apply
equally to hillforts, where the labour force would also have been
organized along family and community lines. Again, participation in
these projects encouraged individuals and families to display their
tribal loyalty.

My own view, and I know it is shared by many colleagues, is that
the hillforts were an expression of local pride and were constructed as
much to impress the community that built them as to deter incomers.
Rather like their later counterparts – the town walls of the Middle
Ages – they were also built to impress visitors. It might perhaps be
worth mentioning here that in areas subject to constant raids and
feuding (like the Scottish Borders), town walls were rarely constructed; such work usually began once a degree of order had been
re-established.[34] At that point, for example in the Welsh Marches in
the time of Edward I (1239–1307), the new walls and castles were
symbols of a changed controlling authority.[35]

One might have expected that the hillfort phenomenon would have
reached its zenith at the time of the Roman conquest (AD 43), but it
didn't. In fact, viewed historically, it seemed to have peaked too early.
Between about 200 and 100 BC, hillforts ceased to be elaborated and
many were abandoned in favour of undefended or 'open' settlements
in the valleys and plains, where people had been living in growing
numbers throughout the Iron Age. Again, this is not what one would
have anticipated at a time when the population was still steadily rising, with consequent pressure on limited farmland. So what was going
on? My feeling is that the hillforts had largely served their purpose:
they had provided permanent expressions in the landscape of tribal
territory and identity – rather like the towers and spires of the thousands of parish churches that still epitomize local identity. I know of
no examples where hillforts were flattened or obliterated, as might
have happened had they indeed been military in the modern sense of
the word. More to the point, when the Romans did eventually arrive,
they often constructed temples or shrines within prominent hillforts,

the best-known example being Maiden Castle, in Dorset.[36] This would strongly suggest that the old hillforts still represented something of enduring importance to the communities that erected them. Then, much later, in post-Roman times, we see a large number of hillforts, especially in the south-west, being rebuilt and reoccupied in late and post-Roman times. The best known of these forts is, of course, South Cadbury, in Somerset (the mythical Camelot).[37] So it would seem that in many instances their potency as symbols of local identity endured for the best part of a millennium.

Of all the sites of Iron Age Britain, one might expect hillforts to have produced the clearest evidence for social ranking and hierarchy. But the evidence is surprisingly thin on the ground, which is not to say, however, that it is entirely absent. It is, however, very subtly expressed. One example that springs to mind is high in the Cheviot Hills of Northumberland, about 12 miles inland from the undulating coast of Lindisfarne and Bamburgh Castle. This is indeed historic territory. These two places aside, the area is best known to archaeologists for its Anglo-Saxon regal centre at Yeavering, which has revealed royal buildings belonging to the ruling dynasty of the kingdom of Bernicia, dating to the 620s AD.[38] I don't think it a coincidence that this important post-Roman centre was located in the flat valley of the River Glen, directly below the towering ramparts of the Iron Age hillfort of Yeavering Bell.[39]

A few years ago I had the great pleasure of walking over the interior of Yeavering Bell with its most recent surveyor, Stewart Ainsworth of English Heritage (and *Time Team* fame). He showed me some of the 125 houses his team had revealed (double the number of any other hillfort in northern England). Identifying them took experience and a good eye for a 'house platform': shallow scoops back into the hillside to level the ground for a house floor. Sometimes the doorways were marked by larger stones and often, too, one could spot the remains of collapsed drystone walls. The doorways of the houses all faced east or south-east, with the exception of two slightly larger buildings which were set on either side of the roadway leading in from the main southern entrance to the hillfort (see Fig. 7.4). The doorways of this pair of houses faced due south, towards the fort entrance. To my mind this

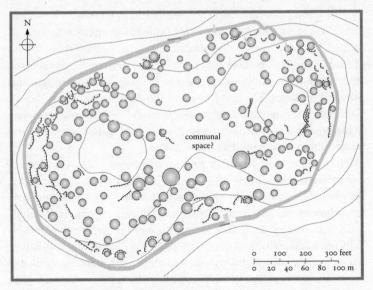

Fig. 7.4 Plan of the hillfort at Yeavering Bell, Northumberland. Note the two large round-houses set back from the main, southern, entrance into the fort, and how their doorways face towards the entrance to the fort. These houses would probably have belonged to the leaders of the tribal group that built and occupied this important hillfort.

positioning is crucial. It reminds me of those dressers in the Neolithic Orcadian houses, which were directly opposite the door, but on the far side of the hearth (Fig. 7.3 (d)). These houses are far more than just guard-buildings or gatehouses. They must have been intended for the resident tribal leaders, who could have dispensed with the usual rules of doorway alignment. It is also clear that the two houses were intended to impress visitors, and, indeed, locals. They could have been set away from the other houses, but they were not. Instead, their positioning within the larger settlement suggests to me that the leaders were still very much a part of the community: in a real sense that was their wider family and they would have been responsible for everyone who looked up to them as they passed by their homes.

DISCOVERING ROUND-HOUSES

Prehistorians are not very good at blowing their own trumpets. To make matters worse, the media like to puff the obviously appealing: Stonehenge (anything, however relevant), henges in general, burials (especially kings in car parks) and so forth. As a consequence, the true achievements of prehistory often remain hidden from public view. Round-houses are a good example of this.

The serious study of Iron Age round-houses only began in the 1930s, continuing during the Second World War.[40] Prior to this work, people generally believed that the prehistoric population lived in hypothetical 'pit dwellings', which (as any practical person would know) would rapidly have filled with water in winter. After the war research gathered momentum, and during the 1960s and '70s there was a spate of new discoveries; indeed, our own work in the Peterborough area added about 70 to the known total of round-houses. And as we have seen, we now know of many thousands of examples from right across the British Isles. Even so, for most people they remain something strange and remote. One can relate, for example, to an ancient church: something that most people in Britain either grow up with, or close to; even those of us who no longer believe, feel at home and often at peace within them. Similarly, stone or brick houses, even the smallest rustic mud-and-stud cottage, are familiar spaces. But this does not apply to round-houses, even if you have visited and entered them at places like Little Butser, Hampshire, Flag Fen, or the Cranborne Ancient Technology Centre, Dorset. Over the years, I have realized that familiarity needs more than just casual exposure; it can require immersion.

My time of immersion came between 1989 and 1995 when I would conduct regular tours through the archaeology park at Flag Fen. We were open all week in those days and I would do two or three tours a day; indeed, sometimes I would do considerably more, to such an extent that my voice failed and I developed polyps on my vocal cords, which then had to be removed surgically. It took a year for my voice to recover completely. I well remember one particular day. I had been trying to interest a group of visitors to Flag Fen and had not been succeeding. I could see in their faces that they viewed our rebuilt round-houses as a sort of archaeologist's fantasy. Somehow, I had to get them to think differently. Then it began to rain, so naturally we moved into one while the shower passed. While we were inside, somebody asked me if I had ever excavated a round-house. By that point I was tired and was about to respond with a put-down, to the effect that I had probably dug about a hundred, when something made me pause. Perhaps I could get the visitors to take our reconstruction more seriously if I explained how I had discovered round-houses for myself? I have learned that if you make things personal they often strike home. Anyhow, I'm glad to say that it seemed to work, and this is more or less what I told them.

I first read about round-houses at university, but learning from books is one thing, experience is quite another; and I first *experienced* a round-house in the winter vacation of 1965/6, during my second year reading archaeology and anthropology at Cambridge. One of the other students at Trinity College, by then in his third year, was Tim Potter. Tim was both highly intelligent and practical and we both shared a deep and abiding interest in gin.

Sadly Tim is no longer with us, but we were very good friends at Trinity. Later he went on to achieve great things in Italy and then at the British Museum. One day, in 1965, I went round to his rooms in Great Court to find him filling in an official expenses form for the Ministry of Works, Ancient Monuments Inspectorate (the 1960s' equivalent of English Heritage). Being a penniless and nosey student, I looked over his shoulder and was astounded by the money he was claiming: truly, here lay riches beyond the dreams of avarice. Tim looked up as I passed him a gin and lime.

'Are you interested?' he asked.

Interested? For money like that, I would have bitten his hand off. So we arranged that I would join him at the now-famous excavations at Mucking, near Thurrock, overlooking the Thames Estuary, in south-east Essex.[41]

It was a Sunday in late December and I was in the passenger seat of Tim's aged black Ford Popular. We stopped for an obligatory lunch-time pint in Potters Bar; no student called Potter could have resisted that, but as a result we arrived in Southend-on-Sea around six o'clock, well after dark. We had to find somewhere to live. The Ministry of Works, in its infinite wisdom, paid a fixed amount for board and lodging, so we felt honour bound to find somewhere cheaper. Then we'd have more money for beer. I can remember walking the empty streets of outer Southend, up and down the A127, the main London road. The place was cold, damp, dark and deserted. At the best of times, seaside resorts can be grim places in the off-season, and on that winter's evening Southend was indeed bleak. Eventually we found a shared room above a run-down transport caff – it certainly lacked the gentility of a café.

We drowned our sorrows somewhere in town and fell into our cold, damp beds; but being young, we slept like logs. The next morning was wet and grey, but we were in fine fettle after a huge, greasy fry-up. Tim introduced me to Margaret Jones, the site director, and then showed me around the site. I had read about it at Cambridge, but the published plans simply could not convey the vastness of the real thing. Mucking was the first of the great open-area excavations that were to become such an important feature of British archaeology in the last four decades of the century. In those days, huge gravel-pits routinely trashed thousands of acres of archaeology every year: hundreds of prehistoric and Roman graves and settlements, Viking and medieval farms, even deserted medieval villages were simply smashed by the bulldozers, completely unrecorded. Today we are slowly piecing together how much might have been destroyed in this orgy of archaeological destruction, but if Mucking was a representative sample of what we have lost, then I would rather not think about it.

I will never forget that tour of Mucking. The precise details became blurred as we walked around. It covered acre after acre and there was simply too much to take in: dozens of Roman graves, prehistoric round-houses, Saxon burials, prehistoric, Roman and early medieval farmsteads, sunken-floored Saxon houses, Bronze Age fields and droveways – I could go on and on. It was like opening the pages of a vast illuminated manuscript and we were walking through the fine illustrations down the margins. At this stage, we could see what each feature was quite clearly, because Margaret had persuaded the gravel company – Hoveringham and Co., long since disappeared, but all credit to them – to strip off the topsoil carefully, so as not to damage what lay directly beneath. Then the excavation would add colour to the picture, by giving dates and revealing details of daily life, and, of course, death.

It was light gravel land, without any clay to cause sticky mud, so the process of topsoil stripping was clean and efficient: the result was that the darker earth of graves and other ancient features stood out clearly against the much paler sands and gravels into which they had been cut. In many ways the actual process of excavation and recording was pretty simple: dark was ancient and man-made, while pale was the untouched geological 'natural'. It was an excellent and straightforward site for a beginner like me.

I had been on a couple of digs in my gap year before starting my degree, but these had been relatively small, well-organized but essentially amateur affairs. This was my introduction to the world of professional, commercial archaeology. In those days we called it 'rescue archaeology' because we were, in theory, rescuing the past from the developers. I say 'in theory', because we were doing nothing of the sort. In reality, we were salvaging a very partial – dare I say it, possibly even an inadequate? – record of sites and features that would then be obliterated, and were certainly never 'rescued', by us, or anyone else.

But to return to that first day on site. We finished the tour and it was time for the morning tea-break, which I took on my own in the diggers' shed. Tim, Margaret and Tom Jones, the site photographer (and Margaret's husband), took theirs in the supervisors' hut. That was the way things were done in those days. I have to say, the solitariness of my cuppa made me rather resentful, but afterwards Tim laughed it off. I can't remember for certain, but he probably told me to think about the fat cheque that would be coming my way to pay next term's college bar bill. Anyhow, I soon got over it.

Back out on site we had been told to record features which had been dug the previous week. These included a number of Iron Age pits, ditches and post-holes that had once belonged to a series of farm buildings. In among them was the farmhouse itself, and being Iron Age (and I recall it fell somewhere in the middle of the Iron Age, maybe around 300–250 BC), it was of the standard round-house form. Over the years, ploughing had done a fair bit of damage, so that only the deeper features survived. I cannot recall if there was a central hearth, but there were two substantial door-posts and short lengths of the shallow circular gully that ran beneath the building's low thatched eaves and caught the rainwater running off the roof. The gullies were essential, because without them the base of the walls, and even the edges of the main house floor, would get damp in very wet weather. Those eaves-drip ring-gullies were the defining feature of round-houses. And now I was recording one. It was about 12 metres (40 feet) in diameter. If we allow for an eaves-width of no more than a metre – and you need low, wide eaves to keep the clay walls dry – then that gives an overall floor space of about 10 metres in diameter. Even my terrible maths can work out that the area of a circle, radius 5 metres, is 78.5 square metres (845 square feet).

I can remember working this out on the back of an envelope. That evening I took a tape measure back to our horrible room above the transport caff. I cannot recall the precise dimensions, but I would guess it measured roughly 2.4 by 3 metres (8 by 10 feet, the size of my garden tool shed), giving it a floor area of about 7.5 square metres. I was astounded: so you could fit our modern room into that middle Iron Age round-house about ten times.

And while we are on the subject of numbers, I didn't know it then, but over the thirteen years of the project, Margaret and Tom Jones's team at Mucking would excavate about 18 hectares (45 acres) and reveal 44,000 archaeological features, including about 110 round-houses, all closely similar to the one Tim and I worked on all those years ago.[42]

There were a number of things that intrigued me about that round-house at Mucking. For a start, the walls seemed remarkably slight. I would have expected much larger posts, sunk deeper into the ground, to support such a substantial area of roof, especially given the fact that Mucking was on the very edge of the Thames Estuary, where, as Tim and I knew only too well, the winds of winter could blow with bone-shattering ferocity. While I was there I looked at some of the earlier excavation plans, and again, wall foundations seemed remarkably slight. When the complete plans were eventually published, they showed that the walls of only a very few houses had survived at all intact, and again, they were remarkably slim, although the two upright posts that framed the front doorway were always substantial. These things set me thinking. I was not aware of it at the time, but Mucking had kindled an interest in prehistoric reconstruction – some call it experimental archaeology – that has never left me.

Over the years, I have rebuilt a number of Iron and Bronze Age houses and in the process have learned a great deal about their construction. For example, those large door-posts and slender walls were soon explained when we built the first of our houses in the Flag Fen Archaeology Park, back in the early 1990s. It was then I discovered that the roof becomes a self-supporting cone if you build it right; and then all that the wall posts have to do is carry its weight and distribute any outward thrust not taken up by the purlins (the smaller timbers that tie the spoke-like main rafters together). But if you break the circle of the wall, you immediately create an area of weakness and small posts tend to splay or bend outwards. To avoid this you need two large door-posts and an equally substantial lintel over the top.

I can remember thinking, as we made all the mistakes that are inherent in experimental archaeology, how good it would be if we could talk to an Iron Age builder. And then I wondered whether such people existed, or did anyone share in this knowledge? I still don't know if there was ever a simple answer to that question, because some of the very largest round-houses, such as some well-known examples from Dorset, have diameters well in excess of 15 metres (50 feet).[43] One of these has been reconstructed at the Cranborne Ancient Technology Centre, in Dorset, and its sheer size and the sophistication of the carpentry needed to build it surely suggest that specialist carpenters must have been used in the Iron Age. We also have good reason to believe that other highly skilled trades, such as metal smiths, wheelwrights and boat-builders, would have been performed by specialists, so this need cause no surprise.

But my interest in ancient reconstruction has affected my own life, too, and that, in turn, has influenced the way I think about the past. I have discussed (in the Introduction) whether there is such a thing as 'accurate' or 'unbiased' prehistory, and came to the conclusion that we cannot, indeed should not, eliminate our personal views and experiences from our thoughts about the past. But it might help, if from time to time (as I'm doing in this book), we made them explicit. And

I'm by no means alone here: in the last three decades, most prehistorians have given up striving for an 'objective' view of the past, and have sought instead approaches that are more relativist, that paint a picture, to use a current phrase, in different shades of grey.[44]

One way I can illustrate how non-archaeological experiences can throw unexpected light on one's personal appreciation of the past, is by describing how the building of our own house has been a profoundly important experience for me and my wife, not just in our lives together, but in our outlook on prehistory and the world in general.

BUILDING HOMES AND RELATIONSHIPS

We constantly hear that we don't have enough housing stock. New houses are not being built. For many people mortgages are cripplingly expensive – and hard to get in the first place. One result of the housing shortage is that people are delaying starting their families. Laying aside the problems this might cause in the future, it does clearly show that a home – a physical place, a building – is needed if a family is to be started and raised. Of course, the prospective parents don't have to own the building, but some form of long-term secure tenure is essential if children are to be brought into the world.

In many societies, the act of building a house is seen as sufficient. No further title to the building would be required. The building process would inevitably involve friends and family to provide practical and financial assistance. (In a non-coin-using society, such assistance would be in the form of gifts, or of binding promises as to future action.) This group of people would not have gathered together unless all were agreed that the young couple had a stable relationship, and had done everything the community required to erect their new home in its chosen place. So concepts of land-ownership, as such, are probably irrelevant here. It would all have been about relationships with different clans and influential people in the community. Following the complex negotiations leading up to marriage, the most important aspect of establishing a new family in prehistoric times would then have been the building of the house. But what I did not realize until we did it ourselves is the profound effect house-building can have on relationships, and not just between the couple who are setting-up the home, but on other people living in the neighbourhood. While we were building our house, we must have been visited by everyone in the area, with offers of advice, help or practical assistance (only a few were just plain nosey); more to the point, those relationships are still strong, and in most instances we have been able to repay some of the favours we received; but it has inevitably taken time – something that is still available in rural communities.

In addition to our own house, I have also built three replica prehistoric round-houses in the archaeology park at Flag Fen. Now you might suppose that it was the construction of these ancient buildings, rather than our new home, that gave me the greater insights into past lives, but you would be mistaken. The former were interesting projects – fascinating even – but they were not done at the same emotional level at all; because the fact is, I was not planning to live in them. If they failed (and some early efforts nearly did), I still had a roof over my head – and of course I was not using my own money, as all the reconstructions were paid for with various grants and donations. Put another way, only a small part of myself, and none of my future, nor my marital relationship, was invested in them.

What I still think of as the 'real' house-building process was, however, very different. In fact, at times it could be quite fraught. For example, we had problems selling our old house and we desperately needed the capital it would raise, because we could only afford a small mortgage on our tiny joint income as freelance archaeologists. Delay might mean that something crucial, like the brick delivery, would fall through, yet we would still have to pay brick-layers. There were also big problems with the uneven load-bearing qualities of the fen sub-soil, and also the power supply and a host of other things. By the end of the process we felt battered; despite this, our relationship was a great deal stronger. We had built our house in middle life, but I can remember thinking at the time that a young couple doing the same thing would now be in a far better position to confront the vicissitudes of raising a family, once, that is, they had built their home.

Nothing can beat the feeling of being surrounded by your own bricks and mortar. The house becomes a symbol of the strength of the human relationship that gave rise to it in the first place. I strongly suspect that would have applied just as much in prehistory as it does today. So now, when I write about how we built our round-houses, I find it much easier to put myself into the emotional state of the original builders. They had so much invested in the process. So it was not just about carpentry, thatching and mud-wall building, as many rather dry prehistory textbooks would have us believe. In many respects, such accounts are missing the point entirely: there's far more to house-building than mere construction.

After a young couple and their two families have agreed where precisely to locate it, the first step in building their round-house would have been to mark the centre point. I can remember opening a bottle of something fizzy when the contractors started erecting the timber frame of our new house. It had been such a struggle just to reach that moment: planning permission had dragged on and on. Our first design had been a simple square box with a chimney at both ends. It was a good strong shape and traditional in the area, as the fireplaces at the gable ends spread the weight and provided balance in the silty fen sub-soils. We had spent several months driving around the district, examining the way farmhouses had been built, and this square form generally seemed to subside less frequently. Most were erected in the 19th and earlier 20th centuries, but quite a few were still being built after the last war.

Imagine our surprise when the local planning officer told us we were wrong: hadn't we observed that square box houses were rare in the Fens? Of course we immediately conceded to his superior knowledge, as we were well aware he had the discretionary powers to deny us permission. Why not, he suggested, have a layout with a turned-in gable end? It would be so much more interesting. Of course we agreed: what a great idea. Clearly he was a man of taste and discernment. We could see how he had progressed so far and so fast in the planning world. Towards the end of the meeting, Maisie casually asked him how long he had been working for the district council. Three weeks, came the reply. And where was he previously? He mentioned a town in Surrey. Maisie comes from Dorking and knew it well. Our new house, which incidentally we've grown very fond of, could be duplicated in any suburban streetscape there. So much for regional distinctiveness.

Next we experienced problems with foundations and electricity supply, but these had been overcome after a series of very happy coincidences, which I don't have space to discuss here; but the point is, it all took time. So when we saw those first timber joists being set up, we broke open a bottle of Cava from the little fridge in the barn we had erected the previous summer. In it we had established a comfortable kitchen – which we shared amicably with several dozen field mice and our dozy cats. We slept in a small caravan around the back.

Archaeologists often discover offerings in the wall footings or in post-holes. Sometimes these may be the bones of adults or children, and they are often described as 'foundation deposits'; they are normally explained in anthropological terms as efforts to appease the ancestors, or some such. That may well be the case. Personally, I favour something a bit less pretentious: when you are building a house, you think a lot about the future; about the life you will lead inside it, and the mark you are making on the landscape, which will remain there long after your own death. I can remember throwing a handful of small change into the concrete of the foundations. Was I appeasing ancestors? I don't know: I just did it. Today many people erect a date stone which usually carries their initials or just the year the house was built. You rarely see date stones on estate houses, built in large numbers by commercial developers. They are the clearest sign that the house was built by its first inhabitants, if not with their own hands, then in close collaboration with a local builder. These stones are the modern equivalent of 'foundation deposits'. Sadly, our own budget was too tight: any spare cash went into our only luxury: an Aga. Ask any archaeologist; he or she will always opt for diet over display.

The point I'm trying to make here is that building your own home is a fraught process and it always must have been. You could only do it in the quiet times of the farming year, which normally meant late autumn, winter or very early spring. In winter you have to contend with frost and snow and in spring and autumn it's the equinoctial gales. So each step in the process needs to be honoured or celebrated in some way. You can never be certain, but I can bet that our prehistoric house-builders would on occasion have quaffed a few mugs of strong ale or mead, and then maybe buried the ceramic mugs beneath the newly completed floor. And I'm equally sure that at some point they would have given thanks to the ancestors, just as today religious people will ask the local priest or vicar to say a few words of blessing once the house has been finished. More secular people (like us) have a house-warming party, which they then regret for ever, as new-laid floors are often soft, and scratch badly.

In the modern world we are rather brutal when it comes to quitting or tearing down a house. We sell up and go, generally leaving absolutely nothing in our wake. If we happen to be very notorious, someone might one day erect a plaque to say that we lived there. But in prehistory, largely I suspect because families were more closely identified with the homes they had built for themselves, abandoned houses were often given ceremonial burial, with a small heap of stones – essentially a cairn or burial mound – placed within the interior of the building, often close to the doorway and/or hearth.

I was able to excavate one of these sites on Bodmin Moor, in Cornwall, with *Time Team* (in 2006), and there could be no doubt that the small cairn we came across in a Bronze Age house had, indeed, been carefully and deliberately positioned there, and was not the remains of collapsed walls, as is sometimes claimed (see Plate 26). As we excavated I can clearly remember thinking that this cairn mattered to people at the time (around 1500 BC). It was a powerful symbol then, as now. Maybe the children erected it after their parents had died. We will never know. But what is quite clear is that whoever it was did not want others to live where their loved ones had spent their lives together. Put another way, the house, in their minds, had become a symbol of a relationship, of happy times, and doubtless, too, of love. I sometimes think that in the Bronze Age, people may have been better at handling such deep and complex emotions than we are today, less 'bottled-up' and able to share their emotions with family and community, largely I suspect because ritual and the spiritual world intervened in all aspects of their daily lives. In the light of my own personal experiences, I found, and still find, the exposure of that house cairn strangely moving.

The small-scale celebrations and ceremonies that are a part of house-building not only established the new family in the area, they also cemented other relationships and encouraged new partnerships. In the later Bronze Age many houses were built within existing fields and paddocks, whose layout was subtly altered to accommodate them – gateways were moved, new drainage gullies were dug, yards were sub-divided etc. This reflected the fact that the house and the farm were part of an integrated set-up, and both were firmly rooted within the family-based system of land tenure.

I'm of course fully aware that any comparisons between what happens today, in a free-market-based economy, and the remote past is at best tenuous: as we saw in Chapter 4, prehistoric economies were based essentially on the relationships between different clans and families; marriage settlements and similar long-term obligations would also have played a major role.[45] But I'm not seeking direct parallels here. I'm looking for something other than analogy. It was as if our new house and its little farm had suddenly acquired some kind of magnetic force, but without any publicity on our part. I can well remember being approached by several feed and fodder merchants, agricultural engineers, fencing contractors, hauliers and neighbouring farmers, while our timber barn was being erected (about a year before work began on the house). It acted like a magnet for any travelling salesman. The same can be said for the house, only this time it was butchers and fishmongers, central-heating oil suppliers, insurance salesmen (several of these) and people who fitted burglar alarms. Again, one can never be certain, but I'm in little doubt myself that similar things must have happened in prehistory. The point to note is that the building of a new house is not like the erection of a new allot-ment shed. It was, and still is, an event and a very important one in the lives, not just of the people directly concerned, but of the commu-nity round about. If a new husband or wife needed an in-depth introduction to local people, building a house was an excellent way to achieve it.

When it came to the building of a round-house, the marking of the precise centre point was followed by the setting out of the walls, which simply required a length of twine. The wall posts were usually spaced at intervals of roughly one metre (a pace), and on soft sub-soils were sunk about a third of their height into the ground. On chalk or limestone, the holes could be far shallower. I will not go into the various types of wall construction revealed by excavation, but these vary from dry stone, sometimes bonded with clay, to turf, to woven wattle hurdle-like panels and finally to the most common of all: the pleasant-sounding 'wattle-and-daub'. Wattle is simply a word to describe long, thin pliant sticks, about as thick as a man's thumb and usually cut from willow or hazel. These are woven between the wall posts, sometimes with a few intermediary stakes. It sounds a simple task, but each wattle must be woven from the opposite direction (because one end is thicker than the other and these need to be balanced as the wall builds up). Then they have to be beaten down firmly to lock them into place. In my experience this can be a very slow and energetic process. I normally use a heavy wooden hammer or beetle (and these have been found on Bronze and Iron Age sites), but a good stout stake or post will also do the job.

Once the weave of wattle has reached the top of the wall posts, usually some 1.5 metres (about 5 feet) above ground, the house-to-be resembles a neat circular sheep pen, with two extra-large posts framing the front door.[46] One reason why houses of this period rarely have two doors is that the doorway (as we have seen) is also a point of structural weakness. This is exacerbated by building-up the wattle-work walls: as you batter the woven wattle down, it actually creates considerable outward pressure on the walls because the straight wattle rods 'resent' being woven into a curve. As the walls grow in height, this outward force accumulates, which is yet another reason why wall posts need to be quite stout. Another, and almost certainly more important, reason for stout door-posts is that the entrance matters. It's a visitor's first impression and one that symbolizes the status of the people within.

The 'daub' component of wattle-and-daub is usually applied to the woven wattles of the wall after the roof has gone on, as this keeps off the rain and allows the wet mix to dry slowly and evenly; it would soon crack in direct sunshine. Animal dung – and I'm reliably informed that horse dung is the best – is traditionally added to a mix of clay and straw to make the finest daub, but it has to be kneaded very thoroughly; this takes much doing and might well have involved the community's children. I was only able to use dung for one of the three round-houses I have built, because we were warned (mistakenly) that visitors to Flag Fen might catch CJD (Creutzfeldt-Jakob disease, the human form of BSE: bovine spongiform encephalopathy). It takes a couple of weeks for the daub to dry, but when it does the finished walls are hard and remarkably well insulated. We gave ours as smooth a finish as we could manage, and then painted them with a white lime wash. This pale surface treatment greatly brightened the otherwise rather gloomy interior.

The roof of a round-house is easy to erect badly. The main rafters – the equivalent of the ribs of an umbrella – need to be selected carefully. We used ash taken from an overgrown coppice, which was probably last cut down in the 1950s. The poles were long and straight and about 15 to 23 centimetres (6 to 9 inches) in diameter. The rafters were linked together by smaller purlins. Our purlins were made from hazel or from ash, which we split down from the off-cuts of the rafters. The purlins were lashed onto the rafters with a plant-fibre twine we bought from a garden centre. In the past they would probably have used string made from flax, nettle stems or lime tree bast (the strong fibres that can be found immediately below the bark). Our bought string rotted quite fast, but by then the roof had settled down and become stable. I suspect the twine used in prehistory would have been far more durable.

The house we were trying to replicate was based on one I had excavated at Fengate in the mid-1970s. The original probably dated to the latter part of the Early Bronze Age, around 1500 BC. As far as Britain is concerned, this was quite an early round-house, so we dug it with a great deal of care. The eaves-drip gully around the outside of the walls drained directly into a dyke which ran alongside one of the main droves leading down to the Flag Fen Basin. I was also pleased to see that the doorway was aligned slightly south of east (about ESE), in precisely the same direction as those Iron Age houses I described earlier, although, of course, a good millennium older.[47] We were excavating stains in the ground left by posts, the walls, the hearth, etc., but we did come across one surprising feature: a concentric ring of posts about a metre in from the circular outer wall. I say surprising, because by the late 1980s several round-houses had been constructed and everyone agreed that with a conical roof you don't need any supporting posts – not even one at the centre. It's the cone shape that gives the roof its strength. The strongest roof-pitch is 45 degrees, which also happens to be the best (i.e. most efficient) slope for thatch to shed water. So why did those Bronze Age builders need the extra ring of posts?

Long before I started to build one for myself, I had been worried about the straw thatch I saw on the few British round-houses and on reconstructions I had visited in France and Germany. Inevitably, it was thick, neat and well trimmed, just like a rose-girt Cotswold cottage on a chocolate box: beautiful, warm and dry. Almost too good to be true. But the farmer in me looked at that thatch with rather different eyes. My sheep adore wheat or barley straw and I often give it to them as fodder when I bring them into the barn after Christmas, for the weeks running up to lambing. Sometimes they even prefer it to hay. Put another way, those luxuriantly thatched roofs represented a huge amount of wasted fodder.

Then I can remember thumbing through a book about Napoleon's Russian campaign where there were paintings of famine-ridden, desperate peasants tearing the thatch off the roofs of their humble cottages to feed to their livestock. At that, the penny dropped. In prehistory, the thatch on a roof would not always have been straw, or even reed (which my sheep will eat in preference even to grass). Maybe by the Iron Age, cereal farming had become sufficiently well established to produce a reliable surplus of good long straw, but in the Bronze Age things were rather different. For a start, the farming economy was more livestock based, cattle and sheep being the major components. As we have already seen in large areas of lowland Britain, cereals were grown in smaller garden-like plots near the houses, rather than further afield, as was to happen in the Iron Age. So I strongly suspect that straw was far from plentiful, and most of what they did have would be needed for fodder.

So what did they use for thatch? Then I just happened to read about the black houses of the Scottish Western Isles, whose roofs were covered with turves cut from the fields around them. Well-grazed, closely cropped grassland is very much a feature of farmland where cattle and sheep are run together, which was traditional in many parts of Britain until very recently. Sheep don't like to graze grass much over 10 centimetres (4 inches) long, which is what cattle actually prefer. So sheep follow the cattle and the result is beautifully managed grazing. Turves cut from such pasture are very strong and mat-like, and if you cut them carefully, you don't have to take much topsoil with them, either. Surprisingly, too, removing turves for roofing can also have a long-term beneficial effect on the grazing.

I'm becoming increasingly convinced that the cutting of turf to go on house roofs was a significant part of the prehistoric farmer's year. If it was done when the ground became softer in autumn, a thinnish layer (say 10–15 cm, 4–6 inches) of dried reeds or cereal straw would first be spread on the purlins, then the turves would simply be laid on this new bed. In my experience, the straw or reed bedding needs to be tied into place, but not as tightly as with conventional thatch, for the simple reason that the pitch of the roof would have been flatter: 35 rather than 45 degrees of pitch. You cannot make a turf roof with such a steep pitch: anything much over 35 degrees causes the turves to slither off in heavy rain.

Cutting the turves used on the roof would have formed part of the farming cycle. During winter, the house's central hearth would have been permanently alight and inevitably smoking. I briefly mentioned before (p. 237) that early experiments in building reconstruction saw one or two minor disasters, where the draught from the front door funnelled smoke through a hole in the roof, converting the hearth into a sort of blast furnace. To avoid this, smoke must be allowed to accumulate high in the roof space where eventually it filters through the thatch to the outside. In the process, however, it coats the reeds, and even the turf above, with thick deposits of potash. So I would suggest – and this is known to have happened in parts of north-western Europe – that the potash-enriched turves were removed from roofs every year or two and were then broken up and spread over the fields as a potent natural fertilizer. A composite reed-and-turf roof is also remarkably well insulated and very strong. A prehistoric family would have felt very snug and secure in such a house – and that surely is what home life is all about.

One final point: that inexplicable inner circle of roof support posts. A flatter roof pitch needs more support than a true cone. So it's my belief that those posts were there because they were needed to support the flatter pitch and greater weight of a wet turf-and-reed roof. Unlike straw or reed thatch, turf tends to absorb, rather than shed rain, and it can get very heavy in wet weather. It is also interesting to note that ordinary-sized domestic houses with internal roof support posts are usually confined to the Bronze Age. In the Iron Age, only the largest round-houses have them. This suggests to me that turf as a roof-covering was replaced by thatch in the Early Iron Age; that was also the time when cereals began to play a far larger part in the mixed-farming economy.

When I began to study archaeology, it was generally believed that most round-houses had a useful life of perhaps ten or twenty years, after which the posts and rafters began to rot. Our own round-houses at Flag Fen have survived for over twenty years, and others around the country are even older. What the earlier estimates were ignoring was the care, attention and, yes, love that prehistoric families would lavish on their houses. These, after all, were their homes and people then, as now, were house-proud. The houses were not just symbols of family, but of the village too. We know that in the Iron Age communities lavished attention on external symbols of their strength and cohesion, such as the elaboration and over-construction of the ramparts of hillforts; and we have also seen that excavations or surveys of their interiors, at places like Maiden Castle or Danebury, have revealed that the houses within them were carefully laid out, sometimes along streets. Given such strong communal feelings, it seems impossible to me that individual families would have been solely responsible for the upkeep and maintenance of their houses, especially in old age. Just like in any modern British community, there would have been ways and means of ensuring that homes were kept in good repair. Then, as now, appearances would have mattered to everybody: one scruffy house would let down an entire neighbourhood.

In Chapter 4, I had the temerity to poke fun at Church of England-style modern Druids. I saw it as a reflection of our tendency to see past religion in terms of its modern equivalent. By contrast, we tend to view ancient domestic life as something rather more nasty and bru-tish. People lived in 'huts', or were 'nomadic'. We cannot imagine that life in Neolithic, Bronze or Iron Age Britain even remotely resembled that of our own times. And of course in some respects that is quite correct: a time traveller going back to prehistory would discover that social organization was different and the integration of religion and ideology into everyday life would seem even stranger. But by the start of the Iron Age, the population of Britain was well over a million and possibly approaching twice that; there was a network of roads, lanes and local trackways; much of the forests had been felled and the landscape was parcelled up into fields, commons and meadows. Most of the Iron Age villages that we know of had roots extending back to the mid-1st millennium BC, or frequently, very much earlier. And as we have seen, most families lived in their own houses and would probably have handed them on to their children. Religion was locally based, and it existed to solemnize the major events of people's lives: birth, marriage, death. To my eye, this short list is very reminiscent of life in rural Britain, even today.

The archaeological evidence shows that Iron Age life was ordered: the layout and arrangement of field systems, for example, reflects and responds to changes in the underlying geology, drainage and topography. But there is also a tendency to align fields NW–SE, which could be to make the best use of sunshine, but might also reflect some of the thoughts behind the arrangement of round-houses. It would be a mistake to assume that the farmed landscape was seen in practical terms only. If a house's layout could be affected by ideology, I can see no reason why something similar shouldn't apply to the layout of fields, droves and farmyards, too. After all, people in prehistoric times did not partition the different aspects of their lives, the way we do today.

We also see how communities dealt with some of the problems and opportunities they came across. For example, good and bad areas of the land tend to be apportioned among the different farms in the area; so a farm would have areas of open scrub or boggy land, as well as well-drained ground for crops or grazing. By the same token, settlements are always sited in the most sheltered places. Nothing is random or haphazard. Just like today, a lot of thought went into such things. This suggests strongly that each community would have had a form of what today we would call local government, with committees that met regularly to discuss what we would now call planning or maintenance issues. Doubtless, too, there were other groups that handled liaison with surrounding communities and the larger tribal authority, which, by the close of the Iron Age, resembled that of a regional kingdom. Indeed, that is certainly how Roman authors described tribal leaders, such as the rebellious Boudicca of the Iceni, or the powerful leader of the Catuvellauni, Cunobelin.

In view of these many similarities I don't think it is too far-fetched to suppose that later Bronze and Iron Age people shared many of our attitudes to their homes, families and local governance. Building a house would have been important to the establishment of a new family within the village. And domestic life, too, would have been carefully ordered. It would have been supported by family and community, and not just because the raising of children was the guarantee of a future. By the 1st millennium BC, prehistory had come a long way: community now came first; life was about far more than the mere struggle for survival. Although they still lacked writing, it seems to me that these people were entirely civilized, in every sense of that often misused word.

FEEDING THE FAMILY: CROPS AND HORTICULTURE

Before we built our house we were very concerned to ensure that the vegetable garden should be positioned on the best soil available. We also considered its exposure to the biting north-easterly gales that blow from off the Wash. So before we did anything else, we carefully examined the field we had bought and noticed that an old (probably Iron Age) tidal creek had once flowed across the southern side. These creeks are filled with much coarser silty deposits than the heavier, silty clays of the surrounding land, so their soils drain much better and are far more fertile. The next thing we did was to plant a substantial hornbeam hedge around the area we had selected. If I had had the money, I would have built a high brick wall, as it took about seven years before the hedge became established: in the early days, it was not unusual to walk out on a winter's morning to discover the broccoli plants had been blown out of the ground overnight.

I don't think I'm obsessed with my vegetable garden, but it does run a very close second to the three females in my life: my wife, my daughter and my sheep-dog. And why? Because I know that food I have grown myself is safe. It is also far more fresh and tasty than the stuff you get from supermarkets. And to this day I still cannot understand why so many small urban and suburban gardens are given over to patchy lawns or, worse, to mini car parks, when they could be growing wholesome food.

In the premodern past, all families, even many people living close to the centre of towns, would have grown a substantial proportion of the food they ate. So the positioning of gardens was very important. Indeed, the lavish flower and pleasure gardens that arose around larger houses from late medieval and Tudor times were making a strong social statement to the effect that 'we are so wealthy and important that we don't need to devote our land to the mere growing of food'. I suspect it was a message that would have struck home forcefully. It is also interesting to note that the productive area of such houses was often concealed within high walls, presided over by a dragon of a head gardener. These gardens were too important to allow ordinary mortals to enter. Later, of course, they would provide exotic fruits and vegetables that would further enhance the prestige of the great family at feasts, balls and other gatherings.

Having been a keen vegetable-grower all my life, I'm still constantly amazed that archaeologists seem to take so little interest in this subject. Instead, all their attention is focused on other aspects of their diet: on meat, milk and cereals. Indeed, it's a shame that university archaeology courses rarely included one of Jacqui Wood's books on prehistoric food and cooking in their List of Required Reading.[48] Did you know, for example, that young hawthorn leaves have a delicious, slightly nutty taste when included in a salad? Plants that we now treat as weeds, such as nettle, chickweed and fat-hen, make delicious and nutritious vegetables, and there are a whole host of herbs that still grow along the edges of our woods, fields and country lanes. The wood that surrounds my own garden is full of ramsons, or wild garlic, which is delicious when added to salads, but tends to lose its flavour once cooked. I have walked across acres of sea kale – a sort of wild brassica, distantly related to cabbage – when filming on the coast of West Wales. I now grow it in my garden and I swear that its forced shoots, when cut in very early spring, are more tender and succulent than asparagus.

The point I'm trying to make here is that these foods were never of marginal interest alone, to be gathered by people who enjoyed 'foraging'. Everyone ate them, and like the hazelnuts of Mesolithic times, I'm sure that many must have been grown in cultivated plots closer to home as well. It all seems so obvious to me, but I doubt if it would be accepted in the academic mainstream. Look up 'vegetables' in most standard textbooks on later prehistory and you will not find them. The index of the superb standard work on the Iron Age, for example, moves seamlessly from 'Varley' to 'Venice'.[49]

Less than twenty years ago I can remember hearing Maisie being told authoritatively by an eminent prehistorian that 'people didn't coppice' in Neolithic times. Then we discovered the stumps of coppiced willows that once grew in the enclosure ditch at Etton. Next we learned that 'nobody practised coppicing in the Mesolithic', and now Maisie has found abundant evidence for it at Star Carr, as early as 8500 BC. I suspect the same sort of leaden conservatism goes for vegetables, too. The words of people like Jacqui Wood, who cooks superbly and understands ancient food to the tips of her fingers, fail to carry the same weight as those of someone who has never left the library, let alone entered a kitchen. The trouble is, this lack of imagination diminishes our perception of domestic life in prehistoric times. An Iron Age meal, just like one today, would have been either delicious, mediocre or disgusting. It entirely depended on the ability of the cook, because a range of ingredients would have been available. Admittedly, times could have been hard, in cold years and in the depths of winter, but in general most people would have eaten well. And if you want proof, it is unusual to find evidence for malnutrition in British prehistoric bones.

At this point I want to return to a topic we first encountered when we discussed the very first Neolithic farmers, back in Chapter 3. I have just mentioned vegetables, but I also believe that cereals, too, would have been grown in gardens or plots, close by the areas where people actually lived. For me, the quest for evidence of growing-grounds began when I was digging at Fengate, back in the 1970s. At first our work revealed massive evidence for large-scale and well-organized animal husbandry. This seems to have been well under way by the start of the Bronze Age, around 2500 BC. But slowly, as we excavated more and more of the land, I began to suspect that some time just before the start of the Iron Age, say by 1000 BC, cereals and other food and non-food crops (such as flax) were being grown on a far larger scale than hitherto. The sheer quantity of evidence was hard to miss: there were grain-impressions on pottery; carbonized wheat and barley lay around hearths, and quern-stone fragments seemed to be turning up in and around every house and outbuilding. But where were these crops being grown?

I had always supposed that these growing-grounds would have been close by settlements, but the scale would probably have been quite small, certainly by modern standards. My instinct was that these plots would have been more horticultural in scale, maybe resembling the allotment gardens one can still see in and around many British towns and cities. I love allotments, with their higgledy-piggledy sheds and leaning frames of runner beans; but they are far more than mere vegetable patches. I have a suspicion they have replaced churches as the true spiritual home of many Britons.

It would have made practical sense to place these growing-grounds near to the farmyards and settlement, as this was where manure would have been produced, and of course kitchen waste would have found its way onto the manure heaps (or middens, as archaeologists call them), just as it does on my own small farm to this day. Being located close by the settlement, people could have ensured that live-stock never strayed onto the growing areas and they would also have kept the plots weeded and watered. But these were just bright ideas of mine. I had no proof whatsoever that such plots existed.

Then, in 1997, I found myself directing excavations at a site on the northern side of the Welland Valley, a few miles downstream of Maxey, right on the very edges of the fen. The site in question was a commercial gravel-pit, known as Welland Bank Quarry – and what a superb site it proved to be.[50] I have already briefly referred to it in Chapter 3, when discussing Neolithic growing-grounds. I cannot describe it in any detail here, but it did provide important confirmation that the theoretical growing-grounds of prehistoric communities were indeed located immediately alongside, and even within, settlements. The evidence consisted of a deposit of 'dark earth' about 30 centimetres (a foot) thick. This charcoal-rich layer which our now-visiting soil scientist, Charly French, reckoned was made up from hearth-sweepings, domestic rubbish and manure, had probably been added to the topsoil to make it more fertile. And the only reason it had not been destroyed by subsequent ploughing was a thick layer of river-borne flood-clay which covered and protected it.

The dark earth covered an area of about 90 by 130 metres (nearly 2.5 acres) in the area we had cleared, and for all we know may originally have extended over an area up to twice that – say, 1 to 2.5 hectares (from 3 to 6 acres; see Plate 28). It seems to have started accumulating in the Middle Bronze Age (c. 1300 BC), and continued to be maintained into the Iron Age until about 600/500 BC, long after the earlier – Bronze Age – settlement had been abandoned. On closer examination it proved to be very rich indeed in finds of small pieces of bone, pottery and flint – entirely typical of settlement debris. This material was distributed across the site quite evenly, which suggested it had been spread there, probably along with the manure (see Plate 29). Then, beneath the dark earth we came upon the pits and post-holes of the Bronze Age settlement, whose upper levels were all filled with dark earth – which would suggest that it had begun to accumulate during the later life of the settlement (see Plate 30).

We know of at least one other, probably contemporary, local site with dark earth, at a nearby Iron Age fort,[51] but by far and away the thickest and most unusual deposit is at a site just outside the village of Potterne, in Dorset.[52] Here the dark earth is so thick and poorly mixed up that it actually contains evidence for the hearths and buildings that contributed to its gradual accumulation, between about 1200 and 600 BC. These dates coincided almost exactly with those of Welland Bank.

ROADS: WHAT THE ROMANS DID NOT DO FOR US

I can well remember at school being taught how the Romans were the source of all enlightenment: how they brought with them writing, Latin, numeracy, history, literature, culture, central government, a civil service, a disciplined military, not to mention towns and roads; then in the 4th century AD, they gave us Christianity, too.[53] In short, although I don't think this was ever stated explicitly, I was taught that the Romans civilized the woad-painted savages of Iron Age Britain. Myths also persist about pre-Roman Britain that continue to irritate prehistorians. So let me finish this chapter with one I find particularly annoying. Put simply, it is the patronizing idea that the Romans 'gave' Britain its roads.

Laying aside the fact that the building of the timber trackway in the Somerset Levels, known as the Sweet Track, has been precisely dated by tree-rings to the winter of 3807/6 BC, it is still widely believed that British communities were somehow incapable of linking their farms and villages together with roads. Since the last war, a host of aerial photographs and other images have shown that the British Isles have been criss-crossed with tens of thousands of roads, lanes and trackways. Dozens have been excavated in, for example, the Somerset Levels, where they can be dated to the Neolithic, Bronze and Iron Ages. They linked drier islands and communities around the fringes of the wetlands and then joined the dry land roads of what would very much later be called the County of Somerset. We have seen how the post alignment at Flag Fen was probably controlled and maintained by a central authority of some sort, who supervised the replacement and repair of timbers. In much later times, roads became the responsibility of individual parishes, and I suspect something very similar would have applied in prehistory, too.

But versions of the myth continue to survive, and the latest states that the Iron Age British did not know how to build or engineer a 'proper' road, with a cambered surface, that shed rainwater. If we bear in mind that Neolithic communities were perfectly capable of fine masonry and smooth, often elegant paving, this accusation is the more preposterous.[54] So it came as a considerable relief when a recent excavation proved beyond a shadow of doubt that Iron Age engineers were capable of constructing a proper, weatherproof metalled road. The discovery was made along a stretch of the ancient route, known as the Portway, which ran along the ridge of Sharpstone Hill, in Shropshire, thereby linking together a series of hillforts.[55] The latest, topmost layer of road surface may just have been constructed in

Roman times, but earlier roads there were just as carefully engineered and were first built, starting almost two and a half centuries before the Roman Conquest, in the years around 200 to 205 BC. As the excavator observed, this road was clearly intended to be used for the transport of heavy loads between the fertile agricultural areas of the Midland plain and the rich mineral mines of the Shropshire and Welsh uplands. The cambered stone-built road is accompanied by banks on either side to mark the line of its route. Perhaps, more remarkably, the surface was formed of hard, rounded cobbles, transported to the area from the foreshore of the Severn, some 2 miles away.

This discovery fits well with what we now know about Iron Age communities in Britain. There is no doubt that the building and re-working of many hillforts was a co-ordinated undertaking: the seemingly chaotic and overcrowded pattern of Early Iron Age times gradually coalesces into a more rational, spaced-out distribution. Similarly, new tracts of Iron Age fields, the so-called 'Celtic Fields', were carefully laid out over huge tracts of chalk downlands, again in a rational and well-organized fashion. In short, there can be absolutely no doubt that the communities of Iron Age Britain were in regular contact with one another, and over long distances, too. The point I want to emphasize here is that this communication happened because that is what people wanted to do. Again, there was no top-down command that somehow roads had to be built, any more than orders were issued to introduce farming, or to re-settle the British Isles after the last Ice Age. So far as we can tell, the construction of Britain's prehistoric roads, like the much later building of the first horse-drawn railways, were local initiatives, undertaken by people who, for various reasons, wanted the work done. Indeed, had the Romans not invaded in AD 43, I'm in little doubt that Britain's subsequent history would not have been adversely affected.

For some two thousand years, we have largely ignored the achievements of Britain's prehistoric communities. Indeed, twenty-five years after it was created, the National Curriculum, which is still largely controlled by Westminster politicians, remains a sad reflection of their short-term view of the world. Prior to 2013 it began English history with the Romans; before 2013 prehistory was ignored for all children in secondary schools.[56] Such attitudes might have been forgivable in the 18th century, when all we had were the written records of Roman authors and a handful of post-Roman tales and 'histories', many of them semi-mythical, and none of them written as history, in the modern sense of that word. This attitude ignores the fact that the discipline of prehistory has been with us since at least the 1860s, and it has revealed that communities of the Neolithic, Bronze and Iron Ages essentially created the modern British landscape, and also established regional economies and cultural identities. Indeed, British prehistorians and field archaeologists in general are widely regarded as being among the best in the world. I suspect that scholars in the future will demonstrate that the pre-Roman influence on Britain's national character was even more profound than we currently believe.

What concerns me considerably is that prehistory is seen in terms of sites and monuments alone. In the media, people discuss the Stones of Stonehenge and why they might have been erected; but nobody enquires about the hundreds of other henges across Britain, nor, indeed, why they are not found across the Channel. There seems, in other words, no interest in the communities who built these great sites; yet I know I'm not alone among prehistorians in my firm belief that they have vitally important lessons to teach us for today. By far their greatest achievement was not to erect a globally renowned temple on Salisbury Plain, but to create Britain.

Without the efforts of prehistoric people, there would be no distinctively British landscape, nor culture. We take these things for granted and never pause in our daily lives to consider their implications. The world is changing, too. Many misguided political leaders think that history is increasingly irrelevant, and that, if anything, it has become a brake on Britain's progress, by constraining development. These people believe that everything can somehow be 'managed', without any help from the past: the pragmatism of top-down central government has triumphed over custom and practice, and as a result, ordinary people and their families are losing influence. Yet in prehistoric times, we, the ordinary people and our families, were the workers, the thinkers, the managers and the planners who spontaneously created Britain.

BRITISH PREHISTORY: A CYCLICAL VIEW

I want to finish the main, prehistoric chapters of this book with some thoughts on underlying social processes, because if I have learned one thing after my personal journey into the archaeological past, it is that nothing ever stayed still. To adapt the well-known Bob Dylan song, 'Prehistoric times, they were a-changin''. If one steps back and takes a longer view, then I think that British prehistory, like ancient approaches to time itself, can be seen as cyclical, with recurring phases of expansion (Pioneering) followed by Establishment (both of which I will temporarily capitalize to make what comes next easier to follow). The less stable Pioneering phases required communities and families to remain in contact through seasonal visits to important central ceremonial sites, and although it is still just one solitary site, I would see those massive posts in the old Stonehenge car park as evidence for such a place. And it is interesting that it is so very early (8000 BC). We have no idea how long this earlier Mesolithic Pioneering phase lasted, but let us suppose it was over around, or just after, 7000 BC. It was followed by an Establishment phase when places like the posts in the car park were either abandoned or were visited less frequently. That stable period then ended around 4000 BC, with the arrival of farming, and the start of a second Pioneering phase. New monuments were then constructed on a grander scale. That phase ended, as we have seen earlier, around 1500 BC, to be followed by a second, Bronze and Early Iron Age, phase of Establishment. So far so good: the situation seems clear enough. But what happened next: why did hillforts suddenly start to appear in such numbers around 500 BC, after a millennium of stability?

My own view is that Britain had embarked on yet another Pioneering or expansion phase, this time brought about by growing populations of people living in the fertile river valleys and lowland plains. Put another way, the developed landscape had begun to fill up and there was expansion into land that had hitherto been regarded as more marginal. It is not for nothing that many well-known hillforts, like Yeavering Bell, Maiden Castle, Hambledon Hill and Ivinghoe

Beacon, were positioned atop escarpments that dominated large, low-lying plains.[57] But it would be a mistake to see these newer land-scapes as being remote and inaccessible: one would hardly say that, for example, of the Dunstable Downs of Bedfordshire, or the rolling chalk hills around the famous White Horse of Uffington, Oxfordshire (previously Berkshire).[58] There is also no reason to suppose they had previously been abandoned, and perhaps we are looking here at a change in the intensity of their use – maybe from open seasonal graz-ing to permanent pasture, and with that came new outlying farmsteads. At the same time, settlement and land-use in the lowlands became far more intensive – leading to increased competition and added social tensions. People needed to emphasize their place in the landscape – and hence the sudden rash of hillforts.

One thing that has always surprised me about hillforts is the fact that they were not thriving when the Romans arrived in AD 43. Had that been the case, then the Conquest would probably have been far less rapid. But no, most hillforts had been abandoned for several gen-erations when the legionaries actually marched in. Nobody has satisfactorily explained that gap: why hillfort building did not con-tinue, let alone gather pace, as the threats from the other side of the Channel became so evident, especially after Caesar's two visits in 55 and 54 BC. I would suggest that the explanation here is quite sim-ple. Hillforts were never intended to be fortifications in the modern, indeed in the Roman, sense of the term. By the end of the 2nd century BC, they had served their social purpose, and most of southern Britain had returned to a more stable Establishment phase.

It is certainly true that this stability was rocked by the events lead-ing up to the Roman Conquest and then by the Boudiccan Revolt of AD 60–61. But it was only rocked: remember, these were relatively superficial political events, and *we* are dealing here with far more pro-found, long-term social processes. Meanwhile, what was happening? Was Britain in turmoil? And the answer, rather surprisingly, is no. Indeed, far from it.

The later 1st and 2nd centuries AD were a time of consolidation. New roads and towns were soon established, and for the duration of the Roman period most of southern Britain grew prosperous, but in a uniquely British way, where the new Roman towns diminished in importance, to be replaced by country estates (termed villas), which were often on the sites of important Iron Age settlements.[59] In rural areas, the pre-existing Iron Age social structure persisted, and in the 4th century gave rise to what has been called the Golden Age of Roman Britain.[60] My own view is that our historical obsession with the Classical World has prevented us from appreciating the true importance of Roman Britain. Behind the attention-grabbing historical events surrounding the Roman Conquest, British communities were quietly growing in size, and were acquiring the flexible identities that would equip them well for the more turbulent centuries that followed the slow breakdown of Roman rule. Personally, I see Roman Britain as the final Establishment phase of British prehistory. And what did the Romano-British ever do for us? They gave us a Britain fit to engage with the emerging medieval world.

Epilogue

The Persistence of Family Life as an Engine of Change

This book has been about home and family life and the way ordinary people managed their affairs in the nine or so millennia between the end of the Ice Age and the coming of the Romans. But it has not been a story of domestic complacency. Instead we have seen how families and communities were able to change and to organize the world around them. They established networks of communication over huge distances, and we have seen how they were able to plan and synchronize expansion and development. As a visible legacy, they bequeathed us the remarkable barrows, henges and hillforts that still adorn the British landscape. But these are mere things. To my mind, their greatest contribution was a pattern of regional cultures whose flexibility has allowed the British to play such an extraordinarily creative role on the world's stage. If I had my way, I would organize an annual holiday in honour of the Unknown Britons.

The arrival of centralized Roman authority, first at Colchester, then soon after at London, marked a fundamental change. I still hold that it was a change ahead of its time, which would have been more appropriate in, say, the 8th and 9th centuries AD, when Middle Saxon England was beginning to trade actively with Carolingian Europe. It was then that the first successful towns began to appear, and with them came the beginnings of the modern world. But sadly, history cannot be rewritten, even to please prehistorians. So I would like to finish this book with some thoughts on how families and ordinary people continued to exert an important stabilizing influence in Roman and early medieval times. Some might see this as the final throes of prehistoric independence, but I'm less pessimistic. I believe that families and family life have continued to play a much larger role in subsequent British history than is generally appreciated. And a good example of this may be found in the social background to the diverse origins of the early Industrial Revolution.[1] But that would be another book. Indeed, I would not be surprised if the development of the internet were to trigger yet another series of changes, whose roots lay ultimately in hearth and home. But now we must return briefly to those incoming Romans, and my personal views on them, which I have to confess have not always been very favourable. But again, if I were to be objective, have I been entirely fair? Surely I must concede that Classical civilization was most remarkable? And yes, it probably was, but why do people still think that change can only happen through the use of force? I would suggest that true, lasting transformation can only come from within individuals, families and societies, via education and rational argument. And to be frank, that is why I still regard the Romans in Britain with some distaste.

ROMAN, OR ROMANO-BRITISH?

When I emerged after celebrating being accepted by Cambridge, I can remember wondering what on earth I ought to be reading during the months of my gap year. So I sought advice from James Dyer, perhaps the most important pioneer of archaeological education in English schools – although I did not know that, then. To me, James was the smiling and very personable director of the excavations at Ravensburgh hillfort, high in the Dunstable Downs, not far from Luton – where I was working as a youthful volunteer. I remember he didn't give me a reading list, but suggested various authors I should look out for when in a library or bookshop. It was a very intelligent suggestion, as it allowed me to use my own discretion. Today, things are more prescriptive: Reading Lists dominate everything and students are not encouraged to use their own judgement – nor, indeed, to make their own mistakes, which can ultimately teach even more. Anyhow, James told me to read anything by Professor Sheppard Frere, of Oxford University. The great man happened to live at Stamford and I met him several times when I was starting work in Peterborough, from 1970. Frere's superb overview of Roman Britain appeared during my last year at Cambridge, and mindful of James's advice, I bought a copy – and I still find myself referring to it from time to time.[2] On the very first page he makes the point that there was no such thing as a truly Roman Britain, because the province of Britannia was a relative late-comer and although it was a part of the Empire for some three and a half centuries, it never became as closely integrated within the system as many contemporary provinces on the European mainland.

In recognition of this, archaeologists refer to the people, the culture and economy of Britain during the Roman period as Romano-British, or R-B for short. The time period involved (AD 43 to *c.* 410), is known as Roman (and *never* Romano-British). I usually try to steer clear of such seemingly narrow distinctions, but in this instance the difference is important; so I abide by the rules.[3]

Anyone with even a slight interest in Britain's ancient history will know that the Roman period began in AD 43 with the Conquest. But it is less well known that people across quite a large area of what would later be known as south-eastern England had already adopted a more Roman-style of self-image, complete with Romanized toilet equipment (such as tweezers, fingernail cleaners, ear-wax scoops and compact pestles and mortars for grinding make-up) and large safety-pin-style fibula brooches, which were better suited to holding together the finer fabrics of Roman costume. Both the toilet equipment and the fibula brooches are first found not on early Roman sites, but in Late Iron Age contexts, towards the end of the 1st century BC and into AD – up to two generations prior to the Conquest.[4] Indeed, a particularly fine pestle and mortar make-up set was found at Flag Fen.

There has been much discussion as to whether the latest Iron Age communities in Britain included urban settlements, as we would understand the term today. My own feeling is that true towns were a Mediterranean concept, and that the large defended town-like settlements of pre-Roman Britain, which prehistorians of the mid-20th century labelled *oppida* (from *oppidum*, the Latin for town), are very different. They included substantial open spaces and they lacked the regular street-patterns which are such a clear indication of the strong central planning authority needed to make, and to run, a true town. They also lacked other infrastructural services, such as sewage or refuse disposal. Essentially, they were sizeable villages, but surrounded

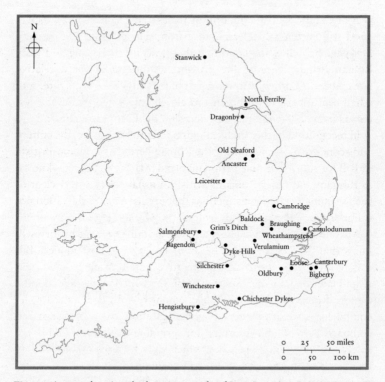

Fig. 8.1 A map showing the known *oppida* of Late Iron Age Britain.

or partially protected by earthworks or other defensive structures (see Fig. 8.1). Their presence does however suggest that some British tribal kingdoms of the Late Iron Age possessed quite a well-developed hierarchical social structure.

It is interesting that the distribution of known Late Iron Age *oppida* coincides quite well with that of Roman villas, many of which grew and expanded in the latter part of the Roman period, in the 4th century AD (see Fig. 8.2).[5] This large area comprises most of England: the south, south-east, east Midlands and Yorkshire – all but the western-most Midlands, and the south-west, and of course most of Wales, too (with the notable exception of the south). This part of Britain is generally taken as the most Romanized region of the province of Britannia.

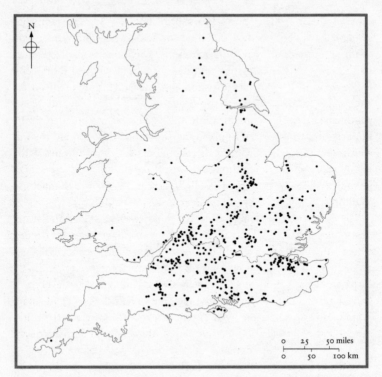

Fig. 8.2 A map of Roman villas in Britain. This is taken from Millett (1990), Fig. 48; I have included both 'certain' and 'probable' examples here, as time has shown many of the latter to have been 'certain'.

But even here, the political systems were far from homogeneous and the populations would have been partitioned into at least eleven tribal kingdoms in, that is, the final centuries of the Iron Age. These kingdoms were used by the Roman administration as the principal sub-divisions of the new province, and were given the name *civitates*, which roughly translates into 'counties' – although in reality most were the size of two or three modern (i.e. Saxon) counties.[6]

Evidence for cultural continuity from Iron Age to Roman can be found at almost every level of Romano-British society; it is likely, as we have already seen, that many of the villa owners belonged to families that had been powerful in pre-Conquest times. Again, this suggests considerable social stability, and with it continuity, over two to three centuries and several generations. The most Romanized parts of Britain were those regions that had already developed more centralized forms of tribal authority and were therefore more predisposed to accept Roman ways of top-down government. Beyond these south-eastern areas, 'Romanization' was less readily accepted, if at all, in parts of north-western England, most of upland Wales and the far south-west (Devon and Cornwall). Scotland, north of Hadrian's Wall, lay outside the Empire, although it was heavily influenced, especially in southern, lowland areas. The Highlands and Islands, like much of Scandinavia, lay well beyond the reach of Rome.

The question that then arises is, to what extent was the population of southern Britain, roughly within the zone of villas, a clone of Rome; or was it something new, and different? For a start, I doubt whether the majority of the rural population were Romanized much, if at all. Most would have continued to speak Celtic languages, and everyone had Celtic names. For the first two or three generations of the Roman period, most rural people lived in wooden round-houses, in the traditional style. But eventually stone replaced wood and British round yielded to Roman rectangular.

When I first read how rectangular buildings replaced round ones in most of the 'core' Romanized areas of southern Britain, it rather depressed me. Instinctively, I felt that when families changed something as fundamental as the shape of their houses, then they were somehow 'selling out', or turning their backs on their traditional culture and way of life. Strangely, I had no trouble accepting that the more Romanized elites would build themselves courtyard villas that quite closely echoed the architectural styles of the Classical world, right down to mosaics and hypocaust (underfloor) central-heating. Somehow, what the elites did back then didn't matter so much, just as today I don't care if bankers and footballers build themselves vast and silly-looking mansions with enormous swimming pools and golden bath taps. They are welcome to them. But I was sad that so many ordinary, sensible Britons in Roman Britain seemed quite happy to turn their backs on over eight millennia of tradition.

Now if there is one thing that archaeologists must beware of, it's jumping to conclusions based on obvious signs of change. And it was a trap I had fallen into. Yes, the shape of houses did change profoundly, but so too did the building materials and the new skills needed to be a builder. Stonework became more fashionable and stone more freely available, thanks to new quarries, quarrying tools and techniques. Roads were better and there was also a more highly developed market system, based around the new Mediterranean-style towns, that were now to be found over most of what was later to become England. Effective saws transformed both carpentry and woodworking, and new, larger and more efficient kilns allowed the production of cheap bricks and tiles for floors, heating ducts and roofs. Hard lime plaster and mortar appeared for the first time. The building trade was transformed and even in more outlying areas, people would mimic the new styles, but in traditional materials: wood, thatch, mud-and-stud, rather than bricks, tiles and mortar. But what I had failed to realize was that the organization of the interior of the new rectangular buildings closely echoed that of round-houses.

As we saw in the previous chapter, everything in a round-house effectively revolved around the central 'core', surrounding the hearth, and an outer 'periphery', where people ate, socialized, worked and slept, beyond the immediate heat of the fire.[7] We see a near-identical core/periphery arrangement in many Roman houses and barns, which were built in a 3-aisled arrangement, with a central and two side-aisles. Indeed, a leading authority on Iron Age houses was so struck by the similarity of the spatial arrangement between traditional round-houses and the new Roman-style 3-aisle buildings, that he saw the persistence of round-houses – well into the Roman period at places like Piercebridge, in County Durham – as 'a positive statement of cultural conservatism'.[8] This should cause few surprises, given that Piercebridge was within the *civitas* of the Brigantes, which lay well outside the more highly Romanized area of the south-east.

Taken together, the evidence from Britain in the Roman period suggests that the Romano-British possessed a culture that had a strong identity in its own right, and was more than merely an absence of *Romanitas*, that is to say, of Classical influence. In fact, there can be no doubt that members of the higher echelons of R-B society would have appeared Roman, because it was in their interests to do so. They would have travelled widely and spoken Latin when required; indeed they often had Latinized British names themselves.

Post-war excavations in London and other cities have revealed a wealth of inscriptions on buildings, tombstones and suchlike, but also smaller and more informal, short-lived writing on tablets, such as 'curses' and wish-lists placed in springs, or offered at shrines. These were always in Latin, and it is hard to avoid the impression that the language was spoken quite widely in cities, if not in the country. I would suspect that the situation in Roman London might have been similar to that in Indian cities under the British Raj, in the 19th and early 20th centuries, where a significant proportion of the population were bilingual.

I'm sure that there would have been a social divide between the elite and the rest, but on the other hand from the late 3rd and through-out the 4th century AD, towns in Roman Britain declined at the expense of country estates, and the social implications of this are still not fully understood. It was a fascinating time, when Romano-British culture seems to have developed a unique and insular character that was recognizably Romanized, but at the same time very British. This was the so-called Golden Age of Roman Britain, and I find it hard to believe that the owners of many rural estates, whose families were, after all, British too and were raised in the area, suddenly decided to sever relations with the bulk of the population living around them. Were that the case, one might expect to find signs that villas had sprouted defences, or were being attacked, and there is little evidence for this, even towards the close of the Roman period in Britain, when the Empire and the Roman army were growing very much weaker and were under constant threat. So I'm inclined to view the changes in later Romano-British society as a sign, not so much of stress, as of communal coherence and stability. It is worth recalling here that during the late 4th century the province of Britannia was still supplying men and corn to the Roman army, although this was soon to cease.

The nominal date for the withdrawal of Roman authority from

Britain is AD 410, but the process had been under way for at least twenty years, or more, prior to that. The Roman-style money-based market economy had reverted more to the earlier, Iron Age, way of doing things, where goods were exchanged, often within and between families, as part of wider social networks. Back in the first and second centuries AD, the Romans had had the good sense to found their new towns close to traditional Iron Age places of exchange and bartering. Then, and as the money-based economy fell out of use towards the end of the 4th century, many of these locations continued to be used, much as in pre-Roman times, although not necessarily as official (i.e. tax-paying) market-places. In other words, southern British society and economy were proving very good at adapting to what would have seemed like powerful global changes going on around them.

The final events of Roman Britain are fascinating. In 408 there was a major incursion by 'barbarians' from continental Europe. By then the Roman army was too weak and disorganized to reject these intruders from Britain. So the British elite took charge and removed them themselves. The following year, and probably as part of the same process, they removed what was left of the governing Roman bureaucracy, too. Presumably they saw little sense in continuing to pay taxes to a government and military who were incapable of looking after their interests. This revolt has traditionally been seen as led by peasants, but as the general level of upheaval seems to have been quite slight, it makes much better sense to attribute it, instead, to the existing Romano-British elite, who didn't do it on their own and who must have collaborated closely with the rest of British society.[9] In other words, it was a broadly based revolt that got rid of the creaking authority of Rome, yet retained society's coherence and allowed Britain to survive into the post-Roman era, without too much strife and bloodshed. Indeed, recent excavations at places like York, Wroxeter and Silchester have demonstrated that while life in and around these towns may not have been the bustling 'town-life' of Roman times, it was prosperous nonetheless, and was enjoyed by quite substantial populations, most probably under the care and protection of the emerging Christian Church.[10]

ENGLAND INVENTS ITSELF
(AD 450–650):
THE POST-ROMAN IRON AGE?

Ever since I was a boy I have enjoyed a good mystery. But I have always been interested in unravelling, in explaining, them. I don't share the fascination of some for those events we will never understand, like the abandonment of the *Mary Celeste* in 1872. Any chances of finding new evidence vanished when the ship was intentionally wrecked by its owner, as part of an insurance fraud, in 1885; when I discovered this, my childhood fascination also vanished. But the Dark Ages are very different. True, there are not many sound written sources to cover the three post-Roman centuries, but the ship of Britain (if I may over-extend a metaphor) has certainly not been wrecked, because we do have archaeology – and lots of it. In fact, I would say we now know as much about the settlements, infrastructure and economy of Early Saxon Britain as of any other period of British history, or prehistory – and I add that, not as an afterthought, but as a realistic contribution. Dominic Powlesland, a good friend over the past four decades, and a man who has made a huge contribution to our understanding of the earlier 1st millennium AD, likes to describe the period as the Post-Roman Iron Age. And as we will see very shortly, he has a wealth of evidence to back him up. But first I must introduce the period.

I very much doubt if archaeologists and historians will ever be able to eliminate that name, the Dark Ages, however much we would like to see it go. Certain terms are unlikely ever to be dislodged. The 'Dark Ages' were first mentioned in the 17th and 18th centuries to describe the onset of medieval darkness that was only to become 'enlightened' by the Renaissance of the 15th and 16th centuries. Latterly, the term has been used to describe the paucity of written sources on Britain – and hence the historical darkness – in the three centuries following the end of the Roman period. I don't find the term remotely helpful and prefer to think of British early medieval history in three broad eras, each of roughly two centuries: Early Saxon (AD 410–650), Middle Saxon (650–850) and Late Saxon (850–1066). As all British readers will be aware, 1066 was the date of the Battle of Hastings and the Norman Conquest.

The Saxon period has not fared very well in the hands of historians, who have generally underplayed its significance, but it is worth noting here that a lot of the innovations popularly believed to have been introduced by the Normans had actually occurred in Saxon times. Many of Britain's great cathedrals, for example, had Saxon origins; some of them, as at Canterbury, were vast. Saxon Benedictine monasteries, like those at Glastonbury and Peterborough, were already very prosperous before the Norman Conquest. The famous medieval system of collective farming, known as the open field system, had been widely adopted in England before 1066. Even castles, the ultimate symbols of Norman power, were being built on top of large mounds by Saxon earls (the oldest title of the established nobility). But perhaps most important of all, people in the Saxon period created the English language.

I'm not a linguist and I don't intend to discuss the origins of the English language, but I do know that its closest modern relative is Frisian, a form of so-called 'Low German'. English is a Germanic language, but one with many classical and other influences, including, of course, French. But how, and why, did it arise? It is quite possible that some people in Britain may have been speaking a Germanic language shortly before the Roman Conquest; as Caesar explicitly states, there was at least one limited migration to Britain from the continent, by a people he describes as the 'Belgae'.[11] Personally I very much doubt whether their influence would have survived long into the Roman period, let alone into Early Saxon times.

I think the answer lies firmly in the Roman period and with the Romano-British population, who, as we have seen, had acquired a strong identity, which doubtless grew even stronger in the post-Roman decades. There is good evidence for Romano-British contacts with the continental mainland during the 4th century, as Britain was an important supplier of grain, and men, to the Roman army. I think it natural that as the influence of Rome diminished, British society turned to its continental neighbours as part of a broader process of cultural realignment. One might wonder why southern Britain did not return to, or retain, earlier, Celtic, roots, but I would suggest that the process of forming the new Romano-British identity had gone too far for that. It would have been easier and more familiar to have turned to similar Romano-hybrid cultures on the European mainland. Of course, we will never know for sure, but I don't think that the new Saxon-based emerging English culture and language came about through cataclysmic events, such as plague, wholesale invasion or mass-migration – and all three have been proposed. No, I would prefer to see such major changes as the result of longer-term processes of social evolution that had been under way for several centuries.

On the continent, the Early Saxon period is known as the Migration Period, because people were moving around, in the aftermath of the shrinking Western Empire. The Vikings marked the final set of migrations – and just like them, I suspect other groups would have arrived in Britain in earlier post-Roman times. But the archaeological evidence does not suggest that there was wholesale population change in the conventional way, through simple invasion and displacement. If that had happened, then over a million Celtic people from what was later to become England would have fled as refugees to Wales, Cornwall and Scotland; but there is no evidence whatsoever for this. I suspect the change from Southern Briton to English happened quite gradually and was the result of two things: a strong, well-defined Romano-British culture, combined with closer social and economic links to the near continent. It is interesting, for example, that many supposedly straightforwardly Germanic (i.e. from Angeln or Saxony) burial practices in pagan 'Saxon' graves in East Anglia can be shown on close analysis to be subtly different from what was happening across the North Sea: the items used are identical or very similar, but they were placed and arranged in the grave in a different, and presumably British, fashion.[12]

The results of scientific analyses of DNA evidence are starting to throw new light on the composition and origin of the English population in the Saxon period, but as we noted in Chapter 3, this is still a relatively new subject and liable to change. There is, however, firm evidence for the arrival of new people in eastern England at this time. We are not talking about mass-migration, so much as a significant influx. Interestingly, genetic links with people in Angeln can clearly be seen in the counties around the Wash, which ties in well with those graves in East Anglia; but given the subtle changes in the way the 'foreign' objects were arranged in the graves, this might suggest that the newcomers had settled into existing social groups who had already modified continental practices. In other words, this limited 'invasion' was not necessarily hostile, and even in the region around the Wash (where the concentration of continental DNA was the highest in England), it amounted to no more than 9–15 per cent of the population.[13] Stephen Oppenheimer reckons that the average figure for England as a whole was about 5.5 per cent. To put these figures into some kind of perspective, estimates of current immigration into Lincolnshire, largely based on National Insurance Numbers allocated to overseas nationals, suggests there were some 45,000 migrants in 2010/11, out of a total county population of 713,665.[14] This would suggest that in one year alone, the Lincolnshire population increased by 6.3 per cent, due to immigration. The Saxon figure is the total spread over a *very* much longer period – maybe a century or more, giving an annual rate of well under 1 per cent. Although today, in towns like Boston and Peterborough, where numbers of migrants are high, some tensions have emerged, local communities are already working to accept the new residents, who are themselves adapting to local ways. Indeed, relations have improved hugely over the past two or three years – and I can speak from personal experience, as I live in the heart of the Lincolnshire Fens, where most of the immigrant workers earn their living.

The way the post-Roman cultural changes happened will, I think, be worked out in the next decade or two, and our understanding of the various processes will certainly be greatly aided by detailed studies of DNA and stable isotope analyses – a technique that can produce surprises, as we saw in the case of the Amesbury Archer. Science, however, is unlikely to answer *why* these changes occurred, and again, I'm in no doubt they were not the result of a single, or indeed a series of, top-down decisions. I suspect that with the rapid decline of the Roman Empire, the Romano-British of southern Britain were spontaneously seeking new identities. Maybe we can see evidence for changes in attitude towards outsiders in what has been termed an Anglo-Saxon 'presence' in Britain well into the Roman period; this was, moreover, long before the Empire would have been showing any signs of military or political weakness.[15] Without further coordinated research, we cannot state positively whether these were early indications of changes that were really happening, or were merely a coincidence; but I suspect the former.

Very often in prehistory, and in archaeology, we can throw light on wider interpretive problems by 'drilling down' to the detail, as we saw earlier at Durrington Walls and Flag Fen. Sometimes the answers to quite difficult questions suddenly become apparent. I can recall there was a huge debate in the 1950s and '60s about the extent to which the many changes observable in British Iron Age culture could be attributed to innovation brought about by 'invaders' from the continental mainland. These ideas were strongly backed by no less an authority than Christopher Hawkes, Professor of Archaeology at Oxford University.[16] I remember reading about his suggestions – which amounted to a fresh invasion every few generations – and coming to the conclusion that the whole of southern Britain would have resembled Heathrow in mid-August. These ideas could not be demolished by citing common sense, but by looking at certain sites in detail, where the evidence showed no sign of any change during one of Hawkes's periods of 'invasion'. In fact, the quite widely accepted idea of incursions of Celtic newcomers early in the Iron Age was firmly rejected when detailed studies – including projects like our own at Fengate and Flag Fen – showed clear evidence for continuity and none for change of population. Using the same argument, it seems to me that our best chance of understanding what was going on in the Early Saxon period lies not so much in grand ideas of social realignment and changing identities, enjoyable as these can be, but in detailed analysis of information out there, in the trenches. And when it comes to the Saxon period, nobody understands its landscapes better than Dominic Powlesland, who has lived in, surveyed, excavated and closely analysed the country around West Heslerton, in North Yorkshire, continuously since the later 1970s.

The landscape in question is almost within sight of Star Carr, that remarkable post-Glacial settlement with which I opened this book. Both are positioned in the Vale of Pickering, but the later landscapes of West Heslerton are towards the southern edge of the Vale, extending up the lower slopes of the most northern of the Yorkshire Wolds. Dominic and his team have pioneered techniques of remote-sensing and geophysical survey that have allowed them to construct detailed plans of a huge area (almost 10 miles across) along the southern margins of the Vale. They were also pioneers of digital archaeology and have an excellent website.[17] Their best-known discovery was the so-called 'Ladder Settlements', which began in later prehistoric times and flourished in the Iron Age and Roman period.[18] They were given the name because of their distinctive shape when seen from the air: a series of routes and droveways linking the 'rungs' that were the boundary ditches of farms and settlements, each one of which had its own cemetery.

To date, the Ladder Settlements have been found in line extending for over 9 miles. These settlements and cemeteries were continuously used and occupied for over a millennium, but the very latest inhabitants, in the 4th and 5th centuries AD, had already adopted Anglo-Saxon houses (distinctive structures, with underfloor cellars, otherwise known as SFBs, or Sunken Floor Buildings), pottery and burial rites. Dominic is firmly of the opinion that these people were not invaders from outside as they occupied precisely the same settlements as their immediate R-B predecessors; their graves in the cemeteries, like those of the Roman period in general, honour those of the Iron and Bronze Ages. Again, this isn't what one would expect of unwanted newcomers. As time passed, and as conditions in the Vale altered, the settlement pattern shifted, but again continuity is evident: certain routes and field boundaries continued to be respected. There was absolutely no evidence for disjunction or conflict – hence Dominic's deliberate use of the term 'post-Roman Iron Age' to describe the period.

The biggest surprise, however, came when they carried out a survey on bodies from the West Heslerton cemetery.[19] The technique used was stable isotope analysis, which I have already mentioned. This process can determine from tooth enamel whether a person grew up in the same area where he or she was buried. The results from eight prehistoric graves showed that all bodies probably came from North Yorkshire. This was what had been expected. But the samples from the earliest Anglo-Saxon (Anglian, in actual fact) graves were surprising. The artefacts found in the graves were all typical of what one might expect to find in the Angeln heartlands, around the southern Baltic and Jutland region. Indeed, any visiting authority on the subject might well have declared that these were the bodies of pioneering Anglian warriors, from overseas. Twenty-four bodies were analysed and of these, just four proved to have been from the continent. But were these the warriors? No, far from it. In fact they were female and one of them was a juvenile. Even more peculiar, none of them (to judge by the possessions buried with them) was particularly well off; so ideas of 'high-status wives' from overseas don't apply, either. And what about the remaining twenty bodies: where did they come from? And again, there were more surprises: ten were local, but the others all came from west of the Pennines – which would suggest that even in the depths of the so-called 'Dark Ages', the infrastructure of north- ern England was in a good state and people could move around with ease. So this does not agree remotely with conventional notions of post-Roman Britain, which supposedly 'reverted' to dark forest and muddy, rutted trackways.[20]

Towards the end of the Early Saxon period, Dominic's 'post-Roman Iron Age' societies of south-eastern Britain had developed into the early Anglo-Saxon kingdoms, much as they had done in late pre-Roman times. The best known of these early rulers is King Raed- wald, who died around 625 and was ruler of Essex (the East Saxons). He is well known today, not for any particularly great deeds, but for his fabulously wealthy tomb in a ship beneath a great mound at Sut- ton Hoo, in Suffolk. We now know – thanks to a recent discovery at Prittlewell – that very rich burials were not confined to royalty in the emerging Kingdom of Essex. I can remember being very forcibly struck by the similarity of the arrangement of the Prittlewell tomb with another very rich and possibly 'royal' burial, this time from the Late Iron Age (15–10 BC), beneath the huge mound of the Lexden Tumulus, on the outskirts of Colchester. The closely similar arrange- ment of the two tombs surely suggests that the early Saxon kingdoms were essentially a reinvention of a much earlier tradition, which was put on hold, as it were, during the Roman period.[21]

That earlier tradition was, of course, tribal, and was therefore embedded within a family structure. Indeed, there is no other way that such close continuity can be explained. But these rich Saxon graves, with their lavish use of imported wine and of exotic objects, would not have seemed out of place in the Iron Age: Lexden was by no means unique. Others have been found, for example at Welwyn, in Hertfordshire, and at Snailwell, Cambridgeshire.[22] Earlier examples in broadly the same tradition can be found as far north as East Yorkshire, where they date back to the late 5th century BC.[23]

It would be a mistake, however, to assume that wealth in Saxon Britain, like today, was mostly confined to the south-east, as the recent discovery of the breath-taking Staffordshire Hoard so vividly illustrates.[24] The process we are witnessing here began to gather pace in the later Iron Age and might best be described as the centralization of power, and with it, wealth. But it would be unwise to view this as a simple process, because it was embedded within many centuries of tradition, custom and practice, all of which were ultimately based on tribe, clan and family structure. As we have seen throughout this book, it was these structures that provided the checks and balances necessary for the regulation of any system of governance. But what I find truly remarkable is that they still persist and affect the lives of everyone living in Britain today.

Notes

For abbreviations used in the notes, see List of References.

INTRODUCTION

1. BBC World Service, 4.55 am, 10 January 2011.
2. I use the term 'prehistory' to describe the time in Britain before the Roman Conquest of AD 43. The principal prehistoric periods covered in this book are the Mesolithic (or Middle Stone Age: 9600–4000 BC), the Neolithic (or New Stone Age: 4000–2500 BC), the Bronze Age (2500–800 BC) and the Iron Age (800 BC–AD 43).
3. Cunliffe (2005), pp. 147, 540.
4. My introduction to social history was by the eminent historian G. M. Trevelyan (published between 1949 and 1952). It has stood the test of time very well and is still available as a boxed set (Penguin Books). There are far too many social histories to list, but a particular favourite is by Orme (2001). The still-classic television introduction to the subject was, of course, *Upstairs, Downstairs*, produced by London Weekend Television from 1971 to 1975. Set between 1903 and 1930, it ran for a total of 68 episodes.
5. For a well-informed jargon-free account of our primate cousins, see Dunbar and Barrett (2000).
6. The story of early human (hominin) development and ancestry is being transformed by the study of DNA, but it isn't a matter of simple descent and development. There are many branches and dead-ends. For an excellent summary, with its archaeological implications, see Foley (2002).
7. By far the best general reference book on early human prehistory is Scarre (2005).
8. I discuss it in Pryor (2003), pp. 411–13. See also Gregory (1991).
9. I cover the Viking Age in Pryor (2010), pp. 235–65, and Pryor (2006a), pp. 68–107.
10. Leahy (2004).
11. Milner et al. (2013), p. 4.

1. AFTER THE AGES OF ICE (9600–8000 BC)

1. For a very good account of Britain's earliest post-Glacial history, see ch. 2 of Cunliffe (2013); this includes an excellent satellite image of the Continental Shelf (p. 36).
2. Milner et al. (2013).
3. For a graph of temperature fluctuations in late and post-Glacial times, see Scarre (2005), p. 178, Fig. 5.1. See also Mithen (2003).
4. The *Colinda* spearhead is in Norwich Castle Museum.
5. Clark and Godwin (1956).
6. Louwe Kooijmans (1970).
7. Coles (1998); Bailey (2007).
8. Gaffney et al. (2007).
9. Smith (1997), p. vii.
10. Parfitt et al. (2010).
11. I cover the first two dates in Pryor (2003), pp. 1–30. The sites involved are Boxgrove, West Sussex, and Happisburgh, Norfolk.
12. Oppenheimer (2006), pp. 114–55.
13. For a superb illustration of life in the middle of the Ice Ages, around half a million years ago, see Roberts and Parfitt (1999).
14. The book that changed archaeological attitudes to hunter-gatherer communities was Lee and de Vore (1968). Interestingly, this book was dedicated to the social anthropologist Claude Lévi-Strauss.
15. Reynier (2005).
16. The site was first brought to public attention in 2003. See Waddington et al. (2003).
17. Gooder (2007).
18. I have reproduced Clive's photo of it in Pryor (2010), p. 29, Fig. 1.3.
19. Later 20th-century research is summarized in Mellars and Dark (1998).
20. Clark (1954).
21. Godwin (1978), pp. 161–2.
22. Ibid., pp. 91–100.
23. Recent environmental research at Star Carr is summarized in various papers in vol. 11 of the *Journal of Wetland Archaeology* (2011).
24. Milner et al. (2013), p. 61.
25. Conneller et al. (2012).
26. Smith (1997).
27. Taylor (1998a).
28. Conneller et al. (2012), p. 1015.
29. Milner et al. (2013), pp. 94–5.

NOTES

2. THE RE-SETTLEMENT GATHERS PACE
(8000–4000 BC)

1. Fagan and Van Noten (1966).
2. Milner et al. (2013), p. 33.
3. Conneller et al. (2012).
4. I discuss Thatcham, with references, in Pryor (2003), pp. 90–95.
5. Ibid., p. 103.
6. Collard et al. (2010).
7. Clarke (1976).
8. Ibid., pp. 472–6.
9. See the post: 'Hazelnuts: Britain's first farmed food? Part 3', in my blog (29 Dec. 2012) *In the Long Run*: http://pryorfrancis.wordpress.com
10. https://www.reading.ac.uk/news-and-events/releases/PR480551.aspx
11. Clark (1954).
12. I discuss the Stonehenge car park discoveries in Pryor (2003), pp. 174–7.
13. Parker Pearson (2012), p. 137.
14. Ibid., p. 230 and p. 236 (the settlement near the car park).
15. Ibid., pp. 147–50.
16. Pryor (2004), pp. 211, 218, also photo.
17. I discuss prehistoric attitudes to time in Pryor (2001b), pp. 282–3.
18. For example, Smith (1997), pp. 96–8.
19. Solstices occur on 21 December (the shortest day) and 21 June (the longest day); the equinoxes (when days and nights are of equal duration) occur midway between the solstices on 21 March and 21 September.
20. Parker Pearson (2012), pp. 243–5.
21. For a summary of the evidence (with references) see Milner et al. (2013), pp. 34–5.
22. *Past* 69 (November 2011).
23. Aurochs were the massive wild cattle native to northern Europe. They did not interbreed with the early domesticated cattle brought to Britain by the first farmers of the Neolithic.
24. *British Archaeology* (January/February 2013), p. 8. 'Mesolithic Merseyside', *Current Archaeology* (January 2013), p. 6.
25. 'Scottish hunters left wolf pelt at home', *British Archaeology* (January/February 2013), p. 6. 'Scotland's First House?', *Current Archaeology* (January 2013), p. 6.
26. Pryor (2001b), pp. 32–5.

27. I discuss the impact of the Black Death on population in Pryor (2010), pp. 183–8.
28. Ibid., p. 340: Fig. 9.4 shows a graph of Peterborough market trade between 1300 and 1400, with years of famine preceding the Black Death.
29. This discussion of Ireland is largely based on Mallory (2013); for Irish food resources, see pp. 42–7.

3. EARLY FARMERS (4000–3000 BC)

1. Cole (1959).
2. Pryor (2010), pp. 46–8.
3. Whittle et al. (2011).
4. Burleigh (1981).
5. Pryor (2003), p. 111 (with refs.).
6. Whittle et al. (2011). The spread of the Neolithic way of life has been dramatically revealed by radiocarbon dating; see the final chapter (and particularly the chart on p. 841) of this important study.
7. Ibid., p. 839.
8. Oppenheimer (2006), pp. 197–280; Pryor (2003), ch. 5 (with refs.); Parker Pearson (2012), pp. 16–21.
9. Hall and Coles (1994), p. 46.
10. For early farming, see Pryor (2006b).
11. Quoted in *Past* (Newsletter of the Prehistoric Society) 67, pp. 11–12.
12. http://journal.antiquity.ac.uk/ant/085/ant/0850395.htm and http://www.sheffield.ac.uk/archaeology/research/csi
13. Pryor (2006b), caption to photo 16.
14. Card (2013).
15. Pryor (1998).
16. Ibid., pp. 5–7.
17. Smith (1965).
18. Mercer (1990) is still an excellent summary of causewayed enclosures. There is a photo of a Hambledon skull on p. 50.
19. For example, French (1994).
20. Taylor (1981).
21. Pryor and French (1985).
22. I illustrate a simplified plan of the Maxey crop-marks in Pryor (2003), pp. 184–5.
23. Pryor (2001b), pp. 109–30; Pryor (2003), pp. 164–73.
24. Healy et al. (2011), pp. 314–32; the tables on p. 325 refer specifically to Etton.

25. Taylor (1998b), p. 157, Fig. 174.
26. Ibid., p. 124, Fig. 133.
27. Ibid., pp. 156–7 (wood 1271), figs. 172–3.
28. Ibid., p. 124, Fig. 133.
29. Ibid., p. 156 (wood 184).
30. Kinnes (1998), p. 163 (pot M3).
31. Ibid., p. 170 (pot M79).
32. Pryor (1998), p. 33, figs. 30–31.
33. The complete human cranium is illustrated *in situ*, in ibid., p. 32, Fig. 25.
34. Frere (1987), pp. 251, 289.
35. 'Ebbsfleet Saxon Mill', *Current Archaeology* 183 (2002), p. 93.
36. For example, Finley (2006).
37. Kinnes (1998), p. 168 (pot M78).
38. Armour-Chélu (1998), p. 284; the quotation is from the first paragraph of the section 'Summary and discussion'.
39. Oswald et al. (2001) has many instances, for example p. 107.
40. Recent research into life in the Irish Neolithic has been well summarized and illustrated in Smyth (2014).
41. Pryor (1974), pp. 6–7.
42. Cross (2003).
43. In actual fact this date was expressed as a range of dates, from 3310 to 2910 BC. The single date I use here is the mid-point of this range. See Pryor (2001a), table 16.1 (lab. no. GaK-4197).
44. See, for example, Oxford Archaeology Unit (2000). See also Kennedy and Davidson (2006); Wessex Archaeology (2008), p. 7; 'Isle of Man house is one of Britain's first', *British Archaeology* (September/October 2009), p. 9; and 'Rare house continues first farmers debate', *British Archaeology* (September/October 2008), p. 9. See also Brophy (2007); Murray et al. (2009); Rowley-Conwy (2002).
45. For an excellent summary of British Neolithic houses, see Darvill and Thomas (1996).
46. Thomas (1991); for an enlarged and revised version of his original thoughts, see Thomas (1999).
47. Pryor (1988).
48. Grogan (1996).
49. Barclay (1996).
50. For example, 'News: Third Neolithic longhouse found in Scotland', *British Archaeology* (September 2004), p. 6.
51. Whittle et al. (2011), p. 832.
52. Childe (1931).

53. Shepherd (2000) has some superb pictures of this extraordinary site.
54. Ashmore (2000), p. 300: Knap of Howar.
55. For Barnhouse, see Richards (2005); for the Links of Noltland, see Moore and Wilson (2013).
56. Taylor and Parker Pearson (1999).
57. The first 7 colour photos in Pryor (2003) show examples of the way the Orcadian sandstone was used. There is also a view of a beach outcrop.
58. Parker Pearson et al. (2004).
59. Thomas (1996).
60. Mercer (1981).
61. Parker Pearson (2012), p. 30.
62. Ibid., p. 31.
63. Richards (1991), p. 32.
64. Parker Pearson (2012), ch. 5, pp. 70–91.
65. Richards (2005).
66. Clarke and Sharples (1985).
67. Parker Pearson (2012), p. 97.
68. Pryor (2003), photos 6 and 7.
69. Bradley (2007), p. 47.

4. THE EMERGENCE OF RURAL BRITAIN
(3000–2000 BC)

1. Parker Pearson (2012), ch. 7.
2. For example, Chippindale (1983), p. 269.
3. Parker Pearson (2012), p. 118.
4. Ibid., p. 111.
5. Ibid., chs. 6 and 7 (pp. 92–127).
6. Ibid., p. 125.
7. Renfrew and Shennan (1982) and Renfrew and Cherry (1986).
8. Renfrew (1973).
9. Pryor and French (1985).
10. Pryor (1988).
11. Pryor (2006a), p. 198.
12. MacKie (1977).
13. Hawkins (1965).
14. Allen and Snashall (2009).
15. *Webster's New World Dictionary* defines numinous thus: '1. Of or characteristic of a numen; supernatural; divine. 2. Having a deeply spiritual

or of mystical effect.' In Roman mythology a *numen* is a 'presiding spirit' or 'guardian deity'.

16. Chippindale (1983), pp. 190–91.
17. Piggott (1968). For an excellent, balanced modern view of the Druids, see Aldhouse-Green (2010).
18. Chippindale (1983), p. 191, photo 163.
19. Parker Pearson (2012), pp. 120–21.
20. Pryor (2010), pp. 138–41.
21. Bradley (2007), p. 53.
22. Smith (1965).
23. Evans and Hodder (2006a).
24. Saville (1990).
25. Dixon et al. (2011), p. 466, Fig. 9.23.
26. Evans and Simpson (1991).
27. Pryor (2011), pp. 107–14.
28. Pryor (1998), p. 16, table 1.
29. Pryor (2003), pp. 182–9.
30. Ibid., pp. 371, 377 (with refs.).
31. Ibid., pp. 197–8.
32. Ibid., p. 202.
33. Thomas (1996), pp. 141–82.
34. Bradley (2007), p. 148.
35. Vander Linden (2007).
36. Fitzpatrick (2002).
37. Cleal (2011).
38. Williams (2011).
39. Mukherjee et al. (2011).
40. Fitzpatrick (2011).
41. McKinley (2011).
42. Ibid., p. 80.
43. Chenery and Evans (2011).
44. Šoberl et al. (2009), pp. 6–8.
45. Parker Pearson (2012), p. 348.

5. THE AGE OF STONEHENGE
(2500–1500 BC)

1. Harding and Lee (1987), list 324 in their catalogue. Many more have been found subsequently.
2. Pryor (2001a), p. 45, Fig. 3.9.

3. For a general account of the project, see Pryor (2001b), Champion (2000).

4. Brennand and Taylor (2003).

5. Pryor and French (1985), pp. 62–6.

6. Brennand and Taylor (2003), p. 28.

7. Ellison and Drewett (1971), pp. 190–93.

8. Parker Pearson (2012), pp. 275–80.

9. It took twenty or so archaeologists and army cadets to drag a slightly lighter (1.5 as opposed to 2.5 tons) tree any distance when we filmed the *Time Team* documentary *Seahenge*.

10. Dyer (1961).

11. Evans (2009).

12. Parker Pearson (2012), p. 193.

13. Pryor (2010), pp. 83–117; Yates (2001).

14. Although the site is generally agreed to be in fields close by Battle Abbey, other plausible suggestions, some much further afield, have been put forward.

15. Blockley (1993).

16. Richards (1990), pp. 275–80, Fig. 160.

17. Information from Dr Adam Gwilt, Department of Archaeology and Numismatics, National Museum Cardiff.

18. RCHM (1969).

19. The first report on Flag Fen is Pryor et al. (1986); the most recent is Pryor and Bamforth (2010). The main excavations are described in Pryor (2001a).

20. Pryor (2005).

21. Pryor (1974).

22. Evans (2009).

23. For the Ouse, see Evans and Knight (2001); for south Lincolnshire: Pryor (2006b), pp. 109–23.

24. Yates (2007).

25. Pryor and French (1985).

26. Mills (1991), p. 226.

27. Parker Pearson (2012), p. 352.

28. I give an account (with references) of La Tène in Pryor (2001a), pp. 434–6. Today I am much less sceptical about the two timber bridges than I was in 2001.

29. Hodson (1962) and (1964).

30. For an overview, see Yates (2007), pp. 1–3.

31. The original dyke survey of Flag Fen is reported in French and Pryor (1993), pp. 94–7.

32. Halliday (1986), in Pryor et al. (1986), p. 2.
33. Field and Parker Pearson (2003), pp. 136–48.
34. Barrowclough (2013), p. 33.
35. For others in the Witham Valley see Catney and Start (2003).
36. Pryor (2001a), pp. 432–4 (with refs.).

6. THE NEW ORDER (1500–1000 BC)

1. Evans (2009); Pryor and Bamforth (2010).
2. Waller (1994), pp. 67–80, maps 3–11.
3. Hall and Coles (1994).
4. Pryor (2001a), pp. 74, 412 (with refs.).
5. Godwin (1978), pp. 161–3.
6. Wheeler (1990).
7. Hall and Coles (1994), pp. 105–31.
8. Pryor (1980), p. 126, Fig.75, no. 7.
9. Burgess and Coombs (1979).
10. Britton (1960).
11. Pryor (2003), pp. 289–91 (with refs.).
12. DBH (2001), 'Coronations', p. 176.
13. Catney and Start (2003).
14. See the collections of the museums in Nottingham and Lincoln. For the Thames, see the Museum of London and the British Museum (which also displays the famous Iron Age Witham shield).
15. Bridgeford (2001), pp. 310–15.
16. Kristiansen (2013), p. 241, Fig. 13.4.
17. Cunliffe (2005), pp. 557–8.
18. Pryor (2003), pp. 250–1.
19. See Somerset Levels Papers from 1975 (vol. 1), published by the Departments of Archaeology at Cambridge and Exeter Universities; also Coles and Coles (1986). For the Vale of Pickering, see Powlesland et al. (1986), and for Dartmoor, see Fleming (1988).
20. West (1985), pp. 169–70.
21. Service (1971), pp. 207–28.
22. Oceania forms an important component of Elman Service's (1975) 'Primitive State' stage of social development, which Wessex and Stonehenge were also supposed to have achieved. It is worth noting that the carving and erecting of the Easter Island statues ultimately destroyed the economy and social structure of the island. For a revealing modern study of a single Easter Island statue, see Pitts et al. (2013).

23. Parker Pearson and Godden (2002).
24. Barrett (2012): this excellent paper from a leading academic is very timely, and his bibliography is instructive; field reports are vastly outnumbered by theoretical papers.

7. AFTER THE NEW ORDER: CELTIC BRITAIN
(1000 BC–AD 43)

1. I discuss some of the problems attached to the word 'Celt' in Pryor (2003), p. 118.
2. Sykes (2006), Oppenheimer (2006).
3. Cunliffe (2001).
4. Pryor (2003), pp. 371, 377.
5. Cunliffe (2001), pp. 352–9.
6. Harding (2009), p. 297.
7. Pryor (2001a), pp. 210–11.
8. Harding (2009).
9. The Broch of Mousa in the Shetland Islands is the tallest one surviving; I have included a photo of it in Pryor (2003), opposite p. 417.
10. Pryor (2010), pp. 367–70.
11. Harding (2009), p. 288.
12. For a discussion of the Iron Age village buildings and their parallels elsewhere, see Pryor (1984), pp. 28–128.
13. See, for example, Harding (2009), figs. 24 and 26.
14. Oswald (1997), p. 90.
15. O'Kelly (1982).
16. Watson and Keating (2000).
17. Burl (1976).
18. Richards (2005). I show a plan of Barnhouse in Pryor (2003), p. 249.
19. Later Bronze Age rectangular, timber hall-like buildings have been found, for example, in the Fens: Evans and Knight (2000). Oval or rectangular buildings (the blockhouses and some duns) are known in Highland and Island Scotland: Cunliffe (2005), pp. 328–31. Perhaps the best-known rectangular structures were found at Danebury hillfort, Hampshire: Cunliffe and Poole (1991), pp. 104–39.
20. For a good example of an easterly doorway orientation, see the Haddenham V enclosure: Evans and Hodder (2006b), p. 100.
21. Parker Pearson (1996).
22. See, for example, Pryor (1984), p. 53: the grave F773 and structure 15, directly below it.

23. I describe the site, Fison Way, near Thetford, in some detail in Pryor (2003), pp. 411–13. The superb original report is by the late Tony Gregory (1991).

24. At Borough Fen, near Peterborough, and at Stonea, near March, Cambs.

25. See Forde-Johnston (1976), Harding (1976).

26. See, for example, Cunliffe (2005), p. 389.

27. The extraordinary diversity of hillforts in a given area is well illustrated by research in Wessex: Payne et al. (2006).

28. Carman and Harding (1999).

29. Mercer (1999).

30. Harding (1999).

31. Kristiansen (1999).

32. Sharples (1991), pp. 124–5.

33. Pryor (2010), p. 141.

34. For an excellent review of research into town walls, see Creighton and Higham (2005).

35. Pryor (2010), pp. 276, 327–32.

36. Sharples (1991), pp. 125–30.

37. Alcock (1972).

38. Hope-Taylor (1977).

39. I discuss Yeavering in Pryor (2006a), pp. 27–31.

40. The eminent German scholar Gerhard Bersu (1889–1964) was the pioneer of round-house studies. His pre-war work at Little Woodbury was published a few years later: Bersu (1940). His wartime researches, while interned on the Isle of Man, did not appear until long after his death: Bersu (1977).

41. I'm very grateful to Chris Evans, Director of the Cambridge University Archaeological Unit, who asked me for my recollections of the site for the major report he is preparing. Without him jogging my memory, I'd have forgotten all of the material in the following paragraphs. For a comprehensive site atlas and summary report of the Mucking excavations see Clark (1993).

42. Clark (1993), p. vi.

43. Harding (2009), p. 58.

44. See for example Hodder (1982) and (1986).

45. I discuss the development of a truly free market in Pryor (2010), pp. 381–3.

46. There are pictures of us reconstructing a round-house in Pryor (2003), photos between pp. 368 and 369.

47. Pryor (1980), pp. 54–5.

48. Wood (2001) and (2009).
49. Cunliffe (2005), p. 740.
50. The quarry operators were taken over by a much larger corporation shortly after the dig and in the consequent administrative disruption some archaeological budgets were 'lost', including the post-excavation writing-up fee for Welland Bank. On my own initiative, I published a short interim report in *Current Archaeology* 160 (1998), pp. 139–45. See also Pryor (2006b), pp. 113–23.
51. Ibid., photo 17.
52. Lawson (2000).
53. The precise date when Christianity arrived in Britain is hard to pin down, but the mid-4th century seems likely. For a balanced account, see Salway (1993), pp. 526–49.
54. See, for example, the extraordinary discoveries at the continuing excavations at the Ness of Brodgar, Orkney: Card (2013).
55. Malim and Hayes (2011).
56. At long last this may be changing. From 2014 prehistory featured in the curriculum of primary schools in England. To find out more, go to and follow @SchPrehistory on Twitter.
57. I discuss all four (with references) in Pryor (2010), ch. 4.
58. I discuss both in ibid., pp. 138–40 (Uffington), and pp. 126–7 (Ivinghoe Beacon).
59. I give examples of this in Pryor (2004), pp. 117–19.
60. de la Bédoyère (1999).

EPILOGUE: THE PERSISTENCE OF FAMILY LIFE AS AN ENGINE OF CHANGE

1. I discuss the social background to the Industrial Revolution in Pryor (2010), ch. 11.
2. Frere (1987) was first published in 1967.
3. Frere's book is now somewhat outdated and I have drawn more heavily on Salway (1993) and Millett (1990) in the following general discussion of the Roman period.
4. Hill (1997), p. 96; Haselgrove (1997), p. 62.
5. De la Bédoyère (1999), pp. 77–98.
6. Millett (1990), pp. 65–9.
7. Harding (2009), pp. 276–7, 290–91.
8. Ibid., p. 277.
9. Millett (1990), pp. 227–8.

10. I discuss this further in Pryor (2004), ch. 5 (with refs.).

11. Cunliffe (2005), p. 582, refers to Caesar's *Gallic Wars*.

12. Lucy (2000), pp. 119–22.

13. Oppenheimer (2006), p. 438.

14. Two PDF files from the website http://www.research-lincs.org.uk
    International Migration Information Sheet_2011.pdf
    Census Estimates Info Sheet_Lincolnshire unrounded.pdf

15. The 'presence' is said to have taken the form of *foederati*, or mercenary troops, from Saxony, but the vast majority of graves show no indication whatsoever that the people in question served in the Roman army. Perhaps the best-known examples come from Mucking, in Essex, and are discussed in Pryor (2004), pp. 150–51 (with refs.).

16. Hawkes (1959).

17. http://www.landscaperesearchcentre.org

18. See Pryor (2004), pp. 204–10 (with refs.).

19. Haughton and Powlesland (1999).

20. Indeed, Hoskins saw the situation as being so bleak that the Anglo-Saxons essentially re-opened the landscape, rather like in early Mesolithic times. See 'The English Settlement', ch. 2 in Hoskins (1955).

21. Both tombs are illustrated in Pryor (2004), pp. 228–9.

22. Cunliffe (2005), pp. 155–9.

23. Stead (1991); Cunliffe (2005), pp. 544–51.

24. The hoard may not be as simple as we once believed: see 'News from the field: Rethinking the Staffordshire Hoard', *Current Archaeology* 276 (March 2013), pp. 24–7.

References

Alcock, L. (1972), *'By South Cadbury is that Camelot ...'* Excavations at *Cadbury Castle 1966–70* (Thames and Hudson, London).

Aldhouse-Green, M. (2010), *Caesar's Druids: Story of an Ancient Priesthood* (Yale University Press, New Haven and London).

Allen, M., and Snashall, N. (2009), 'New Features at Avebury from Hand Coring: Geoarchaeology in Action!', *Past* (Newsletter of the Prehistoric Society) 63, pp. 12–13.

Armour-Chélu, M. (1998), 'The Animal Bone', in Pryor (1998), pp. 273–88.

Ashmore, P. (2000), 'Dating the Neolithic in Orkney', in Ritchie, A. (ed.), *Neolithic Orkney in its European Context* (2000), pp. 299–308 (McDonald Institute for Archaeological Research, Cambridge).

Bailey, G. (2007), 'The Palaeogeography of the North Sea Basin', in Waddington and Pedersen (2007), pp. 3–11.

Barclay, G. J. (1996), 'Neolithic Buildings in Scotland', in Darvill and Thomas (1996), pp. 61–76.

Barnwell, P. S., Palmer, M., and Airs, M. (eds.) (2004), *The Vernacular Workshop: From Craft to Industry, 1400–1900*, Council for British Archaeology Research Report 140 (York).

Barrett, J. C. (2012), 'Are Models of Prestige Goods Economies and Conspicuous Consumption Applicable to the Archaeology of the Bronze to Iron Age Transition in Britain?', in Jones, A. M., Pollard, J., Allen, M. J., and Gardiner, J., *Image, Memory and Monumentality. Archaeological Engagements with the Material World: A Celebration of the Academic Achievements of Professor Richard Bradley* (2012), pp. 6–17 (Oxbow Books, Oxford).

Barrowclough, D. (2013), 'The Identification of a Late Bronze Age Hoard at Barway and Consideration of the Association between Metalwork and Causeways', *Proceedings of the Cambridge Antiquarian Society* 102, pp. 29–36.

Bayliss, A., Healy, F., Whittle, A., and Cooney, G. (2011), 'Neolithic narratives: British and Irish enclosures in their timescapes', in Whittle et al. (2011), pp. 716–19.

Bédoyère, G. de la (1999), *The Golden Age of Roman Britain* (Tempus Books, Stroud).

Bersu, G. (1940), 'Excavations at Little Woodbury, Wiltshire, part I', *Proceedings of the Prehistoric Society* 6, pp. 30–111.

— (1977), *Three Iron Age Round Houses in the Isle of Man* (Manx Museum and National Trust, Douglas).

Binford, L. W. (1962), 'Archaeology and Anthropology', *American Antiquity*, Vol. 28, Part 2, pp. 217–25.

— (1972) *An Archaeological Perspective* (Seminar Press, New York).

Blockley, K. (1993), 'Canterbury Cathedral', *Current Archaeology* 136, pp. 124–30.

Bradley, R. J. (2007), *The Prehistory of Britain and Ireland* (Cambridge University Press).

Brennand, M., and Taylor, M. (2003), 'The Survey and Excavation of a Bronze Age Timber Circle at Holme-next-the-Sea, Norfolk, 1998–9', *Proceedings of the Prehistoric Society* 69, pp. 1–84.

Bridgeford, S. D. (2001), 'Late Bronze Age Swords and Spears from the Power Station and Flag Fen', in Pryor (2001a), pp. 309–17.

Britton, D. (1960), 'The Isleham Hoard, Cambridgeshire', *Antiquity*, Vol. 34, pp. 279–82.

Brophy, K. (2007), 'From Big Houses to Cult Houses: Early Neolithic Timber Halls in Scotland', *Proceedings of the Prehistoric Society* 73, pp. 75–96.

Buckley, D. G., and Ingle, C. J. (2001), 'The Saddle Querns from Flag Fen', in Pryor (2001a), pp. 322–8.

Burgess, C., and Coombs, D. G. (eds.) (1979), *Bronze Age Hoards – Some Finds Old and New*, British Archaeological Reports 67 (Oxford).

Burl, A. (1976), *The Stone Circles of the British Isles* (Yale University Press, New Haven and London).

Burleigh, R. (1981), 'W. F. Libby and the Development of Radiocarbon Dating', *Antiquity*, Vol. 55, pp. 96–8.

Card, N. (2013), 'The Ness of Brodgar: More than a Stone Circle', *British Archaeology* 128, pp. 14–21.

Carman, J., and Harding, A. F. (1999), 'Epilogue: The Future Study of Ancient Warfare', in Carman, J., and Harding, A. F. (eds.), *Ancient Warfare: Archaeological Perspectives* (1999), pp. 249–54 (Sutton Publishing, Stroud).

Catney, S., and Start, D. (eds.) (2003), *Time and Tide: The Archaeology of the Witham Valley*, Witham Valley Archaeology Research Committee (Heckington, near Sleaford).

Champion, M. (2000), *Seahenge: A Contemporary Chronicle* (Barnwell's Timescape Publishing, Aylsham, Norfolk).

Chenery, C. A., and Evans, J. A. (2011), 'Isotope Analyses', in Fitzpatrick (2011), p. 87.

Childe, V. G. (1931), *Skara Brae, a Pictish Village in Orkney* (Kegan Paul, London).

Chippindale, C. (1983), *Stonehenge Complete* (Thames and Hudson, London).

Clark, A. (1993), *Excavations at Mucking*, Vol. 1: *The Site Atlas*, English Heritage Archaeological Report 20 (London).

Clark, J. G. D. (1954), *Excavations at Star Carr, An Early Mesolithic Site at Seamer, near Scarborough, Yorkshire* (Cambridge University Press).

Clark, J. G. D., and Godwin, H. (1956), 'A Maglemosian Site at Brandesburton, Holderness, Yorkshire', *Proceedings of the Prehistoric Society* 22, pp. 6–22.

Clarke, D. L. (1968) *Analytical Archaeology* (Methuen, London).

— (1976), 'Mesolithic Europe: The Economic Basis', in Sieveking, G. de G., Longworth, I. H., and Wilson, K. E. (eds.), *Problems in Economic and Social Archaeology* (1976), pp. 449–81 (Duckworth, London).

Clarke, D. V., and Sharples, N. (1985), 'Settlements and Subsistence in the Third Millennium BC', in Renfrew, A. C. (ed.), *The Prehistory of Orkney*: *BC 4000–1000 AD* (1985), pp. 54–82 (Edinburgh University Press).

Clarke, D. V., Cowie, T. G., and Foxon, A. (1985), *Symbols of Power at the Time of Stonehenge* (National Museum of Scotland, Edinburgh).

Cleal, R. M. J. (2011), 'Pottery', in Fitzpatrick (2011), pp. 140–54.

Cole, S. (1959), *The Neolithic Revolution* (British Museum Press, London).

Coles, B. J. (1998), 'Doggerland: A Speculative Survey', *Proceedings of the Prehistoric Society* 64, pp. 45–81.

Coles, B. J., and Coles, J. M. (1986), *Sweet Track to Glastonbury: The Somerset Levels in Prehistory* (Thames and Hudson, London).

Collard, M., Edinborough, K., Shennan, S. J., and Thomas, M. G. (2010), 'Radiocarbon Evidence Indicates that Migrants Introduced Farming to Britain', *Journal of Archaeological Science*, Vol. 37, Issue 4, pp. 866–70.

Conneller, C., Milner, N., Taylor, B., and Taylor, M. (2012), 'Substantial Settlement in the European Early Mesolithic: New Research at Star Carr', *Antiquity*, Vol. 86, pp. 1004–1020.

Creighton, O., and Higham, R. (2005), *Medieval Town Walls: An Archaeological and Social History of Urban Defence* (Tempus Books, Stroud).

Cross, S. (2003), 'Irish Neolithic Settlement Architecture – A Reappraisal', in Armit, I., Murphy, E., Nelis, E., and Simpson, D. (eds.), *Neolithic Settlement in Ireland and Western Britain* (2003), pp. 195–202 (Oxbow Books, Oxford).

Cunliffe, B. W. (2001), *Facing the Ocean: The Atlantic and its Peoples, 8000 BC–AD 1500* (Oxford University Press).

— (2005), *Iron Age Communities in Britain*, 4th edn (Oxford University Press).

— (2013), *Britain Begins* (Oxford University Press).

Cunliffe, B. W., and Poole, C. (1991), *Danebury, An Iron Age Hillfort in Hampshire*, Vol. 4:*The Excavations 1979–1988: The Site*, Council for British Archaeology Research Report 73 (London).

Darby, H. C. (1940), *The Draining of the Fens* (Cambridge University Press).

Darvill, T., and Thomas, J. C. (eds.) (1996), *Neolithic Houses in Northwest Europe and Beyond*, Oxbow Monograph 57 (Oxbow Books, Oxford).

DBH (2001), *A Dictionary of British History*, Cannon, J. (ed.) (Oxford University Press).

de la Bédoyère, G. (1999), *The Golden Age of Roman Britain* (Tempus Books, Stroud).

Dixon, P., Bayliss, A., Healy, F., Whittle, A., and Darvill, T. (2011), 'The Cotswolds', in Whittle et al. (2011) pp. 434–75.

Dunbar, R., and Barrett, L. (2000), *Cousins: Our Primate Relatives* (BBC Worldwide, London).

Dyer, J. F. (1961), 'Dray's Ditches, Bedfordshire, and Early Iron Age Territorial Boundaries in the Eastern Chilterns', *Antiquaries Journal* 41, pp. 32–43.

Earle, T. K., and Ericson, J. E. (eds.) (1977), *Exchange Systems in Prehistory* (Academic Press, New York).

Ellison, A., and Drewett, P. (1971), 'Pits and Post-holes in the British Early Iron Age: Some Alternative Explanations', *Proceedings of the Prehistoric Society*, Vol. 37, Part 1, pp. 183–94.

Evans, C. J. (2009), *Fengate Revisited: Further Fen-edge Excavations, Bronze Age Fieldsystems and Settlement and the Wyman Abbott/Leeds Archives* (Cambridge Archaeological Unit, Cambridge).

Evans, C. J., and Hodder, I. R. (2006a), *A Woodland Archaeology: Neolithic Sites at Haddenham*, Haddenham Project, Vol. 1 (McDonald Institute for Archaeological Research, Cambridge).

— (2006b), *Marshland Communities and Cultural Landscapes from the Bronze Age to Present Day*, Haddenham Project, Vol. 2 (McDonald Institute for Archaeological Research, Cambridge).

Evans, C. J., and Knight, M. (2000), 'A Fenland Delta: Later Prehistoric Land-use in the Lower Ouse Reaches', in Dawson, M. (ed.), *Prehistoric, Roman and Saxon Landscape Studies in the Great Ouse Valley* (2000), pp. 89–106, Council for British Archaeology Research Report 119 (York).

— (2001), 'The "community of builders": the Barleycroft Post Alignments', in Brück, J. (ed.), *Bronze Age Landscapes: Tradition and Transformation* (2001), pp. 83–98 (Oxbow Books, Oxford).

Evans, J. G., and Simpson, D. D. A. (1991), 'Giants' Hills 2 Long Barrow, Skendleby, Lincolnshire', *Archaeologia* 109, pp. 1–46.

Fagan, B. M., and Van Noten, F. L. (1966), 'Wooden Implements from Late Stone Age Sites at Gwisho Hot-springs, Lochinvar, Zambia', *Proceedings of the Prehistoric Society* 32, pp. 246–61.

Field, N., and Parker Pearson, M. (2003), *Fiskerton – An Iron Age Timber Causeway with Iron Age and Roman Votive Offerings: The 1981 Excavations* (Oxbow Books, Oxford).

Finley, N. (2006), 'Gender and personhood', in Conneller, C., and Warren, G. (eds.), *Mesolithic Britain and Ireland: New Approaches* (2006), pp. 35–60 (Tempus Books, Stroud).

Fitzpatrick, A. P. (2002), '"The Amesbury Archer": A Well-furnished Early Bronze Age Burial in Southern England', *Antiquity*, Vol. 76, No. 293, pp. 629–30.

— (2011), *The Amesbury Archer and the Boscombe Bowmen: Bell Beaker Burials at Boscombe Down, Amesbury, Wiltshire*, Wessex Archaeology Report 27 (Salisbury).

Fleming, A. (1988), *The Dartmoor Reaves: Investigating Prehistoric Land Divisions* (Batsford Books, London).

Foley, R. (2002), 'Parallel Tracks in Time: Human Evolution and Archaeology', in Cunliffe, B. W., Davies, W., and Renfrew, A. C. (eds.), *Archaeology: The Widening Debate* (2002), pp. 3–42 (British Academy, London).

Forde-Johnston, J. (1976), *Hillforts of the Iron Age in England and Wales* (Liverpool University Press).

French, C. A. I. (1994), *Excavation of the Deeping St Nicholas Barrow Complex, South Lincolnshire*, Lincolnshire Archaeology and Heritage Report Series 1 (Heckington).

French, C. A. I., and Pryor, F. M. M. (1993), *The South-West Fen Dyke Project 1982–86*, East Anglian Archaeology 59 (Fenland Archaeological Trust, Peterborough).

Frere, S. (1987), *Britannia: A History of Roman Britain*, 3rd edn (Pimlico, London).

Gaffney, V., Thomson, K., and Fitch, S. (2007), *Mapping Doggerland: The Mesolithic Landscapes of the Southern North Sea* (Archaeopress, Oxford).

Godwin, H. (1978), *Fenland: Its Ancient Past and Uncertain Future*, pp. 161–2 (Cambridge University Press).

Gooder, J. (2007), 'Excavation of a Mesolithic House at East Barns, East Lothian, Scotland: an Interim View', in Waddington and Pedersen (2007), pp. 49–59.

Gregory, A. (1991), *Excavations in Thetford, 1980–1982, Fison Way*, 2 vols., East Anglian Archaeology 53 (Norwich).

Grogan, E. (1996), 'Neolithic Houses in Ireland', in Darvill and Thomas (1996), pp. 41–60.

Hall, D. N., and Coles, J. M. (1994), *Fenland Survey: An Essay in Landscape and Persistence*, English Heritage Archaeological Report 1 (London).

Halliday, T. M. (1986), 'A Note on the Flag Fen Site and its Recent History', in Pryor et al. (1986).

Harding, A. F. (1999), 'Warfare: A Defining Characteristic of Bronze Age Europe?', in Carman, J., and Harding, A. F. (eds.), *Ancient Warfare: Archaeological Perspectives* (1999), pp. 157–74 (Sutton Publishing, Stroud).

Harding, A. F., and Lee, G. E. (1987), *Henge Monuments and Related Sites of Great Britain*, British Archaeological Reports 175 (Oxford).

Harding, D. W. (ed.) (1976) *Hillforts: Later Prehistoric Earthworks in Britain and Ireland* (Seminar Press, London).

— (2009), *The Iron Age Round-house: Later Prehistoric Buildings in Britain and Beyond* (Oxford University Press).

Haselgrove, C. (1997), 'Iron Age Brooch Deposition and Chronology', in Gwilt, A., and Haselgrove, C. (eds.), *Reconstructing Iron Age Societies* (1997), pp. 51–72, Oxbow Monograph 10 (Oxbow Books, Oxford).

Haughton, C. A., and Powlesland, D. J. (1999), *West Heslerton: The Anglian Cemetery* (Landscape Research Centre, Yedingham, Yorkshire).

Hawkes, C. F. C. (1959), 'The ABC of the British Iron Age', *Antiquity*, Vol. 33, pp. 170–82.

Hawkins, G. S. (1965), *Stonehenge Decoded* (Dell Publishing, New York).

Healy, F., Bayliss, A., Whittle, A., Pryor, F. M. M., French, C. A. I., Allen, M. J., Evans, C., Edmonds, M., Meadows, J., and Hey, G. (2011), 'Eastern England', in Whittle et al. (2011), pp. 314–32.

Hill, J. D. (1997) '"The end of one kind of body and the beginning of another kind of body"? Toilet Instruments and "Romanization" in Southern

England during the First Century AD', in Gwilt, A., and Haselgrove, C. (eds.), *Reconstructing Iron Age Societies* (1997), pp. 96–107, Oxbow Monograph 10 (Oxbow Books, Oxford).

Hodder, I. R. (1982), *Symbols in Action: Ethnoarchaeological Studies of Material Culture* (Cambridge University Press).

— (1986), *Reading the Past: Current Approaches to Interpretation in Archaeology* (Cambridge University Press).

Hodder, I. R., and Orton, C. R. (1976), *Spatial Analysis in Archaeology* (Cambridge University Press).

Hodson, F. R. (1962), 'Some Pottery from Eastbourne, the "Marnians" and the pre-Roman Iron Age in Southern England', *Proceedings of the Prehistoric Society* 28, pp. 140–55.

— (1964), 'Cultural Groupings within the British pre-Roman Iron Age', *Proceedings of the Prehistoric Society* 30, pp. 99–110.

Hope-Taylor, B. (1977), *Yeavering: An Anglo-British Centre of Early Northumbria* (HMSO, London).

Hoskins, W. G. (1955), *The Making of the English Landscape* (Penguin Books, London).

Kennedy, J., and Davidson, A. (2006), 'Neolithic Houses – and More Besides – at Llandygai', *Current Archaeology* 203, pp. 592–7.

Kinnes, I. A. (1998), 'The pottery', in Pryor (1998), pp. 161–214.

Kristiansen, K. (1999), 'The Emergence of Warrior Aristocracies in Later European Prehistory and their Long-term History', in Carman, J., and Harding, A. F. (eds.), *Ancient Warfare: Archaeological Perspectives* (1999), pp. 175–90 (Sutton Publishing, Stroud).

— (2013), 'Households in Context. Cosmology, Economy and Long-term Change in the Bronze Age of Northern Europe', in Madella et al. (2013), pp. 235–68.

Lawson, A. J. (2000), *Potterne 1982–5: Animal Husbandry in Later Prehistoric Wiltshire*, Wessex Archaeology Report 17 (Salisbury).

Leach, E. (1974), *Lévi-Strauss*, rev. edn (Fontana, London).

Leahy, K. (2004), 'Detecting the Vikings in Lincolnshire', *Current Archaeology* 190, pp. 462–8.

Lee, R. B., and de Vore, I. (1968), *Man the Hunter* (Aldine, Chicago).

Louwe Kooijmans, L. P. (1970), 'Mesolithic Bone and Antler Implements from the North Sea and from the Netherlands', *Berichten van de Rijksdienst voor het Oudheidkundig Bodemonderzoek* 20–21, pp. 97–173.

Lucy, S. (2000), *The Anglo-Saxon Way of Death* (Sutton Publishing, Stroud).

MacKie, E. W. (1977), *Science and Society in Prehistoric Britain* (Paul Elek, London).

Madella, M., Kovács, G., Berzsényi, B., and Briz i Godino, I. (eds.) (2013), *The Archaeology of Household* (Oxbow Books, Oxford).

Malim, T., and Hayes, L. (2011),'When is a "Roman" Road Roman? An Iron Age Engineered Road at Sharpstone Hill, Bayston, Shropshire', *Past* (Newsletter of the Prehistoric Society) 67, pp. 3–5.

Mallory, J. P. (2013), *The Origins of the Irish* (Thames and Hudson, London).

Mauss, M. (1969), *The Gift: Forms and Functions of Exchange in Archaic Societies* (Cohen and West, London).

McKinley, J. I. (2011), 'Human Remains (Graves 1236 and 1289)', in Fitzpatrick (2011), pp. 77–87.

Mellars, P., and Dark, P. (eds.) (1998), *Star Carr in Context: New Archaeological and Palaeoecological Investigations at the Early Mesolithic Site of Star Carr, North Yorkshire*, McDonald Institute Monograph (Cambridge).

Mercer, R. J. (1981), 'Excavations at Carn Brea, Illogan, Cornwall, 1970–73', *Cornish Archaeology* 20, pp. 1–204.

— (1990), *Causewayed Enclosures*, Shire Archaeology (Princes Risborough).

— (1999), 'The Origins of Warfare in the British Isles', in Carman, J., and Harding, A. F. (eds.), *Ancient Warfare: Archaeological Perspectives*, pp. 143–56 (Sutton Publishing, Stroud).

Millett, M. (1990), *The Romanization of Britain: an essay in archaeological interpretation* (Cambridge University Press).

Mills, A. D. (1991), *A Dictionary of English Place-Names* (Oxford University Press).

Milner, N., Taylor, B., Conneller, C., and Schadla-Hall, T. (2013), *Star Carr: Life in Britain After the Ice Age* (Council for British Archaeology, York).

Mithen, S. (2003), *After the Ice: A Global Human History, 20,000–5000 BC* (Weidenfeld and Nicolson, London).

Moore, H., and Wilson, G. (2013), 'Sands of Time: Domestic Rituals at the Links of Noltland', *Current Archaeology* 275, pp. 12–19.

Mukherjee, A. J., Evershed, R. P., and Gibson, A. (2011), 'Organic Residue Analysis', in Fitzpatrick (2011), pp. 154–6.

Murray, H., Murray, C., and Fraser, S. (2009), 'Crathes Warren Field', *British Archaeology*, pp. 12–17.

Nevell, M. (2005), 'Industrialisation, Ownership, and the Manchester Methodology: The Role of the Contemporary Social Structure During Industrialisation, 1600–1900', *Industrial Archaeology Review* 27, pp. 87–95.

O'Kelly, M. J. (1982), *Newgrange: Archaeology, Art and Legend* (Thames and Hudson, London).

Oppenheimer, S. (2006), *The Origins of the British* (Constable, London).

Orme, N. (2001), *Medieval Children* (Yale University Press, London).

Oswald, A. (1997), 'A Doorway on the Past: Practical and Mystic Concerns in the Orientation of Roundhouse Doorways', in Gwilt, A., and Haselgrove, C. (eds.), *Reconstructing Iron Age Societies* (1997), pp. 87–95, Oxbow Monograph 10 (Oxbow Books, Oxford).

Oswald, A., Dyer, C., and Barber, M. (2001), *The Creation of Monuments: Neolithic Causewayed Enclosures in the British Isles* (English Heritage, Swindon).

Oxford Archaeology Unit (2000), 'White Horse Stone: A Neolithic Longhouse', *Current Archaeology* 168, pp. 450–53.

Palmer, M. (2005), 'The Country House: Technology and Society', *Industrial Archaeology Review* 27, pp. 97–103.

Parfitt, S., Ashton, N., and Lewis, S. (2010), 'Happisburgh', *British Archaeology* 114, pp. 14–23.

Parker Pearson, M. (1993), *Bronze Age Britain* (English Heritage, London).

— (1996), 'Food, Fertility and Front Doors in the First Millennium BC', in Champion, T. C., and Collis, J. R. (eds.), *The Iron Age in Britain and Ireland: Recent Trends* (1996) (J. R. Collis Publications, Department of Archaeology and Prehistory, Sheffield University).

— (2007), 'Before Stonehenge: Village of Wild Parties', *Current Archaeology* 208, pp. 17–21.

— (2012), *Stonehenge: Exploring the Greatest Stone Age Mystery* (Simon and Schuster, London).

Parker Pearson, M., and Godden, K. (2002), *In Search of the Red Slave: Shipwreck and Captivity in Madagascar* (Sutton Publishing, Stroud).

Parker Pearson, M., Sharples, N., and Symonds, J. (2004), *South Uist: Archaeology and History of a Hebridean Island* (Tempus Books, Stroud).

Payne, A., Corney, M., and Cunliffe, B. W. (2006), *The Wessex Hillforts Project: Extensive Survey of Hillfort Interiors in Central Southern England* (English Heritage, London).

Piggott, S. (1968), *The Druids* (Thames and Hudson, London).

Pitts, M., Miles, J., Pagi, H., and Earl, G. (2013), 'The Story of Hoa Hakananai'a', *British Archaeology* 130, pp. 24–31.

Platt, C. (1996), *King Death: The Black Death and its Aftermath in Late-Medieval England* (University of Toronto Press).

Powlesland, D. J., Haughton, C. A., and Hanson, J. H. (1986), 'Excavations at Heslerton, North Yorkshire, 1978–82', *Archaeological Journal* 143, pp. 53–173.

Pryor, F. M. M. (1974), *Excavations at Fengate, Peterborough, England: The First Report*, Royal Ontario Museum Archaeology Monograph No. 3 (Toronto).

— (1980), *Excavation at Fengate, Peterborough, England: The Third Report*, Northamptonshire Archaeological Society, Monograph 1, and Royal Ontario Museum Archaeology Monograph 6 (Northampton and Toronto).

— (1984), *Excavation at Fengate, Peterborough, England: The Fourth Report*, Northamptonshire Archaeological Society, Monograph 2, and Royal Ontario Museum Archaeology Monograph 7 (Northampton and Toronto).

— (1988), 'Earlier Neolithic Organised Landscapes and Ceremonial in Lowland Britain', in Barrett, J. C., and Kinnes, I. A. (eds.), *The Archaeology of Context in the Neolithic and Bronze Age: Recent Trends* (1988), pp. 63–72 (Department of Archaeology and Prehistory, University of Sheffield).

— (1998), *Etton: Excavations at a Neolithic Causewayed Enclosure near Maxey, Cambridgeshire, 1982–7*, English Heritage Archaeological Report (London).

— (2001a), *The Flag Fen Basin: Archaeology and Environment of a Fenland Landscape*, English Heritage Archaeology Report (London).

— (2001b), *Seahenge: A Quest for Life and Death in Bronze Age Britain* (HarperCollins, London).

— (2003), *Britain BC* (HarperCollins, London).

— (2004), *Britain AD: A Quest for Arthur, England and the Anglo-Saxons* (HarperCollins, London).

— (2005), *Flag Fen: Life and Death of a Prehistoric Landscape* (Tempus Books, Stroud).

— (2006a), *Britain in the Middle Ages* (HarperCollins, London).

— (2006b), *Farmers in Prehistoric Britain*, 2nd edn (Tempus Books, Stroud).

— (2010), *The Making of the British Landscape* (Penguin Books, London).

— (2011) *The Birth of Modern Britain* (HarperCollins, London).

Pryor, F. M. M., and Bamforth, M. (eds.) (2010), *Flag Fen, Peterborough: Excavation and Research, 1995–2007* (Oxbow Books, Oxford).

Pryor, F. M. M., and French, C. A. I. (1985), *The Fenland Project, Number 1: Archaeology and Environment in the Lower Welland Valley*, 2 vols., East Anglian Archaeological Report 27 (Peterborough).

Pryor, F. M. M., French, C. A. I., and Taylor, M. (1986), 'Flag Fen, Peterborough, I: Discovery, Reconnaissance and Initial Excavation (1982–85)', *Proceedings of the Prehistoric Society* 52, pp. 1–24.

RCHM (1969), *Peterborough New Town: A Survey of Antiquities in the Areas of Development*, Royal Commission on Historical Monuments (England) (HMSO, London).

Renfrew, A. C. (1973), 'Monuments, Mobilisation and Social Organisation in Neolithic Wessex', in Renfrew, A. C. (ed.), *The Explanation of Culture Change: Models in Prehistory* (1973), pp. 539–58 (Duckworth, London).

Renfrew, A. C., and Bahn, P. (2004), *Archaeology: Theories, Methods and Practice*, 4th edn (Thames and Hudson, London).

Renfrew, A. C., and Cherry, J. F. (1986), *Peer Polity Interaction and Socio-Political Change* (Cambridge University Press).

Renfrew, A. C., and Shennan, S. (1982), *Ranking, Resource and Exchange: Aspects of the Archaeology of Early European Society* (Cambridge University Press).

Renfrew, A. C., and Zubrow, E. B. W. (1994), *The Ancient Mind: Elements of Cognitive Archaeology* (Cambridge University Press).

Reynier, M. J. (2005), *Early Mesolithic Britain: Origins, Development and Directions*, British Archaeological Reports, British Series 393 (Oxford).

Richards, C. (ed.) (2005), *Dwelling Among Monuments: The Neolithic Village of Barnhouse, Maeshowe Passage Grave and Surrounding Monuments at Stenness, Orkney* (McDonald Institute for Archaeological Research, Cambridge).

Richards, J. (1990), *The Stonehenge Environs Project*, English Heritage Archaeological Report 16 (London).

— (1991), *The English Heritage Book of Stonehenge* (Batsford Books, London).

Roberts, M. B., and Parfitt, S. A. (1999), *Boxgrove: A Middle Pleistocene Hominid Site at Eartham Quarry, Boxgrove, West Sussex*, English Heritage Archaeological Report 17 (London).

Rowley-Conwy, P. (2002), 'Great Sites: Balbridie', *British Archaeology* 64, pp. 22–4.

Sahlins, M. (1974), *Stone Age Economics* (Tavistock Publications, London).

Salway, P. (1993), *A History of Roman Britain* (Oxford University Press).

Saville, A. (1990), *Hazleton North: The Excavation of a Neolithic Long Cairn of the Cotswold-Severn Group*, English Heritage Archaeological Report 13 (London).

Scarre, C. (2005), *The Human Past: World Prehistory and the Development of Human Societies* (Thames and Hudson, London).

Service, E. R. (1971), *Profiles in Ethnology*, rev. edn (Harper and Row, New York).

— (1975), *Origins of the State and Civilization: The Process of Cultural Evolution* (Norton, New York).

Sharples, N. M. (1991), *Maiden Castle* (English Heritage/Batsford, London).

Shepherd, A. (2000), 'Great Sites: Skara Brae', *British Archaeology* 55, pp. 8–13.

Smith, C. (1997), *Late Stone Age Hunters of the British Isles* (Routledge, London).

Smith, I. F. (1965), *Windmill Hill and Avebury: Excavations by Alexander Keiller, 1925–1939* (Clarendon Press, Oxford).

Smyth, J. (2014), *Settlement in the Irish Neolithic: New Discoveries at the Edge of Europe*, Prehistoric Society Research Paper 6 (Oxbow Books, Oxford).

Šoberl, L., Pollard, J., and Evershed, E. (2009), 'Pots for the Afterlife: Organic Residue Analysis of British Bronze Age Pottery from Funerary Contexts', *Past* (Newsletter of the Prehistoric Society) 63.

Stead, I. M. (1991), *Iron Age Cemeteries in East Yorkshire*, English Heritage Archaeological Report 22 (London).

Sykes, B. (2006), *Blood of the Isles* (Bantam, London).

Taylor, M. (1981), *Wood in Archaeology*, Shire Archaeology (Princes Risborough).

— (1998a), 'Identification of the Wood and Evidence for Human Working', in Mellars and Dark (1998), pp. 52–63.

— (1998b), 'Wood and Bark from the Enclosure Ditch', in Pryor (1998), pp. 115–59.

Taylor, M., and Parker Pearson, M. (1999), 'The Wood', in Parker Pearson, M., and Sharples, N. (1999), *Between Land and Sea: Excavations at Dun Vulan, South Uist*, p. 57 (Sheffield Academic Press).

Taylor, W. W. (1948), *A Study of Archaeology* (reprinted 1971, Southern Illinois University Press, Carbondale).

Thomas, C. (2002), *The Archaeology of Medieval London* (Sutton Publishing, Stroud).

Thomas, J. S. (1991), *Rethinking the Neolithic* (Cambridge University Press).

— (1996), 'Neolithic houses in mainland Britain and Ireland: a sceptical view', in Darvill and Thomas (1996), pp. 1–12.

— (1999), *Understanding the Neolithic* (Routledge, London).

Trevelyan, G. M. (1949–52), *Illustrated English Social History* (Penguin, Harmondsworth).

Vander Linden, M. (2007), 'What Linked the Bell Beakers in Third Millennium BC Europe?', *Antiquity*, Vol. 81, No. 312, pp. 343–52.

Waddington, C. (2007), 'Rethinking Mesolithic Settlement and a Case Study from Howick', in Waddington and Pedersen (2007), pp. 101–13.

Waddington, C., Bailey, G., Bayliss, A., Boomer, I., Milner, N., Pedersen, K., and Stevenson, T. (2003), 'A Mesolithic Settlement Site at Howick, Northumberland: A Preliminary Report', *Archaeologia Aeliana* (5th series), vol. 3, pp. 159–61.

Waddington, C., and Pedersen, K. (eds.) (2007), *Mesolithic Studies in the North Sea Basin and Beyond: Proceedings of a Conference Held at Newcastle in 2003* (Oxbow Books, Oxford).

Waller, M. (1994), *The Fenland Project, Number 9: Flandrian Environmental Change in Fenland*, East Anglian Archaeology Report 70 (Cambridge).

Watson, A., and Keating, D. (2000), 'The Architecture of Sound in Neolithic Orkney', in Ritchie, A. (ed.), *Neolithic Orkney in its European Context* (2000), pp. 259–63 (McDonald Institute, Cambridge).

Wessex Archaeology (2008), '5,000-year-old Log House near Windsor Castle', *Current Archaeology* 222, p. 7.

West, S. (1985), *The Anglo-Saxon Village at West Stow*, 2 vols., East Anglian Archaeology Report 24 (Suffolk County Planning Department, Ipswich).

Wheeler, W. H. (1990), *A History of the Fens of South Lincolnshire*, reprint of 1896 edn (Paul Watkins, Stamford).

Whittle, A., Healy, F., and Bayliss, A. (2011), *Gathering Time: Dating the Early Neolithic Enclosures of Southern Britain and Ireland*, 2 vols. (Oxbow Books, Oxford).

Williams, D. (2011), 'Petrology of the Beakers', in Fitzpatrick (2011), p. 154.

Wood, J. (2001), *Prehistoric Cooking* (republished in 2011, History Press, Stroud).

— (2009), *Tasting the Past: Recipes from the Stone Age to the Present* (History Press, Stroud).

Yates, D. T. (2001), 'Bronze Age Agricultural Intensification in the Thames Valley and Estuary', in Brück, J. (ed.), *Bronze Age Landscapes: Tradition and Transformation* (2001), pp. 65–82 (Oxbow Books, Oxford).

— (2007), *Land, Power and Prestige: Bronze Age Field Systems in Southern England* (Oxbow Books, Oxford).

Index